# WORLD POVERTY

ISSN 1930-3300

# WORLD POVERTY

Mark Lane

**INFORMATION PLUS® REFERENCE SERIES**
Formerly Published by Information Plus, Wylie, Texas

GALE
CENGAGE Learning

Farmington Hills, Mich • San Francisco • New York • Waterville, Mai
Meriden, Conn • Mason, Ohio • Chicago

## GALE
### CENGAGE Learning®

**World Poverty**

Mark Lane
Kepos Media, Inc.: Steven Long and
Janice Jorgensen, Series Editors

Project Editors: Laura Avery, Tracie Moy

Rights Acquisition and Management: Lynn Vagg

Composition: Evi Abou-El-Seoud, Mary Beth
   Trimper

Manufacturing: Rita Wimberley

For product information and technology assistance, contact us at
**Gale Customer Support, 1-800-877-4253.**
For permission to use material from this text or product,
submit all requests online at **www.cengage.com/permissions.**
Further permissions questions can be e-mailed to
**permissionrequest@cengage.com**

Cover photograph: © imanhakim/Shutterstock.com

Gale
27500 Drake Rd.
Farmington Hills, MI 48331-3535

ISBN-13: 978-0-7876-5103-9 (set)
ISBN-13: 978-1-57302-707-6

ISSN 1930-3300

This title is also available as an e-book.
ISBN-13: 978-1-57302-674-1 (set)
Contact your Gale sales representative for ordering information.

Printed in the United States of America
1 2 3 4 5 6 7 18 17 16 15 14

# TABLE OF CONTENTS

progress toward the elimination of the most serious forms of deprivation associated with poverty. In describing the world's progress since 1990, the chapter also offers insights into what works and what does not work in the fight against poverty.

# PREFACE

*World Poverty* is part of the *Information Plus Reference Series*. The purpose of each volume of the series is to present the latest facts on a topic of pressing concern in modern American life. These topics include the most controversial and studied social issues of the 21st century: abortion, capital punishment, care for the elderly, crime, endangered species, health care, immigration, race and ethnicity, social welfare, women, youth, and many more. Although this series is written especially for high school and undergraduate students, it is an excellent resource for anyone in need of factual information on current affairs.

By presenting the facts, it is the intention of Gale, Cengage Learning to provide its readers with everything they need to reach an informed opinion on current issues. To that end, there is a particular emphasis in this series on the presentation of scientific studies, surveys, and statistics. These data are generally presented in the form of tables, charts, and other graphics placed within the text of each book. Every graphic is directly referred to and carefully explained in the text. The source of each graphic is presented within the graphic itself. The data used in these graphics are drawn from the most reputable and reliable sources, such as from the various branches of the U.S. government, from well-respected worldwide sources such as the United Nations and the World Bank, and from private organizations and associations. Every effort has been made to secure the most recent information available. Readers should bear in mind that many major studies take years to conduct and that additional years often pass before the data from these studies are made available to the public. Therefore, in many cases the most recent information available in 2014 is dated from 2010 or 2011. Older statistics are sometimes presented as well, if they are landmark studies or of particular interest and no more-recent information exists.

Although statistics are a major focus of the *Information Plus Reference Series*, they are by no means its only

content. Each book also presents the widely held positions and important ideas that shape how the book's subject is discussed in the United States. These positions are explained in detail and, where possible, in the words of their proponents. Some of the other material to be found in these books includes historical background, descriptions of major events related to the subject, relevant laws and court cases, and examples of how these issues play out in American life. Some books also feature primary documents or have pro and con debate sections that provide the words and opinions of prominent Americans on both sides of a controversial topic. All material is presented in an evenhanded and unbiased manner; readers will never be encouraged to accept one view of an issue over another.

## HOW TO USE THIS BOOK

It can be argued that poverty is the most widespread and serious problem confronting the modern world. Billions of people are so poor that they struggle, and sometimes fail, to meet their needs for sustenance, shelter, and security. Even among those who can meet these basic needs, there are many who cannot afford adequate medical care, a good education, and other aspects of a decent standard of living. The problems posed by poverty are especially acute in what is generally called the developing world—those countries that have not fully industrialized and developed their economies. When judged in relative terms, however, poverty afflicts substantial numbers of people in even the richest nations on the earth. This book examines the forms that poverty takes around the world, its many causes, the serious negative consequences that it has for individuals and societies, and the efforts that are being employed to eliminate it.

*World Poverty* consists of 10 chapters and three appendixes. Each chapter is devoted to a particular aspect of poverty throughout the world. For a summary of the information that is covered in each chapter, please see the synopses that are provided in the Table of Contents. Chapters generally begin with an overview of the basic facts and background information on the chapter's topic, then proceed to examine subtopics of particular interest. For example, Chapter 3: Poverty in Sub-Saharan Africa provides a statistical overview of poverty in the region as well as a geographical, cultural, and historical context. The chapter then moves on to a consideration of the region's most pressing forms of deprivation and the considerable progress the region has made in combating them. These deprivations include health problems such as malnutrition, high rates of human immunodeficiency virus (HIV) and malaria infection, and a lack of access to clean water and sanitation facilities; educational and literacy levels that lag behind most other world regions; and gender inequalities that hold back progress in the region. Readers can find their way through a chapter by looking for the section and subsection headings, which are clearly set off from the text. They can also refer to the book's extensive Index if they already know what they are looking for.

### Statistical Information

The tables and figures featured throughout *World Poverty* will be of particular use to readers in learning about this issue. These tables and figures represent an extensive collection of the most recent and important statistics on poverty, hunger, and related issues—for example, graphics cover the number of undernourished people by world region, HIV trends in sub-Saharan Africa, Millennium Development Goal data on various countries, and gender parity in school enrollment statistics. Gale, Cengage Learning believes that making this information available to readers is the most important way to fulfill the goal of this book: to help readers understand the issues and controversies surrounding poverty around the world and reach their own conclusions.

Each table or figure has a unique identifier appearing above it, for ease of identification and reference. Titles for the tables and figures explain their purpose. At the end of each table or figure, the original source of the data is provided.

To help readers understand these often complicated statistics, all tables and figures are explained in the text. References in the text direct readers to the relevant statistics. Furthermore, the contents of all tables and figures are fully indexed. Please see the opening section of the Index at the back of this volume for a description of how to find tables and figures within it.

### Appendixes

Besides the main body text and images, *World Poverty* has three appendixes. The first is the Important Names and Addresses directory. Here, readers will find contact information for a number of government and private organizations that can provide further information on aspects of world poverty. The second appendix is the Resources section, which can also assist readers in conducting their own research. In this section, the author and editors of *World Poverty* describe some of the sources that were most useful during the compilation of this book. The final appendix is the detailed Index. It has been greatly expanded from previous editions and should make it even easier to find specific topics in this book.

### COMMENTS AND SUGGESTIONS

The editors of the *Information Plus Reference Series* welcome your feedback on *World Poverty*. Please direct all correspondence to:

Editors
*Information Plus Reference Series*
27500 Drake Rd.
Farmington Hills, MI 48331-3535

# CHAPTER 1
# WHAT IS POVERTY?

*Massive poverty and obscene inequality are such terrible scourges of our times—times in which the world boasts breathtaking advances in science, technology, industry and wealth accumulation—that they have to rank along-side slavery and apartheid as social evils.*

—Nelson Mandela, Speech in Trafalgar Square (London, England), February 3, 2005

Poverty is a multidimensional human problem with many causes and many contributing factors. People on every continent (except Antarctica, which does not have permanent human residents) and people of all races, cultures, and backgrounds are impacted by poverty. In addition to causing numerous problems related to health, education, housing, political opportunities, social status, and community involvement, poverty is also frequently the result of problems in these same realms. Poverty thus often operates in a circular, self-perpetuating fashion in many parts of the world, and combating it requires an in-depth understanding of its human as well as its economic dimensions.

In spite of its prevalence at all stages of human history, poverty is a complex topic that can be difficult to describe in objective terms. Most governments and social service agencies have their own definitions of poverty, including how it is measured and who is considered poor. This chapter will explain the means that are used by the United States and the international community to define and measure poverty.

## DEFINING AND MEASURING POVERTY INTERNATIONALLY

Governments and organizations frequently describe poverty according to an individual's or household's income level, and these income levels are determined by the amount of purchasing power they afford the person or household. Two basic kinds of income-based poverty measures exist: those that quantify absolute poverty and those that quantify relative poverty. Increasingly, the international community has also sought to quantify the human dimensions of poverty that go beyond these basic income and consumption measures.

### Absolute Poverty Measures

**U.S. POVERTY GUIDELINES.** Absolute poverty measures attempt to quantify the amount of income a person or household needs for basic subsistence (food, clothing, sanitation, and shelter). The U.S. Census Bureau, for example, quantifies absolute poverty for statistical purposes by calculating the cost of a no-frills food basket meeting minimal nutritional requirements and then determining how much income a person or household would have left over after the purchase of such a basket of goods. Based on survey findings from the late 1950s, U.S. government officials concluded that a typical family spends one-third of its total income on food. Accordingly, people and families who must spend more than one-third of their incomes to purchase such a food basket fall below the U.S. poverty thresholds as calculated by the Census Bureau. These thresholds are updated each year to account for inflation, and they vary by family size and composition. In 2012 the Census Bureau considered an individual poor if his or her annual income was $11,720 or less. (See Table 1.1.) For a household consisting of one adult and two children under 18, the poverty threshold was an annual income of $18,498.

The U.S. Department of Health and Human Services (HHS) uses a simplified version of the Census Bureau's thresholds to arrive at a separate measure of poverty, which it publishes at the outset of each year so that the many federal agencies charged with administering government assistance can calculate eligibility for their programs. In addition to varying by household size, the HHS guidelines vary depending on whether the household is

# TABLE 1.1

## U.S. poverty thresholds, 2012

[In dollars]

| Size of family unit | Weighted average thresholds | Related children under 18 years | | | | | | | | |
|---|---|---|---|---|---|---|---|---|---|---|
| | | None | One | Two | Three | Four | Five | Six | Seven | Eight or more |
| One person (unrelated individual) | 11,720 | | | | | | | | | |
|    Under 65 years | 11,945 | 11,945 | | | | | | | | |
|    65 years and over | 11,011 | 11,011 | | | | | | | | |
| Two people | 14,937 | | | | | | | | | |
|    Householder under 65 years | 15,450 | 15,374 | 15,825 | | | | | | | |
|    Householder 65 years and over | 13,892 | 13,878 | 15,765 | | | | | | | |
| Three people | 18,284 | 17,959 | 18,480 | 18,498 | | | | | | |
| Four people | 23,492 | 23,681 | 24,069 | 23,283 | 23,364 | | | | | |
| Five people | 27,827 | 28,558 | 28,974 | 28,087 | 27,400 | 26,981 | | | | |
| Six people | 31,471 | 32,847 | 32,978 | 32,298 | 31,647 | 30,678 | 30,104 | | | |
| Seven people | 35,743 | 37,795 | 38,031 | 37,217 | 36,651 | 35,594 | 34,362 | 33,009 | | |
| Eight people | 39,688 | 42,271 | 42,644 | 41,876 | 41,204 | 40,249 | 39,038 | 37,777 | 37,457 | |
| Nine people or more | 47,297 | 50,849 | 51,095 | 50,416 | 49,845 | 48,908 | 47,620 | 46,454 | 46,165 | 44,387 |

SOURCE: "Poverty Thresholds for 2012 by Size of Family and Number of Related Children under 18 Years," in *Poverty*, U.S. Census Bureau, 2013, http://www.census.gov/hhes/www/poverty/data/threshld/thresh12.xls (accessed September 23, 2013)

# TABLE 1.2

## U.S. poverty guidelines, 2013

**2013 poverty guidelines for the 48 contiguous states and the District of Columbia**

| Persons in family/household | Poverty guideline |
|---|---|
| 1 | $11,490 |
| 2 | 15,510 |
| 3 | 19,530 |
| 4 | 23,550 |
| 5 | 27,570 |
| 6 | 31,590 |
| 7 | 35,610 |
| 8 | 39,630 |

For families/households with more than 8 persons, add $4,020 for each additional person.

**2013 poverty guidelines for Alaska**

| Persons in family/household | Poverty guideline |
|---|---|
| 1 | $14,350 |
| 2 | 19,380 |
| 3 | 24,410 |
| 4 | 29,440 |
| 5 | 34,470 |
| 6 | 39,500 |
| 7 | 44,530 |
| 8 | 49,560 |

For families/households with more than 8 persons, add $5,030 for each additional person.

**2013 poverty guidelines for Hawaii**

| Persons in family/household | Poverty guideline |
|---|---|
| 1 | $13,230 |
| 2 | 17,850 |
| 3 | 22,470 |
| 4 | 27,090 |
| 5 | 31,710 |
| 6 | 36,330 |
| 7 | 40,950 |
| 8 | 45,570 |

For families/households with more than 8 persons, add $4,620 for each additional person.

SOURCE: "2013 Poverty Guidelines for the 48 Contiguous States and the District of Columbia," "2013 Poverty Guidelines for Alaska," "2013 Poverty Guidelines for Hawaii," in "Annual Update of the HHS Poverty Guidelines," *Federal Register*, vol. 78, no. 16, January 24, 2013, http://www.gpo.gov/fdsys/pkg/FR-2013-01-24/pdf/2013-01422.pdf (accessed September 23, 2013)

located in the 48 contiguous states and the District of Columbia or in Alaska or Hawaii (the cost of living in Alaska and Hawaii is typically higher than in the rest of the United States). In 2013 an individual living in the contiguous 48 states or the District of Columbia was considered poor, according to this measure, if that individual had less than $11,490 in annual income. (See Table 1.2.) A family of three living in the 48 contiguous states or the District of Columbia was considered poor if its annual income was $19,530 or lower.

**ABSOLUTE POVERTY THRESHOLDS IN OTHER COUNTRIES.** Outside of the United States, absolute poverty lines are most commonly used in the developing world (which consists of those countries that have not fully industrialized and developed their economies). This does not mean that the level of income corresponding to absolute poverty in the United States is identical or even remotely comparable to the level of income corresponding to absolute poverty in China, Mexico, or other developing countries. When countries establish their own absolute poverty lines, they usually attempt to account for the cost of basic nutritional needs, but these costs vary widely based on currency valuations, wages, cost of living, and other factors. For example, the national poverty line in China as of 2013 was 6.3 yuan per day, slightly more than $1, and the national poverty line in Mexico was 2,329 pesos per month, which was the equivalent of approximately $180 (or $6 per day). Martin Ravallion of the World Bank reports in

"A Relative Question" (*Finance and Development*, vol. 49, no. 4, December 2012) that the average poverty line of the 20 or so poorest countries in the world in 2012 was around $1.25 per day, which is the standard international line below which people are considered extremely poor, as described below.

INTERNATIONAL MEASURES. For the purposes of international cooperation in the fight against poverty, national poverty measures are of limited use. To grapple with poverty in various countries using national poverty lines would require in-depth knowledge of each country's currency, costs of living, regional variations in prices, and rates of inflation, among other factors. In order to reduce global poverty and promote economic development in impoverished countries in accordance with its mandate, the World Bank, an international organization that provides a range of technical and other forms of assistance to developing countries, maintains an absolute poverty measure meant to apply globally. From 1990 to 2008 this absolute poverty measure was set at US$1 per day, or an annual income of $370 per year in 1985 U.S. dollars. Anyone living below this threshold, regardless of country or global region, was considered to be experiencing extreme poverty. In 2008 the World Bank announced that it was updating this standard to $1.25 per day in 2005 U.S. dollars. This remains the most widely accepted global definition of extreme poverty as of 2014.

The $1.25-per-day figure used by the World Bank does not equal that literal amount of money as it would be used by an ordinary citizen of the United States today. In calculating poverty across the world, this figure is adjusted using the concept of purchasing power parity (PPP), which accounts for differences in exchange rates, wages, and costs of living. Adjusting for PPP allows economists to quantify the amount of income needed to buy an essential basket of goods and services regardless of national differences in these factors. The poverty line

of $1.25 per day is thus more precisely defined (and provided in statistical sources) as "$1.25 (PPP)," or $1.25 at purchasing power parity, and it is quantified in U.S. dollars at their level of valuation in 2005. Thus, when international organizations note the number of people living on less than $1.25 per day in 2014, they are not referring to that exact amount of money in 2014 dollars.

Although the eradication of extreme poverty is a top priority for many international organizations, the World Bank and other international organizations likewise frequently use an additional absolute poverty measure, US$2 per day (PPP). The $2-per-day threshold is generally considered the level below which individuals are poor, as opposed to extremely poor. Many statistical sources provide information about poverty in individual countries and regions using both the $1.25 threshold for extreme poverty and the $2 threshold for poverty.

Table 1.3 shows the number and proportion of people in the developing world (areas that have not fully industrialized and developed their economies), by region, who were living at or below the $1.25-per-day extreme poverty line in 1990 and 2010. The number of extremely poor people in the developing world fell from 1.9 billion to 1.2 billion during this two-decade period, even as the population across these regions grew from 4.4 billion to 5.9 billion. Much of this progress is attributable to economic development in China. The World Bank notes in "Poverty Overview: Results" (2014, http://www.worldbank.org/en/topic/poverty/overview) that between 1981 and 2010 an estimated 680 million residents of China moved out of extreme poverty.

As Table 1.4 reveals, the number of people in the developing world who were living on $2 per day or less (this group includes those making $1.25 per day as well as those making between $1.25 and $2) also decreased markedly between 1990 and 2010, falling from 2.9 billion (64.6% of the developing world's population) to 2.4 billion (40.7% of the developing world's population). Again, these

**TABLE 1.3**

**People in the developing world living on $1.25 per day or less, by region, 1990 and 2010**

| Region | 1990 | | | 2010 | | |
|---|---|---|---|---|---|---|
| | Headcount (%) | Num of poor (mil.) | Population (mil.) | Headcount (%) | Num of poor (mil.) | Population (mil.) |
| East Asia and Pacific | 56.2 | 926.4 | 1,647.3 | 12.5 | 250.9 | 2,010.4 |
| Europe and Central Asia | 1.9 | 8.6 | 464.3 | 0.7 | 3.2 | 477.1 |
| Latin America and the Caribbean | 12.2 | 53.4 | 436.6 | 5.5 | 32.3 | 583.9 |
| Middle East and North Africa | 5.8 | 13.0 | 225.4 | 2.4 | 8.0 | 331.3 |
| South Asia | 53.8 | 617.3 | 1,147.1 | 31.0 | 506.8 | 1,633.2 |
| Sub-Saharan Africa | 56.5 | 289.7 | 512.4 | 48.5 | 413.7 | 853.6 |
| **Total** | **43.1** | **1,908.5** | **4,433.1** | **20.6** | **1,215.0** | **5,889.4** |

SOURCE: Adapted from "PovcalNet: The On-line Tool for Poverty Measurement Developed by the Development Research Group of the World Bank," World Bank, 2013, http://iresearch.worldbank.org/PovcalNet/index.htm (accessed October 2, 2013). The World Bank: The World Bank authorizes the use of this material subject to the terms and conditions on its website, http://www.worldbank.org/terms.

**TABLE 1.4**

**People in the developing world living on $2.00 per day or less, by region, 1990 and 2010**

| Region | 1990 | | | 2010 | | |
|---|---|---|---|---|---|---|
| | Headcount (%) | Num of poor (mil.) | Population (mil.) | Headcount (%) | Num of poor (mil.) | Population (mil.) |
| East Asia and Pacific | 81.0 | 1,333.8 | 1,647.3 | 29.7 | 597.7 | 2,010.4 |
| Europe and Central Asia | 6.8 | 31.5 | 464.3 | 2.4 | 11.2 | 477.1 |
| Latin America and the Caribbean | 22.4 | 97.6 | 436.6 | 10.4 | 60.6 | 583.9 |
| Middle East and North Africa | 23.5 | 52.9 | 225.4 | 12.0 | 39.9 | 331.3 |
| South Asia | 83.6 | 958.8 | 1,147.1 | 66.7 | 1,089.5 | 1,633.2 |
| Sub-Saharan Africa | 76.0 | 389.2 | 512.4 | 69.9 | 596.4 | 853.6 |
| **Total** | **64.6** | **2,863.8** | **4,433.1** | **40.7** | **2,395.2** | **5,889.4** |

SOURCE: Adapted from "PovcalNet: The On-line Tool for Poverty Measurement Developed by the Development Research Group of the World Bank," World Bank, 2013, http://iresearch.worldbank.org/PovcalNet/index.htm (accessed October 2, 2013). The World Bank: The World Bank authorizes the use of this material subject to the terms and conditions on its website, http://www.worldbank.org/terms.

declines were largely driven by dramatic decreases in East Asia and the Pacific, the developing region that includes China. Sizable though these gains in the fight against poverty are, over one-third of the world's population (2.4 billion of an estimated world population of 6.9 billion) remained poor by this measure as of 2010.

**Relative Poverty Measures**

By contrast with absolute poverty, the concept of relative poverty calls for assessing income and purchasing power in relation to the standard of living in the country or population group to which an individual or household belongs. This approach is often justified according to two lines of argument. The first line of argument holds that people make judgments about whether or not they are poor in relation to average incomes and standards of living in their societies. If a person has only enough income to satisfy his or her baseline nutritional requirements and pay for shelter, that person is likely to feel poor if a neighbor lives in a mansion with a garage full of sports cars and takes lavish vacations.

The second line of argument holds that poverty should be defined as the inability to participate in society, and as a society becomes richer (as average incomes rise), the costs of participating in society at even a minimal level rise. In practice, when relative poverty measures are used, a country's poverty line rises as standards of living rise. Relative poverty is particularly useful in assessing poverty in developed countries, where an individual or household might have enough income to meet basic survival needs while falling so far below the average income in those countries as to be alienated from mainstream society.

Most developed countries other than the United States use relative measures to quantify poverty, as Ravallion points out. Luxembourg, the nation with the highest poverty line in the world in 2012, classified those living on less than the equivalent of US$43 per day as poor. Although U.S. citizens on average demonstrate consumption patterns similar to those of Luxembourg's citizens, meaning that participation in society would require roughly the same amount of income in both countries, only those making less than $13 per day were considered to be poor in the United States in 2012.

In this book, many of the statistics for the developed world (which consists of those countries that have fully industrialized and developed their economies) are derived from Eurostat, the statistical bureau of the European Union (EU; an economic and political alliance of 28 European countries), and from the Organisation for Economic Cooperation and Development (OECD), a group of 34 developed countries including the United States, Canada, many European countries, and other high-income countries worldwide. Eurostat releases a wide range of data on poverty in the EU using an "at-risk of poverty threshold" set at 60% of a country's national median after-tax income. The OECD likewise releases a wide range of data on poverty in the developed world using a poverty line of 50% of median after-tax income.

**Composite Poverty Measures**

Since the mid-1990s national and international agencies have attempted to broaden the analysis of poverty by accounting for its composite, multidimensional nature. Although income and consumption habits remain primary indicators of poverty, the United Nations (UN) and its subordinate agencies, along with other antipoverty groups, often use two other metrics, the Human Development Index (HDI) and the Multidimensional Poverty Index (MPI), to arrive at a fuller view of the interrelated problems of poverty and development.

HUMAN DEVELOPMENT INDEX. In 1997 the UN Development Programme (UNDP) introduced the first of these metrics, the HDI, which is used to assess development in individual countries and regions according to three separate dimensions: health (measured according to life expectancy), education (measured according to mean years of schooling as well as expected years of schooling), and standards of living (measured according to gross national income per capita). (See Figure 1.1.) Each dimension is rated on a scale between 0 and 1, and the composite of the three values represents a country's overall HDI. The higher the HDI value, the higher the level of a country's development.

Table 1.5 depicts the UNDP's 2012 rankings of countries in terms of their HDI values, in descending order, and it classifies countries in the following groups: very high human development, high human development, medium human development, and low human development. The country with the highest human development in 2012 was Norway, with an HDI of 0.955, and the countries with the lowest human development were the Democratic Republic of the Congo and Niger, both of which had an HDI of 0.304. Data were unavailable for a number of countries in the low human development category, including North Korea, which is closed to international observers. The countries in the very high human development category include those that experts frequently classify as "developed" or "industrialized," such as the United States, Canada, the countries of western Europe, and some countries in the Asia-Pacific region (Australia, Japan, South Korea, Hong Kong, and Singapore). The high human development category includes much of Central Asia,

Latin America, and the Caribbean; and the medium and low human development categories include much of South Asia and sub-Saharan Africa.

The UNDP further notes in *Human Development Report 2013—The Rise of the South: Human Progress in a Diverse World* (2013, http://www.undp.org/content/dam/undp/library/corporate/HDR/2013GlobalHDR/English/HDR 2013%20Report%20English.pdf) that countries at the lower end of the HDI spectrum made the most progress in human development between 2000 and 2012, and that "no country for which data was available had a lower HDI value in 2012 than in 2000." The agency also observed that, although progress varied across and within global regions, the faster progress in countries with low HDI values meant that global HDI levels were converging rather than diverging. Although rapid economic development in countries such as Brazil, China, and India accounted for some of the most dramatic gains in HDI, the UNDP cautions against relying on economic progress alone, arguing that government policies that aid the poor, along with investments in education, health, and employment skills, are necessary for the continued promotion of human development gains.

**MULTIDIMENSIONAL POVERTY INDEX.** In 2010 the UNDP introduced the MPI as a further advance in the attempt to understand the dimensions of poverty beyond income and consumption habits. The MPI offers a picture of poverty comparable to the picture of development provided by the HDI, but it focuses on the prevalence and intensity of poverty as distinguished from the level of

**FIGURE 1.1**

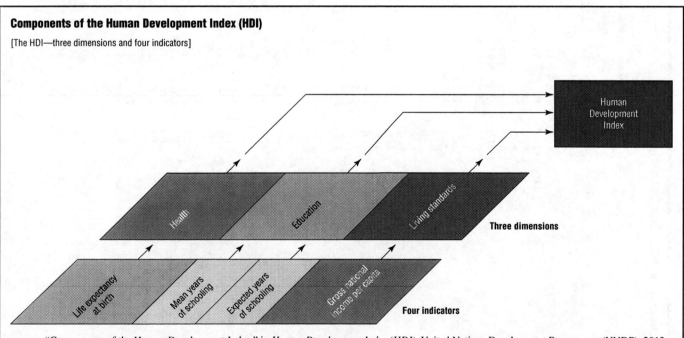

Components of the Human Development Index (HDI)

[The HDI—three dimensions and four indicators]

SOURCE: "Components of the Human Development Index," in *Human Development Index (HDI)*, United Nations Development Programme (UNDP), 2013, http://hdr.undp.org/en/statistics/hdi/ (accessed October 2, 2013)

**TABLE 1.5**

## Human Development Index (HDI) trends, by country, 1980–2012

| HDI rank | Human Development Index (HDI) Value | | | | | | | | HDI rank Change | | Average annual HDI growth (%) | | | |
|---|---|---|---|---|---|---|---|---|---|---|---|---|---|---|
| | 1980 | 1990 | 2000 | 2005 | 2007 | 2010 | 2011 | 2012 | 2007–2012[a] | 2011–2012[a] | 1980/1990 | 1990/2000 | 2000/2010 | 2000/2012 |
| **Very high human development** | | | | | | | | | | | | | | |
| 1 Norway | 0.804 | 0.852 | 0.922 | 0.948 | 0.952 | 0.952 | 0.953 | 0.955 | 0 | 0 | 0.59 | 0.79 | 0.32 | 0.29 |
| 2 Australia | 0.857 | 0.880 | 0.914 | 0.927 | 0.931 | 0.935 | 0.936 | 0.938 | 0 | 0 | 0.27 | 0.37 | 0.23 | 0.22 |
| 3 United States | 0.843 | 0.878 | 0.907 | 0.923 | 0.929 | 0.934 | 0.936 | 0.937 | 0 | -1 | 0.40 | 0.33 | 0.29 | 0.27 |
| 4 Netherlands | 0.799 | 0.842 | 0.891 | 0.899 | 0.911 | 0.919 | 0.921 | 0.921 | 2 | 0 | 0.52 | 0.56 | 0.31 | 0.28 |
| 5 Germany | 0.738 | 0.803 | 0.870 | 0.901 | 0.907 | 0.916 | 0.919 | 0.920 | 5 | 0 | 0.85 | 0.81 | 0.53 | 0.47 |
| 6 New Zealand | 0.807 | 0.835 | 0.887 | 0.908 | 0.912 | 0.917 | 0.918 | 0.919 | -1 | 0 | 0.34 | 0.60 | 0.33 | 0.29 |
| 7 Ireland | 0.745 | 0.793 | 0.879 | 0.907 | 0.918 | 0.916 | 0.915 | 0.916 | -3 | 0 | 0.62 | 1.04 | 0.42 | 0.35 |
| 7 Sweden | 0.792 | 0.823 | 0.903 | 0.905 | 0.909 | 0.916 | 0.915 | 0.916 | 0 | 0 | 0.38 | 0.93 | 0.11 | 0.12 |
| 9 Switzerland | 0.818 | 0.840 | 0.882 | 0.898 | 0.901 | 0.913 | 0.912 | 0.913 | 3 | 0 | 0.27 | 0.49 | 0.33 | 0.29 |
| 10 Japan | 0.788 | 0.837 | 0.878 | 0.896 | 0.903 | 0.909 | 0.910 | 0.912 | 1 | 0 | 0.61 | 0.48 | 0.35 | 0.32 |
| 11 Canada | 0.825 | 0.865 | 0.887 | 0.906 | 0.909 | 0.909 | 0.910 | 0.911 | -4 | -1 | 0.48 | 0.25 | 0.24 | 0.22 |
| 12 Korea, Republic of | 0.640 | 0.749 | 0.839 | 0.875 | 0.890 | 0.905 | 0.907 | 0.909 | 4 | 0 | 1.58 | 1.14 | 0.76 | 0.67 |
| 13 Hong Kong, China (SAR) | 0.712 | 0.788 | 0.815 | 0.857 | 0.877 | 0.900 | 0.904 | 0.906 | 10 | 1 | 1.02 | 0.34 | 1.00 | 0.89 |
| 13 Iceland | 0.769 | 0.815 | 0.871 | 0.901 | 0.908 | 0.901 | 0.905 | 0.906 | -4 | 0 | 0.58 | 0.67 | 0.34 | 0.33 |
| 15 Denmark | 0.790 | 0.816 | 0.869 | 0.893 | 0.898 | 0.899 | 0.901 | 0.901 | -2 | 0 | 0.33 | 0.63 | 0.34 | 0.30 |
| 16 Israel | 0.773 | 0.809 | 0.865 | 0.885 | 0.892 | 0.896 | 0.899 | 0.900 | -2 | 0 | 0.45 | 0.68 | 0.34 | 0.33 |
| 17 Belgium | 0.764 | 0.817 | 0.884 | 0.884 | 0.891 | 0.896 | 0.897 | 0.897 | -2 | 0 | 0.67 | 0.79 | 0.14 | 0.12 |
| 18 Austria | 0.747 | 0.797 | 0.848 | 0.867 | 0.879 | 0.892 | 0.894 | 0.895 | 2 | 0 | 0.66 | 0.62 | 0.51 | 0.46 |
| 18 Singapore | — | 0.756 | 0.826 | 0.852 | 0.885 | 0.892 | 0.894 | 0.895 | 7 | 0 | — | 0.89 | 0.77 | 0.67 |
| 20 France | 0.728 | 0.784 | 0.853 | 0.877 | 0.885 | 0.891 | 0.893 | 0.893 | -1 | 0 | 0.75 | 0.85 | 0.44 | 0.38 |
| 21 Finland | 0.766 | 0.801 | 0.845 | 0.882 | 0.890 | 0.890 | 0.892 | 0.892 | -5 | 0 | 0.45 | 0.54 | 0.52 | 0.45 |
| 21 Slovenia | — | — | 0.842 | 0.876 | 0.888 | 0.892 | 0.892 | 0.892 | -3 | 0 | — | — | 0.58 | 0.48 |
| 23 Spain | 0.698 | 0.756 | 0.847 | 0.865 | 0.874 | 0.884 | 0.885 | 0.885 | 1 | 0 | 0.80 | 1.15 | 0.43 | 0.37 |
| 24 Liechtenstein | — | — | — | — | — | 0.882 | 0.883 | 0.883 | — | 0 | — | — | — | — |
| 25 Italy | 0.723 | 0.771 | 0.833 | 0.869 | 0.878 | 0.881 | 0.881 | 0.881 | -2 | 0 | 0.64 | 0.78 | 0.56 | 0.46 |
| 26 Luxembourg | 0.735 | 0.796 | 0.861 | 0.875 | 0.879 | 0.875 | 0.875 | 0.875 | -5 | 0 | 0.81 | 0.78 | 0.16 | 0.14 |
| 26 United Kingdom | 0.748 | 0.784 | 0.841 | 0.865 | 0.867 | 0.874 | 0.875 | 0.875 | -1 | 0 | 0.47 | 0.70 | 0.39 | 0.33 |
| 28 Czech Republic | — | — | 0.824 | 0.862 | 0.869 | 0.871 | 0.872 | 0.873 | -3 | 0 | — | — | 0.56 | 0.48 |
| 29 Greece | 0.726 | 0.772 | 0.810 | 0.862 | 0.865 | 0.866 | 0.862 | 0.860 | 0 | 0 | 0.62 | 0.48 | 0.67 | 0.50 |
| 30 Brunei Darussalam | 0.765 | 0.782 | 0.830 | 0.848 | 0.853 | 0.854 | 0.854 | 0.855 | 0 | 0 | 0.22 | 0.59 | 0.28 | 0.25 |
| 31 Cyprus | 0.715 | 0.779 | 0.808 | 0.817 | 0.827 | 0.849 | 0.849 | 0.848 | 4 | 0 | 0.86 | 0.36 | 0.50 | 0.41 |
| 32 Malta | 0.713 | 0.757 | 0.801 | 0.827 | 0.829 | 0.844 | 0.846 | 0.847 | 2 | 0 | 0.59 | 0.57 | 0.52 | 0.46 |
| 33 Andorra | — | — | — | 0.831 | — | 0.846 | 0.847 | 0.846 | -1 | -1 | — | — | — | — |
| 33 Estonia | — | 0.728 | 0.786 | 0.830 | 0.841 | 0.839 | 0.844 | 0.846 | -2 | 1 | — | 0.76 | 0.65 | 0.62 |
| 35 Slovakia | — | 0.754 | 0.785 | 0.814 | 0.830 | 0.836 | 0.838 | 0.840 | -1 | 0 | — | 0.40 | 0.64 | 0.57 |
| 36 Qatar | 0.729 | 0.743 | 0.801 | 0.828 | 0.833 | 0.827 | 0.832 | 0.834 | -3 | 0 | 0.18 | 0.76 | 0.32 | 0.33 |
| 37 Hungary | 0.709 | 0.714 | 0.790 | 0.820 | 0.826 | 0.829 | 0.830 | 0.831 | 2 | 0 | 0.07 | 1.02 | 0.48 | 0.42 |
| 38 Barbados | 0.706 | 0.760 | 0.790 | 0.798 | 0.808 | 0.823 | 0.824 | 0.825 | 3 | 0 | 0.73 | 0.38 | 0.41 | 0.37 |
| 39 Poland | — | — | 0.778 | 0.798 | 0.806 | 0.817 | 0.819 | 0.821 | 5 | 0 | — | — | 0.49 | 0.46 |
| 40 Chile | 0.638 | 0.702 | 0.759 | 0.789 | 0.800 | 0.813 | 0.817 | 0.819 | -2 | 2 | 0.96 | 0.78 | 0.68 | 0.64 |
| 41 Lithuania | — | 0.732 | 0.756 | 0.802 | 0.810 | 0.810 | 0.814 | 0.818 | -5 | 0 | — | 0.32 | 0.68 | 0.65 |
| 41 United Arab Emirates | — | — | — | 0.831 | 0.827 | 0.816 | 0.817 | 0.818 | -1 | -3 | — | — | — | — |
| 43 Portugal | 0.644 | 0.714 | 0.783 | 0.796 | 0.806 | 0.817 | 0.817 | 0.816 | -4 | 0 | 1.04 | 0.93 | 0.43 | 0.35 |
| 44 Latvia | 0.675 | 0.699 | 0.738 | 0.792 | 0.808 | 0.805 | 0.809 | 0.814 | 4 | -1 | 0.35 | 0.55 | 0.87 | 0.82 |
| 45 Argentina | 0.675 | 0.701 | 0.755 | 0.771 | 0.787 | 0.805 | 0.810 | 0.811 | 1 | 0 | 0.38 | 0.74 | 0.64 | 0.60 |
| 46 Seychelles | — | — | 0.774 | 0.781 | 0.792 | 0.799 | 0.804 | 0.806 | -1 | 0 | — | — | 0.31 | 0.33 |
| 47 Croatia | — | 0.716 | 0.755 | 0.787 | 0.798 | 0.804 | 0.804 | 0.805 | -1 | -1 | — | 0.52 | 0.63 | 0.54 |

## TABLE 1.5

## Human Development Index (HDI) trends, by country, 1980–2012 [CONTINUED]

| HDI rank | | Human Development Index (HDI) Value | | | | | | | | HDI rank Change | | Average annual HDI growth (%) | | | |
|---|---|---|---|---|---|---|---|---|---|---|---|---|---|---|---|
| | | 1980 | 1990 | 2000 | 2005 | 2007 | 2010 | 2011 | 2012 | 2007–2012[a] | 2011–2012[a] | 1980/1990 | 1990/2000 | 2000/2010 | 2000/2012 |
| **High human development** | | | | | | | | | | | | | | | |
| 48 | Bahrain | 0.644 | 0.713 | 0.781 | 0.802 | 0.802 | 0.794 | 0.795 | 0.796 | −4 | 0 | 1.02 | 0.92 | 0.16 | 0.15 |
| 49 | Bahamas | — | — | — | — | — | 0.791 | 0.792 | 0.794 | 0 | 0 | — | — | — | — |
| 50 | Belarus | — | — | — | 0.730 | 0.756 | 0.785 | 0.789 | 0.793 | 12 | 1 | — | — | — | — |
| 51 | Uruguay | 0.664 | 0.693 | 0.741 | 0.744 | 0.771 | 0.785 | 0.789 | 0.792 | 3 | 0 | 0.42 | 0.68 | 0.58 | 0.55 |
| 52 | Montenegro | — | — | 0.765 | 0.756 | 0.775 | 0.787 | 0.791 | 0.791 | 0 | −2 | — | — | — | — |
| 52 | Palau | — | — | 0.781 | 0.786 | 0.792 | 0.779 | 0.786 | 0.791 | −4 | 2 | — | — | 0.18 | 0.27 |
| 54 | Kuwait | 0.695 | 0.712 | 0.781 | 0.784 | 0.787 | 0.786 | 0.788 | 0.790 | −4 | −1 | 0.25 | 0.92 | 0.06 | 0.10 |
| 55 | Russian Federation | — | 0.730 | 0.713 | 0.753 | 0.770 | 0.782 | 0.784 | 0.788 | 0 | 0 | — | −0.23 | 0.93 | 0.84 |
| 56 | Romania | — | 0.706 | 0.709 | 0.756 | 0.772 | 0.783 | 0.784 | 0.786 | −3 | −1 | — | −0.05 | 0.99 | 0.86 |
| 57 | Bulgaria | 0.673 | 0.704 | 0.721 | 0.756 | 0.766 | 0.778 | 0.780 | 0.782 | 0 | 0 | 0.45 | 0.24 | 0.77 | 0.67 |
| 57 | Saudi Arabia | 0.575 | 0.653 | 0.717 | 0.748 | 0.756 | 0.777 | 0.780 | 0.782 | 5 | 0 | 1.29 | 0.93 | 0.81 | 0.74 |
| 59 | Cuba | 0.626 | 0.681 | 0.690 | 0.735 | 0.770 | 0.775 | 0.777 | 0.780 | −4 | 0 | 0.83 | 0.14 | 1.17 | 1.02 |
| 59 | Panama | 0.634 | 0.666 | 0.724 | 0.746 | 0.758 | 0.770 | 0.776 | 0.780 | 1 | 1 | 0.49 | 0.85 | 0.62 | 0.62 |
| 61 | Mexico | 0.598 | 0.654 | 0.723 | 0.745 | 0.758 | 0.770 | 0.773 | 0.775 | −1 | 0 | 0.89 | 1.00 | 0.64 | 0.59 |
| 62 | Costa Rica | 0.621 | 0.663 | 0.705 | 0.732 | 0.744 | 0.768 | 0.770 | 0.773 | 4 | 0 | 0.65 | 0.62 | 0.85 | 0.76 |
| 63 | Grenada | — | — | — | — | — | 0.768 | 0.770 | 0.770 | −1 | −1 | — | — | — | — |
| 64 | Libya | — | — | — | — | 0.760 | 0.773 | 0.725 | 0.769 | −5 | 23[b] | — | — | — | — |
| 64 | Malaysia | 0.563 | 0.635 | 0.712 | 0.746 | 0.753 | 0.763 | 0.766 | 0.769 | 1 | 1 | 1.21 | 1.15 | 0.69 | 0.64 |
| 64 | Serbia | — | — | 0.726 | 0.751 | 0.760 | 0.767 | 0.769 | 0.769 | −5 | 0 | — | — | 0.56 | 0.49 |
| 67 | Antigua and Barbuda | — | — | — | — | — | 0.761 | 0.759 | 0.760 | — | −1 | — | — | — | — |
| 67 | Trinidad and Tobago | 0.680 | 0.685 | 0.707 | 0.741 | 0.752 | 0.758 | 0.759 | 0.760 | −1 | −1 | 0.08 | 0.32 | 0.70 | 0.60 |
| 69 | Kazakhstan | — | — | 0.663 | 0.721 | 0.734 | 0.744 | 0.750 | 0.754 | 2 | −1 | — | — | 1.15 | 1.08 |
| 70 | Albania | — | 0.661 | 0.698 | 0.729 | 0.737 | 0.746 | 0.748 | 0.749 | −1 | −1 | — | 0.54 | 0.66 | 0.59 |
| 71 | Venezuela, Bolivarian Republic of | 0.629 | 0.635 | 0.662 | 0.694 | 0.712 | 0.744 | 0.746 | 0.748 | 9 | −1 | 0.11 | 0.41 | 1.17 | 1.03 |
| 72 | Dominica | — | — | 0.722 | 0.732 | 0.739 | 0.743 | 0.744 | 0.745 | −3 | 0 | — | — | 0.28 | 0.26 |
| 72 | Georgia | — | — | — | 0.713 | 0.732 | 0.735 | 0.740 | 0.745 | 0 | 3 | — | — | — | — |
| 72 | Lebanon | — | — | — | 0.714 | 0.728 | 0.743 | 0.744 | 0.745 | 3 | 0 | — | — | — | — |
| 72 | Saint Kitts and Nevis | — | — | — | — | — | 0.745 | 0.745 | 0.745 | 0 | — | — | — | — | — |
| 76 | Iran, Islamic Republic of | 0.443 | 0.540 | 0.654 | 0.685 | 0.706 | 0.740 | 0.742 | 0.742 | 7 | −2 | 1.99 | 1.94 | 1.25 | 1.05 |
| 77 | Peru | 0.580 | 0.619 | 0.679 | 0.699 | 0.716 | 0.733 | 0.738 | 0.741 | 3 | −1 | 0.65 | 0.93 | 0.78 | 0.73 |
| 78 | The former Yugoslav Republic of Macedonia | — | — | — | 0.711 | 0.719 | 0.736 | 0.738 | 0.740 | 1 | −2 | — | — | — | — |
| 78 | Ukraine | — | 0.714 | 0.673 | 0.718 | 0.732 | 0.733 | 0.737 | 0.740 | −5 | 0 | — | −0.58 | 0.85 | 0.80 |
| 80 | Mauritius | 0.551 | 0.626 | 0.676 | 0.708 | 0.720 | 0.732 | 0.735 | 0.737 | −2 | −1 | 1.28 | 0.77 | 0.81 | 0.73 |
| 81 | Bosnia and Herzegovina | — | — | — | 0.724 | 0.729 | 0.732 | 0.734 | 0.735 | −6 | −1 | — | — | — | — |
| 82 | Azerbaijan | — | — | — | — | — | 0.734 | 0.732 | 0.734 | — | −1 | — | — | — | — |
| 83 | Saint Vincent and the Grenadines | — | — | — | — | — | 0.731 | 0.732 | 0.733 | — | −2 | — | — | — | — |
| 84 | Oman | — | — | — | — | — | 0.728 | 0.729 | 0.731 | — | −1 | — | — | — | — |
| 85 | Brazil | 0.522 | 0.590 | 0.669 | 0.699 | 0.710 | 0.726 | 0.728 | 0.730 | 0 | 0 | 1.23 | 1.26 | 0.82 | 0.73 |
| 85 | Jamaica | 0.612 | 0.642 | 0.679 | 0.695 | 0.701 | 0.727 | 0.726 | 0.730 | 4 | −2 | 0.47 | 0.57 | 0.69 | 0.61 |
| 87 | Armenia | — | 0.628 | 0.648 | 0.695 | 0.723 | 0.722 | 0.726 | 0.729 | −7 | −1 | — | 0.33 | 1.08 | 0.98 |
| 88 | Saint Lucia | — | — | — | — | — | 0.723 | 0.724 | 0.725 | 0 | 0 | — | — | — | — |
| 89 | Ecuador | 0.596 | 0.635 | 0.659 | 0.682 | 0.688 | 0.719 | 0.722 | 0.724 | 10 | 0 | 0.63 | 0.37 | 0.89 | 0.79 |
| 90 | Turkey | 0.474 | 0.569 | 0.645 | 0.684 | 0.702 | 0.715 | 0.720 | 0.722 | −1 | 0 | 1.85 | 1.26 | 1.04 | 0.95 |
| 91 | Colombia | 0.556 | 0.600 | 0.658 | 0.681 | 0.698 | 0.714 | 0.717 | 0.719 | 0 | 0 | 0.76 | 0.93 | 0.82 | 0.75 |
| 92 | Sri Lanka | 0.557 | 0.608 | 0.653 | 0.683 | 0.693 | 0.705 | 0.711 | 0.715 | 5 | 0 | 0.88 | 0.72 | 0.78 | 0.76 |
| 93 | Algeria | 0.461 | 0.562 | 0.625 | 0.680 | 0.691 | 0.710 | 0.711 | 0.713 | 5 | −1 | 2.01 | 1.07 | 1.28 | 1.10 |
| 94 | Tunisia | 0.459 | 0.553 | 0.642 | 0.679 | 0.694 | 0.710 | 0.710 | 0.712 | 2 | 0 | 1.87 | 1.51 | 1.01 | 0.86 |

## TABLE 1.5

**Human Development Index (HDI) trends, by country, 1980–2012** [CONTINUED]

| HDI rank | Human Development Index (HDI) — Value | | | | | | | | HDI rank — Change | | Average annual HDI growth (%) | | | |
|---|---|---|---|---|---|---|---|---|---|---|---|---|---|---|
| | 1980 | 1990 | 2000 | 2005 | 2007 | 2010 | 2011 | 2012 | 2007–2012[a] | 2011–2012[a] | 1980/1990 | 1990/2000 | 2000/2010 | 2000/2012 |
| **Medium human development** | | | | | | | | | | | | | | |
| 95 Tonga | — | 0.656 | 0.689 | 0.704 | 0.705 | 0.709 | 0.709 | 0.710 | −7 | 0 | — | 0.49 | 0.28 | 0.25 |
| 96 Belize | 0.621 | 0.653 | 0.672 | 0.694 | 0.696 | 0.700 | 0.701 | 0.702 | −4 | 0 | 0.51 | 0.29 | 0.40 | 0.35 |
| 96 Dominican Republic | 0.525 | 0.584 | 0.641 | 0.669 | 0.683 | 0.697 | 0.700 | 0.702 | 4 | 2 | 1.07 | 0.93 | 0.85 | 0.76 |
| 96 Fiji | 0.572 | 0.614 | 0.670 | 0.693 | 0.695 | 0.699 | 0.700 | 0.702 | −3 | 2 | 0.71 | 0.87 | 0.43 | 0.39 |
| 96 Samoa | — | — | 0.663 | 0.689 | 0.695 | 0.699 | 0.701 | 0.702 | −3 | 0 | — | — | 0.52 | 0.48 |
| 100 Jordan | 0.545 | 0.592 | 0.650 | 0.684 | 0.695 | 0.699 | 0.699 | 0.700 | −7 | 0 | 0.83 | 0.95 | 0.72 | 0.62 |
| 101 China | 0.407 | 0.495 | 0.590 | 0.637 | 0.662 | 0.689 | 0.695 | 0.699 | 4 | 4 | 1.96 | 1.78 | 1.55 | 1.42 |
| 102 Turkmenistan | — | — | — | — | — | 0.688 | 0.693 | 0.698 | −1 | 0 | — | — | — | — |
| 103 Thailand | 0.490 | 0.569 | 0.625 | 0.662 | 0.676 | 0.686 | 0.686 | 0.690 | −1 | 1 | 1.50 | 0.94 | 0.93 | 0.82 |
| 104 Maldives | — | — | 0.592 | 0.639 | 0.663 | 0.683 | 0.687 | 0.688 | 1 | −1 | — | — | 1.43 | 1.26 |
| 105 Suriname | — | — | — | 0.666 | 0.672 | 0.679 | 0.681 | 0.684 | −2 | 0 | — | — | — | — |
| 106 Gabon | 0.526 | 0.610 | 0.627 | 0.653 | 0.662 | 0.676 | 0.679 | 0.683 | 0 | 0 | 1.49 | 0.27 | 0.75 | 0.72 |
| 107 El Salvador | 0.471 | 0.528 | 0.620 | 0.655 | 0.671 | 0.678 | 0.679 | 0.680 | −3 | −1 | 1.14 | 1.62 | 0.90 | 0.78 |
| 108 Bolivia, Plurinational State of | 0.489 | 0.557 | 0.620 | 0.647 | 0.652 | 0.668 | 0.671 | 0.675 | 0 | 0 | 1.31 | 1.08 | 0.75 | 0.71 |
| 108 Mongolia | — | 0.559 | 0.564 | 0.622 | 0.638 | 0.657 | 0.668 | 0.675 | 4 | 2 | — | 0.08 | 1.54 | 1.51 |
| 110 Palestine, State of | — | — | — | — | — | 0.662 | 0.666 | 0.670 | 1 | 1 | — | — | — | — |
| 111 Paraguay | 0.549 | 0.578 | 0.617 | 0.641 | 0.650 | 0.668 | 0.670 | 0.669 | −1 | −2 | 0.52 | 0.66 | 0.79 | 0.67 |
| 112 Egypt | 0.407 | 0.502 | 0.593 | 0.625 | 0.640 | 0.661 | 0.661 | 0.662 | 0 | 0 | 2.12 | 1.68 | 1.08 | 0.92 |
| 113 Moldova, Republic of | — | 0.650 | 0.592 | 0.636 | 0.644 | 0.652 | 0.657 | 0.660 | −2 | 0 | — | −0.93 | 0.96 | 0.91 |
| 114 Philippines | 0.561 | 0.581 | 0.610 | 0.630 | 0.636 | 0.649 | 0.651 | 0.654 | 0 | 0 | 0.35 | 0.49 | 0.61 | 0.58 |
| 114 Uzbekistan | — | — | — | 0.617 | 0.630 | 0.644 | 0.649 | 0.654 | 1 | 1 | — | — | — | — |
| 116 Syrian Arab Republic | 0.501 | 0.557 | 0.596 | 0.618 | 0.623 | 0.646 | 0.646 | 0.648 | 0 | 0 | 1.07 | 0.67 | 0.80 | 0.70 |
| 117 Micronesia, Federated States of | — | — | — | — | — | 0.639 | 0.640 | 0.645 | 0 | 0 | — | — | — | — |
| 118 Guyana | 0.513 | 0.502 | 0.578 | 0.610 | 0.617 | 0.628 | 0.632 | 0.636 | 1 | 1 | −0.21 | 1.41 | 0.83 | 0.79 |
| 119 Botswana | 0.449 | 0.586 | 0.587 | 0.604 | 0.619 | 0.633 | 0.634 | 0.634 | −1 | −1 | 2.71 | 0.00 | 0.77 | 0.66 |
| 120 Honduras | 0.456 | 0.520 | 0.563 | 0.582 | 0.594 | 0.629 | 0.630 | 0.632 | 3 | 0 | 1.33 | 0.79 | 1.12 | 0.97 |
| 121 Indonesia | 0.422 | 0.479 | 0.540 | 0.575 | 0.595 | 0.620 | 0.624 | 0.629 | 1 | 3 | 1.26 | 1.21 | 1.39 | 1.28 |
| 121 Kiribati | — | — | — | — | — | 0.628 | 0.627 | 0.629 | 0 | −2 | — | — | — | — |
| 121 South Africa | 0.570 | 0.621 | 0.622 | 0.604 | 0.609 | 0.621 | 0.625 | 0.629 | 1 | 1 | 0.87 | 0.01 | −0.01 | 0.11 |
| 124 Vanuatu | — | — | — | — | — | 0.623 | 0.625 | 0.626 | −2 | 0 | — | — | — | — |
| 125 Kyrgyzstan | — | 0.609 | 0.582 | 0.601 | 0.612 | 0.615 | 0.621 | 0.622 | −3 | 0 | — | −0.45 | 0.54 | 0.56 |
| 126 Tajikistan | — | 0.615 | 0.529 | 0.582 | 0.587 | 0.612 | 0.618 | 0.622 | 3 | 1 | — | −1.50 | 1.47 | 1.36 |
| 127 Viet Nam | — | 0.439 | 0.534 | 0.573 | 0.590 | 0.611 | 0.614 | 0.617 | −2 | 0 | — | 1.98 | 1.37 | 1.22 |
| 128 Namibia | — | 0.569 | 0.564 | 0.579 | 0.592 | 0.604 | 0.606 | 0.608 | 0 | 0 | — | −0.10 | 0.69 | 0.64 |
| 129 Nicaragua | 0.461 | 0.479 | 0.529 | 0.572 | 0.583 | 0.593 | 0.597 | 0.599 | −1 | 0 | 0.37 | 1.01 | 1.15 | 1.04 |
| 130 Morocco | 0.371 | 0.440 | 0.512 | 0.558 | 0.571 | 0.586 | 0.589 | 0.591 | 0 | 0 | 1.71 | 1.54 | 1.35 | 1.20 |
| 131 Iraq | — | — | — | 0.564 | 0.567 | 0.578 | 0.583 | 0.590 | 1 | 1 | — | — | — | — |
| 132 Cape Verde | — | — | 0.532 | 0.551 | 0.570 | 0.581 | 0.584 | 0.586 | −1 | 0 | — | — | 0.88 | 0.81 |
| 133 Guatemala | 0.432 | 0.464 | 0.523 | 0.551 | 0.570 | 0.579 | 0.580 | 0.581 | 5 | 0 | 0.72 | 1.20 | 1.02 | 0.89 |
| 134 Timor-Leste | — | — | 0.418 | 0.491 | 0.519 | 0.565 | 0.571 | 0.576 | 7 | 0 | — | — | 3.06 | 2.71 |
| 135 Ghana | 0.391 | 0.427 | 0.461 | 0.523 | 0.533 | 0.540 | 0.553 | 0.558 | −2 | 0 | 0.90 | 0.77 | 1.58 | 1.60 |
| 136 Equatorial Guinea | — | 0.410 | 0.498 | 0.507 | 0.525 | 0.547 | 0.551 | 0.554 | −1 | 0 | — | 1.98 | 0.96 | 0.90 |
| 136 India | 0.345 | 0.410 | 0.463 | 0.501 | 0.520 | 0.547 | 0.551 | 0.554 | 3 | 0 | 1.75 | 1.23 | 1.67 | 1.50 |
| 138 Cambodia | — | — | 0.444 | 0.494 | 0.510 | 0.532 | 0.538 | 0.543 | 1 | 0 | — | — | 1.82 | 1.68 |
| 138 Lao People's Democratic Republic | — | 0.379 | 0.453 | 0.494 | 0.510 | 0.534 | 0.538 | 0.543 | 3 | 1 | — | 1.80 | 1.66 | 1.53 |
| 140 Bhutan | — | — | — | — | 0.506 | 0.525 | 0.532 | 0.538 | 1 | 1 | — | — | — | — |
| 141 Swaziland | — | 0.533 | 0.502 | 0.504 | 0.520 | 0.532 | 0.536 | 0.536 | −3 | −1 | — | −0.59 | 0.58 | 0.55 |

# TABLE 1.5

Human Development Index (HDI) trends, by country, 1980–2012 [CONTINUED]

| HDI rank | Human Development Index (HDI) Value | | | | | | | | HDI rank Change | | Average annual HDI growth (%) | | | |
|---|---|---|---|---|---|---|---|---|---|---|---|---|---|---|
| | 1980 | 1990 | 2000 | 2005 | 2007 | 2010 | 2011 | 2012 | 2007–2012[a] | 2011–2012[a] | 1980/1990 | 1990/2000 | 2000/2010 | 2000/2012 |
| **Low human development** | | | | | | | | | | | | | | |
| 142 Congo | 0.470 | 0.510 | 0.482 | 0.506 | 0.511 | 0.529 | 0.531 | 0.534 | −1 | 0 | 0.82 | −0.56 | 0.94 | 0.86 |
| 143 Solomon Islands | — | — | 0.486 | 0.510 | 0.522 | 0.522 | 0.526 | 0.530 | −6 | 0 | — | — | 0.70 | 0.71 |
| 144 Sao Tome and Principe | — | — | — | 0.488 | 0.503 | 0.520 | 0.522 | 0.525 | 0 | 0 | — | — | — | — |
| 145 Kenya | 0.424 | 0.463 | 0.447 | 0.472 | 0.491 | 0.508 | 0.511 | 0.519 | 1 | 0 | 0.88 | −0.33 | 1.34 | 1.24 |
| 146 Bangladesh | 0.312 | 0.361 | 0.433 | 0.472 | 0.488 | 0.508 | 0.511 | 0.515 | 1 | 1 | 1.49 | 1.83 | 1.61 | 1.46 |
| 146 Pakistan | 0.337 | 0.383 | 0.419 | 0.485 | 0.498 | 0.512 | 0.513 | 0.515 | −1 | 0 | 1.29 | 0.89 | 2.03 | 1.74 |
| 148 Angola | — | — | 0.375 | 0.406 | 0.472 | 0.502 | 0.504 | 0.508 | 1 | 0 | — | — | 2.97 | 2.56 |
| 149 Myanmar | 0.281 | 0.305 | 0.382 | 0.435 | 0.464 | 0.490 | 0.494 | 0.498 | 1 | 0 | 0.83 | 2.27 | 2.52 | 2.23 |
| 150 Cameroon | 0.373 | 0.431 | 0.429 | 0.453 | 0.459 | 0.488 | 0.492 | 0.495 | 1 | 0 | 1.46 | −0.05 | 1.29 | 1.20 |
| 151 Madagascar | — | — | 0.428 | 0.467 | 0.478 | 0.484 | 0.483 | 0.483 | −3 | 0 | — | — | 1.24 | 1.02 |
| 152 Tanzania, United Republic of | — | 0.353 | 0.369 | 0.395 | 0.408 | 0.466 | 0.470 | 0.476 | 15 | 1 | — | 0.43 | 2.36 | 2.15 |
| 153 Nigeria | 0.322 | 0.368 | 0.405 | 0.434 | 0.448 | 0.470 | 0.471 | 0.471 | 1 | 1 | 1.32 | 0.97 | 1.50 | 1.25 |
| 154 Senegal | 0.340 | 0.357 | 0.418 | 0.441 | 0.454 | 0.470 | 0.467 | 0.470 | −2 | −2 | 0.48 | 1.61 | 1.04 | 0.92 |
| 155 Mauritania | 0.324 | 0.368 | 0.415 | 0.441 | 0.454 | 0.464 | 0.464 | 0.467 | −3 | 0 | 1.29 | 1.22 | 0.99 | 0.96 |
| 156 Papua New Guinea | — | — | 0.401 | 0.429 | — | 0.458 | 0.462 | 0.466 | 1 | 0 | — | — | 1.35 | 1.21 |
| 157 Nepal | 0.234 | 0.341 | 0.401 | 0.429 | 0.440 | 0.458 | 0.460 | 0.463 | 2 | 1 | 3.85 | 1.62 | 1.35 | 1.21 |
| 158 Lesotho | 0.422 | 0.474 | 0.429 | 0.425 | 0.431 | 0.452 | 0.456 | 0.461 | 2 | 1 | 1.18 | −0.99 | 0.53 | 0.61 |
| 159 Togo | 0.357 | 0.382 | 0.426 | 0.428 | 0.442 | 0.452 | 0.455 | 0.459 | −2 | 1 | 0.67 | 1.11 | 0.60 | 0.62 |
| 160 Yemen | — | 0.286 | 0.376 | 0.437 | 0.444 | 0.450 | 0.459 | 0.458 | −4 | −2 | — | 2.78 | 2.16 | 1.66 |
| 161 Haiti | 0.335 | 0.399 | 0.422 | 0.408 | — | 0.450 | 0.453 | 0.456 | −6 | 1 | 1.77 | 0.56 | 0.64 | 0.65 |
| 161 Uganda | — | 0.306 | 0.375 | 0.399 | 0.427 | 0.450 | 0.454 | 0.456 | 0 | 0 | — | 2.06 | 1.84 | 1.65 |
| 163 Zambia | 0.405 | 0.398 | 0.376 | 0.405 | 0.411 | 0.438 | 0.443 | 0.448 | 3 | 0 | −0.18 | −0.56 | 1.52 | 1.46 |
| 164 Djibouti | — | — | — | 0.405 | 0.419 | 0.431 | 0.442 | 0.445 | 0 | 0 | — | — | — | — |
| 165 Gambia | 0.279 | 0.323 | 0.360 | 0.375 | 0.383 | 0.437 | 0.440 | 0.439 | 5 | 0 | 1.47 | 1.09 | 1.95 | 1.65 |
| 166 Benin | 0.253 | 0.314 | 0.380 | 0.414 | 0.420 | 0.432 | 0.434 | 0.436 | −3 | 0 | 2.16 | 1.95 | 1.28 | 1.14 |
| 167 Rwanda | 0.277 | 0.233 | 0.314 | 0.377 | 0.400 | 0.425 | 0.429 | 0.434 | 2 | 0 | −1.74 | 3.05 | 3.07 | 2.73 |
| 168 Côte d'Ivoire | 0.348 | 0.360 | 0.392 | 0.405 | 0.412 | 0.427 | 0.426 | 0.432 | −3 | 1 | 0.34 | 0.85 | 0.86 | 0.81 |
| 169 Comoros | — | — | — | 0.425 | 0.425 | 0.426 | 0.428 | 0.429 | −7 | −1 | — | — | — | — |
| 170 Malawi | 0.272 | 0.295 | 0.352 | 0.363 | 0.381 | 0.413 | 0.415 | 0.418 | 1 | 1 | 0.83 | 1.78 | 1.61 | 1.44 |
| 171 Sudan | 0.269 | 0.301 | 0.364 | 0.390 | 0.401 | 0.411 | 0.419 | 0.414 | −3 | −1 | 1.15 | 1.89 | 1.22 | 1.08 |
| 172 Zimbabwe | 0.367 | 0.427 | 0.376 | 0.352 | 0.355 | 0.374 | 0.387 | 0.397 | 0 | 1 | 1.53 | −1.26 | −0.04 | 0.46 |
| 173 Ethiopia | — | — | 0.275 | 0.316 | 0.350 | 0.387 | 0.392 | 0.396 | 1 | 1 | — | — | 3.49 | 3.09 |
| 174 Liberia | 0.298 | — | 0.304 | 0.301 | 0.334 | 0.367 | 0.381 | 0.388 | 3 | 0 | — | — | 1.88 | 2.04 |
| 175 Afghanistan | 0.209 | 0.246 | 0.236 | 0.322 | 0.346 | 0.368 | 0.371 | 0.374 | 0 | 0 | 1.63 | −0.41 | 4.54 | 3.91 |
| 176 Guinea-Bissau | — | — | — | 0.348 | 0.355 | 0.361 | 0.364 | 0.364 | −4 | 0 | — | — | — | — |
| 177 Sierra Leone | 0.255 | 0.247 | 0.244 | 0.315 | 0.331 | 0.346 | 0.348 | 0.359 | 1 | 2 | −0.28 | −0.15 | 3.58 | 3.29 |
| 178 Burundi | 0.217 | 0.272 | 0.270 | 0.298 | 0.323 | 0.348 | 0.352 | 0.355 | 2 | −1 | 2.26 | −0.07 | 2.59 | 2.31 |
| 178 Guinea | — | — | — | 0.331 | 0.342 | 0.349 | 0.352 | 0.355 | −2 | −1 | — | — | — | — |
| 180 Central African Republic | 0.285 | 0.312 | 0.294 | 0.308 | 0.316 | 0.344 | 0.348 | 0.352 | 2 | −1 | 0.94 | −0.59 | 1.59 | 1.50 |
| 181 Eritrea | — | — | — | — | — | 0.342 | 0.346 | 0.351 | −2 | −1 | — | — | — | — |
| 182 Mali | 0.176 | 0.204 | 0.270 | 0.312 | 0.328 | 0.344 | 0.347 | 0.344 | −2 | −1 | 1.50 | 2.86 | 2.45 | 2.04 |
| 183 Burkina Faso | — | — | — | 0.301 | 0.314 | 0.334 | 0.340 | 0.343 | 1 | 0 | — | — | — | — |
| 184 Chad | — | — | 0.290 | 0.317 | 0.319 | 0.336 | 0.336 | 0.340 | −2 | 0 | — | — | 1.47 | 1.32 |
| 185 Mozambique | 0.217 | 0.202 | 0.247 | 0.287 | 0.301 | 0.318 | 0.322 | 0.327 | 0 | 0 | −0.70 | 2.00 | 2.57 | 2.37 |
| 186 Congo, Democratic Republic of the | 0.286 | 0.297 | 0.234 | 0.258 | 0.280 | 0.295 | 0.299 | 0.304 | 0 | 0 | 0.37 | −2.34 | 2.35 | 2.19 |
| 186 Niger | 0.179 | 0.198 | 0.234 | 0.269 | 0.278 | 0.298 | 0.297 | 0.304 | 1 | 1 | 0.98 | 1.72 | 2.42 | 2.20 |

## TABLE 1.5

## Human Development Index (HDI) trends, by country, 1980–2012 [CONTINUED]

| HDI rank | Human Development Index (HDI) Value | | | | | | | | HDI rank Change | | Average annual HDI growth (%) | | | |
|---|---|---|---|---|---|---|---|---|---|---|---|---|---|---|
| | 1980 | 1990 | 2000 | 2005 | 2007 | 2010 | 2011 | 2012 | 2007–2012[a] | 2011–2012[a] | 1980/1990 | 1990/2000 | 2000/2010 | 2000/2012 |
| **Other countries or territories** | | | | | | | | | | | | | | |
| Korea, Democratic People's Rep. of | — | — | — | — | — | — | — | — | — | — | — | — | — | — |
| Marshall Islands | — | — | — | — | — | — | — | — | — | — | — | — | — | — |
| Monaco | — | — | — | — | — | — | — | — | — | — | — | — | — | — |
| Nauru | — | — | — | — | — | — | — | — | — | — | — | — | — | — |
| San Marino | — | — | — | — | — | — | — | — | — | — | — | — | — | — |
| Somalia | — | — | — | — | — | — | — | — | — | — | — | — | — | — |
| South Sudan | — | — | — | — | — | — | — | — | — | — | — | — | — | — |
| Tuvalu | — | — | — | — | — | — | — | — | — | — | — | — | — | — |
| **Human Development Index groups** | | | | | | | | | | | | | | |
| Very high human development | 0.773 | 0.817 | 0.867 | 0.889 | 0.896 | 0.902 | 0.904 | 0.905 | — | — | 0.56 | 0.59 | 0.40 | 0.36 |
| High human development | 0.605[c] | 0.656[c] | 0.695 | 0.725 | 0.738 | 0.753 | 0.755 | 0.758 | — | — | 0.81 | 0.58 | 0.80 | 0.72 |
| Medium human development | 0.419[c] | 0.481 | 0.549 | 0.589 | 0.609 | 0.631 | 0.636 | 0.640 | — | — | 1.38 | 1.32 | 1.41 | 1.29 |
| Low human development | 0.315 | 0.350 | 0.385 | 0.424 | 0.442 | 0.461 | 0.464 | 0.466 | — | — | 1.05 | 0.95 | 1.82 | 1.62 |
| **Regions** | | | | | | | | | | | | | | |
| Arab States | 0.443 | 0.517 | 0.583 | 0.622 | 0.633 | 0.648 | 0.650 | 0.652 | — | — | 1.56 | 1.21 | 1.07 | 0.94 |
| East Asia and the Pacific | 0.432[c] | 0.502[c] | 0.584 | 0.626 | 0.649 | 0.673 | 0.678 | 0.683 | — | — | 1.51 | 1.51 | 1.43 | 1.31 |
| Europe and Central Asia | 0.651[c] | 0.701[c] | 0.709 | 0.743 | 0.757 | 0.766 | 0.769 | 0.771 | — | — | 0.74 | 0.12 | 0.77 | 0.70 |
| Latin America and the Caribbean | 0.574 | 0.623 | 0.683 | 0.708 | 0.722 | 0.736 | 0.739 | 0.741 | — | — | 0.83 | 0.93 | 0.74 | 0.67 |
| South Asia | 0.357 | 0.418 | 0.470 | 0.514 | 0.531 | 0.552 | 0.555 | 0.558 | — | — | 1.58 | 1.19 | 1.60 | 1.43 |
| Sub-Saharan Africa | 0.366 | 0.387 | 0.405 | 0.432 | 0.449 | 0.468 | 0.472 | 0.475 | — | — | 0.58 | 0.44 | 1.47 | 1.34 |
| Least developed countries | 0.290[c] | 0.327[c] | 0.367 | 0.401 | 0.421 | 0.443 | 0.446 | 0.449 | — | — | 1.22 | 1.15 | 1.91 | 1.70 |
| Small island developing states | 0.530[c] | 0.571[c] | 0.600[c] | 0.623 | 0.658 | 0.645 | 0.647 | 0.648 | — | — | 0.75 | 0.50 | 0.73 | 0.65 |
| World | 0.561[c] | 0.600 | 0.639 | 0.666 | 0.678 | 0.690 | 0.692 | 0.694 | — | — | 0.68 | 0.64 | 0.77 | 0.68 |

[a]A positive value indicates an improvement in rank.

[b]The substantial change in rank is due to an updated International Monetary Fund estimate of Libya's GDP growth in 2011.

[c]Based on fewer than half the countries in the group or region.

Notes: Human Development Index (HDI): A composite index measuring average achievement in three basic dimensions of human development—a long and healthy life, knowledge and a decent standard of living.
Average annual HDI growth: A smoothed annualized growth of the HDI in a given period calculated as the annual compound growth rate.

SOURCE: "Table 2. Human Development Index Trends, 1980–2012," in *Human Development Report 2013—The Rise of the South: Human Progress in a Diverse World*, United Nations Development Programme, 2013, http://www.undp.org/content/dam/undp/library/corporate/HDR/2013GlobalHDR/English/HDR2013%20Report%20English.pdf (accessed September 23, 2013)

FIGURE 1.2

**Components of the Multidimensional Poverty Index (MPI)**

[MPI—three dimensions and 10 indicators]

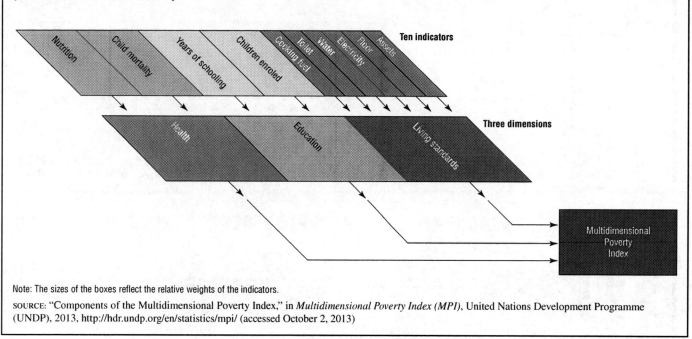

Note: The sizes of the boxes reflect the relative weights of the indicators.

SOURCE: "Components of the Multidimensional Poverty Index," in *Multidimensional Poverty Index (MPI)*, United Nations Development Programme (UNDP), 2013, http://hdr.undp.org/en/statistics/mpi/ (accessed October 2, 2013)

a country or region's development—conditions that are deeply intertwined but distinct from one another. The MPI retains the HDI's focus on the three basic dimensions of health, education, and standards of living, but it breaks these dimensions down into 10 indicators, as Figure 1.2 shows. The health dimension of the metric is calculated according to two indicators, one assessing nutrition and another addressing child mortality; the education dimension is calculated according to two indicators, one assessing years of schooling and another assessing enrollment in school; and the living standards dimension is calculated according to the presence or absence of six indicators in households: cooking fuel, toilets, water, electricity, flooring, and assets. As with the HDI, the goal is not to replace conventional income- and consumption-based measures of poverty but to supplement them.

Table 1.6 shows the MPI values for 104 developing countries, as well as money-based poverty measures for these countries, such as the percentages of people living below $1.25 per day and the percentages living below national poverty lines. MPI values measure both the prevalence and the intensity of poverty. The values range from 0 to 1, like HDI values, but unlike HDI values, higher MPI values indicate higher levels of multidimensional poverty. Although countries with high MPI values also tend to have high percentages of people living under $1.25 per day, more people were living in multidimensional poverty than were living below the $1.25 per day

threshold, and sometimes there are significant disparities between the two measures of poverty.

The countries with the highest MPI values, the largest proportion of their populations living in multidimensional poverty, and the most intense forms of poverty were in sub-Saharan Africa in 2012. Ethiopia had an MPI value of 0.564, and 87.3% of its population lived in multidimensional poverty, whereas only 39% of the country's residents lived below $1.25 per day. Similarly, Burkina Faso had an MPI of 0.535, and 84% of its population lived in multidimensional poverty, while 44.6% of its people lived below $1.25 per day.

In other African countries, measures of poverty intensity (expressed as a percentage) resulted in higher MPI values than in countries with a higher percentage of people living in poverty. For example, Liberia had an MPI value of 0.485, and 83.9% of its population lived in multidimensional poverty, a proportion almost identical to the poverty headcount using the $1.25-per-day threshold (83.8%). Mozambique had a smaller proportion of people living in multidimensional poverty (79.3%) and living below the $1.25-per-day threshold (59.6%), but it had one of the highest measures of poverty intensity (64.6%). Therefore, Mozambique's MPI value of 0.512 was higher than Liberia's, whose intensity of poverty (57.7%) was lower. These variations in poverty data allow researchers to understand the specific forms that poverty takes in individual countries and, hopefully, to begin to craft the most appropriate policy responses.

TABLE 1.6

## Multidimensional poverty in less developed countries

| | Multidimensional Poverty Index | | Population in multidimensional poverty[a] | | | Population vulnerable to poverty (%) | Population in severe poverty (%) | Contribution of deprivation to overall poverty (%) | | | Population below income poverty line (%) | |
|---|---|---|---|---|---|---|---|---|---|---|---|---|
| | Year[b] | Value[a] | Headcount (%) | Headcount (Thousands) | Intensity of deprivation (%) | (%) | (%) | Education | Health | Living standards | PPP $1.25 a day 2002–2011[c] | National poverty line 2002–2012[c] |
| **Estimates based on surveys for 2007–2011** | | | | | | | | | | | | |
| Albania | 2008/2009 (D) | 0.005 | 1.4 | 45 | 37.7 | 7.4 | 0.1 | 32.0 | 44.9 | 23.0 | 0.6 | 12.4 |
| Armenia | 2010 (D) | 0.001 | 0.3 | 6 | 35.2 | 3.0 | 0.0 | 25.8 | 64.8 | 9.4 | 1.3 | 35.8 |
| Bangladesh | 2007 (D) | 0.292 | 57.8 | 83,207 | 50.4 | 21.2 | 26.2 | 18.7 | 34.5 | 46.8 | 43.3 | 31.5 |
| Bhutan | 2010 (M) | 0.119 | 27.2 | 198 | 43.9 | 17.2 | 8.5 | 40.4 | 21.2 | 38.4 | 10.2 | 23.2 |
| Bolivia, Plurinational State of | 2008 (D) | 0.089 | 20.5 | 1,972 | 43.7 | 18.7 | 5.8 | 19.8 | 27.5 | 52.6 | 15.6 | 60.1 |
| Burkina Faso | 2010 (D) | 0.535 | 84.0 | 13,834 | 63.7 | 7.1 | 65.7 | 36.2 | 27.9 | 35.9 | 44.6 | — |
| Cambodia | 2010 (D) | 0.212 | 45.9 | 6,415 | 46.1 | 21.4 | 17.0 | 22.1 | 32.7 | 45.1 | 22.8 | 30.1 |
| Colombia | 2010 (D) | 0.022 | 5.4 | 2,500 | 40.9 | 6.4 | 1.1 | 31.8 | 33.5 | 34.7 | 8.2 | 37.2 |
| Congo | 2009 (D) | 0.208 | 40.6 | 1,600 | 51.2 | 17.7 | 22.9 | 10.4 | 45.6 | 44.0 | 54.1 | 50.1 |
| Congo, Democratic Republic of the | 2010 (M) | 0.392 | 74.0 | 48,815 | 53.0 | 15.1 | 45.9 | 18.0 | 25.1 | 56.9 | 87.7 | 71.3 |
| Dominican Republic | 2007 (D) | 0.018 | 4.6 | 439 | 39.4 | 8.6 | 0.7 | 39.1 | 22.6 | 38.2 | 2.2 | 34.4 |
| Egypt | 2008 (D) | 0.024 | 6.0 | 4,699 | 40.7 | 7.2 | 1.0 | 48.1 | 37.3 | 14.5 | 1.7 | 22.0 |
| Ethiopia | 2011 (D) | 0.564 | 87.3 | 72,415 | 64.6 | 6.8 | 71.1 | 25.9 | 27.6 | 46.5 | 39.0 | 38.9 |
| Ghana | 2008 (D) | 0.144 | 31.2 | 7,258 | 46.2 | 21.6 | 11.4 | 32.1 | 19.5 | 48.4 | 28.6 | 28.5 |
| Guyana | 2009 (D) | 0.030 | 7.7 | 58 | 39.2 | 12.3 | 1.0 | 17.4 | 50.4 | 32.2 | — | — |
| Indonesia | 2007 (D) | 0.095 | 20.8 | 48,352 | 45.9 | 12.2 | 7.6 | 15.7 | 50.6 | 33.8 | 18.1 | 12.5 |
| Jordan | 2009 (D) | 0.008 | 2.4 | 145 | 34.4 | 1.3 | 0.1 | 49.6 | 47.4 | 3.1 | 0.1 | 13.3 |
| Kenya | 2008/2009 (D) | 0.229 | 47.8 | 18,863 | 48.0 | 27.4 | 19.8 | 12.7 | 30.1 | 57.2 | 43.4 | 45.9 |
| Lesotho | 2009 (D) | 0.156 | 35.3 | 759 | 44.1 | 26.7 | 11.1 | 21.9 | 18.9 | 59.2 | 43.4 | 56.6 |
| Liberia | 2007 (D) | 0.485 | 83.9 | 3,218 | 57.7 | 9.7 | 57.5 | 29.7 | 25.0 | 45.3 | 83.8 | 63.8 |
| Madagascar | 2008/2009 (D) | 0.357 | 66.9 | 13,463 | 53.3 | 17.9 | 35.4 | 34.3 | 16.7 | 49.1 | 81.3 | 68.7 |
| Malawi | 2010 (D) | 0.334 | 66.7 | 9,633 | 50.1 | 23.4 | 31.4 | 19.5 | 27.1 | 53.3 | 73.9 | 52.4 |
| Maldives | 2009 (D) | 0.018 | 5.2 | 16 | 35.6 | 4.8 | 0.3 | 13.6 | 81.1 | 5.3 | — | — |
| Mauritania | 2007 (M) | 0.352[d] | 61.7[d] | 1,982[d] | 57.1[d] | 15.1[d] | 40.7[d] | 32.0 | 21.6 | 46.5 | 23.4 | 42.0 |
| Morocco | 2007 (N) | 0.048[d] | 10.6[d] | 3,287[d] | 45.3[d] | 12.3[d] | 3.3[d] | 35.5 | 27.5 | 37.0 | 2.5 | 9.0 |
| Mozambique | 2009 (D) | 0.512 | 79.3 | 18,127 | 64.6 | 9.5 | 60.7 | 23.9 | 36.2 | 39.9 | 59.6 | 54.7 |
| Namibia | 2006/2007 (D) | 0.187 | 39.6 | 855 | 47.2 | 23.6 | 14.7 | 15.1 | 31.0 | 53.9 | 31.9 | 38.0 |
| Nepal | 2011 (D) | 0.217 | 44.2 | 13,242 | 49.0 | 17.4 | 20.8 | 21.8 | 33.7 | 44.4 | 24.8 | 25.2 |
| Nigeria | 2008 (D) | 0.310 | 54.1 | 83,578 | 57.3 | 17.8 | 33.9 | 27.0 | 32.2 | 40.8 | 68.0 | 54.7 |
| Pakistan | 2006/2007 (D) | 0.264[d] | 49.4[d] | 81,236[d] | 53.4[d] | 11.0[d] | 27.4[d] | 30.8 | 37.9 | 31.2 | 21.0 | 22.3 |
| Palestine, State of | 2006/2007 (N) | 0.005 | 1.4 | 52 | 37.3 | 8.8 | 0.1 | 33.9 | 55.3 | 10.8 | 0.0 | 21.9 |
| Peru | 2008 (D) | 0.066 | 15.7 | 4,422 | 42.2 | 14.9 | 3.9 | 18.6 | 20.8 | 60.6 | 4.9 | 31.3 |
| Philippines | 2008 (D) | 0.064 | 13.4 | 12,083 | 47.4 | 9.1 | 5.7 | 15.8 | 56.5 | 27.7 | 18.4 | 26.5 |
| Rwanda | 2010 (D) | 0.350 | 69.0 | 6,900 | 50.8 | 19.4 | 34.7 | 19.5 | 30.9 | 49.6 | 63.2 | 44.9 |
| Sao Tome and Principe | 2008/2009 (D) | 0.154 | 34.5 | 56 | 44.7 | 24.3 | 10.7 | 28.8 | 27.5 | 43.6 | — | 66.2 |
| Senegal | 2010/2011 (D) | 0.439 | 74.4 | 7,642 | 58.9 | 11.7 | 50.6 | 31.8 | 40.6 | 27.6 | 33.5 | 50.8 |
| Sierra Leone | 2008 (D) | 0.439 | 77.0 | 4,321 | 57.0 | 13.1 | 53.2 | 31.5 | 19.3 | 49.2 | 53.4 | 66.4 |
| South Africa | 2008 (N) | 0.057 | 13.4 | 6,609 | 42.3 | 22.2 | 2.4 | 7.5 | 50.5 | 42.0 | 13.8 | 23.0 |
| Swaziland | 2010 (M) | 0.086 | 20.4 | 242 | 41.9 | 23.1 | 3.3 | 16.7 | 29.9 | 53.4 | 40.6 | 69.2 |
| Tanzania, United Republic of | 2010 (D) | 0.332 | 65.6 | 28,552 | 50.7 | 21.0 | 33.4 | 18.3 | 26.4 | 55.3 | 67.9 | 33.4 |
| Timor-Leste | 2009/2010 (D) | 0.360 | 68.1 | 749 | 52.9 | 18.2 | 38.7 | 21.3 | 31.0 | 47.7 | 37.4 | 49.9 |
| Ukraine | 2007 (D) | 0.008 | 2.2 | 1,018 | 35.5 | 1.0 | 0.2 | 4.7 | 91.1 | 4.2 | 0.1 | 2.9 |
| Uganda | 2011 (D) | 0.367 | 69.9 | 24,122 | 52.5 | 19.0 | 31.2 | 15.6 | 34.1 | 50.4 | 51.5 | 31.1 |
| Vanuatu | 2007 (M) | 0.129 | 30.1 | 67 | 42.7 | 33.5 | 6.5 | 29.7 | 17.3 | 53.0 | — | — |
| Viet Nam | 2010/2011 (M) | 0.017 | 4.2 | 3,690 | 39.5 | 7.9 | 0.7 | 32.8 | 25.1 | 42.1 | 40.1 | 28.9 |
| Zambia | 2007 (D) | 0.328 | 64.2 | 7,740 | 51.2 | 17.2 | 34.8 | 17.5 | 27.9 | 54.7 | 68.5 | 59.3 |
| Zimbabwe | 2010/2011 (D) | 0.172 | 39.1 | 4,877 | 44.0 | 25.1 | 11.5 | 10.2 | 33.6 | 56.3 | — | 72.0 |

# TABLE 1.6

## Multidimensional poverty in less developed countries [CONTINUED]

| | Multidimensional Poverty Index | | Population in multidimensional poverty[a] | | | Population vulnerable to poverty (%) | Population in severe poverty (%) | Contribution of deprivation to overall poverty (%) | | | Population below income poverty line (%) | |
|---|---|---|---|---|---|---|---|---|---|---|---|---|
| | Year[b] | Value[a] | Headcount (%) | Headcount (Thousands) | Intensity of deprivation (%) | | | Education | Health | Living standards | PPP $1.25 a day 2002–2011[c] | National poverty line 2002–2012[c] |
| **Estimates based on surveys for 2002–2006** | | | | | | | | | | | | |
| Argentina | 2005 (N) | 0.011[f] | 2.9[f] | 1,160[f] | 37.6[f] | 5.8[f] | 0.2[f] | 41.9 | 12.9 | 45.2 | 0.9 | — |
| Azerbaijan | 2006 (D) | 0.021 | 5.3 | 461 | 39.4 | 12.5 | 0.6 | 24.4 | 49.4 | 26.2 | 0.4 | 15.8 |
| Belarus | 2005 (M) | 0.000 | 0.0 | 0 | 35.1 | 0.8 | 0.0 | 16.6 | 61.8 | 21.7 | 0.1 | 5.4 |
| Belize | 2006 (M) | 0.024 | 5.6 | 16 | 42.6 | 7.6 | 1.1 | 22.8 | 35.8 | 41.4 | — | 33.5 |
| Benin | 2006 (D) | 0.412 | 71.8 | 5,652 | 57.4 | 13.2 | 47.2 | 33.6 | 25.1 | 41.3 | 47.3 | 39.0 |
| Bosnia and Herzegovina | 2006 (M) | 0.003 | 0.8 | 30 | 37.2 | 7.0 | 0.1 | 29.2 | 51.8 | 19.0 | 0.0 | 14.0 |
| Brazil | 2006 (M) | 0.011 | 2.7 | 5,075 | 39.3 | 7.0 | 0.2 | 39.0 | 40.2 | 20.7 | 6.1 | 21.4 |
| Burundi | 2005 (M) | 0.530 | 84.5 | 6,128 | 62.7 | 12.2 | 61.9 | 31.5 | 22.4 | 46.1 | 81.3 | 66.9 |
| Cameroon | 2004 (D) | 0.287 | 53.3 | 9,149 | 53.9 | 19.3 | 30.4 | 25.7 | 24.5 | 49.8 | 9.6 | 39.9 |
| Chad | 2003 (W) | 0.344 | 62.9 | 5,758 | 54.7 | 28.2 | 44.1 | 40.9 | 4.6 | 54.5 | 61.9 | 55.0 |
| China | 2002 (W) | 0.056 | 12.5 | 161,675 | 44.9 | 6.3 | 4.5 | 64.8 | 9.9 | 25.2 | 13.1 | 2.8 |
| Croatia | 2003 (W) | 0.016 | 4.4 | 196 | 36.3 | 0.1 | 0.3 | 45.0 | 46.7 | 8.3 | 0.1 | 11.1 |
| Czech Republic | 2002/2003 (W) | 0.010 | 3.1 | 316 | 33.4 | 0.0 | 0.0 | 0.0 | 99.9 | 0.1 | — | — |
| Côte d'Ivoire | 2005 (D) | 0.353 | 61.5 | 11,083 | 57.4 | 15.3 | 39.3 | 32.0 | 38.7 | 29.3 | 23.8 | 42.7 |
| Djibouti | 2006 (M) | 0.139 | 29.3 | 241 | 47.3 | 16.1 | 12.5 | 38.3 | 24.6 | 37.1 | 18.8 | — |
| Ecuador | 2003 (W) | 0.009 | 2.2 | 286 | 41.6 | 2.1 | 0.6 | 78.6 | 3.3 | 18.1 | 4.6 | 32.8 |
| Estonia | 2003 (W) | 0.026 | 7.2 | 97 | 36.5 | 1.3 | 0.2 | 91.2 | 1.2 | 7.6 | 0.5 | — |
| Gambia | 2005/2006 (M) | 0.324 | 60.4 | 935 | 53.6 | 17.6 | 35.5 | 33.5 | 30.7 | 35.8 | 33.6 | 48.4 |
| Georgia | 2005 (M) | 0.003 | 0.8 | 36 | 35.2 | 5.3 | 0.0 | 23.2 | 33.8 | 43.0 | 15.3 | 24.7 |
| Guatemala | 2003 (W) | 0.127[d] | 25.9[d] | 3,134[d] | 49.1[d] | 9.8[d] | 14.5[d] | 57.2 | 10.0 | 32.8 | 13.5 | 51.0 |
| Guinea | 2005 (D) | 0.506 | 82.5 | 7,459 | 61.3 | 9.3 | 62.3 | 35.5 | 23.0 | 41.5 | 43.3 | 53.0 |
| Haiti | 2005/2006 (D) | 0.299 | 56.4 | 5,346 | 53.0 | 18.8 | 32.3 | 27.0 | 21.5 | 51.5 | — | — |
| Honduras | 2005/2006 (D) | 0.159 | 32.5 | 2,281 | 48.9 | 22.0 | 11.3 | 38.0 | 18.5 | 43.6 | 17.9 | 60.0 |
| Hungary | 2003 (W) | 0.016 | 4.6 | 466 | 34.3 | 0.0 | 0.0 | 1.8 | 95.6 | 2.7 | 0.2 | — |
| India | 2005/2006 (D) | 0.283 | 53.7 | 612,203 | 52.7 | 16.4 | 28.6 | 21.8 | 35.7 | 42.5 | 32.7 | 29.8 |
| Iraq | 2006 (M) | 0.059 | 14.2 | 3,996 | 41.3 | 14.3 | 3.1 | 47.5 | 32.1 | 20.4 | 2.8 | 22.9 |
| Kazakhstan | 2006 (M) | 0.002 | 1.9 | 92 | 36.9 | 5.0 | 0.0 | 14.6 | 56.8 | 28.7 | 0.1 | 8.2 |
| Kyrgyzstan | 2005/2006 (M) | 0.019 | 4.9 | 249 | 38.8 | 9.2 | 0.9 | 36.6 | 36.9 | 26.4 | 6.2 | 33.7 |
| Lao People's Democratic Republic | 2006 (M) | 0.267 | 47.2 | 2,757 | 56.5 | 14.1 | 28.1 | 33.1 | 27.9 | 39.0 | 33.9 | 27.6 |
| Latvia | 2003 (W) | 0.006[d] | 1.6[d] | 37[d] | 37.9[d] | 0.0[d] | 0.0[d] | 0.0 | 88.0 | 12.0 | 0.1 | 5.9 |
| Mali | 2006 (D) | 0.558 | 86.6 | 11,771 | 64.4 | 7.6 | 68.4 | 34.5 | 26.2 | 39.3 | 50.4 | 47.4 |
| Mexico | 2006 (N) | 0.015 | 4.0 | 4,313 | 38.9 | 5.8 | 0.5 | 38.6 | 23.9 | 37.5 | 1.2 | 51.3 |
| Moldova, Republic of | 2005 (D) | 0.007 | 1.9 | 72 | 36.7 | 6.4 | 0.1 | 24.7 | 34.3 | 41.1 | 0.4 | 21.9 |
| Mongolia | 2005 (M) | 0.065 | 15.8 | 403 | 41.0 | 20.6 | 3.2 | 15.4 | 27.9 | 56.6 | — | 35.2 |
| Montenegro | 2005/2006 (M) | 0.006 | 1.5 | 9 | 41.6 | 1.9 | 0.3 | 37.5 | 47.6 | 14.9 | 0.1 | 6.6 |
| Nicaragua | 2006/2007 (D) | 0.128 | 28.0 | 1,538 | 45.7 | 17.4 | 11.2 | 27.9 | 13.6 | 58.5 | 11.9 | 46.2 |
| Niger | 2006 (D) | 0.642 | 92.4 | 12,437 | 69.4 | 4.0 | 81.8 | 35.4 | 21.5 | 43.2 | 43.6 | 59.5 |
| Paraguay | 2002/2003 (W) | 0.064 | 13.3 | 755 | 48.5 | 15.0 | 6.1 | 35.1 | 19.0 | 45.9 | 7.2 | 34.7 |
| Russian Federation | 2003 (W) | 0.005[d] | 1.3[d] | 1,883[d] | 38.9[d] | 0.8[d] | 0.2[d] | 84.2 | 2.5 | 13.3 | 0.0 | 11.1 |
| Serbia | 2005/2006 (M) | 0.003 | 0.8 | 79 | 40.0 | 3.6 | 0.1 | 30.5 | 40.1 | 29.4 | 0.3 | 9.2 |
| Slovakia | 2003 (W) | 0.000[e] | 0.0[e] | 0[e] | 0.0[e] | 0.0[e] | 0.0[e] | 0.0 | 0.0 | 0.0 | 0.1 | — |
| Slovenia | 2003 (W) | 0.000[e] | 0.0[e] | 0[e] | 0.0[e] | 0.4[e] | 0.0[e] | 0.0 | 0.0 | 0.0 | 0.1 | — |
| Somalia | 2006 (M) | 0.514 | 81.2 | 6,941 | 63.3 | 9.5 | 65.6 | 34.2 | 18.6 | 47.2 | — | — |
| Sri Lanka | 2003 (W) | 0.021[d] | 5.3[d] | 1,027[d] | 38.7[d] | 14.4[d] | 0.6[d] | 6.3 | 35.4 | 58.3 | 7.0 | 8.9 |
| Suriname | 2006 (M) | 0.039 | 8.2 | 41 | 47.2 | 6.7 | 3.3 | 36.1 | 18.8 | 45.1 | — | — |
| Syrian Arab Republic | 2006 (M) | 0.021[e] | 5.5[e] | 1,041[e] | 37.5[e] | 7.1[e] | 0.5[e] | 45.4 | 42.7 | 11.8 | 1.7 | — |

# TABLE 1.6

## Multidimensional poverty in less developed countries [CONTINUED]

| | Multidimensional Poverty Index | | Population in multidimensional poverty[a] | | | Population vulnerable to poverty | Population in severe poverty | Contribution of deprivation to overall poverty (%) | | | Population below income poverty line (%) | |
|---|---|---|---|---|---|---|---|---|---|---|---|---|
| | | | Headcount | | Intensity of deprivation | | | | | | PPP $1.25 a day | National poverty line |
| | Value[a] | Year[b] | (%) | (Thousands) | (%) | (%) | (%) | Education | Health | Living standards | 2002–2011[c] | 2002–2012[c] |
| Tajikistan | 0.068 | 2005 (M) | 17.1 | 1,104 | 40.0 | 23.0 | 3.1 | 18.7 | 45.0 | 36.3 | 6.6 | 46.7 |
| Thailand | 0.006 | 2005/2006 (M) | 1.6 | 1,067 | 38.5 | 9.9 | 0.2 | 40.7 | 31.2 | 28.1 | 0.4 | 8.1 |
| The former Yugoslav Republic of Macedonia | 0.008 | 2005 (M) | 1.9 | 39 | 40.9 | 6.7 | 0.3 | 59.9 | 12.8 | 27.3 | 0.0 | 19.0 |
| Togo | 0.284 | 2006 (M) | 54.3 | 3,003 | 52.4 | 21.6 | 28.7 | 28.3 | 25.4 | 46.3 | 38.7 | 61.7 |
| Trinidad and Tobago | 0.020 | 2006 (M) | 5.6 | 74 | 35.1 | 0.4 | 0.3 | 1.3 | 94.3 | 4.4 | — | — |
| Tunisia | 0.010[d] | 2003 (W) | 2.8[d] | 272[d] | 37.1[d] | 4.9[d] | 0.2[d] | 25.0 | 47.3 | 27.6 | 1.4 | 3.8 |
| Turkey | 0.028 | 2003 (D) | 6.6 | 4,378 | 42.0 | 7.3 | 1.3 | 42.3 | 38.4 | 19.2 | 0.0 | 18.1 |
| United Arab Emirates | 0.002 | 2003 (W) | 0.6 | 20 | 35.3 | 2.0 | 0.0 | 94.4 | 0.4 | 5.2 | — | — |
| Uruguay | 0.006 | 2002/2003 (W) | 1.7 | 57 | 34.7 | 0.1 | 0.0 | 96.0 | 0.6 | 3.4 | 0.2 | 18.6 |
| Uzbekistan | 0.008 | 2006 (M) | 2.3 | 603 | 36.2 | 8.1 | 0.1 | 23.2 | 55.7 | 21.1 | — | — |
| Yemen | 0.283 | 2006 (M) | 52.5 | 11,176 | 53.9 | 13.0 | 31.9 | 27.0 | 40.5 | 32.4 | 17.5 | 34.8 |

[a]Not all indicators were available for all countries; caution should thus be used in cross-country comparisons. Where data are missing, indicator weights are adjusted to total 100%.
[b]D indicates data are from Demographic and Health Surveys, M indicates data are from Multiple Indicator Cluster Surveys, W indicates data are from World Health Surveys and N indicates data are from national surveys.
[c]Data refer to the most recent year available during the period specified.
[d]Lower bound estimate.
[e]Upper bound estimate.
[f]Refers to only part of the country.

Notes: Multidimensional Poverty Index: Percentage of the population that is multidimensionally poor adjusted by the intensity of the deprivations.
Multidimensional poverty headcount: Percentage of the population with a weighted deprivation score of at least 33%.
Intensity of deprivation of multidimensional poverty: Average percentage of deprivation experienced by people in multidimensional poverty.
Population vulnerable to poverty: Percentage of the population at risk of suffering multiple deprivations—that is, those with adeprivation score of 20%–33%.
Population in severe poverty: Percentage of the population in severe multidimensional poverty—that is, those with a deprivation score of 50% or more.
Contribution of deprivation to overall poverty: Percentage of the Multidimensional Poverty Index attributed to deprivations in each dimension.
Population below PPP (purchasing power parity) $1.25 a day: Percentage of the population living below the international poverty line $1.25 (in purchasing power parity terms) a day.
Population below national poverty line: Percentage of the population living below the national poverty line, which is the poverty line deemed appropriate for a country by its authorities. National estimates are based on population-weighted subgroup estimates from household surveys.

SOURCE: "Table 5. Multidimensional Poverty Index," in *Human Development Report 2013—The Rise of the South: Human Progress in a Diverse World*, United Nations Development Programme, 2013, http://www.undp.org/content/dam/undp/library/corporate/HDR/2013GlobalHDR/English/HDR2013%20Report%20English.pdf (accessed September 23, 2013)

## Millennium Development Goals

On September 8, 2000, 189 member countries of the UN adopted the Millennium Declaration (http://www.un.org/millennium/declaration/ares552e.htm), an agreement to increase the state of human development worldwide. The declaration includes a commitment to reduce the number of nuclear weapons, protect the environment, and focus attention on Africa. Additionally, a significant section of the declaration outlines the Millennium Development Goals (MDGs; http://mdgs.un.org/unsd/mdg/host.aspx?Content= indicators/officiallist.htm), a list of eight human development goals to be reached by 2015:

1. Eradicate extreme poverty and hunger

2. Achieve universal primary education

3. Promote gender equality and empower women

4. Reduce child mortality

5. Improve maternal health

6. Combat HIV/AIDS, malaria, and other diseases

7. Ensure environmental sustainability

8. Develop a global partnership for development

All eight MDGs involve poverty indicators directly, or they are linked to the problem of poverty in some way. The MDGs have become a standard way to gauge human development progress in all countries and regions of the world. Whether a country is "on target" to reach the goals by the 2015 deadline is a telling indicator in itself of the standard of living in that country. Since the adoption of the MDGs, some progress has been made toward achieving the goals. As the UN concedes, however, progress has been slow and uneven, with some regions moving forward and some falling behind. Table 1.7 presents specific targets for each goal and indicators for monitoring the progress of those targets.

## CLASSIFYING COUNTRIES BY LEVEL OF ECONOMIC DEVELOPMENT

In global determinations of poverty, countries are classified by how "developed" they are economically. During the cold war (the period of escalating tensions between the United States and the Soviet Union that lasted from the 1950s until 1991) the terms *first world*, *second world*, and *third world* came into use. Originally, third-world countries were those that did not align themselves with either the first-world United States and its Western allies, or the second-world Soviet Union and other Eastern bloc countries, such as Bulgaria, Czechoslovakia, East Germany, Hungary, Poland, and Romania. Over time, however, the term *first world* came to refer to those countries that were industrialized and relatively wealthy, whereas *third world* was used to describe countries that were poor, indebted to other nations, and not industrialized.

With the end of the cold war and the dissolution of the Soviet Union in 1991, the term *second world* was abandoned, and *first world* came to refer to all countries that were industrially and technologically developed. *Third world* continued to be used to refer to underdeveloped countries, but over time, that term came to be considered derogatory. Although the term is still used by some people in everyday life, it is not used by researchers, poverty experts, or the international community. In most studies of poverty today, researchers classify countries as either "developed" or "developing." Although both terms represent a spectrum of income levels and poverty rates, the division between them marks the point at which such phenomena as extreme poverty (living on less than $1.25 per day) and many of its worst effects disappear or become exceedingly rare.

Most poverty in the world exists in the developing world, but developing countries are extremely diverse in their levels of economic development and their prevalence of poverty. Some developing countries are well on their way to achieving standards of living comparable to those in the developed world. Other developing countries have rapidly growing economies at the same time that they have large impoverished populations. Still other developing countries have made comparatively little progress in terms of economic development or the alleviation of poverty. It is important, furthermore, to note that a country can remain categorized as "developing" even as it has a very large economy in terms of gross domestic product (GDP; the overall value of goods and services produced in a country in a year). China, for instance, had the world's second-largest economy in 2013 in terms of GDP, but it also had the world's largest population, at over 1.3 billion. Once China's total income has been allocated across its enormous population, average income levels fall well below those that are characteristic of developed economies.

### Least Developed Countries

Researchers often distinguish those developing countries in which poverty is particularly severe and economic growth is particularly hard to engineer, using terms such as *low-income countries*, *least-developed countries*, or *underdeveloped countries*. The UN uses an official classification, Least Developed Countries (LDCs), to set apart those countries whose economies are least developed and whose levels of poverty are among the world's highest. The LDC designation confers eligibility for various forms of international assistance designed to encourage sustained economic growth and development.

**TABLE 1.7**

**Goals and targets from the Millennium Declaration and indicators for monitoring progress**

| Goals and targets from the Millennium Declaration | Indicators for monitoring progress |
|---|---|
| **Goal 1    Eradicate extreme poverty and hunger** | |
| Target 1.A    Halve, between 1990 and 2015, the proportion of people whose income is less than $1 a day | 1.1  Proportion of population below $1 purchasing power parity (PPP) a day[a] |
| | 1.2  Poverty gap ratio [incidence × depth of poverty] |
| | 1.3  Share of poorest quintile in national consumption |
| Target 1.B    Achieve full and productive employment and decent work for all, including women and young people | 1.4  Growth rate of GDP (gross domestic product) per person employed |
| | 1.5  Employment to population ratio |
| | 1.6  Proportion of employed people living below $1 (PPP) a day |
| | 1.7  Proportion of own-account and contributing family workers in total employment |
| Target 1.C    Halve, between 1990 and 2015, the proportion of people who suffer from hunger | 1.8  Prevalence of underweight children under five years of age |
| | 1.9  Proportion of population below minimum level of dietary energy consumption |
| **Goal 2    Achieve universal primary education** | |
| Target 2.A    Ensure that by 2015 children everywhere, boys and girls alike, will be able to complete a full course of primary schooling | 2.1  Net enrollment ratio in primary education |
| | 2.2  Proportion of pupils starting grade 1 who reach last grade of primary education |
| | 2.3  Literacy rate of 15- to 24-year-olds, women and men |
| **Goal 3    Promote gender equality and empower women** | |
| Target 3.A    Eliminate gender disparity in primary and secondary education, preferably by 2005, and in all levels of education no later than 2015 | 3.1  Ratios of girls to boys in primary, secondary, and tertiary education |
| | 3.2  Share of women in wage employment in the nonagricultural sector |
| | 3.3  Proportion of seats held by women in national parliament |
| **Goal 4    Reduce child mortality** | |
| Target 4.A    Reduce by two-thirds, between 1990 and 2015, the under-five mortality rate | 4.1  Under-five mortality rate |
| | 4.2  Infant mortality rate |
| | 4.3  Proportion of one-year-old children immunized against measles |
| **Goal 5    Improve maternal health** | |
| Target 5.A    Reduce by three-quarters, between 1990 and 2015, the maternal mortality ratio | 5.1  Maternal mortality ratio |
| | 5.2  Proportion of births attended by skilled health personnel |
| Target 5.B    Achieve by 2015 universal access to reproductive health | 5.3  Contraceptive prevalence rate |
| | 5.4  Adolescent birth rate |
| | 5.5  Antenatal care coverage (at least one visit and at least four visits) |
| | 5.6  Unmet need for family planning |
| **Goal 6    Combat HIV/AIDS, malaria, and other diseases** | |
| Target 6.A    Have halted by 2015 and begun to reverse the spread of HIV/AIDS | 6.1  HIV prevalence among population ages 15–24 years |
| | 6.2  Condom use at last high-risk sex |
| | 6.3  Proportion of population ages 15–24 years with comprehensive, correct knowledge of HIV/AIDS |
| | 6.4  Ratio of school attendance of orphans to school attendance of nonorphans ages 10–14 years |
| Target 6.B    Achieve by 2010 universal access to treatment for HIV/AIDS for all those who need it | 6.5  Proportion of population with advanced HIV infection with access to antiretroviral drugs |
| Target 6.C    Have halted by 2015 and begun to reverse the incidence of malaria and other major diseases | 6.6  Incidence and death rates associated with malaria |
| | 6.7  Proportion of children under age five sleeping under insecticide-treated bednets |
| | 6.8  Proportion of children under age five with fever who are treated with appropriate antimalarial drugs |
| | 6.9  Incidence, prevalence, and death rates associated with tuberculosis |
| | 6.10  Proportion of tuberculosis cases detected and cured under directly observed treatment short course |
| **Goal 7    Ensure environmental sustainability** | |
| Target 7.A    Integrate the principles of sustainable development into country policies and programs and reverse the loss of environmental resources | 7.1  Proportion of land area covered by forest |
| | 7.2  Carbon dioxide emissions, total, per capita and per $1 GDP (PPP) |
| | 7.3  Consumption of ozone-depleting substances |
| Target 7.B    Reduce biodiversity loss, achieving, by 2010, a significant reduction in the rate of loss | 7.4  Proportion of fish stocks within safe biological limits |
| | 7.5  Proportion of total water resources used |
| | 7.6  Proportion of terrestrial and marine areas protected |
| | 7.7  Proportion of species threatened with extinction |
| Target 7.C    Halve by 2015 the proportion of people without sustainable access to safe drinking water and basic sanitation | 7.8  Proportion of population using an improved drinking water source |
| | 7.9  Proportion of population using an improved sanitation facility |
| Target 7.D    Achieve by 2020 a significant improvement in the lives of at least 100 million slum dwellers | 7.10  Proportion of urban population living in slums[b] |

In "Criteria for Identification and Graduation of LDCs" (2014, http://unohrlls.org/about-ldcs/criteria-for-ldcs/), the UN Office of the High Representative for the Least Developed Countries, Landlocked Developing Countries, and Small Island Developing States provides the technical criteria for classifying a nation as an LDC and for determining when a nation has developed sufficiently to qualify for graduation out of that category. These criteria measure income, human assets, and economic vulnerability. The UN undertakes a review process every three years to determine which countries qualify as LDCs and which should be removed from the category.

A country meets the UN's low-income criterion for classification as an LDC if its gross national income

TABLE 1.7

**Goals and targets from the Millennium Declaration and indicators for monitoring progress** [CONTINUED]

| Goals and targets from the Millennium Declaration | Indicators for monitoring progress |
|---|---|
| **Goal 8**    **Develop a global partnership for development** | |
| Target 8.A    Develop further an open, rule-based, predictable, nondiscriminatory trading and financial system (Includes a commitment to good governance, development, and poverty reduction—both nationally and internationally.) | Some of the indicators listed below are monitored separately for the least developed countries (LDCs), Africa, landlocked developing countries, and small island developing states.<br>**Official development assistance (ODA)**<br>8.1   Net ODA, total and to the least developed countries, as percentage of OECD/DAC donors' gross national income |
| Target 8.B    Address the special needs of the least developed countries (Includes tariff and quota-free access for the least developed countries' exports; enhanced program of debt relief for heavily indebted poor countries (HIPC) and cancellation of official bilateral debt; and more generous ODA for countries committed to poverty reduction.) | 8.2   Proportion of total bilateral, sector-allocable ODA of OECD/DAC donors to basic social services (basic education, primary health care, nutrition, safe water, and sanitation)<br>8.3   Proportion of bilateral official development assistance of OECD/DAC donors that is untied<br>8.4   ODA received in landlocked developing countries as a proportion of their gross national incomes<br>8.5   ODA received in small island developing states as a proportion of their gross national incomes |
| Target 8.C    Address the special needs of landlocked developing countries and small island developing states (through the Programme of Action for the Sustainable Development of Small Island Developing States and the outcome of the 22nd special session of the General Assembly) | **Market access**<br>8.6   Proportion of total developed country imports (by value and excluding arms) from developing countries and least developed countries, admitted free of duty<br>8.7   Average tariffs imposed by developed countries on agricultural products and textiles and clothing from developing countries<br>8.8   Agricultural support estimate for OECD countries as a percentage of their GDP<br>8.9   Proportion of ODA provided to help build trade capacity |
| Target 8.D    Deal comprehensively with the debt problems of developing countries through national and international measures in order to make debt sustainable in the long term | **Debt sustainability**<br>8.10   Total number of countries that have reached their HIPC decision points and number that have reached their HIPC completion points (cumulative)<br>8.11   Debt relief committed under HIPC Initiative and Multilateral Debt Relief Initiative (MDRI)<br>8.12   Debt service as a percentage of exports of goods and services |
| Target 8.E    In cooperation with pharmaceutical companies, provide access to affordable essential drugs in developing countries | 8.13   Proportion of population with access to affordable essential drugs on a sustainable basis |
| Target 8.F    In cooperation with the private sector, make available the benefits of new technologies, especially information and communications | 8.14   Fixed-line telephones per 100 population<br>8.15   Mobile cellular subscribers per 100 population<br>8.16   Internet users per 100 population |

GDP = Gross Domestic Product. PPP = Purchasing Power Parity. OECD = Office of Economic Cooperation and Development. HIPC = Highly indebted poor countries.
aWhere available, indicators based on national poverty lines should be used for monitoring country poverty trends.
bThe proportion of people living in slums is measured by a proxy, represented by the urban population living in households with at least one of these characteristics: lack of access to improved water supply, lack of access to improved sanitation, overcrowding (three or more people per room), and dwellings made of nondurable material.
Note: The Millennium Development Goals and targets come from the Millennium Declaration, signed by 189 countries, including 147 heads of state and government, in September 2000 (www.un.org/millennium/declaration/ares552e.htm) as updated by the 60th UN General Assembly in September 2005. The revised Millennium Development Goal (MDG) monitoring framework shown here, including new targets and indicators, was presented to the 62nd General Assembly, with new numbering as recommended by the Inter-agency and Expert Group on MDG Indicators at its 12th meeting on November 14, 2007. The goals and targets are interrelated and should be seen as a whole. They represent a partnership between the developed countries and the developing countries "to create an environment—at the national and global levels alike—which is conducive to development and the elimination of poverty." All indicators should be disaggregated by sex and urban-rural location as far as possible.

SOURCE: "Millennium Development Goals," in *World Development Indicators 2013*, World Bank, Washington, D.C., 2013, http://databank.worldbank.org/data/download/WDI-2013-ebook.pdf (accessed October 3, 2013). DOI: 10.1596/978-0-8213-9824-1. License: Creative Commons Attribution CC BY 3.0.

(GNI) per capita (the total annual income in a country divided by its population), averaged over three years, falls below $992; and a country qualifies for graduation from LDC status if GNI per capita rises above $1,190. Calculation of a country's human assets and economic vulnerability is more complex. A country's human assets are evaluated based on the percentage of the population that is undernourished, the child mortality rate, the secondary school enrollment rate, and the adult literacy rate. These figures are integrated into a composite Human Assets Index (HAI) score, and eligibility is determined based on thresholds set during the triennial review process.

A country's economic vulnerability is evaluated based on its population size; its remoteness; its levels of merchandise exports; the share of its GDP that comes from agriculture, forestry, and fisheries; the share of its population that lives in low-elevation coastal areas; the level of stability of its exports of goods and services; the number of its people who have been victimized by natural disasters; and the level of stability of its agricultural production. As with the HAI, these figures are integrated into a composite Economic Vulnerability Index, and eligibility is determined according to thresholds set by the committee in charge of the review process.

To be added to the LDC list, a country must meet all three criteria. Eligibility for graduation from LDC status requires that a country exceed two of the three thresholds or that it reach a GNI per capita of at least twice the low-income criterion threshold. For the UN to recommend removal from the LDC category, a country must meet these standards during two consecutive triennial reviews. After this six-year qualifying period, another three-year period passes before actual graduation occurs.

The majority of the countries (33 of 49) classified by the UN in 2013 as LDCs are in sub-Saharan Africa; another 14 are in Asia; one, Sudan, is generally considered part of North Africa (and hence the Arab region) but is also sometimes classified as part of sub-Saharan Africa; and one, Haiti, is part of Latin America and the Caribbean. (See Table 1.8.) LDCs typically have little or no infrastructure—that is, public structures, facilities, and services, such as paved roads, bridges, schools, hospitals, sewer systems, and water purification systems. Many such countries have experienced long-term political unrest in the form of civil war or armed conflict with other nations, or have been subject to unstable governments, dictatorships, and/or corruption. In addition, they may suffer from environmental problems and natural disasters or from other catastrophes such as famine, widespread destruction of property, and the displacement of large segments of their populations.

**TABLE 1.8**

**Nations classified as Least Developed Countries by the United Nations, by continent, 2013**

**Africa**
Angola
Benin
Burkina Faso
Burundi
Central African Republic
Chad
Comoros
Democratic Republic of the Congo
Djibouti
Equatorial Guinea
Eritrea
Ethiopia
Gambia
Guinea
Guinea-Bissau
Lesotho
Liberia
Madagascar
Malawi
Mali
Mauritania
Mozambique
Niger
Rwanda
Sao Tome and Principe
Senegal
Sierra Leone
Somalia
South Sudan
Sudan
Togo
Uganda
United Republic of Tanzania
Zambia

**Asia**
Afghanistan
Bangladesh
Bhutan
Cambodia
Kiribati
Lao People's Democratic Republic
Myanmar
Nepal
Samoa
Solomon Islands
Timor-Leste
Tuvalu
Vanuatu
Yemen

**North America**
Haiti

SOURCE: Created by Mark Lane for Gale, © 2014.

# CHAPTER 2
# THE ECONOMIC AND HUMAN DIMENSIONS OF POVERTY

As noted in Chapter 1, there are a number of overlapping forms of human deprivation that cannot be neatly classified as either causes or effects of poverty. Chronic hunger and malnutrition, for example, are results of poverty, but they also weaken immune systems, undermine maternal health, encourage an unsustainable approach to resource extraction, and reduce school attendance and the ability of students to learn. Saddled with a constellation of problems such as this, an individual or community faces an extremely arduous climb out of poverty. Although national economic development is rightly the focus of many antipoverty programs, these other overlapping forms of deprivation do not necessarily disappear with economic gains at the national level, as measured by growth in gross domestic product (the total value of all goods and services produced by a country in a year).

Moreover, addressing the multiple overlapping components of poverty can bring gains in national economic development beyond those achieved through a strict focus on finance and economics. For example, the gender inequities that characterize many developing societies are frequently an affront to the consensus international view of universal human rights, but they also limit economic development by suppressing the productive potential of women. Finally, economic development programs imposed by outside groups, along with economic policies in the developed world, are themselves sometimes blamed for worsening rather than alleviating poverty in developing countries.

The nature of human and economic development challenges varies from region to region. The countries that have seen the biggest gains in human and economic development since the 1980s, such as China, India, and Brazil, have followed diverse paths rooted in their own unique challenges and institutions, rather than enacting a single authorized set of development strategies such as those commonly recommended by the international community after World War II (1939–1945). Increasingly, international leaders recognize the need for pragmatism, flexibility, and knowledge of a particular country or region's challenges.

Antipoverty efforts in the countries of sub-Saharan Africa, where extremely low average incomes are the norm, must necessarily take different forms from antipoverty efforts in the countries of Latin America and the Caribbean, which have higher average incomes but greater inequality. Indeed, in spite of the fact that Latin American and Caribbean countries are generally more developed and economically dynamic than sub-Saharan African countries, the poorest people in Latin America and the Caribbean are on average poorer than their counterparts in sub-Saharan Africa. (See Figure 2.1.)

Thus, as the economies of the developing world continue to grow at rates that outpace those in the developed world, as in many cases they have since 2000, the need to understand the complex dynamics of poverty is becoming ever more apparent. This chapter will provide a survey of some of the key overlapping dimensions of poverty across the world, paying particular attention to variations in the challenges faced by different global regions.

## ECONOMIC GROWTH AND EMPLOYMENT

Economic growth at the national and regional level has a strong direct correlation with decreasing poverty levels, although it does not solve all of the problems associated with poverty. As mentioned in Chapter 1, China's extraordinarily robust economic development since the 1980s accounts for much of the decrease in poverty worldwide since that time.

One of the central facts pertaining to economic growth in the contemporary world is the increasing interconnectedness of national economies. Globalization, as

FIGURE 2.1

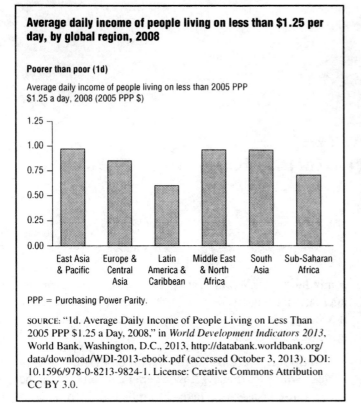

**Average daily income of people living on less than $1.25 per day, by global region, 2008**

Poorer than poor (1d)

Average daily income of people living on less than 2005 PPP $1.25 a day, 2008 (2005 PPP $)

PPP = Purchasing Power Parity.

SOURCE: "1d. Average Daily Income of People Living on Less Than 2005 PPP $1.25 a Day, 2008," in *World Development Indicators 2013*, World Bank, Washington, D.C., 2013, http://databank.worldbank.org/data/download/WDI-2013-ebook.pdf (accessed October 3, 2013). DOI: 10.1596/978-0-8213-9824-1. License: Creative Commons Attribution CC BY 3.0.

this interconnectedness is generally called, has opened up new markets for products, increased companies' ability to obtain financing and affordable labor, and allowed many companies and national economies to operate more efficiently than in the past. With this interconnectedness, however, also comes shared risk.

The effects of the global economic crisis that began with losses in the U.S. housing and financial markets in late 2007 had a profound impact worldwide for many years thereafter because all of the world's major economies are linked in innumerable ways. Increased unemployment rates and decreased rates of economic growth were widespread in the years that followed, even in many regions of the world that did not experience the underlying economic problems that triggered the crisis. Although wealthier countries such as the United States suffer significantly from such economic downturns, the effects of a faltering worldwide economy can be even more catastrophic in regions whose citizens are already extremely vulnerable to poverty and its many related deprivations.

**National Economies**

The most rapidly expanding economies in the developing world were growing faster than the economies of the developed world prior to the years of the global financial crisis, and five years after the crisis began, the developing world continued to outperform the developed

world in terms of growth percentages. According to the International Labour Organization (ILO), in *Global Employment Trends 2013: Recovering from a Second Jobs Dip* (2013, http://www.ilo.org/wcmsp5/groups/public/---dgreports/---dcomm/---publ/documents/publication/wcms_202326.pdf), all regions of the developing world saw their economies grow faster than the economies of the developed world between 2010 and 2012, and this trend was expected to continue through 2014.

As in the developed world, however, economic growth slowed in most of the developing world. The ILO found that growth in the region that comprises central and southeastern Europe and the Commonwealth of Independent States area (a group of nine former Soviet states) fell by 2% in 2012; growth in East Asia slowed by 1.4%, as China experienced its lowest rate of annual economic growth (7.8%) since 1999; growth in South Asia slowed by 1.6%, as India experienced its lowest rate of annual economic growth (4.9%) in a decade; and growth in Latin America and the Caribbean slowed by over 1%, as well.

Only Southeast Asia and the Pacific, North Africa, and sub-Saharan Africa, among the developing regions surveyed by the ILO, saw overall economic growth in 2012. An extreme turnaround in North Africa between 2011 and 2012, from negative to nearly 10% annual growth, was a result of the transition from wartime to peacetime economic conditions in Libya. Libya's economy was one of the largest in the region, and for most of 2011 it was shackled by a civil war that was triggered by the Arab Spring protest movement (which is discussed at greater length in Chapters 4 and 9) that ended with the death of the country's leader, Muammar Qaddhafi (1942–2011). In Southeast Asia and the Pacific, as well as in sub-Saharan Africa, growth appeared relatively unhampered by the global economic crisis.

**Employment and Poverty**

Economic growth lifts people out of poverty primarily through better-paying job and business opportunities and through higher overall rates of employment. The progress that had been made in combating global poverty prior to 2007 thus slowed during the crisis years, and unemployment climbed above precrisis norms. Globally, 197.3 million people were unemployed in 2012, according to the ILO, 28.4 million more than were unemployed in 2007, prior to the crisis. The ILO expected unemployment to reach 6% globally in 2013 and to continue climbing in the years that followed. (See Figure 2.2.)

These figures translated into a global employment-to-population ratio (EPR; the percentage of the total working-age population that is employed) of 60.3%, which was 1% less than in 2007. (See Figure 2.3.) EPR

**FIGURE 2.2**

### Global unemployment trends and projections, 2002–17

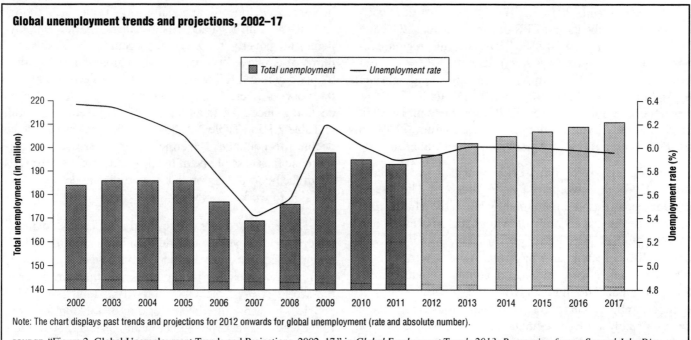

Note: The chart displays past trends and projections for 2012 onwards for global unemployment (rate and absolute number).

SOURCE: "Figure 2. Global Unemployment Trends and Projections, 2002–17," in *Global Employment Trends 2013: Recovering from a Second Jobs Dip*, International Labour Organization, 2013, http://www.ilo.org/wcmsp5/groups/public/---dgreports/---dcomm/---publ/documents/publication/wcms_202326 .pdf (accessed September 23, 2013)

**FIGURE 2.3**

### Global employment-to-population ratios by sex and region, 2007 and 2012

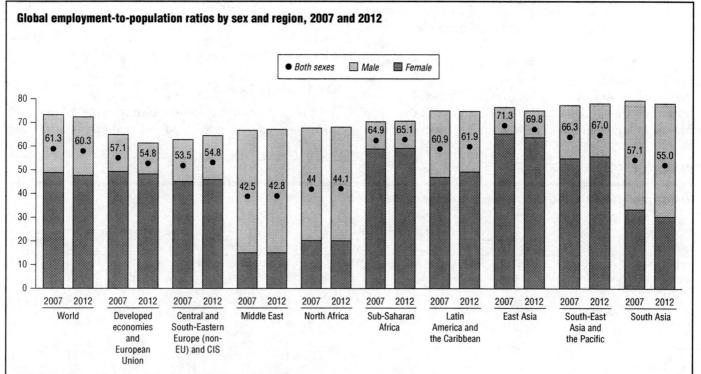

Notes: EU = European Union. CIS = Commonwealth of Independent States.

SOURCE: "Figure 10. Employment-to-Population Ratios by Sex, World and Regions, 2007 and 2012," in *Global Employment Trends 2013: Recovering from a Second Jobs Dip*, International Labour Organization, 2013, http://www.ilo.org/wcmsp5/groups/public/---dgreports/---dcomm/---publ/documents/publication/wcms_202326.pdf (accessed September 23, 2013)

values varied significantly by global region. In *Global Employment Trends 2013*, the ILO reveals that developed economies saw the largest EPR declines between 2002 and 2007, from 57.1% to 54.8%. East Asia (the region economically dominated by China) saw its EPR fall from 71.3% to 69.8%; and South Asia (economically dominated by India) saw its EPR fall from 57.1% to 55%. Other developing regions saw their EPR values remain constant or rise slightly, with the largest increase (from 60.9% to 61.9%) coming in Latin America and the Caribbean.

In all regions of the world, men had substantially higher EPRs than women. (See Figure 2.3.) The largest gender disparities in employment were in the Middle East and North Africa, in both of which regions fewer than 20% of women were employed in 2012, compared with nearly 70% of men; and in South Asia, where roughly 30% of women were employed compared with nearly 80% of men. The regions with the highest levels of female employment were sub-Saharan Africa, where approximately 60% of women were employed, and East Asia, where nearly 65% of women were employed. By comparison, the EPR for women in the developed world was approximately 50%.

In many parts of the world, employment does not necessarily provide a path out of poverty. Indeed, as Figure 2.3 shows, sub-Saharan Africa had one of the highest rates of employment in the world in 2011, and yet it was the world's poorest region. Table 2.1 estimates that 12.9% of the world's employed people made less than $1.25 per day in 2011. Also in 2011 in Southeast Asia and the Pacific, 12.4% of employed people made less than $1.25 per day, and in South Asia 25.7% of employed people made less than $1.25 per day. The proportion of sub-Saharan Africa's employed population that made less than $1.25 per day in 2011 was 41.7%.

When a poverty threshold of $2 per day is used, these percentages climb dramatically, as Table 2.2 shows. Indeed, in South Asia and in sub-Saharan Africa, employment and poverty routinely go together, as nearly two-thirds of employed people in both regions made less than $2 per day in 2011. The number of the extremely poor and the poor as a share of total employed people had been declining since 2000 in all regions of the developing world, as Table 2.1 and Table 2.2 show, and the ILO projected the declines to continue. Nevertheless, these statistics underscore the falseness of one of the most persistent stereotypes about the poor: the notion that poverty is the product of an aversion to work.

The employed are more likely to escape extreme poverty in the developed world than in much of the developing world, but even in the United States, the country with more high-paying jobs, on average, than any other in the world, 7% of the labor force (the total number of people who had either been working or looking for work for at least 27 weeks) lived below the official poverty line in 2011. (See Table 2.3.) This working-poor rate of 7% marked a significant increase since the start of the global economic crisis in 2007, when 5.1% of those in the U.S. labor force for 27 weeks or more lived in poverty. As Table 2.4 shows, the working-poor rate in the United States was much higher for young people, African Americans and Hispanics, and women. Nearly one-third (29%) of all African American women aged 20 to 24 years who had been in the labor force for 27 weeks lived below the poverty line in 2011, as did less than a quarter (18.4%) of African American men in the same age group.

## The Informal Economy

The term *informal economy* refers to the exchange of goods and services outside of national and international

**TABLE 2.1**

**Working poor indicators, US$1.25 per day, selected years 2000–17**

| Both sexes | Numbers of people (millions) | | | | | Share in total employment (%) | | | | |
|---|---|---|---|---|---|---|---|---|---|---|
| | 2000 | 2007 | 2011* | 2012* | 2017* | 2000 | 2007 | 2011* | 2012* | 2017* |
| World | 695.3 | 488.0 | 396.7 | 383.8 | 288.3 | 26.6 | 16.5 | 12.9 | 12.3 | 8.7 |
| Central and South-Eastern Europe (non-EU) and CIS | 7.3 | 3.9 | 3.1 | 2.9 | 1.8 | 5.0 | 2.5 | 1.9 | 1.7 | 1.1 |
| East Asia | 232.2 | 93.3 | 52.2 | 46.3 | 14.6 | 31.2 | 11.5 | 6.3 | 5.6 | 1.7 |
| South-East Asia and the Pacific | 81.7 | 49.0 | 36.8 | 35.4 | 22.2 | 33.7 | 17.9 | 12.4 | 11.7 | 6.9 |
| South Asia | 224.5 | 198.0 | 160.9 | 155.9 | 119.4 | 43.9 | 33.0 | 25.7 | 24.4 | 17.1 |
| Latin America and the Caribbean | 16.1 | 11.3 | 9.7 | 9.6 | 7.7 | 7.8 | 4.6 | 3.6 | 3.5 | 2.6 |
| Middle East | 0.6 | 0.8 | 1.0 | 1.1 | 1.0 | 1.4 | 1.5 | 1.6 | 1.8 | 1.4 |
| North Africa | 4.5 | 3.1 | 3.1 | 4.2 | 4.1 | 9.5 | 5.3 | 4.9 | 6.4 | 5.6 |
| Sub-Saharan Africa | 128.4 | 128.6 | 129.8 | 128.4 | 117.4 | 56.7 | 46.2 | 41.7 | 40.1 | 31.6 |

*2011 are preliminary estimates. 2012/7 are preliminary projections.
Note: Totals may differ due to rounding. EU = European Union. CIS = Commonwealth of Independent States.

SOURCE: "Table A14a. Working Poor Indicators, World and Regions (US$ 1.25 a Day)," in *Global Employment Trends 2013: Recovering from a Second Jobs Dip*, International Labour Organization, 2013, http://www.ilo.org/wcmsp5/groups/public/---dgreports/---dcomm/---publ/documents/publication/wcms_202326 .pdf (accessed September 23, 2013)

**TABLE 2.2**

**Working poor indicators, US$2.00 per day, selected years 2000–17**

| Both sexes | Numbers of people (millions) | | | | | Share in total employment (%) | | | | |
|---|---|---|---|---|---|---|---|---|---|---|
| | 2000 | 2007 | 2011* | 2012* | 2017* | 2000 | 2007 | 2011* | 2012* | 2017* |
| World | 1,195.1 | 991.6 | 868.3 | 853.7 | 730.8 | 45.8 | 33.6 | 28.1 | 27.3 | 22.0 |
| Central and South-Eastern Europe (non-EU) and CIS | 19.1 | 9.3 | 8.1 | 7.8 | 6.3 | 12.9 | 5.9 | 4.9 | 4.7 | 3.7 |
| East Asia | 410.2 | 221.0 | 128.5 | 113.2 | 36.7 | 55.2 | 27.4 | 15.6 | 13.6 | 4.4 |
| South-East Asia and the Pacific | 148.2 | 115.8 | 100.8 | 98.3 | 73.6 | 61.2 | 42.2 | 33.9 | 32.5 | 22.7 |
| South Asia | 397.4 | 414.3 | 391.1 | 391.2 | 371.4 | 77.7 | 69.1 | 62.5 | 61.3 | 53.0 |
| Latin America and the Caribbean | 32.3 | 23.5 | 20.4 | 20.1 | 17.2 | 15.6 | 9.6 | 7.6 | 7.4 | 5.8 |
| Middle East | 3.3 | 4.5 | 4.8 | 5.2 | 5.2 | 8.0 | 8.1 | 7.8 | 8.1 | 7.2 |
| North Africa | 12.6 | 11.3 | 11.4 | 12.9 | 12.8 | 26.7 | 19.2 | 17.8 | 19.7 | 17.5 |
| Sub-Saharan Africa | 172.0 | 191.9 | 203.2 | 204.9 | 207.6 | 75.9 | 68.9 | 65.3 | 64.0 | 55.9 |

*2011 are preliminary estimates. 2012/7 are preliminary projections.
Note: Totals may differ due to rounding. EU = European Union. CIS = Commonwealth of Independent States.

SOURCE: "Table A14b. Working Poor Indicators, World and Regions (US$ 2 a Day)," in *Global Employment Trends 2013: Recovering from a Second Jobs Dip*, International Labour Organization, 2013, http://www.ilo.org/wcmsp5/groups/public/---dgreports/---dcomm/---publ/documents/publication/wcms_202326.pdf (accessed September 23, 2013)

---

**TABLE 2.3**

**Poverty status of persons and primary families in the labor force for 27 or more weeks, United States, 2007–11**

[Numbers in thousands]

| Characteristic | 2007 | 2008 | 2009 | 2010 | 2011 |
|---|---|---|---|---|---|
| Total persons[a] | 146,567 | 147,838 | 147,902 | 146,859 | 147,475 |
| In poverty | 7,521 | 8,883 | 10,391 | 10,512 | 10,382 |
| Working poor rate | 5.1 | 6.0 | 7.0 | 7.2 | 7.0 |
| Unrelated individuals | 33,226 | 32,785 | 33,798 | 34,099 | 33,731 |
| In poverty | 2,558 | 3,275 | 3,947 | 3,947 | 3,621 |
| Working poor rate | 7.7 | 10.0 | 11.7 | 11.6 | 10.7 |
| Primary families[b] | 65,158 | 65,907 | 65,467 | 64,931 | 66,225 |
| In poverty | 4,169 | 4,538 | 5,193 | 5,269 | 5,469 |
| Working poor rate | 6.4 | 6.9 | 7.9 | 8.1 | 8.3 |

[a]Includes persons in families, not shown separately.
[b]Primary families with at least one member in the labor force for more than half the year.
Note: Updated population controls are introduced annually with the release of January data.

SOURCE: "Table A. Poverty Status of Persons and Primary Families in the Labor Force for 27 or More Weeks, 2007–2011," in *A Profile of the Working Poor, 2011*, U.S. Department of Labor, Bureau of Labor Statistics, April 2013, http://www.bls.gov/cps/cpswp2011.pdf (accessed September 23, 2013)

---

regulatory guidelines. The informal economy includes all unincorporated nonagricultural businesses that produce marketable goods and services, but it does not include informal work that goes toward producing goods for one's own household.

The ILO notes in "Informal Economy" (2014, http://www.ilo.org/global/topics/employment-promotion/informal-economy/lang--en/index.htm) that in most countries of the developing world, between half and three-quarters of all nonagricultural jobs are informal rather than official jobs, and conditions in such jobs tend to be less than ideal. "Although it is hard to generalize concerning the quality of informal employment," the ILO states, "it most often means poor employment conditions and is associated with increasing poverty. Some of the characteristic features of informal employment are lack of protection in the event of non-payment of wages, compulsory overtime or extra shifts, lay-offs without notice or compensation, unsafe working conditions and the absence of social benefits such as pensions, sick pay and health insurance. Women, migrants and other vulnerable groups of workers who are excluded from other opportunities have little choice but to take informal low-quality jobs."

The informal economy occupies a larger share of all economic activity in developing countries than in developed countries, but informal labor does exist in wealthier countries as well, mostly in the form of self-employment and part-time and temporary work (the latter two are known as nonstandard wage employment). In the United States informal workers include casual laborers, as well as some employees with nonstandard pay arrangements, including those who work "under the table" (i.e., they are paid in cash and are not reported as official employees).

Although the informal economy resists objective measurement because of its secretive nature, the ILO has since 2003 worked to implement data gathering and reporting efforts aimed at increasing understanding of the informal economy in the developing world, and it has begun issuing reports based on its findings. In *Statistical Update on Employment in the Informal Economy* (June 2012, http://laborsta.ilo.org/applv8/data/INFORMAL_ECONOMY/2012-06-Statistical%20update%20-%20v2.pdf), the ILO distinguishes between "informal employment," which includes jobs with unregistered employers as well as unregistered or under-the-table jobs in the formal sector; and "employment in the informal sector," which includes only those jobs undertaken on behalf of unincorporated businesses. As Figure 2.4 shows, informal work constitutes

TABLE 2.4

**Poverty rate of persons in the labor force for 27 weeks or more by age, sex, and race and Hispanic origin, United States, 2011**

| Age and sex | Total | White | Black or African American | Asian | Hispanic or Latino ethnicity |
|---|---|---|---|---|---|
| | | | Rate[a] | | |
| **Total, 16 years and older** | **7.0** | **6.1** | **13.3** | **5.4** | **12.9** |
| 16 to 19 years | 11.3 | 10.4 | 19.1 | 8.1 | 17.8 |
| 20 to 24 years | 14.0 | 12.0 | 24.1 | 9.7 | 14.5 |
| 25 to 34 years | 9.4 | 8.3 | 17.2 | 5.1 | 14.8 |
| 35 to 44 years | 7.2 | 6.5 | 11.2 | 6.0 | 14.2 |
| 45 to 54 years | 5.1 | 4.2 | 10.3 | 5.6 | 9.6 |
| 55 to 64 years | 3.9 | 3.4 | 8.4 | 3.5 | 9.6 |
| 65 years and older | 1.7 | 1.6 | 2.1 | 1.4 | 4.1 |
| **Men, 16 years and older** | **6.2** | **5.6** | **10.5** | **5.4** | **12.3** |
| 16 to 19 years | 11.8 | 11.1 | 19.4 | [b] | 17.9 |
| 20 to 24 years | 11.2 | 9.9 | 18.4 | 8.4 | 13.0 |
| 25 to 34 years | 7.8 | 7.4 | 11.1 | 5.3 | 13.1 |
| 35 to 44 years | 6.7 | 6.2 | 9.2 | 6.3 | 14.1 |
| 45 to 54 years | 5.0 | 4.3 | 9.1 | 6.0 | 10.3 |
| 55 to 64 years | 3.6 | 3.1 | 8.8 | 3.2 | 9.3 |
| 65 years and older | 0.9 | 0.9 | 1.7 | 0.1 | 1.4 |
| **Women, 16 years and older** | **8.0** | **6.7** | **15.6** | **5.4** | **13.7** |
| 16 to 19 years | 10.9 | 9.7 | 18.8 | [b] | 17.6 |
| 20 to 24 years | 17.0 | 14.5 | 29.0 | 11.2 | 16.4 |
| 25 to 34 years | 11.3 | 9.4 | 22.4 | 4.9 | 17.5 |
| 35 to 44 years | 7.8 | 6.8 | 12.9 | 5.7 | 14.3 |
| 45 to 54 years | 5.2 | 4.1 | 11.3 | 5.2 | 8.6 |
| 55 to 64 years | 4.2 | 3.8 | 8.1 | 3.8 | 10.0 |
| 65 years and older | 2.7 | 2.7 | 2.5 | 3.1 | 7.1 |

[a]Number below the poverty level as a percent of the total in the labor force for 27 or more weeks.
[b]Data not shown where base is less than 80,000.
Note: Estimates for the race groups shown (white, black or African American, and Asian) do not sum to totals because data are not presented for all races. Persons whose ethnicity is identified as Hispanic or Latino may be of any race. Dash represents or rounds to zero.

SOURCE: Adapted from "Table 2. People in the Labor Force for 27 or More Weeks: Poverty Status by Age, Sex, Race, and Hispanic or Latino Ethnicity, 2011," in *A Profile of the Working Poor, 2011*, U.S. Department of Labor, Bureau of Labor Statistics, April 2013, http://www.bls.gov/cps/cpswp2011.pdf (accessed September 23, 2013)

more than half of all nonagricultural work in much of the developing world, with the informal sector generally accounting for most informal work. In Mexico, for example, 54.3% of all nonagricultural work was informal, 34.1% on behalf of unincorporated businesses and 20.2% on behalf of formal employers or otherwise outside of the informal sector. In 15 of the countries for which the ILO had data, informal work constituted more than two-thirds of all employment, and the figure was over 80% in Mali, the Philippines, and India.

Women are more likely than men to be excluded from the formal economy in the developing world, so they account for a larger share of all informal workers than men. As Figure 2.5 shows, in most of the countries for which data were available, informal employment accounted for a larger share of all nonagricultural female employment than nonagricultural male employment. The ILO notes, however, that within the informal sector itself, men constitute the majority of employees in a majority of the countries surveyed.

Although the informal economy acts as a resource for those left out of the formal economy and is in most cases preferable to unemployment, international organizations generally seek to help developing countries transition away from the informal economy. Besides the risks that workers in the informal economy face, informal economic activity imposes costs at the national level, as the World Bank notes in "Workers in the Informal Economy" (2013, http://web.worldbank.org/). Informal work amounts to a loss in tax revenues that countries might have been able to use to improve infrastructure and social services, and it places an extra tax burden on those who are formally employed. In both human rights and development terms, then, formal employment is preferable to informal employment.

## POVERTY, EDUCATION, AND LITERACY

Lack of education is one of the strongest indicators of the likelihood that an individual or household will live in poverty. People who are illiterate or have low levels of education are more likely to be unemployed than their better-educated counterparts, and among employed people, less education corresponds with a greater likelihood of remaining in poverty even while working. Additionally, countries with high levels of illiteracy often have correspondingly underdeveloped economies. According to the United Nations Educational, Scientific, and Cultural Organization (UNESCO), in *Education for All*

**FIGURE 2.4**

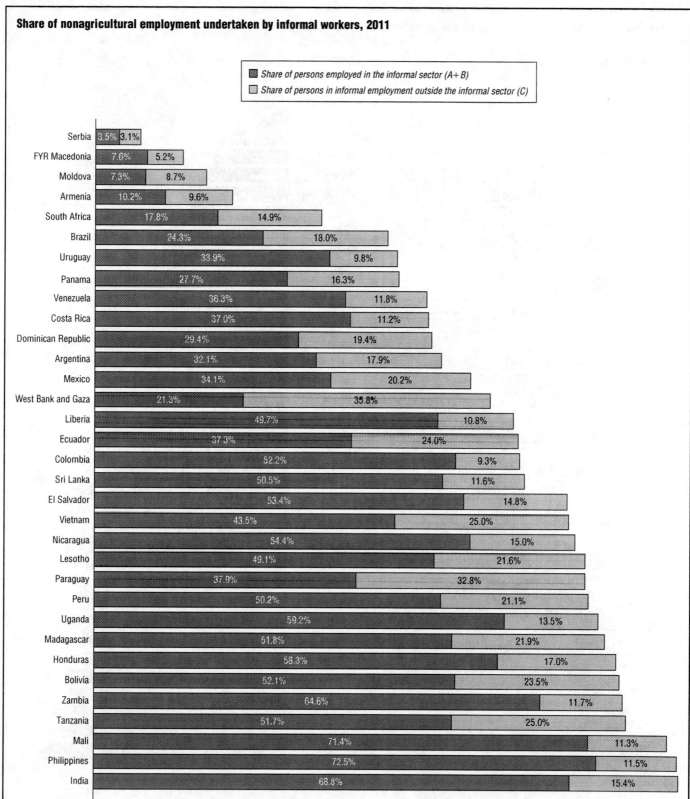

**Share of nonagricultural employment undertaken by informal workers, 2011**

Legend:
- Share of persons employed in the informal sector (A+B)
- Share of persons in informal employment outside the informal sector (C)

| Country | A+B | C |
|---|---|---|
| Serbia | 3.5% | 3.1% |
| FYR Macedonia | 7.6% | 5.2% |
| Moldova | 7.3% | 8.7% |
| Armenia | 10.2% | 9.6% |
| South Africa | 17.8% | 14.9% |
| Brazil | 24.3% | 18.0% |
| Uruguay | 33.9% | 9.8% |
| Panama | 27.7% | 16.3% |
| Venezuela | 36.3% | 11.8% |
| Costa Rica | 37.0% | 11.2% |
| Dominican Republic | 29.4% | 19.4% |
| Argentina | 32.1% | 17.9% |
| Mexico | 34.1% | 20.2% |
| West Bank and Gaza | 21.3% | 35.8% |
| Liberia | 49.7% | 10.8% |
| Ecuador | 37.3% | 24.0% |
| Colombia | 52.2% | 9.3% |
| Sri Lanka | 50.5% | 11.6% |
| El Salvador | 53.4% | 14.8% |
| Vietnam | 43.5% | 25.0% |
| Nicaragua | 54.4% | 15.0% |
| Lesotho | 49.1% | 21.6% |
| Paraguay | 37.9% | 32.8% |
| Peru | 50.2% | 21.1% |
| Uganda | 59.2% | 13.5% |
| Madagascar | 51.8% | 21.9% |
| Honduras | 58.3% | 17.0% |
| Bolivia | 52.1% | 23.5% |
| Zambia | 64.6% | 11.7% |
| Tanzania | 51.7% | 25.0% |
| Mali | 71.4% | 11.3% |
| Philippines | 72.5% | 11.5% |
| India | 68.8% | 15.4% |

Note: The data refer to non-agricultural employment and the latest year available for each country.

SOURCE: "Figure 1. Share of Persons Employed in the Informal Economy, Latest Year Available," in *Statistical Update on Employment in the Informal Economy*, International Labour Organization, Department of Statistics, June 2012, http://laborsta.ilo.org/applv8/data/INFORMAL_ECONOMY/2012-06-Statistical%20update%20-%20v2.pdf (accessed October 7, 2013)

**FIGURE 2.5**

**Share of nonagricultural employment undertaken by informal workers, by sex, 2011**

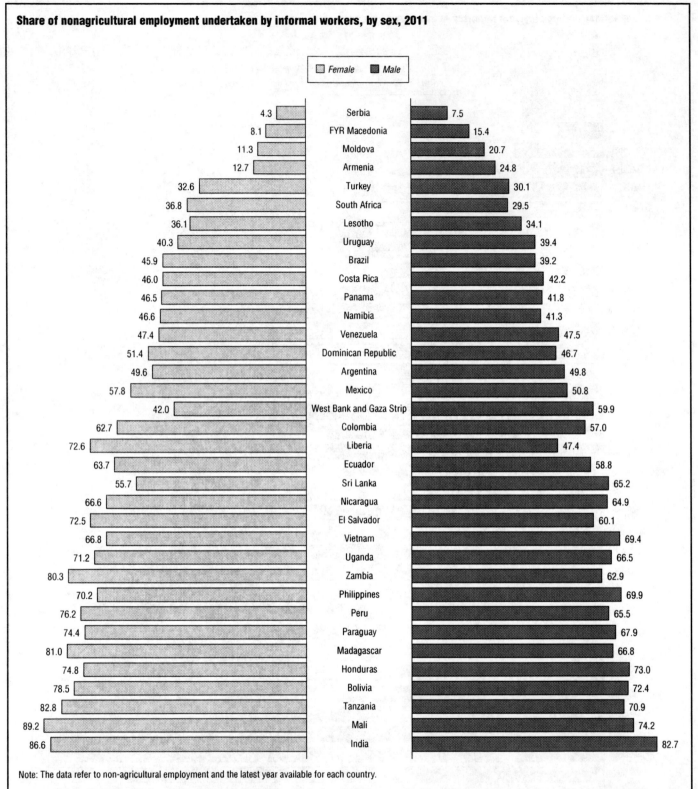

Note: The data refer to non-agricultural employment and the latest year available for each country.

SOURCE: "Figure 2. Share of Informal Employment in Total Non-Agricultural Employment," in *Statistical Update on Employment in the Informal Economy*, International Labour Organization, Department of Statistics, June 2012, http://laborsta.ilo.org/applv8/data/INFORMAL_ECONOMY/2012-06-Statistical%20update%20-%20v2.pdf (accessed October 7, 2013).

*Global Monitoring Report 2012—Youth and Skills: Putting Education to Work* (2012, http://unesdoc.unesco.org/images/0021/002180/218003e.pdf), "Education is not only

about making sure all children can attend school. It is about setting young people up for life, by giving them opportunities to find decent work, earn a living, contribute to their communities and societies, and fulfill their potential. At the wider level, it is about helping countries nurture the workforce they need to grow in the global economy."

Since 1985 the international community has observed substantial progress in reducing illiteracy worldwide, but the number of illiterate adults remained stubbornly high as of 2011, and progress has been uneven. The number of illiterate adults globally fell from 880.5 million in 1990 to 773.5 million in 2011, even as the world population grew by more than 1.5 billion during that same period. (See Table 2.5.) Illiteracy is a problem that is increasingly restricted to the developing world. In the developed world, there were around 1.1 million illiterate people in 2011, down from 4.7 million in 1990. Within the developing world, East Asia, the region that includes China, has seen the most raw numerical progress in combating illiteracy. As Table 2.5 shows, in 1990 there were 230.2 million illiterate people in East Asia, and in 2011 there were 87.7 million, for a decrease of approximately 61.9%. Central and eastern Europe and Central Asia made similarly dramatic progress in reducing illiteracy during the same period, although both regions had far smaller illiterate populations at the outset. Central and eastern Europe's illiterate population fell from 12.1 million to 4.9 million between 1990 and 2011, for a decrease of 59.3%; and Central Asia's illiterate population fell from 937,000 to 290,000, for a decrease of 69%.

The Arab states, along with Latin America and the Caribbean, saw slower progress at fighting illiteracy during this period. The number of illiterate adults in the Arab states fell from 51.7 million in 1990 to 47.6 million in 2011, and Latin America and the Caribbean saw its illiterate population decrease from 42.2 million in 1990 to 35.6 million in 2011. (See Table 2.5.) South and West Asia, as a region, saw its illiterate population climb slightly, from 401 million in 1990 to 407 million in 2011, and sub-Saharan Africa saw its illiterate population grow significantly, from 133.2 million in 1990 to 182 million in 2011.

Across the developing world, illiteracy disproportionately affected women in 2011, which was true in 1990, too. As Table 2.5 reveals, women accounted for 63.8% of the developing world's illiterate population in 2011, little changed from 1990, when women accounted for 62.9% of the developing world's illiterate population. In no region of the developing world except Central Asia (where there were also far fewer illiterate people than in most other developing regions) was substantial progress made in introducing gender parity in literacy levels, as the female share of the illiterate population fell from 76.8% in 1990 to 62.7% in 2011.

These regional totals, however, belie wide variations in the challenges faced by individual developing countries. As indicated in Figure 2.6, 10 countries account for almost three-quarters of the entire world's illiterate population.

Of these 10 countries, India has by far the largest population of illiterate adults, with 287 million in the period 2005–10, followed by China (62 million), Pakistan (50 million), Bangladesh (44 million), Nigeria (35 million), Ethiopia (27 million), Egypt (16 million), Brazil (14 million), Indonesia (13 million), and the Democratic Republic of the Congo (12 million). During the 2005–10 period there were also 11 countries with adult literacy rates below 50%. With the exception of Haiti, which had an adult literacy rate of 49%, all of these countries were in sub-Saharan Africa. Niger and Burkina Faso faced the biggest challenges in this realm, with adult literacy rates of only 29%, followed closely by Mali (31%) and Chad (34%).

## HUNGER AND HEALTH
### Undernourishment and Malnutrition

Undernourishment, or the inability to satisfy dietary requirements either because of an insufficient quantity of food or because of problems with food quality and nutritional value, is largely a problem confined to the developing world. Undernourishment in childhood, and especially the first two years of life, is particularly devastating, causing developmental damage that cannot be undone. Hunger's relation to poverty is reciprocal: poverty usually results in hunger, but hunger is a factor that keeps people in poverty. Deficiencies in nutrients such as iodine, vitamin A, iron, and zinc contribute to weakened immune systems, anemia, learning disabilities, complications in pregnancy and childbirth, and many childhood diseases. These conditions result in poverty-causing problems such as absenteeism and poor performance at school and work, unemployment, illiteracy, and the continuing cycle of poverty. (See Figure 2.7.)

According to the Food and Agriculture Organization (FAO) of the United Nations (UN), in *The State of Food Insecurity in the World 2012: Economic Growth Is Necessary but Not Sufficient to Accelerate Reduction of Hunger and Malnutrition* (2012, http://www.fao.org/docrep/016/ i3027e/i3027e00.htm), 870 million people worldwide were chronically undernourished in 2010–12. Of the world's total of chronically hungry people, 852 million lived in developing countries, a figure equal to 14.9% of the developing world's total population. (See Table 2.6.)

Progress in reducing undernourishment has been significant since 1990, when an estimated 23.2% of the developing world's population suffered from undernourishment, but the pace of reductions slowed with the onset of the global economic crisis in 2007. The Millennium Development Goal (MDG; see Chapter 1) of halving the percentage of people suffering from chronic hunger between 1990 and 2015 would mean arriving at a target of 11.6% of the developing world's population. As of 2012 the FAO projected hunger in the developing world would fall to 12.5% of the total population by 2015, barely missing the MDG.

# TABLE 2.5

**Adult (age 15 and over) illiterate population and female percentage of illiterate population by region, 1990–2015**

[Numbers in thousands]

| EFA region | 1990 (1985–1994 census decade) | | | | 2000 (1995–2004 census decade) | | | | 2011 (2005–2014 census decade) | | | | 2015 projection | | | |
|---|---|---|---|---|---|---|---|---|---|---|---|---|---|---|---|---|
| | MF | M | F | % F | MF | M | F | % F | MF | M | F | % F | MF | M | F | % F |
| Arab states | 51,697 | 18,886 | 32,811 | 63.5 | 51,827 | 18,056 | 33,770 | 65.2 | 47,603 | 16,082 | 31,521 | 66.2 | 47,629 | 15,829 | 31,800 | 66.8 |
| Central and Eastern Europe | 12,077 | 2,529 | 9,548 | 79.1 | 8,589 | 1,758 | 6,831 | 79.5 | 4,919 | 1,104 | 3,815 | 77.5 | 6,506 | 1,307 | 5,199 | 79.9 |
| Central Asia | 937 | 217 | 720 | 76.8 | 483 | 136 | 347 | 71.8 | 290 | 108 | 182 | 62.7 | 247 | 104 | 143 | 57.8 |
| East Asia and the Pacific | 231,557 | 70,927 | 160,630 | 69.4 | 127,564 | 37,583 | 89,981 | 70.5 | 89,478 | 26,356 | 63,122 | 70.5 | 76,014 | 22,314 | 53,701 | 70.6 |
| East Asia | 230,154 | 70,337 | 159,816 | 69.4 | 125,993 | 36,908 | 89,085 | 70.7 | 87,652 | 25,519 | 62,133 | 70.9 | 74,173 | 21,424 | 52,749 | 71.1 |
| Pacific | — | — | — | — | — | — | — | — | — | — | — | — | — | — | — | — |
| Latin America and the Caribbean | 42,204 | 18,794 | 23,410 | 55.5 | 38,316 | 17,236 | 21,080 | 55.0 | 35,614 | 15,994 | 19,620 | 55.1 | 32,681 | 14,980 | 17,701 | 54.2 |
| Caribbean | — | — | — | — | 2,853 | 1,324 | 1,529 | 53.6 | 3,503 | 1,629 | 1,874 | 53.5 | 3,388 | 1,583 | 1,805 | 53.3 |
| Latin America | 39,300 | 17,483 | 21,817 | 55.5 | 35,463 | 15,912 | 19,551 | 55.1 | 32,112 | 14,366 | 17,746 | 55.3 | 29,293 | 13,397 | 15,896 | 54.3 |
| North America and Western Europe | — | — | — | — | — | — | — | — | — | — | — | — | — | — | — | — |
| South and West Asia | 400,974 | 160,188 | 240,786 | 60.1 | 391,704 | 145,392 | 246,312 | 62.9 | 407,021 | 147,352 | 259,669 | 63.8 | 381,909 | 134,166 | 247,743 | 64.9 |
| Sub-Saharan Africa | 133,172 | 50,916 | 82,256 | 61.8 | 156,739 | 59,462 | 97,277 | 62.1 | 181,950 | 70,535 | 111,414 | 61.2 | 191,376 | 74,378 | 116,998 | 61.1 |
| Developed countries | — | — | — | — | — | — | — | — | — | — | — | — | — | — | — | — |
| Countries in transition | 4,698 | 728 | 3,970 | 84.5 | 2,050 | 468 | 1,583 | 77.2 | 1,190 | 364 | 825 | 69.4 | 649 | 259 | 389 | 60.0 |
| Developing countries | 865,961 | 321,076 | 544,885 | 62.9 | 771,308 | 278,461 | 492,847 | 63.9 | 763,987 | 276,498 | 487,490 | 63.8 | 733,847 | 262,093 | 471,754 | 64.3 |
| **World** | **880,504** | **325,465** | **555,039** | **63.0** | **782,469** | **282,548** | **499,921** | **63.9** | **773,549** | **280,366** | **493,184** | **63.8** | **742,799** | **265,870** | **476,929** | **64.2** |

SOURCE: "Table 2. Adult (Aged 15+ Years) Illiterate Population (000) and Female Percentage of Illiterate Population by Region, 1990–2015," in *Adult and Youth Literacy: National, Regional, and Global Trends, 1985–2015*, UNESCO Institute for Statistics (UIS), June 2013, http://www.uis.unesco.org/datacentre (accessed September 23, 2013).

## FIGURE 2.6

**Countries with the most illiterate adults and with literacy rates below 50%, 2005–10**

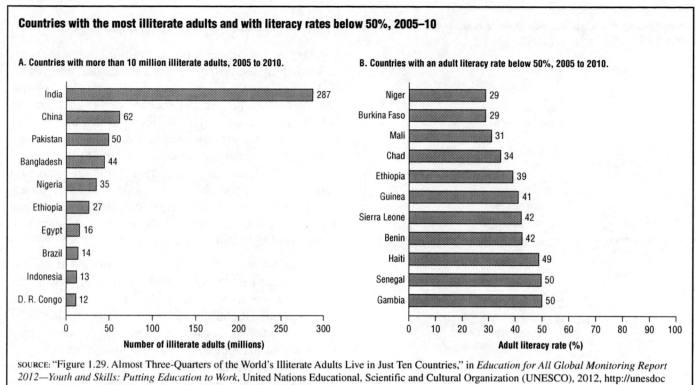

A. Countries with more than 10 million illiterate adults, 2005 to 2010.

| Country | Number of illiterate adults (millions) |
|---|---|
| India | 287 |
| China | 62 |
| Pakistan | 50 |
| Bangladesh | 44 |
| Nigeria | 35 |
| Ethiopia | 27 |
| Egypt | 16 |
| Brazil | 14 |
| Indonesia | 13 |
| D. R. Congo | 12 |

B. Countries with an adult literacy rate below 50%, 2005 to 2010.

| Country | Adult literacy rate (%) |
|---|---|
| Niger | 29 |
| Burkina Faso | 29 |
| Mali | 31 |
| Chad | 34 |
| Ethiopia | 39 |
| Guinea | 41 |
| Sierra Leone | 42 |
| Benin | 42 |
| Haiti | 49 |
| Senegal | 50 |
| Gambia | 50 |

SOURCE: "Figure 1.29. Almost Three-Quarters of the World's Illiterate Adults Live in Just Ten Countries," in *Education for All Global Monitoring Report 2012—Youth and Skills: Putting Education to Work*, United Nations Educational, Scientific and Cultural Organization (UNESCO), 2012, http://unesdoc.unesco.org/images/0021/002180/218003e.pdf (accessed September 23, 2013)

Nevertheless, as with other development and poverty indicators, progress toward eliminating chronic undernourishment varied widely from region to region and country to country in the developing world. Among all regions of the developing world for which the FAO presented data in its 2012 report, only Western Asia saw the percentage of its population experiencing chronic hunger increase, from 6.6% in 1990–92 to 10.1% in 2010–12. (See Table 2.6.) Sub-Saharan Africa accomplished a significant reduction in hunger levels over the course of those two decades: the percentage of people in the region who were undernourished fell from 32.8% in 1990–92 to 26.8% in 2010–12. Nonetheless, the 2010–12 percentage remained unacceptably high, exceeding the 1990–92 hunger levels of most other regions in the developing world.

Most of the total progress at combating hunger in this two-decade period came in the high-population regions of Eastern Asia and Southeastern Asia. Eastern Asia, led by declines in China, saw its hunger levels fall by nearly 100 million people during the period, from 20.8% to 11.5% of the region's population. (See Table 2.6.) Southeastern Asia, led by declines in the populous countries of Indonesia, Thailand, and Vietnam, saw a slightly smaller decline in terms of raw numbers, as the chronically hungry population fell from 134 million to 65 million. Southeastern Asia's progress, however, was larger than Eastern Asia's in percentage terms, as the proportion of

the hungry in the region fell from 29.6% to 10.9%. Latin America and the Caribbean made more modest progress, reducing the number of the hungry by 16 million (from 65 million to 49 million) and the percentage of the hungry by more than 40% (from 14.6% to 8.3%).

Malnutrition refers both to the effects of chronic undernourishment and to obesity. Because maternal undernourishment and/or undernourishment in early childhood can have irreversible cognitive and physical effects, much of the international community's attention to malnutrition focuses on children. The personal and societal burdens created by these forms of malnutrition are at present more significant than those created by obesity, although the rapid growth in obesity rates even in the developing world are cause for great concern among public health officials and experts. Among the most studied indicators of malnutrition are stunting (being too short for one's age) and micronutrient deficiencies (lacking one or more vitamins or minerals that are important for human health). The FAO reports in *The State of Food and Agriculture 2013: Food Systems for Better Nutrition* (2013, http://www.fao.org/docrep/018/i3300e/i3300e.pdf) that as of 2013, 26% of children globally were stunted and 2 billion people experienced one or more micronutrient deficiencies. There were also an estimated 1.4 billion overweight people in the world, and 500 million of these overweight people were obese. "Most countries are burdened by multiple types of

## FIGURE 2.7

**Relationship of hunger and malnutrition to other problems of poverty**

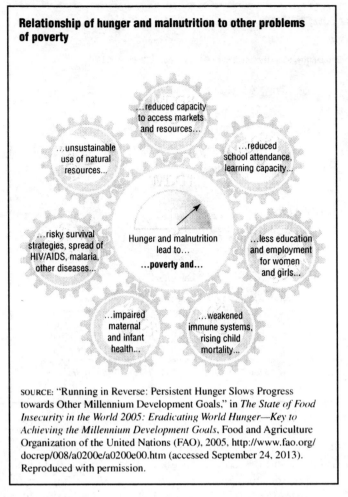

...reduced capacity to access markets and resources...

...unsustainable use of natural resources...

...reduced school attendance, learning capacity...

...risky survival strategies, spread of HIV/AIDS, malaria, other diseases...

Hunger and malnutrition lead to...

...poverty and...

...less education and employment for women and girls...

...impaired maternal and infant health...

...weakened immune systems, rising child mortality...

SOURCE: "Running in Reverse: Persistent Hunger Slows Progress towards Other Millennium Development Goals," in *The State of Food Insecurity in the World 2005: Eradicating World Hunger—Key to Achieving the Millennium Development Goals*, Food and Agriculture Organization of the United Nations (FAO), 2005, http://www.fao.org/docrep/008/a0200e/a0200e00.htm (accessed September 24, 2013). Reproduced with permission.

malnutrition," the FAO concludes, "which may coexist within the same country, household, or individual."

Figure 2.8 shows the prevalence of stunting and micronutrient deficiencies in the developing world. The types of micronutrient deficiency considered are anemia (or anaemia, a sign of iron deficiency), vitamin A deficiency, and iodine deficiency. These are not the only forms of micronutrient deficiency that adversely affect health, but they are the ones for which the most data exist. The data regarding stunting, anemia, and vitamin A deficiency pertain to children under five, the group that is the focus of most research into malnutrition, whereas the iodine-deficiency data pertain to the total population in the developing regions surveyed. As with undernourishment, significant progress has been made throughout the developing world in combating these conditions, but progress has been uneven. Malnutrition levels remain stubbornly high in many regions. In Africa, for example, nearly 40% of children exhibited stunting and vitamin A deficiency; nearly 60% of children were anemic; and approximately 40% of the total population had low levels of urinary iodine in the most recent years for which data were available. (See Figure 2.8.) Latin America and the

Caribbean was the developing region with the lowest levels of each type of malnutrition, although even there, approximately 35% of children were anemic.

The consequences of malnutrition are sometimes quantified in terms of "disability-adjusted life years" (DALYs). One DALY is equivalent to the loss of one year of healthy life, so the number of DALYs and the DALY rate in a country or region provides a picture of the gap between current health conditions and optimal conditions in which people enjoy maximum life expectancy and a disease-free old age. Table 2.7 provides DALY totals for the different regions of the developing world, broken down into DALYs resulting from child and maternal malnutrition, from being underweight, and from being overweight and obese.

Child and maternal malnutrition accounted for the highest quantities of lost years of healthy life in the developing world in 2010, at 164,416 DALYs, a total generated almost entirely in Africa (78,017 malnutrition DALYs) and Asia (80,070). People in the developing world whose undernourishment resulted in being underweight accounted for 77,294 DALYs in 2010, and again these totals were almost entirely the product of underweight people in Africa (43,990) and Asia (32,210). The health effects of both of these forms of malnutrition had decreased by more than half since 1990.

The cumulative lost years of life attributed to overweight and obesity, by contrast, rose sharply between 1990 and 2010 in the developing world and the developed world alike. (See Table 2.7.) Among regions of the developing world, Asia and Latin America and the Caribbean were most adversely affected by overweight and obesity, together accounting for 46,000 of the total 55,882 overweight and obesity DALYs in the developing world.

### Child Mortality and Life Expectancy

Poverty is directly correlated with increased mortality and shorter life spans. Diseases that are preventable or treatable in the developed world remain life threatening to many in the developing world because of the lack of affordable health care, sanitation, clean water sources, and other necessities. While such necessities are widely available to ordinary citizens in the developed world, they are frequently obtainable by only the privileged in the developing world. Additionally, chronic hunger claims the lives of many in the developing world either directly, because of starvation, or indirectly, by weakening the body's resistance to disease.

The UN's Inter-Agency Group for Child Mortality Estimation finds in *Levels & Trends in Child Mortality: Report 2013* (2013, http://www.childinfo.org/files/Child_Mortality_Report_2013.pdf) that the global child mortality rate fell 47% between 1990 and 2012, from

**TABLE 2.6**

**Undernourishment in the developing world, 1990–2012**

| | Number (millions) and prevalence (%) of undernourishment | | | | |
|---|---|---|---|---|---|
| | 1990–92 | 1999–2001 | 2004–06 | 2007–09 | 2010–12* |
| **World** | **1,000** | **919** | **898** | **867** | **868** |
| | **18.6%** | **15.0%** | **13.8%** | **12.9%** | **12.5%** |
| Developed regions | 20 | 18 | 13 | 15 | 16 |
| | 1.9% | 1.6% | 1.2% | 1.3% | 1.4% |
| Developing regions | 980 | 901 | 885 | 852 | 852 |
| | 23.2% | 18.3% | 16.8% | 15.5% | 14.9% |
| Africa | 175 | 205 | 210 | 220 | 239 |
| | 27.3% | 25.3% | 23.1% | 22.6% | 22.9% |
| Northern Africa | 5 | 5 | 5 | 4 | 4 |
| | 3.8% | 3.3% | 3.1% | 2.7% | 2.7% |
| Sub-Saharan Africa | 170 | 200 | 205 | 216 | 234 |
| | 32.8% | 30.0% | 27.2% | 26.5% | 26.8% |
| Asia | 739 | 634 | 620 | 581 | 563 |
| | 23.7% | 17.7% | 16.3% | 14.8% | 13.9% |
| Western Asia | 8 | 13 | 16 | 18 | 21 |
| | 6.6% | 8.0% | 8.8% | 9.4% | 10.1% |
| Southern Asia | 327 | 309 | 323 | 311 | 304 |
| | 26.8% | 21.2% | 20.4% | 18.8% | 17.6% |
| Caucasus and Central Asia | 9 | 11 | 7 | 7 | 6 |
| | 12.8% | 15.8% | 9.9% | 9.2% | 7.4% |
| Eastern Asia | 261 | 197 | 186 | 169 | 167 |
| | 20.8% | 14.4% | 13.2% | 11.8% | 11.5% |
| South-Eastern Asia | 134 | 104 | 88 | 76 | 65 |
| | 29.6% | 20.0% | 15.8% | 13.2% | 10.9% |
| Latin America and the Caribbean | 65 | 60 | 54 | 50 | 49 |
| | 14.6% | 11.6% | 9.7% | 8.7% | 8.3% |
| Latin America | 57 | 53 | 46 | 43 | 42 |
| | 13.6% | 11.0% | 9.0% | 8.1% | 7.7% |
| Caribbean | 9 | 7 | 7 | 7 | 7 |
| | 28.5% | 21.4% | 20.9% | 18.6% | 17.8% |
| Oceania | 1 | 1 | 1 | 1 | 1 |
| | 13.6% | 15.5% | 13.7% | 11.9% | 12.1% |

*Projections.

SOURCE: "Table 1. Undernourishment in the Developing Regions, 1990–92 to 2010–12," in *The State of Food Insecurity in the World 2012: Economic Growth Is Necessary but Not Sufficient to Accelerate Reduction of Hunger and Malnutrition*, Food and Agricultural Organization of the United Nations (FAO), 2012, http://www.fao.org/docrep/016/i3027e/i3027e00.htm (accessed September 24, 2013). Reproduced with permission.

90 deaths per 1,000 live births to 48. Although this represents enormous progress, the MDG for reducing child mortality by two-thirds between 1990 and 2015 was unlikely to be met. There were an estimated 6.6 million deaths of children under the age of five years in 2012, most of which were from preventable causes or treatable diseases, and 98.6% of which were in the developing world. (See Table 2.8.)

More than 80% of global under-the-age-of-five child mortality occurred in sub-Saharan Africa (49.5%) and Southern Asia (32.2%) in 2012, as Table 2.8 indicates. All regions of the developing world saw declines of more than 50% in their child mortality rates between 1990 and 2012, with the exception of sub-Saharan Africa, which achieved only a 14% decline in the under-five death rate. In Eastern Asia, led by China, child mortality declined by 84% during this period, well above the MDG. The only other regions of the developing world that saw declines at or above the MDG were northern Africa and Latin America and the Caribbean, both of which saw child mortality fall by 67%.

Another indicator that demonstrates the severity of the health gap between the developed and the developing world is life expectancy. As Table 2.9 shows, people in developed countries can generally expect to live substantially longer than those in developing countries. Between 1990 and 2011 the developed region consisting of European Union countries saw life expectancy rise from 75 to 80, and North American life expectancy rose from 75 to 79. The developing regions of East Asia and the Pacific (with a 2011 life expectancy of 75), Europe and Central Asia (76), and Latin America and the Caribbean (74) each made gains comparable to those in the developed world over the same period, but 2011 life expectancies in these countries were comparable to 1990 life expectancies in the developed world. Life expectancies in the Middle East and North Africa, South Asia, and sub-Saharan Africa had likewise increased by similar amounts between 1990 and 2011, but the 2011 levels in these countries lagged dramatically behind those in the developed world. South Asia's 2011 life expectancy of 66 and sub-Saharan Africa's life expectancy of 56 were particularly stark reminders of the destructive effects of poverty on health.

**FIGURE 2.8**

Prevalence of malnutrition indicators in the developing world, by region, selected years 1990–2011

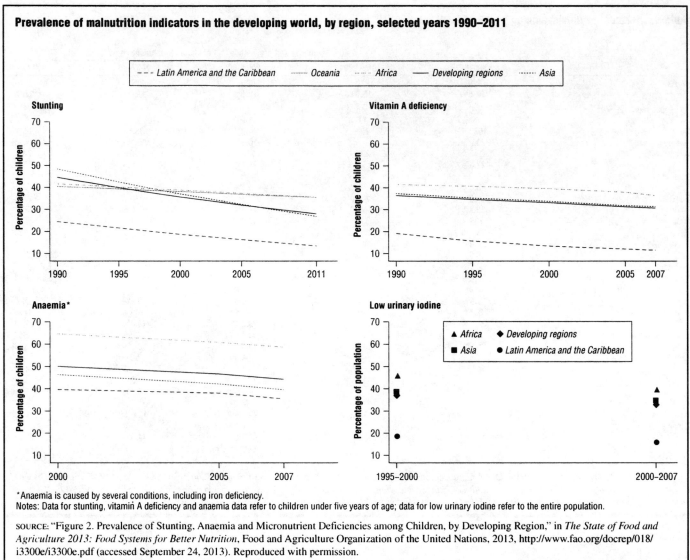

*Anaemia is caused by several conditions, including iron deficiency.

Notes: Data for stunting, vitamin A deficiency and anaemia data refer to children under five years of age; data for low urinary iodine refer to the entire population.

SOURCE: "Figure 2. Prevalence of Stunting, Anaemia and Micronutrient Deficiencies among Children, by Developing Region," in *The State of Food and Agriculture 2013: Food Systems for Better Nutrition*, Food and Agriculture Organization of the United Nations, 2013, http://www.fao.org/docrep/018/i3300e/i3300e.pdf (accessed September 24, 2013). Reproduced with permission.

## POVERTY, GOVERNMENTS, AND GLOBALIZATION

The growing economic interdependence of nations has been one of the most consequential developments in the post–World War II world. Proponents of globalization maintain that opening markets across national borders provides opportunities for both large and small economies. They suggest that freer exchange of money and technology can help develop the world's smaller and poorer economies and therefore help alleviate poverty in developing regions while increasing the wealth of developed ones.

Opponents of globalization argue that the system resulting from this interdependence favors those who are already most advantaged and puts the welfare of multinational corporations above the welfare of poor and indigenous people. Multinational corporations that move into developing countries are often seen to be exploiting the populace in the name of providing

opportunities for them. Critics suggest that people in traditional cultures are often denied the ability to sustain themselves by growing their own food, making their own clothing, and maintaining economic autonomy. Also, many claim that with globalization has come an increase in unjust labor practices that take advantage of the poor, such as sweatshops and the use of child labor.

A major facet of globalization is the forging of free trade agreements (FTAs), which are arrangements between countries that allow the exchange of goods and labor across borders without governmental tariffs (taxes on imported goods) or other trade barriers. Two of the best-known FTAs are the North American Free Trade Agreement (among Canada, Mexico, and the United States) and the Central American Free Trade Agreement (among Costa Rica, the Dominican Republic, El Salvador, Guatemala, Honduras, Nicaragua, and the United States). Despite the increasing number of FTAs, poor

TABLE 2.7

**Disability-adjusted life years (DALYs), by malnutrition-related risk factor, population group, and region, 1990 and 2010**

| Region | Child and maternal malnutrition Total DALYs (thousands) | | Underweight Total DALYs (thousands) | | Underweight DALYs per 1,000 population (number) | | Overweight and obesity Total DALYs (thousands) | | Overweight and obesity DALYs per 1,000 population (number) | |
|---|---|---|---|---|---|---|---|---|---|---|
| | 1990 | 2010 | 1990 | 2010 | 1990 | 2010 | 1990 | 2010 | 1990 | 2010 |
| World | 339,951 | 166,147 | 197,774 | 77,346 | 313 | 121 | 51,613 | 93,840 | 20 | 25 |
| Developed regions | 2,243 | 1,731 | 160 | 51 | 2 | 1 | 29,956 | 37,959 | 41 | 44 |
| Developing regions | 337,708 | 164,416 | 197,614 | 77,294 | 356 | 135 | 21,657 | 55,882 | 12 | 19 |
| Africa | 121,492 | 78,017 | 76,983 | 43,990 | 694 | 278 | 3,571 | 9,605 | 15 | 24 |
| Eastern Africa | 42,123 | 21,485 | 27,702 | 11,148 | 779 | 205 | 353 | 1,231 | 5 | 11 |
| Middle Africa | 18,445 | 17,870 | 12,402 | 11,152 | 890 | 488 | 157 | 572 | 6 | 13 |
| Northern Africa | 10,839 | 4,740 | 4,860 | 1,612 | 216 | 68 | 2,030 | 4,773 | 36 | 47 |
| Southern Africa | 2,680 | 1,814 | 930 | 382 | 155 | 63 | 620 | 1,442 | 36 | 51 |
| Western Africa | 47,405 | 32,108 | 31,089 | 19,696 | 947 | 383 | 412 | 1,588 | 6 | 14 |
| Asia | 197,888 | 80,070 | 115,049 | 32,210 | 297 | 90 | 12,955 | 34,551 | 9 | 16 |
| Central Asia | 3,182 | 1,264 | 967 | 169 | 133 | 27 | 953 | 1,709 | 43 | 57 |
| Eastern Asia | 21,498 | 4,645 | 6,715 | 347 | 53 | 4 | 5,427 | 13,331 | 9 | 14 |
| Southern Asia | 138,946 | 60,582 | 89,609 | 27,325 | 514 | 150 | 2,953 | 9,281 | 6 | 11 |
| South-Eastern Asia | 27,971 | 9,736 | 15,490 | 3,318 | 270 | 61 | 1,045 | 5,032 | 5 | 16 |
| Western Asia | 6,291 | 3,843 | 2,269 | 1,051 | 104 | 41 | 2,577 | 5,198 | 42 | 45 |
| Latin America and the Caribbean | 17,821 | 6,043 | 5,292 | 979 | 94 | 18 | 5,062 | 11,449 | 26 | 36 |
| Caribbean | 2,559 | 1,073 | 849 | 252 | 204 | 67 | 401 | 854 | 25 | 38 |
| Central America | 5,437 | 1,491 | 2,124 | 366 | 133 | 22 | 1,228 | 3,309 | 28 | 42 |
| South America | 9,826 | 3,479 | 2,319 | 361 | 64 | 11 | 3,433 | 7,286 | 25 | 34 |
| Oceania | 507 | 286 | 290 | 115 | 302 | 87 | 69 | 276 | 30 | 67 |

Notes: DALY (disability-adjusted life year) estimates for child and maternal malnutrition include factors such as child underweight, iron deficiency, vitamin A deficiency, zinc deficiency and suboptimal breastfeeding. They also include maternal haemorrhage and maternal sepsis and iron-deficiency anaemia among women. Estimates for overweight and obesity refer to adults aged 25 and older.

SOURCE: "Table 1. Disability-Adjusted Life Years in 1990 and 2010, by Malnutrition-Related Risk Factor, Population Group and Region," in *The State of Food and Agriculture 2013: Food Systems for Better Nutrition*, Food and Agriculture Organization of the United Nations, 2013, http://www.fao.org/docrep/018/ i3300e/i3300e.pdf (accessed September 24, 2013). Reproduced with permission.

TABLE 2.8

**Child (under age five) mortality rate and trends, by region, 1990–2012**

[In thousands, unless otherwise indicated]

| Region | 1990 | 1995 | 2000 | 2005 | 2010 | 2012 | Decline (percent) 1990–2012 | Share of global under-five deaths (percent) 1990 | Share of global under-five deaths (percent) 2012 |
|---|---|---|---|---|---|---|---|---|---|
| Developed regions | 226 | 153 | 131 | 112 | 97 | 90 | 60 | 1.8 | 1.4 |
| Developing regions | 12,394 | 10,701 | 9,568 | 8,123 | 6,901 | 6,463 | 48 | 98.2 | 98.6 |
| Northern Africa | 268 | 188 | 137 | 101 | 91 | 88 | 67 | 2.1 | 1.3 |
| Sub-Saharan Africa | 3,772 | 3,998 | 4,084 | 3,791 | 3,391 | 3,245 | 14 | 29.9 | 49.5 |
| Latin America and the Caribbean | 627 | 500 | 383 | 286 | 249 | 206 | 67 | 5.0 | 3.1 |
| Caucasus and Central Asia | 146 | 122 | 86 | 72 | 69 | 64 | 56 | 1.2 | 1.0 |
| Eastern Asia | 1,675 | 862 | 659 | 426 | 304 | 272 | 84 | 13.3 | 4.2 |
| Excluding China | 28 | 42 | 30 | 17 | 15 | 14 | 51 | 0.2 | 0.2 |
| Southern Asia | 4,784 | 4,096 | 3,492 | 2,835 | 2,277 | 2,108 | 56 | 37.9 | 32.2 |
| Excluding India | 1,459 | 1,241 | 1,078 | 850 | 755 | 694 | 52 | 11.6 | 10.6 |
| South-Eastern Asia | 843 | 692 | 521 | 446 | 380 | 346 | 59 | 6.7 | 5.3 |
| Western Asia | 265 | 229 | 189 | 150 | 125 | 120 | 55 | 2.1 | 1.8 |
| Oceania | 14 | 15 | 16 | 16 | 15 | 15 | −3 | 0.1 | 0.2 |
| World | 12,621 | 10,854 | 9,699 | 8,234 | 6,998 | 6,553 | 48 | 100.0 | 100.0 |

Note: All calculations are based on unrounded numbers.

SOURCE: "Table 2. Levels and Trends in the Number of Deaths of Children under Age Five, by Millennium Development Goal Region, 1990–2012," in *Levels & Trends in Child Mortality: Report 2013*, United Nations, Inter-Agency Group for Child Mortality Estimation, 2013, http://www.childinfo.org/files/Child_ Mortality_Report_2013.pdf (accessed September 24, 2013)

countries are often subject to higher import tariffs and other unfavorable circumstances when they export goods to developed countries. Also, when these FTAs are signed outside of the auspices of the World Trade Organization, they do not always provide poor countries the opportunity to band together to create more favorable

**TABLE 2.9**

**Life expectancy at birth, by region, selected years 1990–2011**

| | 1990 | 1995 | 2000 | 2005 | 2010 | 2011 |
|---|---|---|---|---|---|---|
| World | 66 | 66 | 68 | 69 | 70 | 71 |
| East Asia & Pacific | 69 | 70 | 72 | 73 | 74 | 75 |
| European Union | 75 | 76 | 77 | 78 | 80 | 80 |
| Europe & Central Asia | 72 | 72 | 73 | 74 | 76 | 76 |
| Latin America & Caribbean | 68 | 70 | 72 | 73 | 74 | 74 |
| Middle East & North Africa | 66 | 68 | 70 | 71 | 72 | 72 |
| North America | 75 | 76 | 77 | 78 | 79 | 79 |
| South Asia | 59 | 61 | 63 | 65 | 66 | 66 |
| Sub-Saharan Africa | 50 | 50 | 50 | 52 | 55 | 56 |

SOURCE: Adapted from "Life Expectancy at Birth, Total (Years)," in *World DataBank: World Development Indicators*, World Bank, 2013, http:// databank.worldbank.org/data/views/variableselection/selectvariables.aspx? source=world-development-indicators (accessed September 24, 2013)

rules for themselves. As a result, the rules that favor rich countries often prevail.

## Agricultural Subsidies and Food Exports

Agricultural subsidies are often cited as a factor in either causing or worsening the problems of hunger and economic development. The governments of wealthy countries routinely pay farmers—mostly the owners of large farms—and agribusinesses billions of dollars each year to produce too much or not enough of certain crops to control the prices of crops for export or import.

Farm subsidies in Europe, Japan, and the United States are designed to work in conjunction with trade barriers such as quotas (limitations of imports) and tariffs. When farmers in developed countries are paid to overproduce certain foods (e.g., rice and corn), those countries export the surplus to poor countries for extremely low prices or sometimes without charge as aid. At the same time, trade barriers prevent poor countries from exporting crops and other goods to wealthy countries (this is sometimes called protectionism).

Food dumping, as the export of surplus crops from the developed world is sometimes called, is a matter of official U.S. government policy. Although the United States regularly donates large amounts of food to developing countries, it is not purchasing food grown by farmers in the developing countries—it sends crops grown by American farmers and shipped overseas by U.S. companies. Critics of the policy suggest that the priority of the program is to recoup the United States' food expenses and to aid American agribusiness, rather than to help those in need.

In some emergencies, such as disasters or wars that disrupt supply chains and destroy crops, the importation of American food represents the most sensible food-aid option. In other cases, though, even in emergency situations, food is available in the country or region affected, and U.S. funds could be more efficiently spent on these locally or

regionally sourced foods, because the costs of American food production (which are much higher than the costs of food production in the developing world) and shipping must be factored into the overall price of the food donations.

Additionally, supplying U.S.-grown crops after the early stages of an emergency have passed hurts local economies by driving prices down to levels that local farmers cannot match. Once local farmers have been prevented from competing in this way, a country can become perennially dependent on food aid, and farmers instead use their land to produce crops such as cut flowers or livestock feed for export to developed countries. These countries thus become more vulnerable to international economic trends ranging from rising prices in world commodity markets (which can make food aid less available), to falling prices for the commodities they produce for export, to financial meltdowns such as those that touched off the global economic crisis in 2007. A country that is capable of meeting its own food needs without significant amounts of imported food is, by contrast, better positioned to reduce poverty and increase its levels of human development.

In "Haitian Farmers Undermined by Food Aid" (January 11, 2012, http://www.publicintegrity.org/2012/ 01/11/7844/haitian-farmers-undermined-food-aid), Jacob Kushner of the Center for Public Integrity reports on a prominent example of what many antipoverty advocates believe to be an instance of food dumping that helped U.S. agribusiness at the expense of farmers in one of the world's poorest countries. In the immediate aftermath of the devastating January 2010 earthquake in the Caribbean country of Haiti, which killed an estimated 170,000 to 300,000 people and left more than a million homeless, the country's food supply was so drastically disrupted that sending U.S. food to the country represented the right policy. Nevertheless, the importation of $140 million in U.S.-grown crops over the course of 2010 made it impossible for thousands of local growers to sell their own crops at a profit, and poverty in the country is believed to have worsened as a result.

As Kushner reports, growing recognition of the flaws in U.S. aid policies led the former president Bill Clinton (1946–), who was the UN special envoy to Haiti and one of the leading figures in helping to raise funds for the earthquake recovery, to argue in March 2011 before a U.S. Senate Foreign Relations Committee for the cessation of U.S. food dumping. "Since 1981," Clinton stated, "the United States has followed a policy, until the last year or so when we started rethinking it, that we rich countries that produce a lot of food should sell it to poor countries and relieve them of the burden of producing their own food, so, thank goodness, they can leap directly into the industrial era. ... It has not worked. It may have been good for some of my farmers in Arkansas, but it has not worked."

## International Debt

Lending and debt relief to underdeveloped and developing nations is another controversial issue. Many low-income countries became heavily indebted to wealthy nations during the 1970s, when banks around the world began lending money to developing countries that were rich in resources such as oil. The money, however, was often mismanaged—particularly in the countries of sub-Saharan Africa—and spent on projects to expand the wealth of the upper classes, rather than used to build the infrastructure and make the social investments necessary for economic development. When interest rates on the loans rose and the prices of oil and other resources fell during the 1980s, the indebted countries were unable to repay the loans. Many of these nations turned to the World Bank or the International Monetary Fund (IMF) for help. These organizations underwrote more loans, but required that the poor countries agree to undergo structural adjustment programs (SAPs).

In essence, the World Bank and the IMF demanded that the poor countries restructure their economies by cutting spending and revaluing their currency so that they could begin to repay their loans and emerge from debt. Most low-income countries met the restructuring criteria by limiting their social spending (e.g., on education, health care, and social services), lowering wages, cutting jobs, and taking land from subsistence farmers to grow crops for export. This focus on increasing trade has generated the most severe criticism from opponents of SAPs, who argue that the United States and other wealthy countries encourage such measures to improve their own trading opportunities, which destroys the ability of poor countries to support themselves by encouraging dependence on imports of food and other basic necessities. Supporters of SAPs, however, point out that this economic system allows poor countries to participate more fully in the global market and that the benefits of restructuring will eventually "trickle down" to the poor.

In 1996 the World Bank and the IMF created the Heavily Indebted Poor Countries (HIPC) Initiative. The initiative was intended to reduce the debt of the most heavily indebted poor countries to manageable levels. In 2005 the HIPC Initiative was supplemented by the Multilateral Debt Relief Initiative (MDRI) to help countries make progress toward the UN MDGs.

The MDRI cancels the debt of countries that meet the HIPC Initiative criteria, which include implementing agreed-on reforms and developing a Poverty Reduction Strategy Paper (PRSP; the paper describes the policies and programs that a country will pursue over several years to encourage economic growth and reduce poverty). As a country makes progress toward these goals, a decision point is reached, whereby the International Development Association of the World Bank and the IMF determine whether the country should receive debt relief. If the country is granted debt relief, it may begin receiving interim debt relief at the decision point. Once the PRSP has been adopted and implemented for at least one year, and when other criteria have been met, the country is said to have reached its completion point, and full debt relief is given.

## Other Factors Associated with Hunger and Poverty

A number of other factors cause or contribute to poverty and the many forms of deprivation with which it is associated. One of the most common contributing factors for poverty and hunger is a country's system of governance. The World Bank, through its ongoing Worldwide Governance Indicators research project (http://info.worldbank.org/governance/wgi/index.aspx#home), has compiled several hundred variables and developed indicators that measure six dimensions of a country's governance. Four governance indicators in particular—political stability and absence of violence, government effectiveness, rule of law, and control of corruption—are necessary to achieve hunger reduction in a country. Hunger worsens and per capita food production drops, for example, in countries that are experiencing violent conflict and/or political instability.

Natural disasters, such as droughts, excess rainfall, extreme temperatures, and earthquakes, also cause food crises by slowing food production or halting it altogether. These occurrences have far more serious consequences in poor countries, where food production is already low. Displacement is another consequence of natural disasters that increases the incidence of hunger in poor countries. When people are forced to flee after major disasters such as earthquakes or to migrate because of severe weather conditions, pressure to produce enough food to support them is placed on the areas in which they settle.

# CHAPTER 3
# POVERTY IN SUB-SAHARAN AFRICA

## SUB-SAHARAN AFRICA

Africa is the second-largest continent (after Asia) in both land area and population, with more than 1 billion people living in 55 countries. With a total land area of 11.7 million square miles (30.3 million square kilometers [km]), Africa accounts for slightly more than 20% of the earth's land area, and its population accounts for almost 15% of the global population.

Africa is typically discussed as two distinct regions: northern Africa (the area in and around the Sahara Desert that is inhabited mostly by Arabic-speaking people with many cultural similarities to the peoples of Western Asia) and sub-Saharan Africa (the area south of the Sahara, in which many different tribes and nationalities live). The Sahara, the world's largest non-Arctic desert, is located primarily in the countries of Algeria, Egypt, and Libya, and occupies the northern portion of Mauritania. The countries south of the Sahara are sub-Saharan geographically, but "sub-Saharan Africa" is also frequently discussed as a political entity, given the cultural and economic similarity of the countries in the region. Sudan, in spite of being south of the Sahara, is sometimes considered North African rather than sub-Saharan because of its cultural similarity to other North African states.

The World Bank classifies six countries as North African: Algeria, Djibouti, Egypt, Libya, Morocco, and Tunisia. (Other organizations demarcate the region differently and compile data based on those alternate demarcations.) The economies of these countries are linked with the economies of Europe and the Middle East, and politically these nations are often grouped with other Arab states in Asia. Although none of these North African countries is considered part of the developed world, in general the region is more economically developed than sub-Saharan Africa. Table 3.1 shows the World Bank's 2010 breakdown of African economies by income, as measured by gross national income (GNI) per capita.

The countries of North Africa were all classified as either "lower middle income" or "upper middle income." Although there were numerous sub-Saharan countries in these categories (and the lone "high income" African country, the small oil-producing state of Equatorial Guinea, is in sub-Saharan Africa), sub-Saharan Africa has a much higher concentration of poverty than North Africa. All 26 of the African countries classified as "low income" by the World Bank in 2010 were sub-Saharan. These classifications are consistent with the categorization by the United Nations (UN) of 33 sub-Saharan African countries as Least Developed Countries (LDCs).

## THE IMPACT OF VIOLENCE AND WAR

The concentration of poverty in sub-Saharan Africa is partly due to its recent history. After World War II (1939–1945) the sub-Saharan economies were booming as they sold raw materials to Europe and Asia for their rebuilding and to the United States for its growth. These newly independent nations, once colonies of various European countries, borrowed heavily from abroad, only to face massive monetary problems with the world economic decline during the 1970s. From that time on, many parts of sub-Saharan Africa have become poorer and poorer amid corruption, conflict, and despotism. Long-running civil wars have been a particularly chilling and disruptive feature of sub-Saharan Africa's recent history, displacing millions of people, in some cases triggering famine, and in general setting back economic and human development for generations. The most conflict-ridden parts of sub-Saharan Africa are, on the whole, the poorest and least-developed.

Perhaps the bloodiest and most damaging of these wars occurred in the Democratic Republic of the Congo (DRC), a large, resource-rich country in central Africa. Since the 1990s eight African nations in addition to the DRC (Angola, Chad, Libya, Namibia, Rwanda, Sudan,

TABLE 3.1

**World Bank classification of African economies by GNI per capita, 2010**

| Low income<br>GNI per capita of $1,005 or less | Middle income | | High income<br>GNI per capita of $12,276 and over |
| --- | --- | --- | --- |
| | Lower middle income<br>GNI per capita higher than $1,006 and less than $3,975 | Upper middle income<br>GNI per capita of $3,976 but less than $12,275 | |
| Benin | Angola | Algeria | Equatorial Guinea |
| Burkina Faso | Cameroon | Botswana | |
| Burundi | Cape Verde | Gabon | |
| Central Africa Republic | Congo, Rep. | Libya | |
| Chad | Côte d'Ivoire | Mauritius | |
| Comoros | Djibouti | Namibia | |
| Congo, Dem. Rep. | Egypt, Arab Rep. | Seychelles | |
| Eritrea | Ghana | South Africa | |
| Ethiopia | Lesotho | Tunisia | |
| Gambia, The | Mauritania | | |
| Guinea | Morocco | | |
| Guinea-Bissau | Nigeria | | |
| Kenya | São Tomé and Príncipe | | |
| Liberia | Senegal | | |
| Madagascar | South Sudan | | |
| Malawi | Sudan | | |
| Mali | Swaziland | | |
| Mozambique | Zambia | | |
| Niger | | | |
| Rwanda | | | |
| Sierra Leone | | | |
| Somalia | | | |
| Tanzania | | | |
| Togo | | | |
| Uganda | | | |
| Zimbabwe | | | |

Note: GNI = Gross national income.

SOURCE: "Table 1. World Bank Classification of Economies, 2010," in *Africa Development Indicators 2012/13*, World Bank, Washington, D.C., 2013, https://openknowledge.worldbank.org/bitstream/handle/10986/13504/9780821396162.pdf?sequence=1 (accessed September 26, 2013). DOI: 10.1596/978-0-8213-9616-2. License: Creative Commons Attribution CC BY 3.0.

Uganda, and Zimbabwe) and more than 20 armed groups have been involved in a struggle for control of the country that has involved numerous stages, periods in which the central government consolidated its power, and new outbreaks of violence. Although the heaviest fighting of the Congolese civil war had ended by 2006, militias and splinter groups continued to fight in the eastern part of the country through 2013, and nearly 20,000 UN troops remained on the ground in an attempt to keep the peace.

Another of the region's most costly wars, in terms of human life as well as economic development, was that between Sudan's government and the area of the country that eventually seceded and in 2011 became South Sudan. Conflict between these groups dates to 1955, covers two distinct periods of civil war, and includes multiple episodes of mass killing and other atrocities. The heaviest fighting had ended by the second decade of the 21st century, but conflict had spilled over into the neighboring countries of Chad and the Central African Republic.

Table 3.2 shows economic development indicators for the countries of sub-Saharan Africa in 2010. Although sub-Saharan Africa as a whole had seen average annual

economic growth, as measured by gross domestic product (GDP; the total value of all goods and services produced by a country in a year) per capita, of 2.6% over the preceding decade, growth was uneven across the continent. Numerous low-income African nations (those with GNI per capita of $1,005 or less) had average annual negative growth over the course of the preceding decade. Zimbabwe saw its economy shrink by an annual average of 6.2% from 2000 to 2010, and its 2010 GNI per capita stood at $480. Eritrea's economy contracted by an annual average of 2.9% over the decade, and its 2010 GNI per capita was $340. Other low-income countries that had seen their economies shrink yearly over the preceding decade were the Central African Republic (−0.7%), the Comoros (−0.8%), and Guinea-Bissau (−0.5%). There were, additionally, eight low-income countries that had seen average annual growth of less than 2%, an insufficient rate of growth to drive significant improvements in living standards: Benin (0.8%), Burundi (0.5%), the Gambia (1.4%), Kenya (1.7%), Liberia (1.7%), Madagascar (0.3%), Niger (0.6%), and Togo (0.1%). Still other countries experienced economic growth at an average rate of 2% or more, but this had not been enough to raise them above the World Bank's low-income threshold of

**TABLE 3.2**

**Basic development indicators for countries in sub-Saharan Africa, 2010**

| | Population Total (millions) 2010 | Population Growth (annual %) 2010 | Land area (thousands of sq km) 2010 | Population density (people per sq km) 2010 | GNI per capita, World Bank Atlas method (current $) 2010 | GDP per capita Constant 2000 prices $ 2010[a] | GDP per capita Average annual growth (%) 2000–10 | Life expectancy at birth (years) 2010 | Under-five mortality rate (per 1,000) 2010 | Gini index 2000–10[b] | Adult literacy rate (% ages 15 and older) Male 2009 | Adult literacy rate (% ages 15 and older) Female 2009 | Net official development assistance per capita (current $) 2010 |
|---|---|---|---|---|---|---|---|---|---|---|---|---|---|
| **Sub-Saharan Africa** | **844.0** | **2.5** | **23,616** | **35.7** | **1,202** | **653** | **2.6** | **54.2** | **122** | — | — | — | **52.8** |
| Excluding South Africa | 794.0 | 2.5 | 22,401 | 35.4 | 895 | 458 | 3.2 | 54.3 | 125 | — | 74.5 | 56.1 | 54.7 |
| Excl. S. Africa & Nigeria | 635.6 | 2.5 | 21,491 | 29.6 | 824 | 437 | 3.0 | 55.0 | 120 | — | — | — | 65.1 |
| Angola | 19.1 | 2.8 | 1,247 | 15.3 | 3,960 | 1,369 | 9.4 | 50.7 | 161 | 58.6 | 82.9 | 57.6 | 12.5 |
| Benin | 8.8 | 2.8 | 111 | 80.0 | 780 | 377 | 0.8 | 55.6 | 115 | 38.6 | 54.2 | 29.1 | 77.9 |
| Botswana | 2.0 | 1.3 | 567 | 3.5 | 6,750 | 4,190 | 2.7 | 53.1 | 48 | — | 83.8 | 84.4 | 77.8 |
| Burkina Faso | 16.5 | 3.0 | 274 | 60.2 | 550 | 283 | 2.9 | 54.9 | 176 | 39.8 | — | — | 64.5 |
| Burundi | 8.4 | 2.6 | 26 | 326.4 | 230 | 138 | 0.5 | 49.9 | 142 | 33.3 | 72.6 | 60.9 | 75.2 |
| Cameroon | 19.6 | 2.2 | 473 | 41.5 | 1,200 | 714 | 1.0 | 51.1 | 136 | 38.9 | — | — | 27.6 |
| Cape Verde | 0.5 | 0.9 | 4 | 123.1 | 3,280 | 1,959 | 5.0 | 73.8 | 36 | 50.5 | 90.1 | 80.3 | 661.1 |
| Central African Republic | 4.4 | 1.9 | 623 | 7.1 | 470 | 240 | -0.7 | 47.6 | 159 | 56.3 | 69.1 | 42.1 | 59.3 |
| Chad | 11.2 | 2.6 | 1,259 | 8.9 | 710 | 300 | 6.1 | 49.2 | 173 | 39.8 | 44.5 | 23.1 | 43.3 |
| Comoros | 0.7 | 2.6 | 2 | 395.0 | 750 | 336 | -0.8 | 60.6 | 86 | 64.3 | 79.7 | 68.7 | 91.5 |
| Congo, Dem. Rep. | 66.0 | 2.7 | 2,267 | 29.1 | 180 | 106 | 2.5 | 48.1 | 170 | 44.4 | 79.5 | 54.9 | 53.7 |
| Congo, Rep. | 4.0 | 2.5 | 342 | 11.8 | 2,240 | 1,253 | 1.7 | 57.0 | 93 | 47.3 | — | — | 324.6 |
| Côte d'Ivoire | 19.7 | 2.0 | 318 | 62.1 | 1,170 | 588 | -0.6 | 54.7 | 123 | 41.5 | 64.7 | 45.3 | 42.8 |
| Equatorial Guinea | 0.7 | 2.8 | 28 | 25.0 | 13,720 | 8,537 | 12.4 | 50.8 | 121 | — | 97.0 | 89.8 | 121.0 |
| Eritrea | 5.3 | 3.0 | 101 | 52.0 | 340 | 147 | -2.9 | 61.0 | 61 | — | 77.9 | 56.0 | 30.6 |
| Ethiopia | 82.9 | 2.2 | 1,000 | 83.0 | 390 | 221 | 6.3 | 58.7 | 106 | 29.8 | — | — | 42.5 |
| Gabon | 1.5 | 1.9 | 258 | 5.8 | 7,680 | 4,214 | 0.2 | 62.3 | 74 | 41.5 | 91.4 | 84.1 | 69.1 |
| Gambia, The | 1.7 | 2.7 | 10 | 172.8 | 610 | 704 | 1.4 | 58.2 | 98 | 47.3 | 57.6 | 35.8 | 69.5 |
| Ghana | 24.4 | 2.4 | 228 | 107.2 | 1,250 | 360 | 3.4 | 63.8 | 74 | 42.8 | 72.8 | 60.4 | 69.4 |
| Guinea | 10.0 | 2.2 | 246 | 40.6 | 390 | 550 | 5.2 | 53.6 | 130 | 39.4 | 50.8 | 28.1 | 21.8 |
| Guinea-Bissau | 1.5 | 2.1 | 28 | 53.9 | 580 | 161 | -0.5 | 47.7 | 150 | 35.5 | 66.9 | 38.0 | 92.0 |
| Kenya | 40.5 | 2.6 | 569 | 71.2 | 810 | 469 | 1.7 | 56.5 | 85 | 47.7 | 90.5 | 83.5 | 40.2 |
| Lesotho | 2.2 | 1.0 | 30 | 71.5 | 1,100 | 496 | 2.7 | 47.4 | 85 | 52.5 | 82.9 | 95.3 | 118.0 |
| Liberia | 4.0 | 4.0 | 96 | 41.5 | 210 | 261 | 1.7 | 56.2 | 103 | 38.2 | 63.7 | 54.5 | 355.3 |
| Madagascar | 20.7 | 2.9 | 582 | 35.6 | 430 | 243 | 0.3 | 66.5 | 62 | 44.1 | — | — | 22.7 |
| Malawi | 14.9 | 3.1 | 94 | 158.1 | 330 | 185 | 2.3 | 53.5 | 92 | 39.0 | 80.6 | 67.0 | 68.6 |
| Mali | 15.4 | 3.0 | 1,220 | 12.6 | 600 | 273 | 2.0 | 51.0 | 178 | 33.0 | — | — | 70.8 |
| Mauritania | 3.5 | 2.4 | 1,031 | 3.4 | 1,000 | 609 | 3.1 | 58.2 | 111 | 40.5 | 64.5 | 50.3 | 108.2 |
| Mauritius | 1.3 | 0.5 | 2 | 631.0 | 7,780 | 5,181 | 3.1 | 73.0 | 15 | — | 90.6 | 85.3 | 97.8 |
| Mozambique | 23.4 | 2.3 | 786 | 29.7 | 440 | 384 | 4.9 | 49.7 | 135 | 45.7 | 70.1 | 41.5 | 83.4 |
| Namibia | 2.3 | 1.8 | 823 | 2.8 | 4,250 | 2,696 | 3.1 | 62.1 | 40 | 63.9 | 88.9 | 88.1 | 112.3 |
| Niger | 15.5 | 3.5 | 1,267 | 12.3 | 360 | 179 | 0.6 | 54.3 | 143 | 34.6 | 72.0 | 49.8 | 48.0 |
| Nigeria | 158.4 | 2.5 | 911 | 173.9 | 1,170 | 540 | 4.1 | 51.4 | 143 | 48.8 | 75.0 | 66.8 | 13.0 |
| Rwanda | 10.6 | 3.0 | 25 | 430.6 | 520 | 337 | 4.8 | 55.1 | 91 | 53.1 | 93.7 | 84.1 | 97.2 |
| São Tomé and Principe | 0.2 | 1.8 | 1 | 172.3 | 1,250 | — | — | 64.4 | 80 | 50.8 | — | — | 298.1 |
| Senegal | 12.4 | 2.7 | 193 | 64.6 | 1,080 | 562 | 1.5 | 59.0 | 75 | 39.2 | 61.8 | 38.7 | 74.6 |
| Seychelles | 0.1 | (0.9) | 0 | 188.1 | 10,460 | 8,788 | 1.8 | 73.0 | 14 | 65.8 | — | — | 647.7 |
| Sierra Leone | 5.9 | 2.2 | 72 | 81.9 | 340 | 268 | 5.0 | 47.4 | 174 | 42.5 | 52.7 | 30.1 | 79.6 |
| Somalia | 9.3 | 2.3 | 627 | 14.9 | — | — | — | 50.9 | 180 | — | — | — | 53.3 |
| South Africa | 50.0 | 1.4 | 1,214 | 41.2 | 6,090 | 3,753 | 2.7 | 52.1 | 57 | 63.1 | — | — | 20.6 |
| Sudan | 33.6 | 1.9 | 2,376 | 18.3 | 1,300 | 524 | 4.1 | 61.1 | 103 | 35.3 | — | — | 61.8 |

## TABLE 3.2

**Basic development indicators for countries in sub-Saharan Africa, 2010** [CONTINUED]

| | Population | | Land area (thousands of sq km) 2010 | Population density (people per sq km) 2010 | GNI per capita, World Bank Atlas method (current $) 2010 | GDP per capita Constant 2000 prices | | Life expectancy at birth (years) 2010 | Under-five mortality rate (per 1,000) 2010 | Gini index 2000–10[b] | Adult literacy rate (% ages 15 and older) | | Net official development assistance per capita (current $) 2010 |
|---|---|---|---|---|---|---|---|---|---|---|---|---|---|
| | Total (millions) 2010 | Growth (annual %) 2010 | | | | $ 2010[a] | Average annual growth (%) 2000–10 | | | | Male 2009 | Female 2009 | |
| Swaziland | 1.1 | 1.1 | 17 | 61.4 | 2,930 | 1,811 | 2.1 | 48.3 | 78 | 51.5 | 87.8 | 86.2 | 86.6 |
| Tanzania | 44.8 | 3.0 | 886 | 50.6 | 530 | 459 | 4.2 | 57.4 | 92 | 37.6 | 79.0 | 66.9 | 66.0 |
| Togo | 6.0 | 2.1 | 54 | 110.8 | 550 | 265 | 0.1 | 56.6 | 103 | 34.4 | — | — | 69.5 |
| Uganda | 33.4 | 3.2 | 200 | 167.3 | 500 | 380 | 4.3 | 53.6 | 99 | 44.3 | — | — | 51.6 |
| Zambia | 12.9 | 1.6 | 743 | 17.4 | 1,070 | 432 | 3.1 | 48.5 | 111 | 54.6 | 80.6 | 61.3 | 70.7 |
| Zimbabwe | 12.6 | 0.8 | 387 | 32.5 | 480 | 321 | -6.2 | 49.9 | 80 | — | 94.7 | 89.4 | 58.3 |
| **North Africa** | **166.3** | **1.5** | **5,762** | **28.9** | **3,533** | **2,313** | **3.2** | **72.8** | **27** | — | — | — | **16.4** |
| Algeria | 35.5 | 1.5 | 2,382 | 14.9 | 4,390 | 2,232 | 2.3 | 72.9 | 36 | — | — | — | 5.6 |
| Djibouti | 0.9 | 1.9 | 23 | 38.3 | — | — | 2.0 | 57.5 | 91 | 40.0 | — | — | 148.8 |
| Egypt, Arab Rep. | 81.1 | 1.8 | 995 | 81.5 | 2,420 | 1,976 | 3.2 | 73.0 | 22 | 30.8 | — | — | 7.3 |
| Libya | 6.4 | 1.5 | 1,760 | 3.6 | — | — | 3.3 | 74.8 | 17 | — | 95.2 | 82.0 | 1.3 |
| Morocco | 32.0 | 1.0 | 446 | 71.6 | 2,850 | 1,844 | 3.7 | 71.9 | 36 | 40.9 | 68.9 | 43.9 | 31.1 |
| Tunisia | 10.5 | 1.0 | 155 | 67.9 | 4,140 | 3,144 | 3.7 | 74.6 | 16 | 41.4 | — | — | 52.2 |
| **Africa** | **1,010.3** | **2.3** | **29,378** | **34.4** | **1,586** | **926** | **2.6** | **57.2** | **113** | — | — | — | **47.3** |

[a]Provisional.
[b]Data are for the most recent year available during the period specified.
Notes: GNI = Gross national income. GDP = Gross domestic product.

SOURCE: "Table 1.1. Basic Indicators," in *Africa Development Indicators 2012/13*, World Bank, Washington, D.C., 2013, https://openknowledge.worldbank.org/bitstream/handle/10986/13504/9780821396162.pdf?sequence=1 (accessed September 26, 2013). DOI: 10.1596/978-0-8213-9616-2. License: CreativeCommons Attribution CC BY 3.0.

$1,005 GNI per capita: Burkina Faso (2.9%), Chad (6.1%), the DRC (2.5%), Ethiopia (6.3%), Guinea (5.2%), Malawi (2.3%), Mali (2%), Mauritania (3.1%), Mozambique (4.9%), Rwanda (4.8%), Sierra Leone (5%), Tanzania (4.2%), and Uganda (4.3%).

As Table 1.5 in Chapter 1 shows, the countries of sub-Saharan Africa lag well behind most of the world as measured by the UN's Human Development Index (HDI), an attempt to quantify a country's level of health, education, and living standards. Only one sub-Saharan African country, the small tourist-friendly island nation of the Seychelles (with a 2012 HDI value of 0.806), was among the 47 countries classified as having "very high human development." Likewise, only one sub-Saharan country, Mauritius (with a 2012 HDI of 0.737), was among the 47 nations classified as having "high human development." Botswana, Cape Verde, Equatorial Guinea, Gabon, Ghana, Guyana, Namibia, South Africa, Suriname, and Swaziland were all classified as having "medium human development." Among the 46 nations identified as having "low human development," 36 were in sub-Saharan Africa.

## THE IMPACT OF HEALTH ISSUES
### Undernourishment and Malnutrition

As Figure 3.1 shows, 27% of the population of sub-Saharan Africa suffered from undernourishment during the years 2010 through 2012, down from 32% in 1990 through 1992. The size of the decline in the proportion of the undernourished population, however, was much smaller than elsewhere in the developing world, and the 2010–12 level of hunger was roughly equal to 1990–92 levels in the other most-impoverished parts of the world. Hunger is especially damaging to children, as discussed in Chapter 2, frequently resulting in forms of malnutrition with potentially irreversible effects on mental and physical development. Table 3.3 shows that the prevalence of malnutrition among children in sub-Saharan Africa, in the form of stunting (below-average height) and micronutrient deficiencies, far exceeded the prevalence of malnutrition overall in developing regions. Four in 10 (39.6%) children in sub-Saharan Africa showed signs of stunting in the most recent years for which data were available as of 2013; more than two-thirds (67.8%) were anemic (deficient in iron); 45.6% were deficient in vitamin A; and 36% were deficient in iodine. Although the prevalence of malnutrition varied among individual countries, in very few African countries were the levels of malnutrition prevalence lower than in the developing world overall.

In *International Food Security Assessment, 2013–23* (June 2013, http://www.ers.usda.gov/ersDownloadHandler .ashx?file=/media/1138077/gfa-24a.pdf), Birgit Meade and Stacey Rosen of the U.S. Department of Agriculture (USDA) Economic Research Service estimate that 29%

FIGURE 3.1

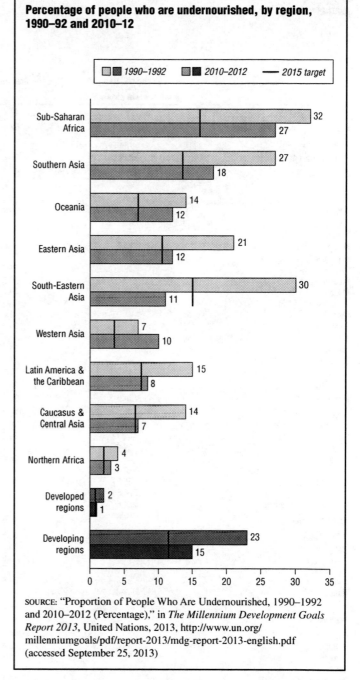

**Percentage of people who are undernourished, by region, 1990–92 and 2010–12**

Legend: 1990–1992 · 2010–2012 · 2015 target

- Sub-Saharan Africa: 32 / 27
- Southern Asia: 27 / 18
- Oceania: 14 / 12
- Eastern Asia: 21 / 12
- South-Eastern Asia: 30 / 11
- Western Asia: 7 / 10
- Latin America & the Caribbean: 15 / 8
- Caucasus & Central Asia: 14 / 7
- Northern Africa: 4 / 3
- Developed regions: 2 / 1
- Developing regions: 23 / 15

SOURCE: "Proportion of People Who Are Undernourished, 1990–1992 and 2010–2012 (Percentage)," in *The Millennium Development Goals Report 2013*, United Nations, 2013, http://www.un.org/millenniumgoals/pdf/report-2013/mdg-report-2013-english.pdf (accessed September 25, 2013)

of the region's people were food insecure (those who experience disruptions in their ability to obtain food in sufficient quantities and of adequate nutritional value) in 2013, down from 56% in 1995 and 41% in 2005. The primary factors in increased food security across the region varied by country. Chad, Ethiopia, Malawi, Mali, and Niger made gains in food security through increases in food production. A combination of production gains and an increase in food imports drove additional gains in Angola, Madagascar, Mozambique, and Tanzania. Finally, in Kenya and Sudan gains in food security came largely through imports of food. The authors note that, as

TABLE 3.3

## Malnutrition in Africa, 2008–13*

| | Prevalence of stunting among children (%) | Prevalence of micronutrient deficiencies and anemia among children (%) | | | Prevalence of obesity among adults (%) |
|---|---|---|---|---|---|
| | | Anaemia | Vitamin A deficiency | Iodine deficiency | |
| | Most recent observation | Most recent observation | | | 2008 |
| **World** | **25.7** | **47.9** | **30.7** | **30.3** | **11.7** |
| **Countries in developing regions** | 28.0 | 52.4 | 34.0 | 29.6 | 8.7 |
| **Africa** | 35.6 | 64.6 | 41.9 | 38.2 | 11.3 |
| **Sub-Saharan Africa** | 39.6 | 67.8 | 45.6 | 36.0 | 7.5 |
| **Eastern Africa** | 42.1 | 65.2 | 46.3 | 38.2 | 3.9 |
| Burundi | 57.7 | 56.0 | 27.9 | 60.5 | 3.3 |
| Comoros | 46.9 | 65.4 | 21.5 | — | 4.4 |
| Djibouti | 32.6 | 65.8 | 35.2 | — | 10.4 |
| Eritrea | 43.7 | 69.6 | 21.4 | 25.3 | 1.8 |
| Ethiopia | 44.2 | 75.2 | 46.1 | 68.4 | 1.2 |
| Kenya | 35.2 | 69.0 | 84.4 | 36.8 | 4.7 |
| Madagascar | 49.2 | 68.3 | 42.1 | — | 1.7 |
| Malawi | 47.8 | 73.2 | 59.2 | — | 4.5 |
| Mauritius | 13.6 | 16.8 | 9.2 | 4.4 | 18.2 |
| Mozambique | 43.7 | 74.7 | 68.8 | 68.1 | 5.4 |
| Réunion | — | — | — | — | — |
| Rwanda | 44.3 | 41.9 | 6.4 | 0.0 | 4.3 |
| Seychelles | 7.7 | 23.8 | 8.0 | — | 24.6 |
| Somalia | 42.1 | — | 61.7 | — | 5.3 |
| Uganda | 38.7 | 64.1 | 27.9 | 3.9 | 4.6 |
| United Republic of Tanzania | 42.5 | 71.8 | 24.2 | 37.7 | 5.4 |
| Zambia | 45.8 | 52.9 | 54.1 | 72.0 | 4.2 |
| Zimbabwe | 32.3 | 19.3 | 35.8 | 14.8 | 8.6 |
| **Middle Africa** | 35.0 | 63.9 | 56.1 | 23.8 | 4.8 |
| Angola | 29.2 | 29.7 | 64.3 | — | 7.2 |
| Cameroon | 32.5 | 68.3 | 38.8 | 91.7 | 11.1 |
| Central African Republic | 40.7 | 84.2 | 68.2 | 79.5 | 3.7 |
| Chad | 38.8 | 71.1 | 50.1 | 29.4 | 3.1 |
| Congo | 31.2 | 66.4 | 24.6 | — | 5.3 |
| Democratic Republic of the Congo | 43.4 | 70.6 | 61.1 | 10.1 | 1.9 |
| Equatorial Guinea | 35.0 | 40.8 | 13.9 | — | 11.5 |
| Gabon | 26.3 | 44.5 | 16.9 | 38.3 | 15.0 |
| Sao Tome and Principe | 31.6 | 36.7 | 95.6 | — | 11.3 |
| **Northern Africa** | 21.0 | 46.6 | 20.4 | 49.3 | 23.0 |
| Algeria | 15.9 | 42.5 | 15.7 | 77.7 | 17.5 |
| Egypt | 30.7 | 29.9 | 11.9 | 31.2 | 34.6 |
| Libya | 21.0 | 33.9 | 8.0 | — | 30.8 |
| Morocco | 14.9 | 31.5 | 40.4 | 63.0 | 17.3 |
| Sudan | 37.9 | 84.6 | 27.8 | 62.0 | 6.6 |
| Tunisia | 9.0 | 21.7 | 14.6 | 26.4 | 23.8 |
| Western Sahara | — | — | — | — | — |
| **Southern Africa** | 30.8 | 27.1 | 18.7 | 28.3 | 31.3 |
| Botswana | 31.4 | 38.0 | 26.1 | 15.3 | 13.5 |
| Lesotho | 39.0 | 48.6 | 32.7 | 21.5 | 16.9 |
| Namibia | 29.6 | 40.5 | 17.5 | 28.7 | 10.9 |
| South Africa | 23.9 | 24.1 | 16.9 | 29.0 | 33.5 |
| Swaziland | 30.9 | 46.7 | 44.6 | 34.5 | 23.4 |
| **Western Africa** | 36.4 | 77.1 | 43.5 | 40.2 | 6.6 |
| Benin | 44.7 | 81.9 | 70.7 | 8.3 | 6.5 |
| Burkina Faso | 35.1 | 91.5 | 54.3 | 47.5 | 2.4 |
| Cape Verde | 21.4 | 39.7 | 2.0 | 77.4 | 11.5 |
| Côte d'Ivoire | 39.0 | 69.0 | 57.3 | 27.6 | 6.7 |
| Gambia | 24.4 | 79.4 | 64.0 | 72.8 | 8.5 |
| Ghana | 28.6 | 76.1 | 75.8 | 71.3 | 8.0 |
| Guinea | 40.0 | 79.0 | 45.8 | 32.4 | 4.7 |
| Guinea-Bissau | 32.2 | 74.9 | 54.7 | — | 5.4 |
| Liberia | 39.4 | 86.7 | 52.9 | 3.5 | 5.5 |
| Mali | 27.8 | 82.8 | 58.6 | 68.3 | 4.8 |
| Mauritania | 23.0 | 68.2 | 47.7 | 69.8 | 14.0 |
| Niger | 54.8 | 81.3 | 67.0 | 0.0 | 2.5 |
| Nigeria | 41.0 | 76.1 | 29.5 | 40.4 | 7.1 |

**TABLE 3.3**

**Malnutrition in Africa, 2008–13\*** [CONTINUED]

| | Prevalence of stunting among children (%) | Prevalence of micronutrient deficiencies and anemia among children (%) | | | Prevalence of obesity among adults (%) |
|---|---|---|---|---|---|
| | | Anaemia | Vitamin A deficiency | Iodine deficiency | |
| | Most recent observation | Most recent observation | | | 2008 |
| Saint Helena | — | — | — | — | — |
| Senegal | 28.7 | 70.1 | 37.0 | 75.7 | 8.0 |
| Sierra Leone | 37.4 | 83.2 | 74.8 | — | 7.0 |
| Togo | 29.5 | 52.4 | 35.0 | 6.2 | 4.6 |

\*The most recent available data for each country and condition comes from numerous surveys conducted between 2008 and 2013.

SOURCE: Adapted from "Annex Table," in *The State of Food and Agriculture 2013: Food Systems for Better Nutrition*, Food and Agriculture Organization of the United Nations, 2013, http://www.fao.org/docrep/018/i3300e/i3300e.pdf (accessed September 24, 2013). Reproduced with permission.

of 2013, in much of sub-Saharan Africa, food production had only recently begun to outpace population growth, and they project that over the decade from 2013 to 2023, many countries will see their populations grow faster than their production or import capabilities. Those countries most at risk of increased food insecurity were Chad, Malawi, and Uganda. Meade and Rosen project that, if current trends hold, 70% of Uganda's population will be food insecure in 2023. Food insecurity was expected to affect 34% of the population of sub-Saharan Africa by 2023. No other region of the developing world was expected to see sizable increases in food insecurity over the course of that decade.

**The HIV Epidemic**

Many parts of sub-Saharan Africa have seen infection from the human immunodeficiency virus (HIV) reach epidemic levels since the 1990s. As shown in Table 3.4, the percentage of adults believed to have the virus that causes AIDS varies widely across the region. A number of countries (Burkina Faso, Burundi, Cape Verde, Eritrea, Liberia, Madagascar, Mali, Mauritania, Niger, São Tomé and Príncipe, and Senegal) had a 2012 HIV prevalence of 1% or less among the adult population. The global prevalence of HIV among adults at this time was an estimated 0.8%, according to the Joint UN Programme on HIV/AIDS (UNAIDS) in *Global Report: UNAIDS Report on the Global AIDS Epidemic 2013* (2013, http://www.unaids.org/en/media/unaids/contentassets/documents/epidemiology/2013/gr013/UNAIDS_Global_Report_2013_en.pdf). Other African countries had 2012 HIV rates 20 or more times higher, such as Botswana, where 23% of adults aged 15 to 49 years were infected; Lesotho, where 23.1% were infected; and Swaziland, where 26.5% were infected. The percentage of adults infected in other countries was lower while remaining alarmingly high: Malawi (10.8%), Mozambique (11.1%), Namibia (13.3%), South Africa (17.9%), Zambia (12.7%), and Zimbabwe (14.7%). Many of these countries, such as Botswana, Malawi, and Zimbabwe, had seen their HIV rates fall

significantly since 2001. Others, such as Mozambique, South Africa, and Swaziland, had seen significant increases in HIV rates. Overall, HIV infection rates in sub-Saharan Africa fell by a little more than 1% between 2001 and 2012.

Although the rates of infection remain high in many sub-Saharan countries, rates of death from conditions associated with AIDS have fallen substantially since 2003 as a result of the increasing availability of antiretroviral drug therapies, which are often effective at containing the progress of the disease but which typically cost more than individuals in developing countries can afford. According to UNAIDS, in *Global Report*, antiretroviral therapy prevented 6.6 million deaths associated with AIDS worldwide between 1995 and 2012, 5.4 million of them in low- and middle-income countries. In 2012 an estimated 57% of men in sub-Saharan Africa who were HIV positive and eligible for treatment received treatment, compared with 73% of women who were infected and eligible for treatment. The U.S. President's Emergency Plan for AIDS Relief (PEPFAR), launched in 2003 under President George W. Bush (1946–) and continued under President Barack Obama (1961–), was, along with funding from European and other high-income countries, instrumental in improving access to antiretroviral drugs in sub-Saharan Africa and other low-income regions.

**Malaria**

Malaria is a highly infectious but preventable disease that is spread through tropical regions by mosquitoes. Malaria is particularly common in sub-Saharan Africa due to the prevalence of *Plasmodium falciparum*, the most deadly of the four species of the *Plasmodium* parasite that causes malaria. In addition, Anopheles mosquitoes, which spread the parasite from person to person when they bite an infected individual and then bite an uninfected one, are prevalent in sub-Saharan Africa. Another complicating factor is the high level of HIV

**TABLE 3.4**

**Percentage of HIV-positive adults aged 15–49 in Sub-Saharan Africa, 2001 and 2012**

| | 2001 Estimate | 2012 Estimate |
|---|---|---|
| Sub-Saharan Africa | 5.8 | 4.7 |
| Angola | 1.8 | 2.3 |
| Benin | 1.6 | 1.1 |
| Botswana | 28.1 | 23.0 |
| Burkina Faso | 2.2 | 1.0 |
| Burundi | 2.9 | 1.3 |
| Cameroon | 5.2 | 4.5 |
| Cape Verde | 0.5 | 0.2 |
| Central African Republic | — | — |
| Chad | 3.8 | 2.7 |
| Comoros | <0.1 | 2.1 |
| Congo | 4.7 | 2.8 |
| Côte d'Ivoire | 6.4 | 3.2 |
| Democratic Republic of the Congo | 1.5 | 1.1 |
| Equatorial Guinea | — | — |
| Eritrea | 2.0 | 0.7 |
| Ethiopia | 3.6 | 1.3 |
| Gabon | 6.1 | 4.0 |
| Gambia | 1.0 | 1.3 |
| Ghana | 2.3 | 1.4 |
| Guinea | 1.3 | 1.7 |
| Guinea-Bissau | 2.8 | 3.9 |
| Kenya | 8.5 | 6.1 |
| Lesotho | 23.4 | 23.1 |
| Liberia | 2.3 | 0.9 |
| Madagascar | 0.7 | 0.5 |
| Malawi | 15.5 | 10.8 |
| Mali | 1.6 | 0.9 |
| Mauritania | 0.6 | 0.4 |
| Mauritius | 1.0 | 1.2 |
| Mozambique | 9.0 | 11.1 |
| Namibia | 15.0 | 13.3 |
| Niger | 1.0 | 0.5 |
| Nigeria | 3.5 | 3.1 |
| Rwanda | 4.4 | 2.9 |
| Sao Tome and Principe | 1.1 | 1.0 |
| Senegal | 0.5 | 0.5 |
| Sierra Leone | 1.0 | 1.5 |
| South Africa | 15.3 | 17.9 |
| South Sudan | 3.1 | 2.7 |
| Swaziland | 24.8 | 26.5 |
| Togo | 4.5 | 2.9 |
| Uganda | 6.8 | 7.2 |
| United Republic of Tanzania | 7.5 | 5.1 |
| Zambia | 15.1 | 12.7 |
| Zimbabwe | 24.3 | 14.7 |

SOURCE: Adapted from "Epidemiology: Estimated HIV Prevalence—Adult (Ages 15–49)," in *Global Report: UNAIDS Report on the Global AIDS Epidemic 2013*, Joint United Nations Programme on HIV/AIDS, 2013, http://www.unaids.org/en/media/unaids/contentassets/documents/epidemiology/2013/gr2013/UNAIDS_Global_Report_2013_en.pdf (accessed September 25, 2013)

infection in sub-Saharan Africa and its effect on contracting malaria. According to the UN Children's Fund (UNICEF), in "Malaria" (2013, http://www.unicef.org/health/index_malaria.html), there is increasing evidence that HIV and malaria interact, in some cases worsening the effects of both conditions and possibly increasing the likelihood of HIV transmission.

Countries with high rates of malarial infection typically have comparatively low levels of economic development, slower rates of economic growth, and higher rates of poverty than countries that have lower rates of malaria. UNICEF notes that those at the highest risk of contracting malaria are "the poor who tend to live in malaria-prone rural areas in poorly-constructed dwellings that offer few, if any, barriers against mosquitoes." The disease also reinforces poverty by significantly impacting labor force participation and school attendance. Children who suffer from repeat infections often develop permanent neurological damage that cuts short their education and hampers their ability to participate fully in the labor force as adults.

In the early 21st century poverty researchers began recognizing malaria's role in increasing impoverishment at the family and community levels and diminishing economic advancement at the national and global levels. Aside from the obvious difficulties facing poor families who cannot afford treatment or prevention, the wider effects of frequent epidemics include impeded market activity and tourism as traders and potential tourists avoid areas with heavy infection rates. Even agricultural trends can shift with malaria rates. Farmers who are dependent on the availability of workers during harvest seasons will be less likely to plant labor-intensive cash crops, instead relying on subsistence crops.

According to the World Health Organization (WHO), in *World Malaria Report 2012* (2012, http://who.int/iris/bitstream/10665/78945/1/9789241564533_eng.pdf), there were 219 million cases of malaria worldwide in 2010, with 174 million (79.5%) of these cases in the African region. Approximately 660,000 people died from malaria that year, with 596,000 (90.3%) of the deaths in Africa. Children are particularly vulnerable to the disease. According to UNICEF, in "Malaria," approximately one in six child deaths in Africa is directly attributable to malaria. Malaria is also a major contributing factor in Africa to the development of anemia, which affects more than two-thirds of children in sub-Saharan Africa. (See Table 3.3.) Malaria is additionally associated with severe anemia in pregnant women, which is a factor in low birth weight, one of the leading indicators of the likelihood of infant mortality and inadequate growth.

In the past the most effective and affordable antimalarial drug was chloroquine. However, the malaria parasite in sub-Saharan Africa developed resistance to this drug, so the WHO no longer recommends chloroquine use. Since 2003 nearly all sub-Saharan countries have shifted to artemisinin-based combination drugs, which are effective in treating multidrug-resistant strains of the malaria parasite.

One of the most effective ways to prevent the spread of malaria is the use of insecticide-treated mosquito nets (ITNs), which are draped over beds at night, when most disease-carrying mosquitoes bite. UNICEF observes that sleeping under ITNs is believed to reduce child mortality by 20% and to save the lives of six children for every 1,000 children who correctly use the nets. With funding and support from a number of agencies, the percentage of sub-Saharan African children sleeping under ITNs has risen dramatically since 2000. (See Figure 3.2.) In 2000 only 3% of households in sub-Saharan Africa owned at least one ITN; by 2012 an estimated 53% of households in the region owned at least one ITN. The proportion of the sub-Saharan African population that sleeps under ITNs increased from near 0% in 2000 to 33% in 2012. Nevertheless, as the WHO notes in *World Malaria Report 2012*, the number of ITNs delivered to at-risk countries in sub-Saharan Africa began decreasing in 2010. Together with the likelihood that existing ITNs were degrading over time with repeated use, this decrease in the supply of ITNs was expected to have significant negative impacts in the years to come.

## Sanitation and Clean Water

Clean water (water that is free of disease-causing organisms) for drinking, food preparation, and bathing is essential to public health. The effective sanitation of wastewater is a key component of the effort to maintain an uncontaminated water supply. Fecal waste must remain separate from water supplies, and wastewater must be treated to kill harmful organisms. Even though urine is virtually free of microbes, fecal waste contains a variety of species of microbes, many of which are capable of causing disease. Drinking or preparing food with contaminated water is one of the most common ways that harmful diseases are transmitted in the developing world. Bathing with contaminated water can result in infections of the skin, mucous membranes, ears, nose, and throat. Diseases that are commonly transmitted by contaminated water include those that cause severe diarrhea. Diarrheal diseases are a common cause of death in sub-Saharan Africa.

Sub-Saharan Africa lags behind other regions of the world in the use of improved drinking water sources that supply clean water. Being without clean water is defined as living more than 0.6 of a mile (1 km) from the nearest safe water source. People without a source of clean water nearby usually collect water from unsafe sources, such as drains, ditches, and streams. These sources are often shared with animals and are likely to be contaminated with disease-causing organisms, such as bacteria and viruses, which may cause severe illness and death. The UN notes in *The Millennium Development Goals Report 2013* (June 2013, http://www.un.org/millenniumgoals/pdf/report-2013/mdg-report-2013-english.pdf) that the proportion of the sub-Saharan African population that uses an improved water source climbed from 49% in 1990 to 63% in 2011. While this represents significant progress, the region was far behind most other parts of the developing world, where the overall rate of access to improved water sources was 87% in 2011. The Millennium Development Goal (MDG) for clean water was the halving of the population without sustainable access to safe drinking water and basic sanitation. As Figure 3.3 shows, progress toward this goal in Africa was uneven. A majority of countries on the continent had either made insufficient progress toward the MDG for clean water as of 2010 or were not on track for meeting the target.

Open defecation remains a common practice among some of the poorest residents of sub-Saharan Africa. In a rural environment this practice may involve defecation on open land; in an urban environment open defecation may mean relieving oneself in a gutter, onto a newspaper, or into a plastic bag. Often the practice results in the contamination of water sources used by a community for drinking, food preparation, and bathing. Other methods of unimproved sanitation that are common in the developing world likewise result in substandard hygiene, such as improperly constructed pit toilets or hanging latrines (structures suspended in the air, often with flimsy materials). Furthermore, in many cultures women are not allowed to be seen uncovered, so they often have to wait

**FIGURE 3.2**

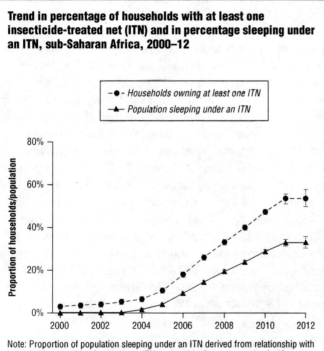

Trend in percentage of households with at least one insecticide-treated net (ITN) and in percentage sleeping under an ITN, sub-Saharan Africa, 2000–12

- ● - Households owning at least one ITN
- ▲ - Population sleeping under an ITN

Note: Proportion of population sleeping under an ITN derived from relationship with household ownership of at least one ITN analyzed by linear regression in 48 household surveys 2001–2011, $y = 0.67x - 0.03$.

SOURCE: "Figure 4.2. Estimated Trend in Proportion of Households with at Least One ITN and Proportion of the Population Sleeping under an ITN in Sub-Saharan Africa, 2000–2012," in *World Malaria Report 2012*, World Health Organization, 2012, http://who.int/iris/bitstream/10665/78945/1/9789241564533_eng.pdf (accessed September 25, 2013). Reproduced with permission of the publisher.

## FIGURE 3.3

**Progress toward MDG drinking-water targets in Africa, 2010**

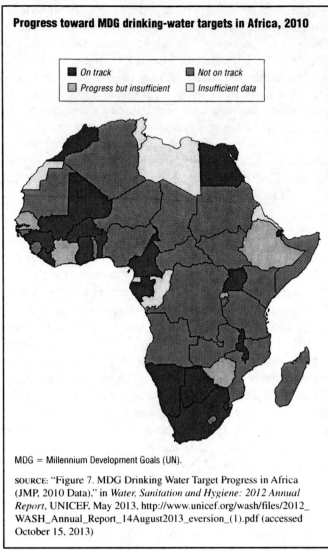

■ On track    ▨ Not on track
▦ Progress but insufficient    □ Insufficient data

MDG = Millennium Development Goals (UN).

SOURCE: "Figure 7. MDG Drinking Water Target Progress in Africa (JMP, 2010 Data)," in *Water, Sanitation and Hygiene: 2012 Annual Report*, UNICEF, May 2013, http://www.unicef.org/wash/files/2012_WASH_Annual_Report_14August2013_eversion_(1).pdf (accessed October 15, 2013)

until dark to relieve themselves either in the open or in shared facilities. As a result, they not only develop health issues from delayed defecation and possibly urination but also risk bodily harm as they travel in the darkness alone. Improved sanitation (the use of toilets) relieves women of these health and safety problems, restores some level of dignity to both genders, dramatically reduces disease, and reduces childhood deaths.

Sanitation improvements lag behind improvements related to clean water, both in sub-Saharan Africa and in the developing world at large. (See Figure 3.4.) In sub-Saharan Africa in 2011 only 30% of the population had access to improved sanitation facilities (such as properly constructed pit toilets or flush toilets, which ensure hygiene by keeping waste from coming into contact with the people who use the facilities), up slightly from 26% in 1990. Another 18% of the region's population had access to shared sanitation facilities (including facilities shared by two or more families as well as public facilities) in 2011, and again this marked only a slight improvement

over 1990 levels (14%). The percentage of people in sub-Saharan Africa who used unimproved sanitation facilities climbed from 24% to 26% between 1990 and 2011. More than a quarter (26%) of sub-Saharan Africans defecated openly in 2011, down from 36% in 1990 but still alarmingly high given the dramatic health consequences resulting from the practice.

## THE IMPACT OF EDUCATION AND LITERACY

In 2011, 77% of all children of primary school age in sub-Saharan Africa were enrolled in primary school, according to the UN, in the *Millennium Development Goals Report 2013*. This was the lowest rate of enrollment in the developing world, for which the overall enrollment rate was 90%. However, the region had made dramatic progress since 1990, when only 53% of primary-age children were enrolled. Children who started primary school were more likely to leave before finishing (and therefore before obtaining basic literacy and mathematical skills) in sub-Saharan Africa than elsewhere in the developing world. According to the UN, two out of five of the region's students who started primary school in 2010 were expected to drop out before finishing.

As Table 3.5 shows, the dimensions of the challenges regarding education and literacy varied among sub-Saharan African nations. Among those countries for which data were available in 2010, Eritrea had the lowest primary-school enrollment rate, at 33.5%. Other countries with notably low 2010 enrollment rates were Burkina Faso (58.1%), Equatorial Guinea (56.3%), The Gambia (65.5%), Mali (62%), Niger (57.2%), and Nigeria (57.6%). Enrollment rate trends varied among these countries, as well. For example, 2010 enrollment rates in Niger and Burkina Faso, while below average for sub-Saharan Africa, represented enormous improvements over their 2000 rates of 27% and 34.1%, respectively. By contrast, Equatorial Guinea, Eritrea, The Gambia, and Nigeria had all seen enrollment rates decline from 2000 levels. A number of sub-Saharan countries, meanwhile, were approaching the MDG of achieving universal primary education, with enrollment rates above 90%: Benin (93.8%), Cameroon (92.4%), Cape Verde (93.2%), Republic of Congo (90.8%), Mauritius (93.4%), Mozambique (91.9%), Rwanda (98.8%), São Tomé and Príncipe (98.4%), Uganda (90.9%), and Zambia (91.4%).

There was also wide variation in the share of students who started grade one and went on to finish their primary education. In general, those countries that had the highest completion rates in 2008–09, such as Botswana (96.6%), Mauritius (98%), Seychelles (94.9%), and Swaziland (96.2%), were among the higher-income sub-Saharan countries. (See Table 3.5.) These and other higher-income countries also tended

**FIGURE 3.4**

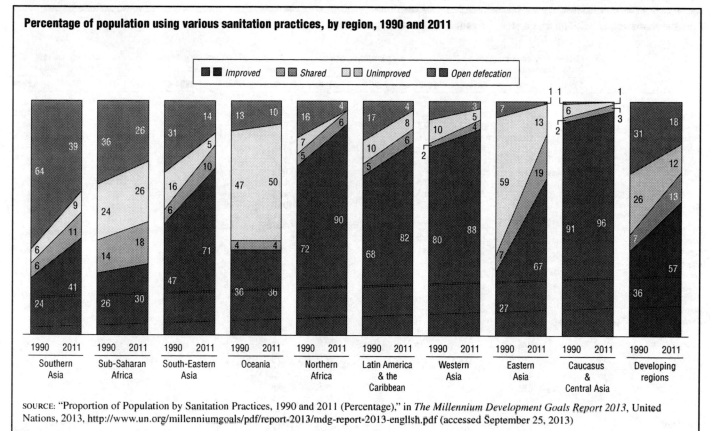

**Percentage of population using various sanitation practices, by region, 1990 and 2011**

Legend: ■■ Improved   ■■ Shared   □□ Unimproved   ■■ Open defecation

SOURCE: "Proportion of Population by Sanitation Practices, 1990 and 2011 (Percentage)," in *The Millennium Development Goals Report 2013*, United Nations, 2013, http://www.un.org/millenniumgoals/pdf/report-2013/mdg-report-2013-engllsh.pdf (accessed September 25, 2013)

to have higher percentages of literate young people (aged 15 to 24 years) than most countries in the region. The countries with the lowest youth literacy rates in 2009, such as Benin (54.3%), Chad (46.3%), and Sierra Leone (57.6%), were among the least developed sub-Saharan countries. Besides the educational challenges that are obviously connected to poverty, such as a lack of resources and facilities, many troubled sub-Saharan countries fall short of educational goals due to a high prevalence of disease and the disruption caused by military conflict.

## Gender Equity

As discussed in Chapter 1, equality between the sexes is not only a vital humanitarian goal but a strategy for economic development. The traditional exclusion of women from productive economic activity, a common feature of many developing countries' cultures, amounts to a major constraint on the potential for economic growth and the alleviation of poverty in those countries. Since 1990 sub-Saharan Africa has made significant progress in increasing women's access to education and nonagricultural career options, but it lags behind most of the world on many measures of equality.

**EDUCATION AND LITERACY.** According to the World Bank's data portal "World DataBank: Millennium Development Goals" (2013, http://databank.worldbank.org/data/views/variableselection/selectvariables.aspx?source=millennium-development-goals), sub-Saharan African boys were more likely than girls to be enrolled in primary school and to be literate. For the region as a whole, 94 girls were enrolled in primary school for every 100 boys in 2011. The female youth literacy rate (the percentage of young people aged 15 to 24 years who were literate) was 65%, and the male youth literacy rate was 76%. There were wide variations among individual countries, however. As Table 3.6 shows, in 2010 girls outnumbered boys among primary school students in many countries, including Cape Verde, Lesotho, Malawi, Mauritania, Mauritius, Rwanda, São Tomé and Príncipe, and Seychelles. Among young people aged 15 to 24 years in 2009, more young women than men were literate in a number of countries as well, including Botswana, Cape Verde, Equatorial Guinea, Kenya, Lesotho, Liberia, Mauritius, Namibia, Rwanda, São Tomé and Príncipe, Swaziland, and Zimbabwe. Not surprisingly, many of the sub-Saharan countries with the lowest rates of female primary school enrollment also had similarly low rates of female youth literacy. These countries included Angola, Benin, the Central African Republic, Chad, Guinea-Bissau, and Mozambique.

The gender imbalance in education worsened at the secondary (middle and high school) and tertiary (college)

TABLE 3.5

## Primary education in sub-Saharan Africa, by country, selected years 1990–2011

| | Net primary enrollment ratio (% of relevant age group) | | | Primary completion rate (% of relevant age group) | | | Share of cohort reaching grade 5 (% of grade 1 students) | | | Youth literacy rate (% ages 15–24) | | |
|---|---|---|---|---|---|---|---|---|---|---|---|---|
| | 1990 | 2000 | 2010 | 1990 | 2000 | 2010 | 1990 | 2000 | 2008–09* | 1991 | 2000 | 2009 |
| **Sub-Saharan Africa** | | | | | | | | | | | | |
| Angola | — | — | 85.7 | — | — | 46.6 | — | — | 44.8 | — | — | 73.1 |
| Benin | 41.2 | — | 93.8 | 19.5 | 39.8 | — | 27.3 | 84.2 | 60.4 | — | — | 54.3 |
| Botswana | 86.9 | 80.9 | — | 89.8 | 89.1 | — | 75.7 | 89.0 | 96.6 | 89.3 | — | 95.2 |
| Burkina Faso | — | 34.1 | 58.1 | 19.3 | 23.8 | 45.1 | 55.6 | 69.1 | 75.1 | 20.2 | — | — |
| Burundi | — | 44.7 | — | 40.9 | 26.3 | 56.1 | 57.2 | 58.8 | 62.4 | 53.6 | 73.3 | 76.6 |
| Cameroon | 71.1 | — | 92.4 | 54.2 | 51.0 | 78.7 | 66.6 | — | 76.3 | — | 83.1 | — |
| Cape Verde | 92.7 | 98.9 | 93.2 | 53.6 | 107.2 | 98.9 | 53.0 | 89.2 | — | 88.2 | — | 98.2 |
| Central African Republic | 57.9 | — | 70.5 | 30.4 | — | 41.1 | 42.7 | — | 56.3 | — | 58.5 | 64.7 |
| Chad | — | 54.5 | — | 16.3 | 22.9 | 34.5 | 35.6 | 54.9 | 36.5 | — | 37.6 | 46.3 |
| Comoros | — | 73.5 | — | — | — | — | — | — | — | — | 80.2 | 85.3 |
| Congo, Dem. Rep. | — | — | — | — | — | 58.7 | — | — | 60.0 | — | — | 67.7 |
| Congo, Rep. | — | — | 90.8 | 58.8 | — | 70.8 | 70.6 | — | — | — | — | — |
| Côte d'Ivoire | — | 56.0 | — | 40.1 | 42.7 | — | 60.8 | 88.0 | 66.1 | — | 60.7 | 66.6 |
| Equatorial Guinea | — | 72.1 | 56.3 | — | — | 52.4 | — | — | 69.6 | — | 94.9 | 97.9 |
| Eritrea | — | 37.7 | 33.5 | — | 36.2 | 39.8 | — | 60.5 | 69.0 | — | — | 88.7 |
| Ethiopia | — | 40.3 | 81.3 | — | 23.0 | 72.2 | — | 64.6 | 50.5 | — | — | — |
| Gabon | — | — | — | — | — | — | — | — | — | — | — | 97.6 |
| Gambia, The | 51.4 | 66.9 | 65.5 | — | 66.6 | 70.5 | — | 73.0 | 65.1 | — | 52.6 | 65.5 |
| Ghana | — | 64.2 | — | — | 71.1 | — | — | 66.3 | 78.4 | — | 70.7 | 80.1 |
| Guinea | 24.9 | 46.6 | 77.0 | 18.8 | 32.3 | 64.1 | 50.6 | — | 68.6 | — | — | 61.1 |
| Guinea-Bissau | — | 51.0 | 73.9 | — | 29.7 | 67.6 | — | — | — | — | 59.5 | 70.9 |
| Kenya | — | 65.1 | — | — | — | — | — | — | — | — | 80.3 | 92.7 |
| Lesotho | 70.7 | 76.0 | 73.4 | 58.4 | 59.8 | 69.6 | 66.3 | 67.2 | 80.4 | — | 90.9 | 92.0 |
| Liberia | — | — | — | — | — | — | — | — | — | — | — | 75.6 |
| Madagascar | 70.3 | 67.0 | — | 37.0 | 37.1 | 72.5 | 34.0 | 36.1 | 34.6 | — | 70.2 | — |
| Malawi | — | — | — | 28.1 | 65.5 | 66.8 | 32.3 | — | 60.9 | — | — | 86.5 |
| Mali | — | — | 62.0 | — | 29.4 | 54.8 | — | — | 84.0 | — | — | — |
| Mauritania | — | 61.1 | 74.0 | 29.1 | — | 74.8 | 63.8 | — | 74.3 | — | 61.3 | 67.7 |
| Mauritius | 97.2 | 92.5 | 93.4 | 113.7 | 95.6 | 96.0 | — | 98.4 | 98.0 | 91.2 | 94.5 | 96.5 |
| Mozambique | 44.0 | 56.0 | 91.9 | 26.5 | 16.2 | 60.6 | 33.8 | 52.5 | 53.7 | — | — | 70.9 |
| Namibia | 79.1 | 88.1 | — | — | 91.4 | — | — | 90.9 | 91.5 | 88.1 | — | 93.0 |
| Niger | 22.8 | 27.0 | 57.2 | 15.8 | 18.7 | 41.2 | 57.0 | 74.0 | 64.3 | — | — | — |
| Nigeria | — | 64.5 | 57.6 | — | — | 74.4 | — | — | 86.3 | 71.2 | — | 71.8 |
| Rwanda | — | — | 98.8 | 49.2 | 22.9 | 69.6 | 51.5 | 41.7 | 47.2 | 74.9 | 77.6 | 77.2 |
| São Tomé and Príncipe | 96.1 | — | 98.4 | 77.9 | — | 85.3 | — | — | 77.4 | 93.9 | — | 95.3 |
| Senegal | 45.1 | 59.6 | 75.5 | 42.0 | 40.3 | 59.2 | 72.8 | 72.3 | 73.7 | — | — | 65.0 |
| Seychelles | — | — | — | — | 106.6 | 133.2 | — | 91.0 | 94.9 | — | — | — |
| Sierra Leone | — | — | — | — | — | — | — | — | — | — | — | 57.6 |
| Somalia | — | — | — | — | — | — | — | — | — | — | — | — |
| South Africa | — | 89.7 | — | — | 86.4 | — | — | — | — | — | — | — |
| Sudan | — | 40.2 | — | — | 36.7 | — | — | — | — | — | — | — |
| Swaziland | 74.3 | 71.8 | 85.6 | 62.7 | 60.7 | 76.9 | 60.0 | 74.0 | 96.2 | — | 88.4 | 93.4 |
| Tanzania | 51.4 | 53.1 | — | — | — | 89.9 | — | 81.4 | 89.8 | — | — | 77.4 |
| Togo | 62.3 | 87.0 | — | 35.0 | 69.0 | 73.7 | 44.5 | 74.7 | 77.7 | — | 74.4 | — |
| Uganda | — | — | 90.9 | — | — | 57.2 | — | 57.1 | 57.1 | 69.8 | — | — |
| Zambia | — | 70.3 | 91.4 | — | 62.7 | 103.3 | — | — | 71.0 | — | — | 74.6 |
| Zimbabwe | — | — | — | 93.6 | — | — | 68.7 | — | — | — | — | 98.9 |
| **North Africa** | | | | | | | | | | | | |
| Algeria | 87.5 | 91.6 | 95.6 | 80.8 | 82.4 | 96.0 | 83.8 | 97.1 | 95.0 | — | — | — |
| Djibouti | 29.3 | 26.7 | — | 32.0 | 27.8 | — | 73.9 | — | 64.3 | — | — | — |
| Egypt, Arab Rep. | — | 90.4 | 94.4 | — | 94.3 | 101.0 | — | — | 97.2 | — | — | — |
| Libya | — | — | — | — | — | — | — | — | — | — | — | 99.9 |
| Morocco | 56.2 | 76.2 | 93.7 | 51.4 | 57.4 | 84.7 | 68.9 | 80.0 | 93.9 | — | — | 79.5 |
| Tunisia | 92.6 | 95.6 | — | 80.3 | 88.2 | — | — | 80.0 | 93.1 | 96.1 | — | — |

*Data are for the most recent year available during the period specified.

SOURCE: "Table 3.2. Millennium Development Goal 2: Achieve Universal Primary Education," in *Africa Development Indicators 2012/13*, World Bank, Washington, D.C., 2013, https://openknowledge.worldbank.org/bitstream/handle/10986/13504/9780821396162.pdf?sequence=1 (accessed September 26, 2013). DOI: 10.1596/978-0-8213-9616-2. License: Creative Commons Attribution CC BY 3.0.

levels in sub-Saharan Africa. According to the World Bank, in "World DataBank," there were only 83 female students for every 100 male students at the secondary level in the region in 2011, and there were only 61 young women for every 100 young men at the tertiary level.

**EMPLOYMENT.** Women in sub-Saharan Africa were also disadvantaged in the labor market, relative to women in most other world regions. In the *Millennium Development Goals Report 2013*, the UN notes that 33% of nonagricultural jobs in sub-Saharan Africa were held

TABLE 3.6

**Gender equity in sub-Saharan Africa, by country, selected years 1990–2010**

| | Ratio of girls to boys in primary and secondary school (%) | | | Ratio of young literate women to men (% ages 15–24) | | | Women in national parliament (% of total seats) | | | Share of women employed in the nonagricultural sector (%) | | |
|---|---|---|---|---|---|---|---|---|---|---|---|---|
| | 1990 | 2000 | 2010 | 1990 | 2000 | 2009 | 1990 | 2000 | 2010 | 1990 | 2000 | 2000–10* |
| **Sub-Saharan Africa** | | | | | | | | | | | | |
| Angola | — | — | 78.9 | — | — | 81.1 | 15.0 | 16.0 | 38.6 | — | — | — |
| Benin | — | 60.9 | — | — | — | 66.9 | 3.0 | 6.0 | 10.8 | — | — | 24.3 |
| Botswana | 108.0 | 101.7 | — | — | — | 103.2 | 5.0 | — | 7.9 | 33.5 | 42.9 | 45.2 |
| Burkina Faso | — | 70.2 | 87.7 | — | — | — | — | 8.0 | 15.3 | 23.0 | 23.2 | 26.5 |
| Burundi | 79.0 | — | 93.9 | 80.7 | 91.7 | 99.2 | — | 6.0 | 32.1 | 14.3 | — | — |
| Cameroon | 82.3 | — | 85.4 | — | 88.2 | — | 14.0 | 6.0 | 13.9 | — | — | 22.2 |
| Cape Verde | 94.0 | — | 104.2 | 96.1 | — | 101.7 | 12.0 | 11.0 | 18.1 | — | 38.9 | 38.9 |
| Central African Republic | 59.1 | — | 69.4 | — | 66.6 | 79.4 | 4.0 | 7.0 | 9.6 | — | — | 46.8 |
| Chad | 40.9 | 55.9 | 65.8 | — | 41.7 | 72.8 | — | 2.0 | 5.2 | 3.8 | — | — |
| Comoros | — | 84.2 | — | — | 92.4 | 98.7 | 0.0 | — | 3.0 | — | — | — |
| Congo, Dem. Rep. | — | — | 78.5 | — | — | 84.8 | 5.0 | — | 8.4 | 25.9 | — | — |
| Congo, Rep | 88.5 | 85.8 | — | — | — | — | 14.0 | 12.0 | 7.3 | 26.1 | — | — |
| Côte d'Ivoire | — | 69.3 | — | — | 73.6 | 84.6 | 6.0 | — | 8.9 | — | — | — |
| Equatorial Guinea | — | 81.3 | — | — | 100.2 | 100.5 | 13.0 | 5.0 | 10.0 | 10.5 | — | — |
| Eritrea | — | 77.3 | 80.1 | — | — | 93.6 | — | 15.0 | 22.0 | — | — | — |
| Ethiopia | — | 65.0 | 88.8 | — | — | — | — | 2.0 | 27.8 | — | — | 47.3 |
| Gabon | — | 95.9 | — | — | — | 98.0 | 13.0 | 8.0 | 14.7 | — | — | — |
| Gambia, The | — | — | 99.4 | — | 64.3 | 84.5 | 8.0 | 2.0 | 7.5 | — | — | — |
| Ghana | 78.0 | 90.2 | — | — | 86.2 | 97.3 | — | 9.0 | 8.3 | — | 31.7 | 31.7 |
| Guinea | 44.0 | — | — | — | — | 79.1 | — | 9.0 | — | — | 24.2 | 28.5 |
| Guinea-Bissau | — | 65.4 | — | — | 61.4 | 81.3 | 20.0 | — | 10.0 | 10.8 | — | — |
| Kenya | — | 97.6 | — | — | 101.1 | 101.8 | 1.0 | 4.0 | 9.8 | 21.4 | — | — |
| Lesotho | 123.8 | 107.5 | 106.1 | — | 114.9 | 114.4 | — | 4.0 | 24.2 | — | — | — |
| Liberia | — | 73.3 | — | — | — | 114.9 | — | — | 12.5 | — | — | 11.4 |
| Madagascar | 95.6 | — | — | — | 93.9 | — | 7.0 | 8.0 | — | — | — | 37.7 |
| Malawi | 80.9 | 92.8 | 101.3 | — | — | 99.0 | 10.0 | 8.0 | 20.8 | 10.5 | — | — |
| Mali | 57.6 | 71.1 | 81.9 | — | — | — | — | 12.0 | 10.2 | — | — | 34.6 |
| Mauritania | 68.9 | 93.1 | 101.2 | — | 81.9 | 90.8 | — | 4.0 | 22.1 | — | 35.8 | 35.8 |
| Mauritius | 100.4 | 98.1 | 100.1 | 101.1 | 101.8 | 102.1 | 7.0 | 8.0 | 18.8 | 37.4 | 38.6 | 36.7 |
| Mozambique | 72.7 | 75.0 | 89.0 | — | — | 81.6 | 16.0 | — | 39.2 | 11.4 | — | — |
| Namibia | 110.8 | 103.7 | — | — | — | 104.2 | 7.0 | 22.0 | 24.4 | — | 42.8 | 41.4 |
| Niger | 53.0 | 65.1 | 78.3 | — | — | — | 5.0 | 1.0 | — | — | — | 36.1 |
| Nigeria | 76.5 | 82.0 | 90.1 | — | — | 83.6 | — | — | 7.0 | — | 18.6 | 21.1 |
| Rwanda | 94.8 | 96.6 | 101.9 | — | 97.9 | 100.5 | 17.0 | 17.0 | 56.3 | — | 33.0 | 33.0 |
| São Tomé and Príncipe | — | — | 100.4 | — | — | 101.0 | 12.0 | 9.0 | 18.2 | — | — | — |
| Senegal | 67.4 | 82.3 | 100.0 | — | — | 75.7 | 13.0 | 12.0 | 22.7 | — | — | 10.6 |
| Seychelles | — | 103.0 | 104.0 | — | — | — | 16.0 | 24.0 | 23.5 | — | — | — |
| Sierra Leone | 61.8 | — | — | — | — | 71.1 | — | 9.0 | 13.2 | — | — | 23.2 |
| Somalia | — | — | — | — | — | — | 4.0 | — | 6.8 | 21.7 | — | — |
| South Africa | 103.5 | 100.4 | — | — | — | — | 3.0 | 30.0 | 44.5 | — | 41.1 | 45.1 |
| Sudan | — | — | — | — | — | — | — | — | 25.6 | 22.2 | — | — |
| Swaziland | — | 96.1 | 94.0 | — | 103.2 | 103.2 | 4.0 | 3.0 | 13.6 | — | — | — |
| Tanzania | 97.1 | — | — | — | — | 97.3 | — | 16.0 | 30.7 | — | — | 30.5 |
| Togo | 58.1 | 69.1 | — | — | 76.0 | — | 5.0 | — | 11.1 | 41.0 | — | — |
| Uganda | 77.9 | 91.1 | 98.5 | — | — | — | 12.0 | 18.0 | 31.5 | — | — | 39.0 |
| Zambia | — | — | — | 97.4 | — | 82.3 | 7.0 | 10.0 | 14.0 | 16.6 | 22.0 | 22.0 |
| Zimbabwe | 96.4 | — | — | — | — | 101.1 | 11.0 | 14.0 | 15.0 | 15.4 | 20.4 | 21.9 |
| **North Africa** | | | | | | | | | | | | |
| Algeria | 81.6 | — | — | — | — | — | 2.0 | 3.0 | 7.7 | — | — | 15.0 |
| Djibouti | 72.3 | 71.0 | — | — | — | — | 0.0 | 0.0 | 13.8 | — | — | 26.7 |
| Egypt, Arab Rep. | 80.5 | 92.1 | 95.9 | — | — | — | 4.0 | 2.0 | 1.8 | 20.5 | 19.0 | 18.1 |
| Libya | — | — | — | — | — | 99.9 | — | — | 7.7 | — | — | 15.8 |
| Morocco | 68.8 | 82.6 | — | — | — | 83.2 | 0.0 | 1.0 | 10.5 | — | — | 20.8 |
| Tunisia | 84.6 | 97.6 | — | — | — | — | 4.0 | 12.0 | 27.6 | — | 24.3 | 25.0 |

*Data are for the most recent year available during the period specified.

SOURCE: "Table 3.3. Millennium Development Goal 3: Promote Gender Equity and Empower Women," in *Africa Development Indicators 2012/13*, World Bank, Washington, D.C., 2013, https://openknowledge.worldbank.org/bitstream/handle/10986/13504/9780821396162.pdf?sequence=1 (accessed September 26, 2013). DOI: 10.1596/978-0-8213-9616-2. License: Creative Commons Attribution CC BY 3.0.

by women in 2011. This figure was up significantly from the 1990 level of 24%, and it was higher than in North Africa, Southern Asia, and Western Asia. In the rest of the developing world women's share of nonagricultural employment ranged between 37% and 44%, and in the developed world women occupied 48% of jobs in the nonagricultural sector. As Table 3.6 shows, African countries with above-average female employment levels included Botswana, where women held 45.2% of nonagricultural jobs in the most recent year for which data were available; the Central African Republic (46.8%); Ethiopia (47.3%); Namibia (41.1%); and South Africa (45.1%).

**PARLIAMENTARY PARTICIPATION.** On one measure of gender equity, the share of women among all parliamentary representatives, a number of sub-Saharan African countries outperform not only the rest of the developing world but most of the developed world, as well. Many human rights advocates measure women's participation in the democratic process relative to the goals set out by the Beijing Declaration and Platform for Action (1995, http://www.un.org/womenwatch/daw/beijing/pdf/BDPfA%20E.pdf), a document drafted by delegates to the UN Fourth World Conference on Women in 1995. In articulating an agenda for women's empowerment, the Platform for Action suggests a goal of seeing women occupy 30% of decision-making positions at all levels of government worldwide. In 2010 women held more than 30% of parliamentary seats in Angola (38.6%), Burundi (32.1%), Mozambique (39.2%), Rwanda (56.3%), South Africa (44.5%), Tanzania (30.7%), and Uganda (31.5%). (See Table 3.6.) By comparison, in that same year women accounted for fewer than 20% of seats in the U.S. Congress.

# CHAPTER 4
# POVERTY IN ASIA AND THE ARAB STATES

## DEFINING ASIA AND ITS REGIONS

In terms of both number of people and land mass, Asia is the largest continent in the world, with approximately 4.3 billion people (about 60% of the world's population) and over 17 million square miles (44 million square kilometers) of land area (30% of the entire land area on the earth). It is commonly regarded as consisting of 55 states, including 6 territories that are not universally recognized as states, and it encompasses several geographically and culturally distinct regions.

Often, international organizations and other experts divide the continent into the regions of North Asia (the Asian portion of Russia), East Asia (China, Japan, Mongolia, North Korea, South Korea, and Taiwan), West Asia (which consists of Middle Eastern countries including Iran, Iraq, Israel, Jordan, Kuwait, Lebanon, Saudi Arabia, Syria, and Turkey, as well as the South Caucasus countries of Armenia, Azerbaijan, and Georgia), South Asia (Afghanistan, Bangladesh, Bhutan, India, the Maldives, Nepal, Pakistan, and Sri Lanka), Southeast Asia (Cambodia, Indonesia, the Lao People's Democratic Republic [Lao PDR, commonly called Laos], Malaysia, Myanmar [also called Burma], the Philippines, Thailand, Vietnam, and other nearby nations), and Central Asia (the former Soviet republics of Kazakhstan, Kyrgyzstan, Tajikistan, Turkmenistan, and Uzbekistan).

Because the borders around Asia have never been permanently defined, and because there are numerous territories on the continent that are recognized as nations by some countries and organizations but not others, experts disagree on the total number of countries on the continent, and different authorities draw regional boundaries such as the above differently. For example, sometimes East and Southeast Asia are discussed together as East Asia and the Pacific; and some researchers consider Central Asia to consist not only of the

countries listed above but of Afghanistan, Mongolia, Tibet, and parts of India, Iran, Pakistan, and Russia, among other countries.

Much of the best available data on poverty in Asia are subject to the vagaries of these inconsistent approaches to classification. Many useful sources for the data and information in this chapter come from the Asian Development Bank (ADB), the United Nations (UN) Economic and Social Commission for Asia and the Pacific (ESCAP), and other UN groups focusing on what is known as the Asia-Pacific region, or Asia and the Pacific. This designation refers to most of Asia north and east of the Middle East, as well as the island nations of the western Pacific Ocean. The Arab countries of the Middle East are not included in most sources of data released by these and other similar organizations, but no overview of economic life in Asia would be complete while ignoring the Middle East.

Data sources that focus on the Arab states of the Middle East, such as those released by the UN Economic and Social Commission for Western Asia (ESCWA) and the League of Arab States (Arab League), are not strictly limited by continental boundaries. Those nations and territories commonly designated Arab states include a number of African countries (Algeria, the Comoros, Djibouti, Egypt, Mauritania, Morocco, Somalia, Sudan, and Tunisia) in addition to the Asian states of Bahrain, Iraq, Jordan, Kuwait, Lebanon, Oman, Qatar, Saudi Arabia, the Syrian Arab Republic, the United Arab Emirates, and Yemen, and the territory of Palestine, which is considered a state by many in the Arab world but a part of the state of Israel by much of the rest of the world. The text and graphics that follow, therefore, are divided into sections pertaining to Asia and the Pacific, on the one hand, and the Arab states, on the other. The chapter should not be considered a comprehensive treatment of poverty within the precise geographical borders of the Asian continent.

Instead, it focuses on the two regions that, while they do not match up precisely with the continent's borders, account for most of the poverty in Asia.

## ASIA AND THE PACIFIC

The ADB has a membership composed both of developing Asian countries and of developed countries outside of Asia. The developing member countries are the focus of the organization's efforts to spur economic development, and they account for the bulk of the continent's population as well as the overwhelming majority of its poor people. Table 4.1 lists those countries by subregion. Most researchers studying poverty in the region exclude Japan, a highly developed country, as well as Australia and New Zealand. Poverty in developed countries will be the focus of Chapter 6.

Asia and the Pacific, as the ADB and other organizations refer to the region, is characterized by extreme geographic, ethnic, and cultural diversity as well as by immense economic differences. The region is home to some of the wealthiest people in the world and some of the poorest, many of whom reside in the least developed countries (LDCs) of Asia and the Pacific. (See Table 1.8 in Chapter 1.) Among the 14 Asian LDCs are tiny island nations such as Kiribati, Samoa, the Solomon Islands, and Tuvalu, as well as nations rocked by decades of war and extremism such as Afghanistan, Cambodia, Myanmar, Nepal, and Timor-Leste (a small island nation, also known as East Timor). Some Asian LDCs, among them Cambodia, Laos, and Nepal, have imperfectly transitioned from socialist or other forms of government and opened their economies to international trade. One LDC, Bangladesh, is Asia's fifth most-populous country. A coastal neighbor to India and Myanmar, Bangladesh has seen little political stability since becoming an independent country in 1971, and the prevalence and depth of its poverty are among the world's most severe.

Nevertheless, large numbers of Asia's poorest people also live in populous countries with large and rapidly growing economies, chief among them the world's two largest countries, China and India, which had populations of 1.3 billion and 1.2 billion, respectively, in 2013. Indonesia, the world's fourth-largest country (after China, India, and the United States), with a population of more than 250 million in 2013, likewise had a large and rapidly developing economy but also high levels of poverty and inequality. Pakistan, Asia's fourth-largest country, with a population of more than 180 million in 2013, had an underdeveloped economy and a large poor population, without being classified as an LDC. Other Asian countries with large impoverished populations included the Federated States of Micronesia, the Philippines, and Vietnam in Southeast Asia; Georgia in West Asia; and Turkmenistan in Central Asia.

**TABLE 4.1**

**Asian Development Bank's (ADB) developing member countries, 2013**

| Central Asia | Southeast Asia |
|---|---|
| Armenia | Brunei Darussalam |
| Azerbaijan | Cambodia |
| Georgia | Indonesia |
| Kazakhstan | Lao People's Dem. Rep. |
| Kyrgyz Republic | Malaysia |
| Tajikistan | Myanmar |
| Turkmenistan | Philippines |
| Uzbekistan | Singapore |
| **East Asia** | Thailand |
| China, People's Rep. of | Viet Nam |
| Hong Kong, China | **The Pacific** |
| Korea, Rep. of | Cook Islands |
| Mongolia | Fiji Islands |
| Taipei, China | Kiribati |
| **South Asia** | Marshall Islands |
| Afghanistan | Micronesia, Fed. States of |
| Bangladesh | Nauru |
| Bhutan | Palau |
| India | Papua New Guinea |
| Maldives | Samoa |
| Nepal | Solomon Islands |
| Pakistan | Timor-Leste |
| Sri Lanka | Tonga |
| | Tuvalu |
| | Vanuatu |

SOURCE: Adapted from *Asian Development Outlook 2013: Asia's Energy Challenge*, Asian Development Bank (ADB), 2013, http://www.adb.org/sites/default/files/pub/2013/ado2013.pdf (accessed September 30, 2013)

Thus, poverty in Asia and the Pacific was tied to a more diverse set of political and economic contexts than poverty in sub-Saharan Africa. The overall prevalence of poverty in the region was lower, but with a population approximately four times the size of Africa's, Asia and the Pacific accounts for the largest share of the world's poverty by many measures. Additionally, in the case of some indicators of poverty, the region's problems are more widespread and intense than sub-Saharan Africa's.

### Poverty Measures and Economic Development

Based on the most recent data available as of 2014, over 60% of those in the developing world who lived on less than $1.25 per day lived in Asia and the Pacific, as did nearly 70% of underweight children under five years old, over 70% of those without basic sanitation facilities, and over 70% of those infected with tuberculosis. More than half of the developing world's births at which no skilled health practitioner was present occurred in Asia and the Pacific. The region was home to nearly half of the developing world's people who had no access to safe drinking water and to more than 40% of the developing world's total incidents of child mortality. Asia and the Pacific likewise accounted for approximately one-third of the developing world's maternal deaths and well over a third of children who were not enrolled in primary school. Table 4.2

## TABLE 4.2

### Economic development and poverty indicators in Asia, by country, selected years 2009–12

| Developing member economy | Proportion of population below the poverty line | | Millennium development goals (latest available year) | | | | |
|---|---|---|---|---|---|---|---|
| | National (% of population) | $1.25 (PPP) a day (% of population) | Growth rate of gross domestic product (GDP) per person employed (% at 1990 PPP dollars) | Employment-to-population ratio (% of population aged 15 years and above) | Proportion of employed people living below $1.25 (PPP) per day (%) | Prevalence of underweight children under 5 years of age (%) | Proportion of population below minimum level of dietary energy consumption (%) |
| | 2011 | 2010 | 2009 | 2011 | 2008 | 2010 | 2010–2012 |
| Afghanistan | 36.0[b] | — | — | — | 38.0* | 33* | — |
| Armenia | 35.0 | 2.5 | — | 45.0[b] | 0.7 | 5 | <5 |
| Azerbaijan | 7.6 | 0.4[b] | 7.4[b] | 60.9 | 0.7 | 8* | <5 |
| Bangladesh | 31.5[d] | 43.3 | — | 56.0* | 50.1 | 36[e] | 17 |
| Bhutan | 23.2[t] | 1.7[t] | 17.3* | 70.9 | 26.9* | 13 | — |
| Brunei Darussalam | — | — | — | 63.1* | — | — | <5 |
| Cambodia | 30.1[a] | 18.6[c] | -7.4* | 87.3 | 25.1[a] | 28 | 17 |
| China, People's Republic of | 10.2[l,o] | 11.8[c] | — | — | — | 4 | 12 |
| Cook Islands | 28.4* | — | — | 60.0* | — | — | — |
| Fiji | 31.0[c] | 5.9[a] | — | 50.3[a] | 18.5[b] | 7[b] | <5 |
| Georgia | 23.0 | 18.0 | 9.0[b] | 55.4 | 10.7 | 1[c] | 25 |
| Hong Kong, China | — | — | -2.6 | 58.2 | — | — | — |
| India | 29.8[d] | 32.7 | 1.2 | 52.9[d] | 39.2* | 43* | 18 |
| Indonesia | 12.5 | 18.1 | 1.2 | 63.9 | 19.8* | 18 | 9 |
| Kazakhstan | 5.3 | 0.1[c] | -2.0 | 67.8 | 0.0[a] | 4* | <5 |
| Kiribati | 21.8* | — | — | 80.1* | — | 15[c] | 8 |
| Korea, Republic of | 5.0* | — | 4.5[d] | 59.1 | — | — | <5 |
| Kyrgyz Republic | 36.8 | 6.7 | — | 60.1* | 1.5[a] | 2* | 6 |
| Lao People's Democratic Republic | 27.6[b] | 33.9[d] | — | 65.7* | 31.5 | 31* | 28 |
| Malaysia | 3.8[c] | 0.0[c] | -5.3 | 60.6[d] | 0.0[c] | 13* | <5 |
| Maldives | 15.0[d] | 1.5* | — | 54.9* | 1.3* | 17[c] | 6 |
| Marshall Islands | 20.0* | — | — | — | — | 13[a] | — |
| Micronesia, Federated States of | 29.9* | 31.2*,[o] | 3.9* | 56.0* | 11.3* | 15* | 24 |
| Mongolia | 29.8 | — | — | — | 31.1* | 5 | — |
| Myanmar | 25.6[d] | — | — | — | — | 23 | — |
| Nauru | — | — | — | — | — | 5[a] | — |
| Nepal | 25.2 | 24.8 | — | 91.6* | 50.4* | 29[e] | 18 |
| Pakistan | 22.3* | 21.0[b] | 2.3[a] | 42.8 | 19.2* | 32[e] | 20 |
| Palau | 24.9* | — | — | — | — | 2 | — |
| Papua New Guinea | 28.0[c] | 35.8* | — | — | 34.0* | 18* | 17 |
| Philippines | 26.5[c] | 18.4[c] | -3.1 | 60.1 | 19.0* | 22[b] | <5 |
| Samoa | 26.9[b] | — | -4.6 | 48.2* | — | 2* | — |
| Singapore | — | — | — | 63.5 | — | 3* | — |
| Solomon Islands | 22.7* | — | 3.2 | 23.1* | 21.5* | 12[a] | 13 |
| Sri Lanka | 8.9[d] | 4.1 | 3.2 | 50.7[d] | 5.8[a] | 21[a] | 24 |
| Taipei,China | 1.4 | — | — | 55.6 | — | — | — |
| Tajikistan | 46.7[c] | 6.6[c] | -7.0* | 58.4* | 19.5* | 15[a] | 32 |
| Thailand | 13.2 | 0.4 | -4.4 | 71.6 | 0.0* | 7* | 7 |
| Timor-Leste | 41.1[c] | — | — | 52.4* | 32.6[a] | 45 | 38 |
| Tonga | 22.5[c] | — | — | 50.6* | — | 2* | — |

**TABLE 4.2**

**Economic development and poverty indicators in Asia, by country, selected years 2009–12** [CONTINUED]

| Developing member economy | Proportion of population below the poverty line — National $1.25 (PPP) a day (% of population) | | Millennium development goals (latest available year) | | | | |
|---|---|---|---|---|---|---|---|
| | | | Growth rate of gross domestic product (GDP) per person employed (% at 1990 PPP dollars) | Employment-to-population ratio (% of population aged 15 years and above) | Proportion of employed people living below $1.25 (PPP) per day (%) | Prevalence of underweight children under 5 years of age (%) | Proportion of population below minimum level of dietary energy consumption (%) |
| | 2011 | 2010 | 2009 | 2011 | 2008 | 2010 | 2010–2012 |
| Turkmenistan | 29.9* | 24.8* | — | — | 19.0* | 8* | <5 |
| Tuvalu | 26.3[d] | — | — | 53.3* | — | 2[a] | — |
| Uzbekistan | 17.7[d] | — | — | — | 35.3* | 4* | 6 |
| Vanuatu | 12.7[d] | — | — | 67.6[c] | — | 16[a] | 9 |
| Viet Nam | 12.6 | 16.9[b] | 3.6* | 75.8 | 12.0 | 12[e] | 9 |

PPP = Purchasing power parity.
* Refers to estimates/preliminary figures; or refers to periods before 2007.
[a] Differs from standard definition; or refers to only part of the country.
[a]2007.
[b]2008.
[c]2009.
[d]2010.
[e]2011.
[f]2012.
—Denotes data not available.
-Denotes value equal to zero.
0 or 0.0 denotes value is less than half of unit employed.

SOURCE: Adapted from "Millennium Development Goals," in *Basic 2013 Statistics*, Asian Development Bank, Economics and Research Department, Development Indicators and Policy Research Division, 2013, http://www.adb.org/sites/default/files/pub/2013/basic-statistics-2013.pdf (accessed October 15, 2013)

provides a further sense of the dimensions of poverty in Asia. In Bangladesh, a country of more than 150 million people, 43.3% of the population lived on $1.25 per day or less in 2010; and 32.7% of India's more than 1.2 billion residents lived on $1.25 per day or less. These two countries alone account for much of the continent's most extreme poverty.

China, the world's largest country by population, had the world's second-largest economy in 2013, trailing only the United States. Economic growth in China had outpaced that of every country in the world for much of the preceding three decades, and China was poised to become the world's leading economic power in another decade and a half, according to many accounts. Although China had made enormous progress in reducing poverty since the 1980s, after 30 years of sustained economic growth it still had one of the world's largest impoverished populations, many of them living in the country's rural interior. Although a lower proportion of the country's more than 1.3 billion people lived in extreme poverty (11.8% in 2009) than in many other Asian countries, this amounted to approximately 150 million people. (See Table 4.2.) In the early 21st century China was home to a rapidly expanding middle class and a burgeoning population of the extremely wealthy.

Other countries in the region, although their economic development has occurred more recently than that of countries in North America and Western Europe, were among the world's most economically developed. As Table 4.3 shows, gross national income (GNI) per capita in Singapore in 2011 was $42,930, little different from that of the United States and the most prosperous countries of Western Europe. Brunei Darussalam ($31,800 in 2009), Hong Kong ($36,010), the Republic of Korea (South Korea; $20,870), and Taipei (Taiwan; $20,200) also had GNIs per capita that placed them among the most economically advanced countries in the world. Each of these countries was also categorized as having "very high human development" as measured by the UN's Human Development Index, an attempt to quantify a country's level of health, education, and living standards. (See Table 1.5 in Chapter 1.)

## Health

UNDERNOURISHMENT AND MALNUTRITION. As reported by ESCAP, the ADB, and the UN Development Programme (UNDP) in the joint publication *Asia-Pacific Aspirations: Perspectives for a Post-2015 Development Agenda* (August 2013, http://www.unescap.org/pdd/CSN/MDG/MDG-Report 2012-2013(lowres).pdf), the country with the most chronically hungry residents as a proportion of population in 2012 was Timor-Leste, where nearly 40% of the population was undernourished. More than

**TABLE 4.3**

### Gross National Income (GNI) per capita in Asia, by country, 2011

| Developing member economy | Per capita Gross National Income (GNI), Atlas method (US$) 2011 |
|---|---|
| Afghanistan | 470 |
| Armenia | 3,360 |
| Azerbaijan | 5,290 |
| Bangladesh | 780 |
| Bhutan | 2,130 |
| Brunei Darussalam | 31,800[a] |
| Cambodia | 820 |
| China, People's Republic of | 4,940 |
| Cook Islands | — |
| Fiji | 3,720 |
| Georgia | 2,860 |
| Hong Kong, China | 36,010 |
| India | 1,420 |
| Indonesia | 2,940 |
| Kazakhstan | 8,260 |
| Kiribati | 2,030 |
| Korea, Republic of | 20,870 |
| Kyrgyz Republic | 900 |
| Lao People's Democratic Republic | 1,130 |
| Malaysia | 8,770 |
| Maldives | 5,720 |
| Marshall Islands | 3,910 |
| Micronesia, Federated States of | 2,860 |
| Mongolia | 2,310 |
| Myanmar | — |
| Nauru | — |
| Nepal | 540 |
| Pakistan | 1,120 |
| Palau | 6,510 |
| Papua New Guinea | 1,480 |
| Philippines | 2,210 |
| Samoa | 3,160 |
| Singapore | 42,930 |
| Solomon Islands | 1,110 |
| Sri Lanka | 2,580 |
| Taipei, China | 20,200 |
| Tajikistan | 870 |
| Thailand | 4,440 |
| Timor-Leste | 2,730[b] |
| Tonga | 3,820 |
| Turkmenistan | 4,800 |
| Tuvalu | 4,950 |
| Uzbekistan | 1,510 |
| Vanuatu | 2,730 |
| Viet Nam | 1,270 |

[a]2009.
[b]2010.
—Denotes data not available.

SOURCE: Adapted from "National Accounts," in *Basic 2013 Statistics*, Asian Development Bank, Economics and Research Department, Development Indicators and Policy Research Division, 2013, http://www.adb.org/sites/default/files/pub/2013/basic-statistics-2013.pdf (accessed October 15, 2013)

30% of the populations of the Democratic People's Republic of Korea (North Korea) and Tajikistan were estimated to be chronically hungry, and Georgia, Laos, Mongolia, and Sri Lanka all had hunger levels near or above 25% of their total populations. Proportionally, these levels of undernourishment were similar to those in the poorest sub-Saharan African countries. Other countries in Asia had lower percentages of undernourished people but more hunger in terms of absolute numbers. These countries included:

Pakistan, where nearly 20% of the total population of more than 180 million were undernourished.

India, where over 15% of the population of more than 1.2 billion were undernourished.

Bangladesh, where over 15% of the population of more than 150 million were undernourished.

the Philippines, where over 15% of the population of more than 95 million were undernourished.

China, where over 10% of the population of more than 1.3 billion were undernourished.

Other smaller countries with undernourished populations of between 10% and 15% of total residents were Cambodia, Nepal, and the Solomon Islands.

Given the prevalence of undernourishment in these countries, some of which are LDCs and some of which are rapidly developing nations, malnutrition is a major challenge in the Asia-Pacific region. The biggest challenge lay in India, which did not have the highest levels of malnutrition prevalence in Asia but did have the largest absolute number of malnourished children. Nearly half (47.9%) of Indian children exhibited signs of stunting in the most recent year for which data were available, 74.3% were anemic, 62% were deficient in vitamin A, and 31.3% were iodine deficient. (See Table 4.4.) Other countries in the Asia-Pacific region where malnutrition levels ranked among the world's worst included Afghanistan, where 59.3% of children were stunted, 64.5% were deficient in vitamin A, and 71.9% were iodine deficient; Timor-Leste, where 57.7% of children were stunted; Laos, where nearly half of children were stunted, anemic, and deficient in vitamin A; Bangladesh, where 43.2% of children were stunted,

## TABLE 4.4

### Malnutrition in Asia and the Pacific, 2008–13*

| | Prevalence of stunting among children (%) | Prevalence of micronutrient deficiencies and anaemia among children (%) | | | Prevalence of obesity among adults (%) |
| | | Most recent observation | | | |
| | Most recent observation | Anaemia | Vitamin A deficiency | Iodine deficiency | 2008 |
|---|---|---|---|---|---|
| **Asia exluding Japan** | 26.8 | 49.6 | 33.9 | 29.8 | 6.0 |
| **Central Asia** | 22.7 (A) | 38.5 | 38.3 | 39.1 | 18.4 |
| Kazakhstan | 17.5 | 36.3 | 27.1 | 53.1 | 24.4 |
| Kyrgyzstan | 18.1 | 49.8 | 26.3 | 88.1 | 17.2 |
| Tajikistan | 39.2 | 37.7 | 26.8 | — | 9.9 |
| Turkmenistan | 28.1 | 35.8 | 28.0 | 18.7 | 14.3 |
| Uzbekistan | 19.6 | 38.1 | 53.1 | 39.8 | 17.3 |
| **Eastern Asia** | 8.5 | 20.1 | 9.4 | 15.0 | 5.6 |
| China | 9.4 | 20.0 | 9.3 | 15.7 | 5.6 |
| Democratic People's Republic of Korea | 32.4 | 31.7 | 27.5 | — | 3.8 |
| Mongolia | 27.5 | 21.4 | 19.8 | 52.8 | 16.4 |
| Republic of Korea | — | 16.5 | 0.0* | — | 7.3 |
| **South-Eastern Asia** | 27.4 | 41.0 | 23.4 | 30.2 | 5.3 |
| Brunei Darussalam | — | 24.2 | 0.0* | — | 7.9 |
| Cambodia | 40.9 | 63.4 | 22.3 | — | 2.3 |
| Indonesia | 35.6 | 44.5 | 19.6 | 16.3 | 4.7 |
| Lao People's Democratic Republic | 47.6 | 48.2 | 44.7 | 26.9 | 3.0 |
| Malaysia | 17.2 | 32.4 | 3.5 | 57.0 | 14.1 |
| Myanmar | 35.1 | 63.2 | 36.7 | 22.3 | 4.1 |
| Philippines | 32.3 | 36.3 | 40.1 | 23.8 | 6.4 |
| Singapore | 4.4 | 18.9 | 0.0* | — | 6.4 |
| Thailand | 15.7 | 25.2 | 15.7 | 34.9 | 8.5 |
| Timor-Leste | 57.7 | 31.5 | 45.8 | — | 2.9 |
| Viet Nam | 30.5 | 34.1 | 12.0 | 84.0 | 1.6 |
| **Southern Asia** | 45.5 (A) | 66.5 | 50.0 | 36.6 | 3.2 |
| Afghanistan | 59.3 | 37.9 | 64.5 | 71.9 | 2.4 |
| Bangladesh | 43.2 | 47.0 | 21.7 | 42.5 | 1.1 |
| Bhutan | 33.5 | 80.6 | 22.0 | 13.5 | 5.5 |
| India | 47.9 | 74.3 | 62.0 | 31.3 | 1.9 |
| Iran (Islamic Republic of) | 7.1 | 35.0 | 0.5 | 19.7 | 21.6 |
| Maldives | 20.3 | 81.5 | 9.4 | 43.1 | 16.1 |
| Nepal | 40.5 | 78.0 | 32.3 | 27.4 | 1.5 |
| Pakistan | 43.0 | 50.9 | 12.5 | 63.6 | 5.9 |
| Sri Lanka | 19.2 | 29.9 | 35.3 | 30.0 | 5.0 |

*The most recent available data for each country and condition comes from numerous surveys conducted between 2008 and 2013.

SOURCE: Adapted from "Annex Table," in *The State of Food and Agriculture 2013: Food Systems for Better Nutrition*, Food and Agriculture Organization of the United Nations, 2013, http://www.fao.org/docrep/018/i3300e/i3300e.pdf (accessed September 24, 2013). Reproduced with permission.

47% were anemic, and 42.5% were iodine deficient; Pakistan, where 43% of children were stunted, 50.9% were anemic, and 63.6% were iodine deficient; Nepal, where 40.5% of children were stunted, and 78% were anemic; and Cambodia, where 40.9% of children were stunted, and 63.4% were anemic.

In other countries in the Asia-Pacific region, adult obesity was becoming a serious public-health issue even as the threat of undernourishment and its attendant forms of malnutrition had not fully abated. (See Table 4.4.) Nearly a quarter (24.4%) of adults in Kazakhstan were obese as of 2008. Other countries with high levels of obesity were Iran (21.6%), Kyrgyzstan (17.2%), the Maldives (16.1%), Mongolia (16.4%), and Uzbekistan (17.3%).

SANITATION AND CLEAN WATER. As of 2011, access to clean water in the Asia-Pacific region was a much more pressing issue for rural populations than for people in urban areas. Table 4.5 shows the percentage of the population with access to improved water sources in the developing member countries of the ADB. The countries with the lowest proportion of their populations using improved water sources were Afghanistan (61%), Cambodia (67%), Kiribati (66%), Papua New Guinea (40%), and Tajikistan (66%). In each of these countries, more than 85% of those living in urban areas had access to clean water, while access in rural areas lagged significantly. In Afghanistan only 53% of the rural population had access to improved water sources. Similar proportions of the rural population had access to safe water in Tajikistan (57%), Cambodia (61%), and Kiribati (50%). Only 33% of Papua New Guinea's rural population had access to improved water sources. Dramatic progress had been made throughout the region since 1990 in this regard.

As in sub-Saharan Africa, improved sanitation facilities in Asia and the Pacific were less common than clean water sources. Again there were disparities between urban and rural populations, but sanitation facilities were not a given in urban areas in many parts of the region. Only 28% of Afghanistan's population (46% of those in urban areas and 23% of those in rural areas) had access to adequate sanitation facilities in 2011. (See Table 4.6.) The prevalence of sanitation facilities was 19% in Papua New Guinea, 27% in the Solomon Islands, 33% in Cambodia, 35% in India and Nepal, 39% in Kiribati, 39% in Timor-Leste, 45% in Bhutan and Micronesia, 47% in Pakistan, 53% in Mongolia, 55% in Bangladesh, 58% in Vanuatu, 59% in Indonesia, 62% in Laos, and 65% in China.

## Education and Literacy

In general, the countries of the Asia-Pacific region have high primary school enrollment and literacy levels by the standards of the developing world, as Table 4.7 shows.

Most countries in the region had total enrollment rates near or above 90% in 2011 (or the most recent year for which data were available), and in some cases these high enrollment rates represent significant progress since 1990. India, for example, saw primary school enrollment rise from 83.5% of primary-age children in 2000 to 98.6% in 2010, on par with enrollment levels in the developed world. This improvement was in large part due to increasing educational access for girls. Cambodia, Georgia, Mongolia, Nauru, and Palau made similar gains between the 1990s and 2011, reaching primary enrollment rates similar to those in the developed world. Some countries made even more dramatic progress, among them Bhutan, which increased total enrollment from 55% in 1998 to 90.2% in 2012; and Laos, where total enrollment climbed from 66.2% in 1990 to 97.4% in 2011. Timor-Leste, a country that is still recovering from the aftereffects of a prolonged struggle for independence from Indonesia, increased its primary school enrollment levels very rapidly, from 66.8% in 2005 to 90.9% in 2011.

The Asian country with the lowest levels of primary school enrollment during the 1990s was Afghanistan, where only 25.7% of the total primary-age population was enrolled in school in 1993. (See Table 4.7.) This low enrollment rate included a wide disparity between male (37.4%) and female (13.1%) enrollment, as well. Although the ADB has published no updated educational data on Afghanistan, a joint briefing paper released by the nonprofit aid group Oxfam International in collaboration with numerous other nongovernmental organizations, *High Stakes: Girls' Education in Afghanistan* (February 24, 2011, http://www.oxfam.org/sites/www.oxfam.org/files/afghanistan-girls-education-022411.pdf), estimates that 60% of all primary-age boys in the country and 42% of all primary-age girls were enrolled in school in 2007–08. This represents enormous progress since the early 1990s, but the overall primary enrollment rate remained the lowest among all Asia-Pacific countries, and Afghanistan's gender disparity in education remained glaring by any standard.

Other Asia-Pacific countries with primary enrollment levels well below those in the developed world were Pakistan (72.1% in 2011), Nepal (71.1% in 2000, the most recent year for which data were available), and Papua New Guinea (74.9% in 2010). In both Pakistan and Nepal, low levels of female enrollment were a major factor in the low total percentages of children enrolled in primary school.

Rates at which students who start their educations attend school through the last grade of primary school were also comparatively high in Asia and the Pacific as of 2011, although they fell below developed-world standards. (See Table 4.8.) Among countries for which completion rates were reported, the countries with the lowest rates of primary-school completion as of 2010 (or the most recent

TABLE 4.5

**Percentage of population using improved water sources, Asia and the Pacific, by region, country, and urban/rural location, 1990 and 2011**

[In percent]

| Regional member | 1990 | | | 2011 | | |
|---|---|---|---|---|---|---|
| | Total | Urban | Rural | Total | Urban | Rural |
| **Developing member economies** | | | | | | |
| **Central and West Asia** | | | | | | |
| Afghanistan | 5 (1991) | 14 (1991) | 3 (1991) | 61 | 85 | 53 |
| Armenia | 91 (1992) | 98 (1992) | 75 (1992) | 99 | 100 | 98 |
| Azerbaijan | 70 | 88 | 49 | 80 | 88 | 71 |
| Georgia | 85 | 95 | 72 | 98 | 100 | 96 |
| Kazakhstan | 96 | 99 | 92 | 95 | 99 | 90 |
| Kyrgyz Republic | 77 (1991) | 97 (1991) | 66 (1991) | 89 | 96 | 85 |
| Pakistan | 85 | 95 | 81 | 91 | 96 | 89 |
| Tajikistan | 61 (1993) | 93 (1993) | 47 (1993) | 66 | 92 | 57 |
| Turkmenistan | 86 (1994) | 99 (1994) | 76 (1994) | 71 | 89 | 54 |
| Uzbekistan | 90 | 97 | 85 | 87 | 98 | 81 |
| **East Asia** | | | | | | |
| China, People's Rep. of | 67 | 97 | 56 | 92 | 98 | 85 |
| Hong Kong, China | — | — | — | — | — | — |
| Korea, Rep. of | 90 (1991) | 97 (1991) | 67 (1991) | 98 | 100 | 88 |
| Mongolia | 54 | 74 | 27 | 85 | 100 | 53 |
| Taipei, China | — | — | — | — | — | — |
| **South Asia** | | | | | | |
| Bangladesh | 76 | 87 | 74 | 83 | 85 | 82 |
| Bhutan | 86 (1997) | 99 (1997) | 82 (1997) | 97 | 100 | 96 |
| India | 70 | 89 | 64 | 92 | 96 | 89 |
| Maldives | 93 | 100 | 91 | 99 | 100 | 98 |
| Nepal | 67 | 96 | 64 | 88 | 91 | 87 |
| Sri Lanka | 68 | 92 | 63 | 93 | 99 | 92 |
| **Southeast Asia** | | | | | | |
| Brunei Darussalam | — | — | — | — | — | — |
| Cambodia | 31 | 48 | 28 | 67 | 90 | 61 |
| Indonesia | 70 | 90 | 61 | 84 | 93 | 76 |
| Lao PDR | 40 (1994) | 70 (1994) | 33 (1994) | 70 | 83 | 63 |
| Malaysia | 88 | 94 | 82 | 100 | 100 | 99 |
| Myanmar | 56 | 80 | 48 | 84 | 94 | 79 |
| Philippines | 85 | 93 | 77 | 92 | 93 | 92 |
| Singapore[a] | 100 | 100 | na | 100 | 100 | na |
| Thailand | 86 | 96 | 82 | 96 | 97 | 95 |
| Viet Nam | 58 | 88 | 50 | 96 | 99 | 94 |
| **The Pacific** | | | | | | |
| Cook Islands | 100 | 100 | 100 | 100 | 100 | 100 |
| Fiji | 85 | 94 | 79 | 96 | 100 | 92 |
| Kiribati | 50 | 74 | 36 | 66 | 87 | 50 |
| Marshall Islands | 92 | 91 | 94 | 94 | 93 | 97 |
| Micronesia, Fed. States of | 91 | 94 | 90 | 90 | 95 | 88 |
| Nauru | 93 (1996) | 93 (1996) | na | 96 | 96 | na |
| Palau | 90 | 98 | 72 | 95 | 97 | 86 |
| Papua New Guinea | 33 | 87 | 24 | 40 | 89 | 33 |
| Samoa | 89 | 97 | 87 | 98 | 97 | 98 |
| Solomon Islands | 78 (2000) | 93 (2000) | 76 (2000) | 79 | 93 | 76 |
| Timor-Leste | 53 (1995) | 67 (1995) | 49 (1995) | 69 | 93 | 60 |
| Tonga | 99 | 98 | 99 | 99 | 99 | 99 |
| Tuvalu | 90 | 92 | 89 | 98 | 98 | 97 |
| Vanuatu | 62 | 94 | 55 | 91 | 98 | 88 |
| **Developed member economies** | | | | | | |
| Australia | 100 | 100 | 100 | 100 | 100 | 100 |
| Japan | 100 | 100 | 100 | 100 | 100 | 100 |
| New Zealand | 100 | 100 | 100 | 100 | 100 | 100 |

— = Data not available at cutoff date.
na = Not applicable.

SOURCE: "Table 7.3—7.8. Population Using Improved Water Sources (%)," in *Key Indicators for Asia and the Pacific 2013*, 44th ed., Asian Development Bank (ADB), 2013, http://www.adb.org/sites/default/files/pub/2013/ki2013.pdf (accessed September 30, 2013)

year for which data were available) were Pakistan, where only 52.2% of students who started first grade finished primary school, Papua New Guinea (56.9%), Cambodia (61.3%), India (61.4%), Nepal (61.7%), Bangladesh (66.2%), and Laos (68%). These countries were, accordingly, among those Asia-Pacific nations with the lowest levels of youth literacy. (See Table 4.9.) Pakistan's youth literacy rate was the region's lowest, at 70.7% in the most

**TABLE 4.6**

**Percentage of population using improved sanitation, Asia and the Pacific, by region, country, and urban/rural location, 1990 and 2011**

[In percent]

| Regional member | 1990 Total | 1990 Urban | 1990 Rural | 2011 Total | 2011 Urban | 2011 Rural |
|---|---|---|---|---|---|---|
| **Developing member economies** | | | | | | |
| **Central and West Asia** | | | | | | |
| Afghanistan | 21 (1991) | 26 (1991) | 20 (1991) | 28 | 46 | 23 |
| Armenia | 89 (1992) | 95 (1992) | 75 (1992) | 90 | 96 | 81 |
| Azerbaijan | 57 (1994) | 70 (1994) | 43 (1994) | 82 | 86 | 78 |
| Georgia | 96 | 97 | 96 | 93 | 96 | 91 |
| Kazakhstan | 96 | 96 | 97 | 97 | 97 | 98 |
| Kyrgyz Republic | 93 (1991) | 94 (1991) | 93 (1991) | 93 | 94 | 93 |
| Pakistan | 27 | 72 | 7 | 47 | 72 | 34 |
| Tajikistan | 89 (1993) | 93 (1993) | 87 (1993) | 95 | 95 | 94 |
| Turkmenistan | 98 | 99 | 97 | 99 | 100 | 98 |
| Uzbekistan | 84 | 95 | 76 | 100 | 100 | 100 |
| **East Asia** | | | | | | |
| China, People's Rep. of | 24 | 48 | 15 | 65 | 74 | 56 |
| Hong Kong, China | — | — | — | — | — | — |
| Korea, Rep. of | 100 | 100 | 100 | 100 | 100 | 100 |
| Mongolia | 50 (1994) | 66 (1994) | 28 (1994) | 53 | 64 | 29 |
| Taipei, China | — | — | — | — | — | — |
| **South Asia** | | | | | | |
| Bangladesh | 38 | 54 | 34 | 55 | 55 | 55 |
| Bhutan | 38 (1997) | 66 (1997) | 30 (1997) | 45 | 74 | 29 |
| India | 18 | 50 | 7 | 35 | 60 | 24 |
| Maldives | 68 | 98 | 58 | 98 | 97 | 98 |
| Nepal | 7 | 36 | 4 | 35 | 50 | 32 |
| Sri Lanka | 68 | 78 | 65 | 91 | 83 | 93 |
| **Southeast Asia** | | | | | | |
| Brunei Darussalam | — | — | — | — | — | — |
| Cambodia | 9 | 36 | 3 | 33 | 76 | 22 |
| Indonesia | 35 | 61 | 24 | 59 | 73 | 44 |
| Lao PDR | 20 (1994) | 61 (1994) | 12 (1994) | 62 | 87 | 48 |
| Malaysia | 84 | 88 | 81 | 96 | 96 | 95 |
| Myanmar | 55 (1991) | 77 (1991) | 47 (1991) | 77 | 84 | 74 |
| Philippines | 57 | 69 | 45 | 74 | 79 | 69 |
| Singapore* | 99 | 99 | na | 100 | 100 | na |
| Thailand | 82 | 87 | 79 | 93 | 89 | 96 |
| Viet Nam | 37 | 64 | 30 | 75 | 93 | 67 |
| **The Pacific** | | | | | | |
| Cook Islands | 100 | 100 | 100 | 95 | 95 | 95 |
| Fiji | 57 | 85 | 37 | 87 | 92 | 82 |
| Kiribati | 28 | 43 | 20 | 39 | 51 | 30 |
| Marshall Islands | 65 | 77 | 41 | 76 | 84 | 55 |
| Micronesia, Fed. States of | 19 | 49 | 9 | 45 | 74 | 37 |
| Nauru | 66 | 66 | na | 66 | 66 | na |
| Palau | 46 | 63 | 8 | 100 | 100 | 100 |
| Papua New Guinea | 20 | 62 | 13 | 19 | 57 | 13 |
| Samoa | 93 | 94 | 92 | 92 | 93 | 91 |
| Solomon Islands | 25 (2000) | 81 (2000) | 15 (2000) | 27 | 81 | 15 |
| Timor-Leste | 37 (1995) | 51 (1995) | 33 (1995) | 39 | 68 | 27 |
| Tonga | 95 | 98 | 95 | 92 | 99 | 89 |
| Tuvalu | 73 | 75 | 71 | 83 | 86 | 80 |
| Vanuatu | 35 (1992) | 50 (1992) | 32 (1992) | 58 | 65 | 55 |
| **Developed member economies** | | | | | | |
| Australia | 100 | 100 | 100 | 100 | 100 | 100 |
| Japan | 100 | 100 | 100 | 100 | 100 | 100 |
| New Zealand | — | — | 88 | — | — | 88 (1996) |

— = Data not available at cutoff date.
na = Not applicable.
*No data for the rural area since the country is 100% urban.

SOURCE: "Table 7.3—7.9. Population Using Improved Sanitation Facilities (%)," in *Key Indicators for Asia and the Pacific 2013*, 44th ed., Asian Development Bank (ADB), 2013, http://www.adb.org/sites/default/files/pub/2013/ki2013.pdf (accessed September 30, 2013)

recent year for which data were available, followed by Papua New Guinea (70.8%), Bhutan (74.4%), Bangladesh (78.7%), Timor-Leste (79.5%), India (81.1%), Nepal (82.4%), Laos (83.9%), and Cambodia (87.1%). In most other Asia-Pacific countries, the youth literacy rate exceeded 95%, comparable to the norms in the developed world.

TABLE 4.7

**Percentage of children enrolled in primary school, Asia and the Pacific, by region and country, 1990 and 2011**

| Regional member | Total | | Girls* | | Boys* | |
|---|---|---|---|---|---|---|
| | 1990 | 2011 | 1990 | 2011 | 1990 | 2011 |
| **Developing member economies** | | | | | | |
| **Central and West Asia** | | | | | | |
| Afghanistan | 25.7 (1993) | — | 13.1 | — | 37.4 | — |
| Armenia | 86.9 (2002) | 96.2 (2007) | 87.8 | 97.6 | 86.1 | 95.0 |
| Azerbaijan | 88.8 (1991) | 87.3 | 88.6 | 86.0 | 89.1 | 88.4 |
| Georgia | 83.8 (1995) | 98.4 | 83.0 | 94.2 (2007) | 84.5 | 96.3 (2007) |
| Kazakhstan | 94.0 (2000) | 99.6 (2012) | 95.3 | 99.6 | 92.8 | 99.6 |
| Kyrgyz Republic | 91.9 (1996) | 96.1 | 89.9 | 95.8 | 93.9 | 96.3 |
| Pakistan | 57.9 (2001) | 72.1 | 46.3 | 65.0 | 68.9 | 79.0 |
| Tajikistan | 96.1 (2000) | 97.6 | 92.8 | 95.7 | 99.3 | 99.5 |
| Turkmenistan | — | — | — | — | — | — |
| Uzbekistan | 93.4 (2007) | 92.8 | 92.2 | 91.5 | 94.5 | 94.1 |
| **East Asia** | | | | | | |
| China, People's Rep. of | 97.8 | 99.8 | — | — | — | — |
| Hong Kong, China | 92.2 (1995) | 97.2 | 92.8 | 99.8 | 91.6 | 94.9 |
| Korea, Rep. of | 99.4 | 98.9 (2010) | 99.5 (1998) | 98.4 | 98.1 (1998) | 99.3 |
| Mongolia | 80.7 (1995) | 98.8 | 81.6 | 98.2 | 79.9 | 99.4 |
| Taipei, China | 98.0 | 97.8 (2012) | 97.9 | 97.7 | 98.2 | 97.9 |
| **South Asia** | | | | | | |
| Bangladesh | 72.7 | — | 66.9 | — | 78.2 | — |
| Bhutan | 55.0 (1998) | 90.2 (2012) | 51.0 | 91.5 | 59.0 | 88.9 |
| India | 83.5 (2000) | 98.6 (2010) | 75.9 | 98.5 | 90.4 | 98.8 |
| Maldives | 97.8 (1999) | 94.6 | 98.0 | 95.1 | 97.5 | 94.1 |
| Nepal | 65.1 (1999) | 71.1 (2000) | 57.0 | 64.0 | 72.7 | 77.9 |
| Sri Lanka | 99.8 (2001) | 93.0 | 99.8 (2006) | 93.3 | 99.9 (2006) | 92.7 |
| **Southeast Asia** | | | | | | |
| Brunei Darussalam | 93.4 (1991) | 99.1 (1995) | 93.2 | 99.7 (1994) | 93.6 | 96.6 (1994) |
| Cambodia | 81.6 (1997) | 98.2 | 75.0 | 95.4 (2010) | 88.0 | 96.4 (2010) |
| Indonesia | 94.6 | 99.0 | 92.7 | 100.0 | 96.6 | 98.0 |
| Lao PDR | 66.2 | 97.4 | 55.1 (1992) | 96.4 | 63.6 (1992) | 98.2 |
| Malaysia | 96.2 (1994) | 95.9 (2005) | 96.4 | 95.9 | 96.0 | 95.9 |
| Myanmar | — | — | — | — | — | — |
| Philippines | 97.7 | 88.7 (2009) | 97.0 | 89.5 | 98.4 | 87.9 |
| Singapore | — | — | — | — | — | — |
| Thailand | 93.6 (2006) | 89.7 (2009) | 92.9 | 89.4 | 94.3 | 90.0 |
| Viet Nam | 98.5 (1998) | 99.4 | — | — | — | — |
| **The Pacific** | | | | | | |
| Cook Islands | 90.8 (1998) | 98.4 (2010) | 89.2 | 95.9 (2000) | 92.3 | 93.0 (2000) |
| Fiji | 94.7 (1998) | 99.0 | 94.7 | 99.3 (2009) | 94.7 | 98.8 (2009) |
| Kiribati | 99.7 (1991) | 99.6 (2002) | — | — | — | — |
| Marshall Islands | 98.1 (2002) | 99.4 | 97.5 | — | 98.7 | — |
| Micronesia, Fed. States of | 93.7 | 95.8 | — | — | — | — |
| Nauru | 75.1 (1992) | 95.0 | — | — | — | — |
| Palau | 81.8 | 90.0 | — | — | — | — |
| Papua New Guinea | 53.1 | 74.9 (2010) | — | — | — | — |
| Samoa | 96.7 (1998) | 93.4 | 98.8 | 96.2 | 94.8 | 90.8 |
| Solomon Islands | 77.0 (2005) | 87.5 (2010) | 76.1 | 87.3 | 78.0 | 87.7 |
| Timor-Leste | 66.8 (2005) | 90.9 | 65.3 | 90.6 | 68.3 | 91.3 |
| Tonga | 92.3 | 98.9 (2006) | 93.2 | 88.7 (1999) | 91.5 | 94.0 (1999) |
| Tuvalu | 99.5 (1991) | 98.1 (2007) | — | — | — | — |
| Vanuatu | 98.3 (1998) | 98.9 (2005) | 98.1 | 97.0 (2004) | 98.4 | 98.1 (2004) |
| **Developed member economies** | | | | | | |
| Australia | 97.5 | 97.2 (2010) | 97.7 | 97.5 | 97.2 | 96.9 |
| Japan | 100.0 | 100.0 (2010) | 100.0 | 99.9 (2007) | 99.9 | 100.0 (2007) |
| New Zealand | 99.5 | 99.5 (2010) | 98.7 (1991) | 99.6 | 99.0 (1991) | 99.3 |

— = Data not available at cutoff date.

*Figures refer to the same year as indicated in the column for "total" unless indicated otherwise.

SOURCE: "Table 2.1—2.1. Net Enrollment Ratio in Primary Education (%)," in *Key Indicators for Asia and the Pacific 2013*, 44th ed., Asian Development Bank (ADB), 2013, http://www.adb.org/sites/default/files/pub/2013/ki2013.pdf (accessed September 30, 2013)

## Gender Equity

In education, many countries in Asia and the Pacific have made substantial progress since the 1990s in introducing equality between the sexes. In other realms of life, however, Asian girls and women frequently face more serious forms of discrimination than do girls and women in any other part of the world. According to ESCAP, the ADB, and the UNDP in *Asia-Pacific Aspirations*, bias

TABLE 4.8

**Percentage of students starting grade 1 who reach the last grade of primary school, Asia and the Pacific, by region and country, 1990 and 2010**

| Regional member | Total | | Girls[a] | | Boys[a] | |
|---|---|---|---|---|---|---|
| | 1990 | 2010 | 1990 | 2010 | 1990 | 2010 |
| **Developing member economies** | | | | | | |
| **Central and West Asia** | | | | | | |
| Afghanistan | 87.8 (1993) | — | 87.8 | — | 87.8 | — |
| Armenia | 96.4 (1997) | 96.0 | 95.6 (2002) | 96.0 | 95.9 (2002) | 96.0 |
| Azerbaijan | 92.0 (1993) | 97.2 | 91.2 | 95.6 | 92.7 | 98.6 |
| Georgia | 99.1 (1999) | 96.2 (2009) | 99.8 | 98.6 | 98.5 | 94.1 |
| Kazakhstan | 97.1 (1994) | 99.6 (2011) | 97.5 | 99.7 | 96.7 | 99.4 |
| Kyrgyz Republic | 95.5 (1995) | 95.3 | 93.9 (1999) | 95.9 | 95.1 (1999) | 94.7 |
| Pakistan | 69.7 (2004) | 52.2 | 72.4 | 51.0 | 67.8 | 53.2 |
| Tajikistan | 70.9 (1997) | 98.9 | 99.2 (2008) | 98.7 | 98.2 (2008) | 99.1 |
| Turkmenistan | — | — | — | — | — | — |
| Uzbekistan | 91.8 (1995) | 98.1 | 96.9 (2000) | 98.3 | 98.6 (2000) | 97.8 |
| **East Asia** | | | | | | |
| China, People's Rep. of | 87.3 | — | — | — | — | — |
| Hong Kong, China | 99.3 (2002) | 99.4 | 100.0 | 99.3 | 98.7 | 99.6 |
| Korea, Rep. of | 99.2 (1998) | 99.3 (2009) | 99.0 | 99.3 | 99.4 | 99.2 |
| Mongolia | 68.2 (1995) | 92.8 | 70.5 | 93.6 | 65.8 | 92.1 |
| Taipei, China | — | — | — | — | — | — |
| **South Asia** | | | | | | |
| Bangladesh | 66.6 (2008) | 66.2 (2009) | 66.1 | 70.6 | 67.1 | 61.9 |
| Bhutan | 31.0 (1993) | 94.9 (2011) | 29.3 | 98.7 | 32.3 | 91.2 |
| India | 57.3 (1995) | 61.4 (2001) | 54.1 | 63.5 | 59.8 | 59.7 |
| Maldives | — | — | — | — | — | — |
| Nepal | 35.7 (1991) | 61.7 (2007) | 32.3 (1992) | 63.7 | 43.9 (1992) | 59.8 |
| Sri Lanka | 93.2 | 97.3 | 94.1 | 94.6 | 92.2 | 100.0 |
| **Southeast Asia** | | | | | | |
| Brunei Darussalam | 79.7 (1991) | 96.6 | 95.1 (2003) | 96.3 (2009) | 99.0 (2003) | 96.0 (2009) |
| Cambodia | 34.4 (1994) | 61.3 | 34.9 (1995) | 62.0 | 44.2 (1995) | 60.7 |
| Indonesia | 79.7 | 88.0 | 92.7 (1995) | 82.8 (2007) | 86.1 (1995) | 77.4 (2007) |
| Lao PDR | 32.7 | 68.0 | 32.1 (1992) | 69.2 | 33.9 (1992) | 66.9 |
| Malaysia | 83.0 | 99.2 (2009) | 83.3 | 99.9 | 82.7 | 98.7 |
| Myanmar | 55.2 (2000) | 74.8 (2009) | 55.2 | 77.5 | 55.3 | 72.2 |
| Philippines | 60.9 | 75.8 (2008) | 75.9 (1998) | 80.0 | 65.3 (1998) | 72.0 |
| Singapore | — | 98.7 (2008) | — | 98.8 | — | 98.5 |
| Thailand | — | — | — | — | — | — |
| Viet Nam | 82.8 (1999) | 93.8 | 86.2 | 85.0 (2002) | 79.9 | 85.7 (2002) |
| **The Pacific** | | | | | | |
| Cook Islands | 99.9 (2001) | 75.0 | — | — | — | — |
| Fiji | 86.5 (1998) | 90.9 (2008) | 89.4 | 88.3 | 84.0 | 93.4 |
| Kiribati | 78.0 (1995) | 78.9 (2003) | 67.2 (2001) | 86.1 | 71.7 (2001) | 72.7 |
| Marshall Islands | 78.4 (2005) | 83.5 (2008) | 72.4 (2006) | 79.5 | 69.4 (2006) | 87.3 |
| Micronesia, Fed. States of | 92.0[b] (2000) | 86.0[b] (2009) | — | — | — | — |
| Nauru | — | 92.8 (2011) | — | — | — | — |
| Palau | — | 93.0 (2005) | — | — | — | — |
| Papua New Guinea | 58.1 | 56.9 (2009) | — | — | — | — |
| Samoa | 82.2 (1996) | 76.6 | 91.7 (1999) | 79.1 | 88.5 (1999) | 74.2 |
| Solomon Islands | 85.0 (1991) | 88.3 (2009) | — | — | — | — |
| Timor-Leste | 74.2 (2008) | 83.6 | 77.9 | 85.1 | 70.8 | 82.1 |
| Tonga | 91.1 (2000) | 90.4 (2005) | — | 91.4 | — | 89.4 |
| Tuvalu | 81.3 (1991) | 91.2 (2004) | — | — | — | — |
| Vanuatu | 68.5 (1992) | 71.5 (2008) | 71.0 (1999) | 69.3 | 67.0 (1999) | 73.5 |
| **Developed member economies** | | | | | | |
| Australia | — | — | — | — | — | — |
| Japan | 100.0 (2008) | 100.0 (2009) | 100.0 | 99.9 | 100.0 | 100.0 |
| New Zealand | — | — | — | — | — | — |

— = Data not available at cutoff date.

[a]Figures refer to the same year as indicated in the column for "total" unless indicated otherwise.

[b]Data for 2000 and 2009 apply to reference period 1997–2000 and 2007–09, respectively.

SOURCE: "Table 2.1—2.2. Proportion of Pupils Starting Grade 1 Who Reach the Last Grade of Primary (%)," in *Key Indicators for Asia and the Pacific 2013*, 44th ed., Asian Development Bank (ADB), 2013, http://www.adb.org/sites/default/files/pub/2013/ki2013.pdf (accessed September 30, 2013)

against women commonly begins prior to birth in the region. Whereas the average male-female sex ratio globally is 101.7 (or 101.7 males for every 100 females), in East Asia the ratio is 106.2, and in South Asia it is 105.7. This is largely the result of two factors: prenatal sex selection (the abortion of fetuses that are determined to

**TABLE 4.9**

**Youth (aged 15–24) literacy rates in Asia and the Pacific, by country, 1990 and 2011**

[In percent]

| Regional member | Total | | Girls[a] | | Boys[a] | |
|---|---|---|---|---|---|---|
| | 1990 | 2011 | 1990 | 2011 | 1990 | 2011 |
| **Developing member economies** | | | | | | |
| **Central and West Asia** | | | | | | |
| Afghanistan | — | — | — | — | — | — |
| Armenia | 99.8 (2001) | 99.8 | 99.9 | 99.8 | 99.8 | 99.7 |
| Azerbaijan | 99.9 (1999) | 100.0 (2009) | 99.9 | 99.9 | 99.9 | 100.0 |
| Georgia | 99.8 (2002) | 99.8 | 99.9 | 99.9 | 99.8 | 99.8 |
| Kazakhstan | 99.8 (1999) | 99.8 (2009) | 99.9 | 99.9 | 99.8 | 99.8 |
| Kyrgyz Republic | 99.7 (1999) | 99.8 (2009) | 99.7 | 99.8 | 99.7 | 99.7 |
| Pakistan | 55.3 (1998) | 70.7 (2009) | 43.1 | 61.5 | 67.1 | 79.1 |
| Tajikistan | 99.8 (2000) | 99.9 | 99.8 | 99.9 | 99.8 | 99.9 |
| Turkmenistan | 99.8 (1995) | 99.8 | 99.8 | 99.9 | 99.8 | 99.8 |
| Uzbekistan | 99.9 (2000) | 99.9 | 99.9 | 100.0 | 99.9 | 99.9 |
| **East Asia** | | | | | | |
| China, People's Rep. of | 94.3 | 99.6 (2010) | 91.5 | 99.6 | 97.0 | 99.7 |
| Hong Kong, China | — | — | — | — | — | — |
| Korea, Rep. of | — | — | — | — | — | — |
| Mongolia | 97.7 (2000) | 95.7 | 98.4 | 97.3 | 97.0 | 94.1 |
| Taipei, China | 92.4[b] | 98.3[b] (2012) | — | — | — | — |
| **South Asia** | | | | | | |
| Bangladesh | 44.7 (1991) | 78.7 | 38.0 | 80.4 | 51.7 | 77.1 |
| Bhutan | — | 74.4 (2005) | — | 68.0 | — | 80.0 |
| India | 61.9 (1991) | 81.1 (2006) | 49.3 | 74.4 | 73.5 | 88.4 |
| Maldives | 98.2 | 99.3 (2006) | 98.3 | 99.4 | 98.1 | 99.2 |
| Nepal | 49.6 (1991) | 82.4 | 32.7 | 77.5 | 68.2 | 89.2 |
| Sri Lanka | 95.6 (2001) | 98.2 (2010) | 96.1 | 98.6 | 95.1 | 97.7 |
| **Southeast Asia** | | | | | | |
| Brunei Darussalam | 98.1 (1991) | 99.7 | 98.1 | 99.7 | 98.1 | 99.8 |
| Cambodia | 76.3 (1998) | 87.1 (2009) | 71.1 | 85.9 | 81.8 | 88.4 |
| Indonesia | 96.2 | 98.8 | 95.1 | 98.8 | 97.4 | 98.8 |
| Lao PDR | 71.1 (1995) | 83.9 (2005) | 64.1 | 78.7 | 78.8 | 89.2 |
| Malaysia | 95.6 (1991) | 98.4 (2010) | 95.2 | 98.5 | 95.9 | 98.4 |
| Myanmar | 94.6 (2000) | 96.1 | 93.5 | 95.8 | 95.8 | 96.3 |
| Philippines | 96.6 | 97.8 (2008) | 96.9 | 98.5 | 96.3 | 97.0 |
| Singapore | 99.0 | 99.8 (2010) | 99.1 | 99.8 | 98.9 | 99.7 |
| Thailand | 98.0 (2000) | 98.1 (2005) | 97.8 | 97.9 | 98.1 | 98.2 |
| Viet Nam | 93.9 (1999) | 97.1 | 93.6 | 96.7 | 94.2 | 97.5 |
| **The Pacific** | | | | | | |
| Cook Islands | 99.0 (2001) | 96.0 | — | — | — | — |
| Fiji | 99.3 (1996) | 99.5 (2008) | — | — | — | — |
| Kiribati | 92.0 (1991) | 98.5 (2010) | — | — | — | — |
| Marshall Islands | 98.3 (1999) | 98.0 | — | — | — | — |
| Micronesia, Fed. States of | 96.4 (1994) | 95.7 (2010) | — | — | — | — |
| Nauru | 99.0 (2002) | 96.5 | — | 97.2 | — | 95.7 |
| Palau | 99.0 (2000) | 99.7 (2005) | — | — | — | — |
| Papua New Guinea | 66.7 (2000) | 70.8 | 64.1 | 74.8 | 69.1 | 67.0 |
| Samoa | 99.0 (1991) | 99.5 | 99.0 | 99.6 | 99.1 | 99.4 |
| Solomon Islands | 62.0 (1991) | 89.5 (2009) | — | — | — | — |
| Timor-Leste | — | 79.5 (2010) | — | 78.6 | — | 80.5 |
| Tonga | 99.3 (1996) | 99.4 (2006) | 99.4 | 99.6 | 99.3 | 99.3 |
| Tuvalu | 98.7 (1991) | 98.6 (2007) | — | — | — | — |
| Vanuatu | 86.3 (1994) | 94.6 | 85.2 | 94.8 | 87.3 | 94.4 |
| **Developed member economies** | | | | | | |
| Australia | — | — | — | — | — | — |
| Japan | — | — | — | — | — | — |
| New Zealand | — | — | — | — | — | — |

— = Data not available at cutoff date.

[a]Figures refer to the same year as indicated in the column for "total" unless indicated otherwise.

[b]Refers to literacy rate among persons aged 15 and above.

SOURCE: "Table 2.1—2.3. Literacy Rate of 15–24 Year-Olds (%)," in *Key Indicators for Asia and the Pacific 2013*, 44th ed., Asian Development Bank (ADB), 2013, http://www.adb.org/sites/default/files/pub/2013/ki2013.pdf (accessed September 30, 2013)

be female), and an excessive amount of female infant mortality whose causes are unknown but suspected of being related to anti-female bias. "This alarming phenomenon," the authors of *Asia-Pacific Aspirations* write, "is what Amartya Sen [1933–; a Nobel Prize–winning economist and philosopher from India] has referred to as 'missing women': in 2007, it was estimated that in seven Asian countries 100 million women were missing."

Women in the Asia-Pacific region also face other challenges. Maternal mortality is a major problem in South Asia, where comparatively few women have access to prenatal care and to a skilled health practitioner at the time of birth, and where there are high levels of unintended pregnancies. According to ESCAP, the ADB, and the UNDP, in *Asia-Pacific Aspirations*, 217 of every 100,000 South Asian mothers died while giving birth in 2010, resulting in female life expectancies below world averages. Among adolescent girls between the ages of 15 and 19 years, maternal mortality is South Asia's leading cause of death.

India, the world's second-largest country in population, is by many accounts one of the most discriminatory toward women, and in 2012 and 2013 international attention became focused on the routine occurrence of rape and other forms of anti-female violence in the country. The article "Rape and Murder in Delhi" (Economist .com, January 5, 2013) states that "the UN's human rights chief calls rape in India a 'national problem.' Rapes and the ensuing deaths (often from suicide) are routinely described in India's press—though many more attacks go unreported to the public or police. Delhi has a miserable but deserved reputation for being unsafe, especially for poor and low-caste women. Sexual violence in villages, though little reported, keeps girls and women indoors after dark. As young men migrate from the country into huge, crowded slums, their predation goes unchecked. Prosecution rates for rape are dismally low and convictions lower still—as in many countries." These alarming facts gained wider coverage in the international press after the December 2012 gang-rape and murder of a 23-year-old medical student on a public bus in Delhi, which led to massive street protests in the city and a growing global outcry against the country's gender norms.

These disturbing symptoms of anti-female bias had their statistical counterparts in indicators suggesting that women in the Asia-Pacific region were less empowered than their counterparts in most other world regions. The authors of *Asia-Pacific Aspirations* point out that women have made little progress in the realm of professional and economic empowerment since 1990. That year 28% of nonagricultural jobs in the Asia-Pacific region were held by women, and by 2009 women's share of nonagricultural employment in the region had risen only minimally, to 31%. As Table 4.10 shows, women's share of non-agricultural jobs in 2010 (or the most recent year for which data were available) was particularly low in Afghanistan (18.4% in 2008), Bangladesh (20.1% in 2009), Bhutan (26.8% in 2009), Fiji (29.6%), India (18.1%), the Marshall Islands (29.3%), Nepal (14%), and Pakistan (12.6%).

Asia and the Pacific likewise lagged behind much of the rest of the world in its share of women in government. According to ESCAP, the ADB, and the UNDP, in *Asia-Pacific Aspirations*, "Even Asian countries with high levels of development have low proportions of women in their national legislatures, as in Japan (11% in the lower house) and the Republic of Korea (16%). The Pacific subregion, despite achieving gender parity in education, has four of the world's six countries with no women legislators." As Table 4.10 shows, those countries were Micronesia, Nauru, Palau, and the Solomon Islands. In fully 20 of the 45 Asia-Pacific countries shown in Table 4.10, moreover, women accounted for fewer than 10% of national parliamentary seats. Among those countries with the highest levels of female parliamentary representation, some were perhaps surprising, given their otherwise poor performance on indicators of female empowerment. Nepal had the region's highest percentage of female parliamentarians, at 33%; and in Afghanistan, where discrimination in education and employment was particularly severe, 28% of parliamentary seats were occupied by women. In Pakistan, another country not known for gender equity, women accounted for 23% of parliamentary seats.

## THE ARAB STATES

The Arab region, as discussed above, includes countries in Western Asia as well as a number of culturally similar countries in North and East Africa. The UN and the Arab League in the joint publication *The Arab Millennium Development Goals Report: Facing Challenges and Looking beyond 2015* (2013, http://www.escwa.un.org/ information/publications/edit/upload/E_ESCWA_EDGD _2013_1_E.pdf) assign the countries of the Arab region to one of four basic categories: the Cooperation Council for the Arab States of the Gulf (GCC), the Least Developed Countries (LDCs), Maghreb (a term historically used to refer to the countries of northwest Africa), and Mashreq (a term historically used to refer to Egypt and the countries to the north of the Arabian Peninsula). For the purposes of the report, the GCC countries are identified as Bahrain, Kuwait, Oman, Qatar, Saudi Arabia, and the United Arab Emirates; the LDCs are the Comoros, Djibouti, Mauritania, Somalia, Sudan, and Yemen; the Maghreb countries are Algeria, Libya, Morocco, and Tunisia; and the Mashreq countries are Egypt, Iraq, Jordan, Lebanon, Palestine, and the Syrian Arab Republic.

### The Impact of Military Conflicts

The Arab region in general is more economically developed than much of developing Asia and Africa, as it includes numerous oil-rich states and has benefited from historically strong economic ties with Europe and the West. The region has endured numerous forms of volatility in the 21st century, however, and its

TABLE 4.10

**Gender equity indicators in Asia, by country, 2010–12**

| | Millennium development goals (latest available year) | | | | |
|---|---|---|---|---|---|
| | Ratio of girls to boys in education | | | Share of women in wage employment in the nonagricultural sector | Proportion of seats held by women in national parliament |
| | 2011 | | | % | % |
| Developing member economy | Primary | Secondary | Tertiary | 2010 | 2012 |
| Afghanistan | 0.71 | 0.55 | 0.24[c] | 18.4[b] | 28 |
| Armenia | 1.03 | 1.03 | 1.30 | 43.1[c] | 8 |
| Azerbaijan | 0.98 | 0.98 | 1.02 | 43.9 | 16 |
| Bangladesh | — | 1.14[d] | 0.61[c] | 20.1* | 20 |
| Bhutan | 1.01[f] | 1.05[f] | 0.68 | 26.8[c] | 9 |
| Brunei Darussalam | 1.01 | 1.02 | 1.69 | 30.3* | — |
| Cambodia | 0.95 | 0.93 | 0.62 | 43.5* | 20 |
| China, People's Republic of | 1.04 | 1.05 | 1.13 | 39.1* | 21 |
| Cook Islands | 1.03 | 1.20 | — | 38.2* | 4[e] |
| Fiji | 1.00 | 1.08 | 1.19* | 29.6* | 9* |
| Georgia | 1.03 | 0.95[b] | 1.20 | 48.5 | 7 |
| Hong Kong, China | 1.04 | 1.02 | 1.10 | 49.5 | — |
| India | 1.00[b] | 0.92[d] | 0.73[d] | 18.1* | 11 |
| Indonesia | 1.02[d] | 1.00[d] | 0.89[d] | 32.4[b] | 18 |
| Kazakhstan | 1.00[f] | 0.97[f] | 1.45[f] | 50.0[b] | 24 |
| Kiribati | 1.04[c] | 1.11[b] | — | 38.5* | 9 |
| Korea, Republic of | 0.99[d] | 0.99[d] | 0.72[d] | 42.6 | 15 |
| Kyrgyz Republic | 0.99 | 1.00 | 1.24 | 50.6[c] | 23 |
| Lao PDR | 0.94 | 0.85 | 0.74 | 32.1* | 25 |
| Malaysia | 1.00* | 1.07[d] | 1.34[d] | 39.2[b] | 10 |
| Maldives | 0.98 | 1.13* | 1.13[b] | 30.0* | 7 |
| Marshall Islands | 0.99 | 1.03[c] | 1.28* | 29.3* | 3 |
| Micronesia, Federated States of | 1.01[a] | 1.08* | — | — | 0 |
| Mongolia | 0.98 | 1.06 | 1.49 | 52.7 | 4 |
| Myanmar | 1.00[d] | 1.06[d] | 1.37 | 35.7* | 4 |
| Nauru | 1.06[b] | 1.20[b] | — | — | 0 |
| Nepal | 0.86* | 0.89* | 0.60* | 14.0* | 33 |
| Pakistan | 0.82 | 0.73 | 0.91 | 12.6[b] | 23 |
| Palau | 1.03[a] | 1.02* | 2.04* | 39.6* | 0 |
| Papua New Guinea | 0.89[b] | 0.70* | 0.57* | 32.1* | 1 |
| Philippines | 0.98[c] | 1.08[c] | 1.24[c] | 41.9 | 23 |
| Samoa | 1.04 | 1.15 | 0.92* | 36.7* | 4 |
| Singapore | — | — | — | 45.4[c] | 22 |
| Solomon Islands | 0.99[d] | 0.88[d] | — | 30.8* | 0 |
| Sri Lanka | 1.00[d] | 1.03[d] | 1.92[d] | 31.0[c] | 6 |
| Taipei, China | 1.01 | 1.01 | 1.08 | — | — |
| Tajikistan | 0.96 | 0.87 | 0.52 | 37.1* | 19 |
| Thailand | 0.99[c] | 1.08 | 1.31 | 45.5[c] | 16 |
| Timor-Leste | 0.96 | 1.03 | 0.70[c] | 35.0* | 32 |
| Tonga | 0.96[a] | 1.00* | 1.66* | 35.6* | 4 |
| Turkmenistan | — | — | — | 42.1* | 17 |
| Tuvalu | 0.95* | 1.10* | — | 33.9* | 7 |
| Uzbekistan | 0.97 | 0.98 | 0.65 | 39.4[a] | 22 |
| Vanuatu | 0.95[d] | 1.02[d] | 0.60* | 38.9[b] | 2 |
| Viet Nam | 0.94 | 1.09[d] | 1.01 | 40.4* | 24 |

*Refers to estimates/preliminary figures; or refers to periods before 2007.
[a]2007.
[b]2008.
[c]2009.
[d]2010.
[e]2011.
[f]2012.
—Denotes data not available.

SOURCE: Adapted from "Millennium Development Goals," in *Basic 2013 Statistics*, Asian Development Bank, Economics and Research Department, Development Indicators and Policy Research Division, 2013, http://www.adb.org/sites/default/files/pub/2013/basic-statistics-2013.pdf (accessed October 15, 2013)

challenges in the realm of economic development cannot be considered separately from these events.

Iraq was the site of two U.S.-led wars, one that lasted from 1990 to 1991 and a second, more destructive and protracted war that lasted from 2003 to 2010. The Second Gulf War resulted in the overthrow of Iraq's leader, Saddam Hussein (1937–2006), and the destruction of substantial amounts of property and infrastructure. Prior to the second war, Iraq was among the most economically developed countries in the Arab region.

The East African country of Somalia, meanwhile, remains embroiled in a civil war that has been ongoing since 1991. The country has enjoyed little stability since that time in spite of international peacekeeping efforts, and as of March 2014 no stable government had emerged from the perpetual struggle for power among rival tribal, military, and religious forces.

Sudan, located in northeastern Africa, is also a country marked by long-running civil war. A first civil war lasted from 1955 to 1972 and eventually led to a second, which lasted from 1983 to 2005. The fallout from these wars included the 2011 secession of the southern portion of the country and the splitting of Sudan into two states, Sudan (which is predominantly Muslim) and South Sudan (where a majority of residents practice indigenous religions or Christianity). Sudan's economic challenges include not only the destruction resulting from the long-running wars but the secession of South Sudan, which contains most of the oil fields that had previously generated much of the country's economic growth.

Yet another part of the region whose economic prospects have been drastically circumscribed by military and social conflict is the State of Palestine, which many in the Arab world consider an independent nation occupied by Israel, the country of which Palestine is officially part. Although not an officially recognized nation by Israel or most of the world, Palestine declared itself a sovereign state in 1988, and in 2012 it was granted the status of nonmember observer state by the UN. The Palestinian-Israeli conflict means that many residents live under conditions of occupation, with limited freedom of movement, interruptions in access to basic necessities, and constrained opportunities for economic development.

## The Arab Spring

Since 2010 the countries of the Arab region have seen a wave of internal uprisings collectively known as the "Arab Spring." Beginning in December 2010, when mass demonstrations in Tunisia led to the January 2011 ousting of the President Zine el-Abidine Ben Ali (1936–), who had ruled since 1987, the Arab Spring protests have been united in their calls for the replacement of dictatorships with democratic governments or democratic reforms. The Tunisian revolution galvanized dissidents in other countries, and with the help of social media, Egyptians took to the streets to demonstrate against the leadership of their president, Hosni Mubarak (1928–), who had ruled the country since 1981. Mubarak's government engaged in violent attempts to repress the uprisings before ceding power to the country's military in February 2011, pending elections to establish a new government. Similar revolutions followed in Bahrain, Jordan, Libya, Syria, and Yemen.

These revolts have met with varying amounts of resistance from the ruling governments in individual countries, and the wide-ranging effects of the Arab

Spring remain yet to be determined, both in the affected countries and in the region as a whole. The uprisings in both Syria and Libya led to protracted civil wars. In the case of Libya, rebel forces prevailed with the help of troops under the command of the North Atlantic Treaty Organization (NATO; a military alliance of 28 countries including the United States and most states in Western Europe), bringing about the ouster and death of Muammar Qaddhafi (1942–2011), who had been in power since 1969. In Syria, by contrast, President Bashar al-Assad (1965–) remained in power, as of early 2014, after two years of violent fighting and the triggering of one of the world's most pressing refugee crises. As of 2014, protests in Bahrain had not proven conclusive in either bringing about a change of government or reinforcing the legitimacy of the country's current leadership. Jordan's King Abdullah (1962–) responded to his country's protestors by promising democratic reforms, but there were doubts as to his intentions to follow through on these promises. In Egypt, meanwhile, the 2012 democratic elections that followed the 2011 revolution led to the election of Mohamed Morsi (1951–), an Islamist, as president, but displeasure with Morsi's rule led to a second wave of demonstrations and a military coup d'état that dissolved the democratically elected government in 2013.

The UN and the Arab League note in the *Arab Millennium Development Goals Report* that dissatisfaction among the citizens who supported the overthrow of their governments goes beyond concerns over economic conditions. Three of the countries that are among the leaders in the Arab region in terms of their progress toward Millennium Development Goals are among those whose people have revolted against their leaders: Egypt, Syria, and Tunisia. The authors of the report note that the countries embroiled in political turmoil are those where citizens, regardless of the country's level of economic development, lack a sense of *voice* and *accountability*; that is, they do not have adequate representation in their country's political decision making, and they lack confidence that their leaders can be held accountable for such decisions.

Figure 4.1 shows the countries of the Arab region as measured on the horizontal access by their level of gross domestic product (GDP; the total value of all goods and services produced by a country in a year) per capita, and on the vertical axis by their governments' levels of voice and accountability. Relative to the rest of the developing world (the unlabeled points on the graph), the countries of the Arab region all score below average on measures of voice and accountability, even when they are high-income countries. For example, the most economically productive Arab state, Qatar, is characterized by lower levels of voice and accountability than the poorest Arab state, the Comoros. Those countries on the lower right

**FIGURE 4.1**

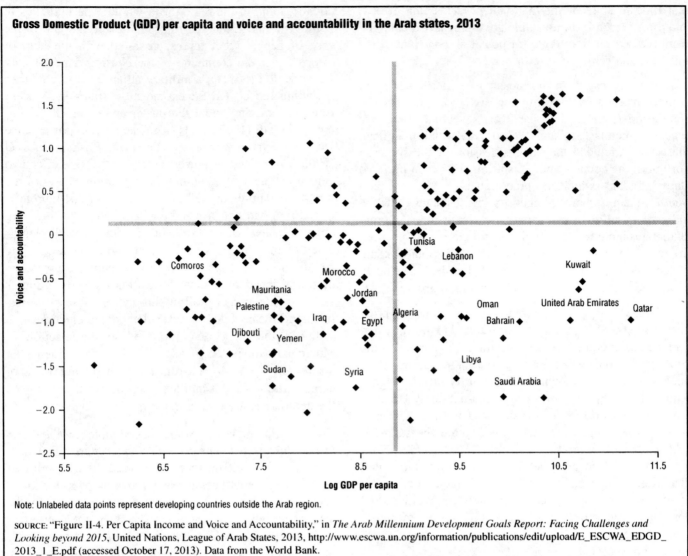

**Gross Domestic Product (GDP) per capita and voice and accountability in the Arab states, 2013**

Note: Unlabeled data points represent developing countries outside the Arab region.

SOURCE: "Figure II-4. Per Capita Income and Voice and Accountability," in *The Arab Millennium Development Goals Report: Facing Challenges and Looking beyond 2015*, United Nations, League of Arab States, 2013, http://www.escwa.un.org/information/publications/edit/upload/E_ESCWA_EDGD_2013_1_E.pdf (accessed October 17, 2013). Data from the World Bank.

quadrant of Figure 4.1 are characterized by a combination of "national wealth and poor governance," in the words of the authors of the *Arab Millennium Development Goals Report*.

The UN and the Arab League further note in their report that the Arab states as a whole had lower rates of extreme poverty than all other regions of the developing world in 2010, with the exception of the developing countries of Europe and Central Asia. In that year only 4.1% of people in the Arab region lived on $1.25 per day or less, compared with 6% in Latin America, 13.5% in East Asia and the Pacific, 32.5% of South Asia, and 48.6% of sub-Saharan Africa.

Poverty levels varied among the different groups of countries in the Arab region, as Figure 4.2 shows, and they increased significantly between 2010 and 2012, in keeping with the increased political instability in the region. The six Arab LDCs had collectively seen poverty

levels rise dramatically since 1990, from 13.9% to 21.6% of their total populations. Likewise the Mashreq subregion (in which five of six countries had been affected either by war, revolution, or occupation) had seen poverty levels rise between 2010, when 1.3% of the population lived on less than $1.25 per day, and 2012, when 5.7% of the population lived on less than $1.25 per day. The Maghreb countries saw poverty levels remain stable between 2010 and 2012.

**Health**

UNDERNOURISHMENT AND MALNUTRITION. Between 1991 and 2011 undernourishment levels in the Arab region grew from 13.9% to 15.3% of the population. (See Figure 4.3.) All subregions saw their undernourishment levels fall slightly during these two decades, according to the UN and the Arab League, in the *Arab Millennium Development Goals Report*, with the

FIGURE 4.2

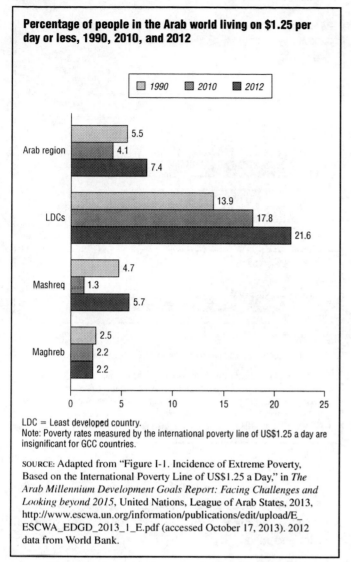

**Percentage of people in the Arab world living on $1.25 per day or less, 1990, 2010, and 2012**

LDC = Least developed country.
Note: Poverty rates measured by the international poverty line of US$1.25 a day are insignificant for GCC countries.

SOURCE: Adapted from "Figure I-1. Incidence of Extreme Poverty, Based on the International Poverty Line of US$1.25 a Day," in *The Arab Millennium Development Goals Report: Facing Challenges and Looking beyond 2015*, United Nations, League of Arab States, 2013, http://www.escwa.un.org/information/publications/edit/upload/E_ESCWA_EDGD_2013_1_E.pdf (accessed October 17, 2013). 2012 data from World Bank.

FIGURE 4.3

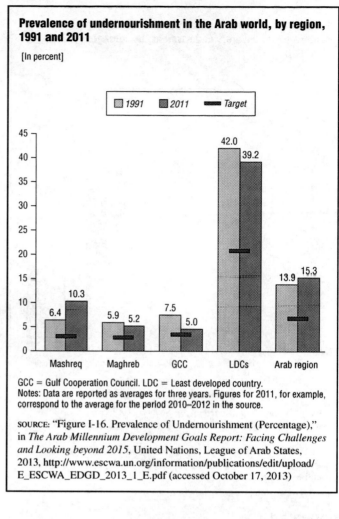

**Prevalence of undernourishment in the Arab world, by region, 1991 and 2011**

[In percent]

GCC = Gulf Cooperation Council. LDC = Least developed country.
Notes: Data are reported as averages for three years. Figures for 2011, for example, correspond to the average for the period 2010–2012 in the source.

SOURCE: "Figure I-16. Prevalence of Undernourishment (Percentage)," in *The Arab Millennium Development Goals Report: Facing Challenges and Looking beyond 2015*, United Nations, League of Arab States, 2013, http://www.escwa.un.org/information/publications/edit/upload/E_ESCWA_EDGD_2013_1_E.pdf (accessed October 17, 2013)

exception of the Mashreq countries, where the undernourished population grew from 6.4% of the population to 10.3%. This increase was largely attributable to escalating levels of hunger in Iraq, which experienced dramatic growth in its undernourished population from 2 million (11% of the population) in 1990 to 8.6 million (26%) in 2011. Palestine, which was also part of the Mashreq subregion, had undernourishment levels of approximately 30%. The Arab LDCs had substantially higher undernourishment levels overall, at 39.2% in 2011. The Comoros and Somalia had the highest hunger levels among individual countries in the region, at approximately 60% of their total populations. Sudan and Yemen, also LDCs, had undernourishment levels of approximately 30%.

The share of underweight children in the Arab states among all children under the age of five years also increased between 1990 and 2010. (See Figure 4.4.) The highest underweight rates, according to the UN and the

Arab League in the *Arab Millennium Development Goals Report*, were in Djibouti, Somalia, Sudan, and Yemen. Stunted growth in children was down slightly in the region as a whole, but it had risen between 2000 and 2010 in the Arab LDCs and in the Mashreq subregion. (See Figure 4.5.) The countries with the highest rates of stunting were Djibouti, Iraq, Morocco, Sudan, Syria, and Yemen.

**CLEAN WATER AND SANITATION.** Access to improved water sources made only a slight gain in Arab states between 1990, when 80% of the population had access to clean water, and 2010, when 81% of the population did. (See Figure 4.6.) The Mashreq (93%) and GCC (98%) subregions were closest to providing universal access to improved water sources, whereas the Maghreb countries lagged (82%). The LDCs as a group had seen access to clean water decline from 58% to 54% during these two decades. As the UN and the Arab League observe in the *Arab Millennium Development Goals Report*, access to clean water had declined not only in the LDCs of Sudan and Yemen but in Algeria, Iraq, and Palestine. These declines were the result of numerous factors, including an insufficient water supply given the

FIGURE 4.4

**Percentage of children under five in the Arab region who are moderately or severely underweight, by subregion, 1990s and 2010**

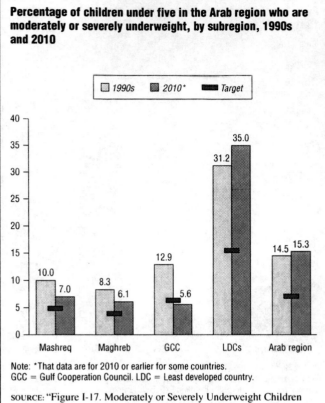

Note: *That data are for 2010 or earlier for some countries.
GCC = Gulf Cooperation Council. LDC = Least developed country.

SOURCE: "Figure I-17. Moderately or Severely Underweight Children under the Age of Five," in *The Arab Millennium Development Goals Report: Facing Challenges and Looking Beyond 2015*, United Nations, League of Arab States, 2013, http://www.escwa.un.org/information/publications/edit/upload/E_ESCWA_EDGD_2013_1_E.pdf (accessed October 17, 2013)

**FIGURE 4.6**

**Percentage of the population in the Arab region with access to improved water sources, by subregion, 1990 and 2010**

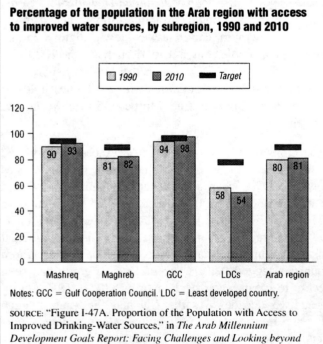

Notes: GCC = Gulf Cooperation Council. LDC = Least developed country.

SOURCE: "Figure I-47A. Proportion of the Population with Access to Improved Drinking-Water Sources," in *The Arab Millennium Development Goals Report: Facing Challenges and Looking beyond 2015*, United Nations, League of Arab States, 2013, http://www.escwa.un.org/information/publications/edit/upload/E_ESCWA_EDGD_2013_1_E.pdf (accessed October 17, 2013)

**FIGURE 4.5**

**Percentage of children under five in the Arab region who are stunted, by subregion, 2000–04 and 2010**

[In percent]

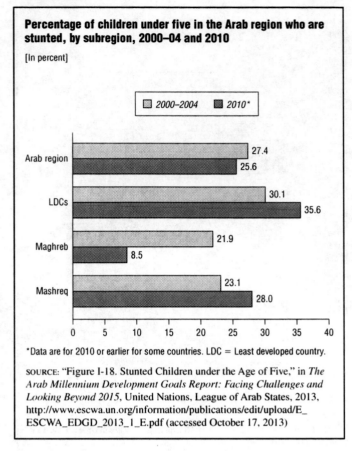

*Data are for 2010 or earlier for some countries. LDC = Least developed country.

SOURCE: "Figure I-18. Stunted Children under the Age of Five," in *The Arab Millennium Development Goals Report: Facing Challenges and Looking Beyond 2015*, United Nations, League of Arab States, 2013, http://www.escwa.un.org/information/publications/edit/upload/E_ESCWA_EDGD_2013_1_E.pdf (accessed October 17, 2013)

aridity of the region, poor strategies for managing the water supply, inadequate financial resources to supply what water there is to a growing population, and political conflict and instability.

Unlike other parts of the developing world, most of the subregions of the Arab region were approaching universal access to sanitation facilities as of 2010. Access in the Mashreq countries had increased from 75% in 1990 to 90% in 2010, access in the Maghreb countries had increased from 73% to 84%, and access in the GCC subregion had increased from 94% to 99%. (See Figure 4.7.) The Arab LDCs, however, lagged far behind the other subregions, with sanitation facilities accessible to only 34% of the population in 2010, up from 25% in 1990. Additionally, as the UN and the Arab League note in the *Arab Millennium Development Goals Report*, the many conflicts in the Arab region since 2010 likely meant that some of these gains had been reversed as of 2013, along with the 2010 levels of access to clean water.

**Education and Literacy**

Between 1999 and 2011 the Arab states as a group had made significant improvements in increasing primary-school enrollment rates, building on progress made since the 1960s, when free primary and secondary

**FIGURE 4.7**

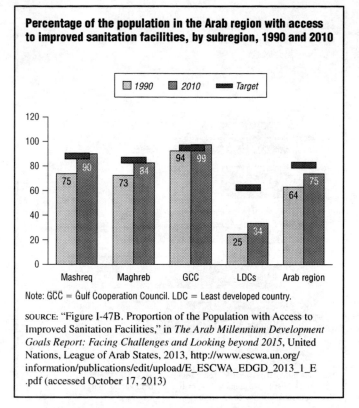

Percentage of the population in the Arab region with access to improved sanitation facilities, by subregion, 1990 and 2010

□ 1990    ▨ 2010    ▬ Target

Mashreq: 75, 90
Maghreb: 73, 84
GCC: 94, 99
LDCs: 25, 34
Arab region: 64, 75

Note: GCC = Gulf Cooperation Council. LDC = Least developed country.

SOURCE: "Figure I-47B. Proportion of the Population with Access to Improved Sanitation Facilities," in *The Arab Millennium Development Goals Report: Facing Challenges and Looking beyond 2015*, United Nations, League of Arab States, 2013, http://www.escwa.un.org/information/publications/edit/upload/E_ESCWA_EDGD_2013_1_E.pdf (accessed October 17, 2013)

**FIGURE 4.8**

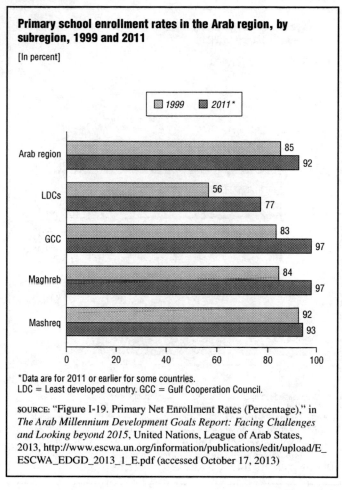

Primary school enrollment rates in the Arab region, by subregion, 1999 and 2011

[In percent]

▨ 1999    ▨ 2011*

Arab region: 85, 92
LDCs: 56, 77
GCC: 83, 97
Maghreb: 84, 97
Mashreq: 92, 93

*Data are for 2011 or earlier for some countries.
LDC = Least developed country. GCC = Gulf Cooperation Council.

SOURCE: "Figure I-19. Primary Net Enrollment Rates (Percentage)," in *The Arab Millennium Development Goals Report: Facing Challenges and Looking beyond 2015*, United Nations, League of Arab States, 2013, http://www.escwa.un.org/information/publications/edit/upload/E_ESCWA_EDGD_2013_1_E.pdf (accessed October 17, 2013)

education became the norm in the region. As Figure 4.8 shows, 85% of primary-age children in the region were enrolled in primary school in 1999, and by 2011, 92% of primary-age children were enrolled. The region's LDCs drove a substantial portion of these overall gains, increasing enrollment levels from 56% to 77% over the period. The GCC and Maghreb states also saw sizable increases, as rates in both subregions rose from 83% and 84%, respectively, to near-universal enrollment (97%). Only in the Mashreq countries were enrollment rates essentially flat, inching upward from 92% to 93%. According to the UN and the Arab League, in the *Arab Millennium Development Goals Report*, half of the Arab region's out-of-school children were concentrated in five countries as of 2011: Egypt, Iraq, Saudi Arabia, Sudan, and Yemen. In Algeria, Iraq, Oman, Syria, and Yemen low enrollment rates were largely a function of the exclusion of large numbers of girls from the education system.

Of those children who started primary school, comparatively high percentages finished primary school across the Arab region in 2010. The exception to this trend was in the Arab LDCs, where only 60% of those children who started primary school attended through the last grade. The LDCs had shown great improvement since 1999, however, when 43% of students completed primary school. In the GCC states, primary completion rates climbed from 90% to 96% during this period; in the Maghreb states, the rates climbed from 73% to 90%; and in Mashreq countries, the rates climbed from 86% to 90%. Literacy rates among

young people increased accordingly between the 1990s and 2010. (See Figure 4.9.) The GCC states had near-universal youth literacy (97%), up from 92% in the 1990s; and the other three Arab subregions all made dramatic improvements during this period. Overall, the youth literacy rate reached 89% in the Arab region as a whole, up from 70% in the 1990s.

**Gender Equity**

Despite having a reputation for confining women to subservient roles in society, the Arab states have made dramatic progress in increasing access to education for girls and young women. Between 1999 and 2011, all subregions moved toward gender parity in education. Only the GCC states boasted a primary-school system characterized by gender parity as of 2011, but the Maghreb and Mashreq regions were expected to arrive at gender parity by 2015. The Arab LDCs, meanwhile, saw their collective gender parity index (with 1 representing full gender parity) rise from 0.62 to 0.85 between 1999 and 2011. The GCC, Maghreb, and Mashreq countries were all approaching parity at the secondary level, as well, while the LDCs lagged further behind. One of the hindrances to achieving gender parity in secondary education was the prevalence of

FIGURE 4.9

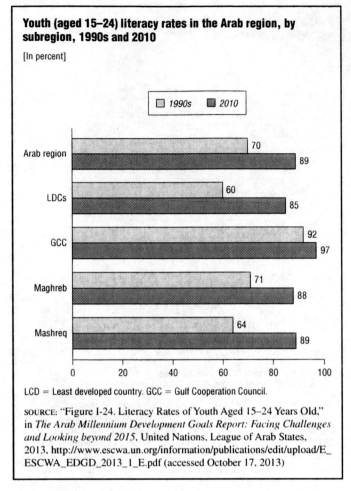

**Youth (aged 15–24) literacy rates in the Arab region, by subregion, 1990s and 2010**

[In percent]

☐ 1990s  ■ 2010

| | 1990s | 2010 |
|---|---|---|
| Arab region | 70 | 89 |
| LDCs | 60 | 85 |
| GCC | 92 | 97 |
| Maghreb | 71 | 88 |
| Mashreq | 64 | 89 |

LCD = Least developed country. GCC = Gulf Cooperation Council.

SOURCE: "Figure I-24. Literacy Rates of Youth Aged 15–24 Years Old," in *The Arab Millennium Development Goals Report: Facing Challenges and Looking beyond 2015*, United Nations, League of Arab States, 2013, http://www.escwa.un.org/information/publications/edit/upload/E_ESCWA_EDGD_2013_1_E.pdf (accessed October 17, 2013)

FIGURE 4.10

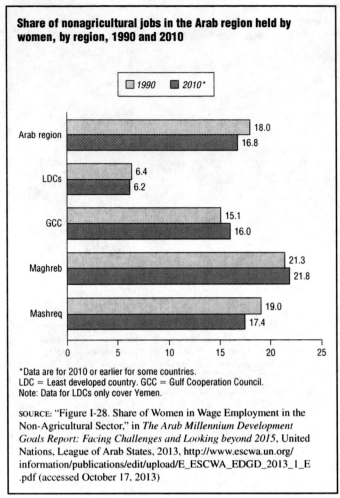

**Share of nonagricultural jobs in the Arab region held by women, by region, 1990 and 2010**

☐ 1990  ■ 2010*

| | 1990 | 2010* |
|---|---|---|
| Arab region | 18.0 | 16.8 |
| LDCs | 6.4 | 6.2 |
| GCC | 15.1 | 16.0 |
| Maghreb | 21.3 | 21.8 |
| Mashreq | 19.0 | 17.4 |

*Data are for 2010 or earlier for some countries.
LDC = Least developed country. GCC = Gulf Cooperation Council.
Note: Data for LDCs only cover Yemen.

SOURCE: "Figure I-28. Share of Women in Wage Employment in the Non-Agricultural Sector," in *The Arab Millennium Development Goals Report: Facing Challenges and Looking beyond 2015*, United Nations, League of Arab States, 2013, http://www.escwa.un.org/information/publications/edit/upload/E_ESCWA_EDGD_2013_1_E.pdf (accessed October 17, 2013)

early marriage among girls living in poverty. As noted in the *Arab Millennium Development Goals Report*, 54% of girls from the poorest households in Sudan married before the age of 18 years in 2010, compared with 17% of girls in the country's richest households. Other states in the region have seen marked increases in gender parity at the secondary level as a result of instituting a minimum marriage age of 18 years. Many human rights activists consider the prohibition of early marriage (usually defined as the marriage of girls under the age of 18 years) a key goal in the pursuit of equal rights between men and women.

In contrast to the region's achievement of relative gender parity in education, women are less likely to be part of the workforce in the Arab states than in other parts of the developing world. Regionally only 16.8% of non-agricultural wage-paying jobs were held by women in 2010, down from 18% in 1990. (See Figure 4.10.) Within the Arab region, the prevalence of women in the non-agricultural sector was extremely low, varying from 6.2% of women in LDCs (down from 6.4% in 1990), to 21.8% (little changed from 1990 levels) in the Maghreb countries. Worldwide, approximately 40% of nonagricultural jobs were held by women in 2010.

Furthermore, as the UN and the Arab League indicate in the *Arab Millennium Development Goals Report*, women who do have paid jobs in the region are generally paid far less than men for the same work. In Palestine, for example, women in manufacturing jobs make 50% of what men performing the same jobs made. Women with manufacturing jobs in Egypt (earning 66% of what men earned for the same job), Jordan (68%), and Syria (79%) fared somewhat better, but inequality remained a pressing issue for the region's economy.

Female representation in Arab parliaments lags behind levels elsewhere in the world, although it has increased rapidly since 2000. (See Figure 4.11.) In 2012 women held 12.7% of seats in the region as a whole, up from a dismal 2.6% in 2000. Only the GCC states had more female representation (18.6%) than the developing world average (18%) in 2012. The Mashreq states had the lowest levels of female representation, at 9.1%, followed by the Maghreb countries, at 14.2%, and the LDCs, at 15%. All regions had seen dramatic increases since 2000, but continued progress was not necessarily inevitable. In spite of the fact that women were an important part of the mass demonstrations of the Arab Spring, they were given

## FIGURE 4.11

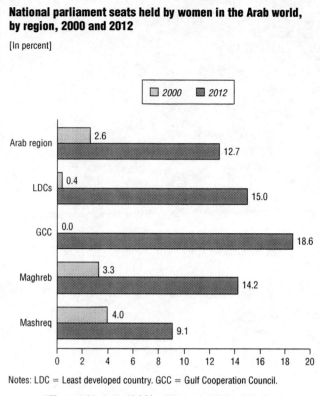

**National parliament seats held by women in the Arab world, by region, 2000 and 2012**

[In percent]

```
            ☐ 2000   ■ 2012

Arab region  ☐ 2.6
             ■■■■■ 12.7

LDCs         ☐ 0.4
             ■■■■■■ 15.0

GCC          ☐ 0.0
             ■■■■■■■ 18.6

Maghreb      ☐ 3.3
             ■■■■■ 14.2

Mashreq      ☐ 4.0
             ■■■ 9.1

             0   2   4   6   8   10  12  14  16  18  20
```

Notes: LDC = Least developed country. GCC = Gulf Cooperation Council.

SOURCE: "Figure I-29. Seats Held by Women in National Parliaments (Percentage)," in *The Arab Millennium Development Goals Report: Facing Challenges and Looking beyond 2015*, United Nations, League of Arab States, 2013, http://www.escwa.un.org/information/publications/edit/upload/E_ESCWA_EDGD_2013_1_E.pdf (accessed October 17, 2013)

little consideration in the transitional governments and processes that resulted from the uprisings. Egypt's 2011 parliamentary elections, for example, saw women win only 2% of seats, whereas under the previous regime there had been a quota system guaranteeing women 12% representation.

Additionally, the UN and the Arab League observe in the *Arab Millennium Development Goals Report* that some forms of violence against women have increased in the wake of the Arab Spring uprisings. There have been numerous cases in which men have publicly humiliated and attacked women who have participated in calls for social and political change. Violence against women in the Arab states largely occurs out of sight, however, and there are few statistical assessments of the threats women face in the region (a fact that is itself perhaps a reflection of the lack of concern for women's health and well-being in the region). A 2011 survey cited by the UN and the Arab League suggests that high proportions of women in some Arab countries (33.2% in Egypt, for example, and 20.6% in Jordan) had been victims of violence at some point in their lives. Health studies have additionally found that the violent practice of female genital mutilation occurs at rates above 90% in Egypt, Djibouti, Somalia, and Sudan.

# CHAPTER 5
# POVERTY IN LATIN AMERICA AND THE CARIBBEAN

The developing region commonly called Latin America and the Caribbean (LAC) consists of those portions of North America that are south of the United States, all of the South American mainland, and the island nations in or bordering the Caribbean Sea (most of which are part of North America). Mainland North American LAC countries include Belize, Costa Rica, El Salvador, Guatemala, Honduras, Mexico, Nicaragua, and Panama. South American mainland countries include Argentina, Bolivia, Brazil, Chile, Colombia, Ecuador, Guyana, Paraguay, Peru, Suriname, Uruguay, and Venezuela. The Caribbean island nations and territories of the region include Antigua and Barbuda, Barbados, the British Virgin Islands, Cuba, Dominica, the Dominican Republic, Grenada, Haiti, Jamaica, Montserrat, Saint Kitts and Nevis, Saint Lucia, Saint Vincent and the Grenadines, Trinidad and Tobago, and the Turks and Caicos Islands. The region is home to approximately 600 million people, more than half of whom live in the two largest countries of Brazil (whose population was just over 200 million in 2013) and Mexico (whose population was nearly 120 million in 2013). The economies of these two countries are responsible for much of the overall growth, as well as much of the poverty, in the LAC region.

## ECONOMIC GROWTH, POVERTY REDUCTION, AND EMPLOYMENT

Generally speaking, the LAC region is among the most developed parts of the developing world, with more advanced economies and higher standards of living than in many parts of sub-Saharan Africa, Asia and the Pacific, and the Middle East/North Africa. The region has seen sustained economic growth since the mid-1990s, with particularly rapid growth beginning in 2000 and continuing through early 2014. Growth slowed measurably following the global financial crisis that began in the developed world in late 2007, but the

region's progress toward increased economic development continued. There were substantial disparities in growth rates between the rapidly developing Latin American economies and the generally less dynamic Caribbean economies. The period 2010–13, during which the world economy's recovery from the crisis years was fitful, saw slowed growth in Latin America, from a gross domestic product (GDP) increase of 5.7% in 2010 to a projected increase of 3% in 2013, according to the UN's Economic Commission for Latin America and the Caribbean, in *Economic Survey of Latin America and the Caribbean, 2013: Three Decades of Uneven and Unstable Growth* (2013, http://www.eclac.org/publicaciones/xml/3/50483/EconomicSurvey2013complete.pdf). These rates were well above growth rates in most developed countries, however. Economic growth accelerated in the Caribbean countries over the same period, from 0.2% in 2010 to 2% in 2013.

International observers such as the World Bank use different absolute measures of poverty in LAC countries than in most of the developing world. Because average incomes and living costs are higher than in other developing regions, extreme poverty in LAC is defined as living on $2.50 per day or less, and poverty is defined as living on $4 per day or less. As a result of the LAC region's sustained economic growth between the mid-1990s and 2011, the number of people falling below both thresholds declined dramatically. The proportion of the LAC population living in extreme poverty declined by almost half during this period, from 26.3% of the population to 13.3% of the population. (See Figure 5.1.) The proportion of the region's population living on less than $4 per day fell from 43.2% in 1995 to 26.6% in 2011. (See Figure 5.2.)

Table 5.1 shows the percentages of people living in extreme poverty in selected LAC countries in the years 2006–11. Argentina, Chile, and Uruguay had the lowest levels of extreme poverty in the region throughout these

**FIGURE 5.1**

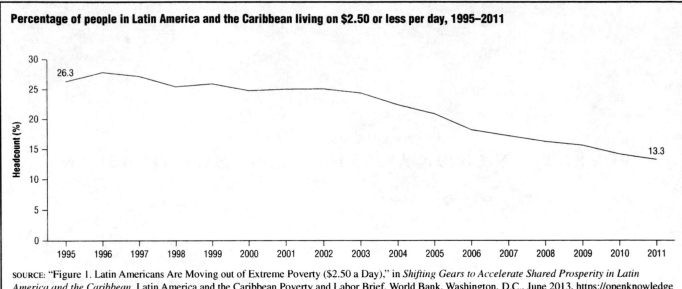

Percentage of people in Latin America and the Caribbean living on $2.50 or less per day, 1995–2011

SOURCE: "Figure 1. Latin Americans Are Moving out of Extreme Poverty ($2.50 a Day)," in *Shifting Gears to Accelerate Shared Prosperity in Latin America and the Caribbean*, Latin America and the Caribbean Poverty and Labor Brief, World Bank, Washington, D.C., June 2013, https://openknowledge .worldbank.org/bitstream/handle/10986/15265/LAC%20Poverty%20and%20Labor%20Brief%20June%202013.pdf?sequence=1 (accessed September 30, 2013). DOI:10.1596/978-1-4648-0078-8. License: Creative Commons Attribution CC BY 3.0.

**FIGURE 5.2**

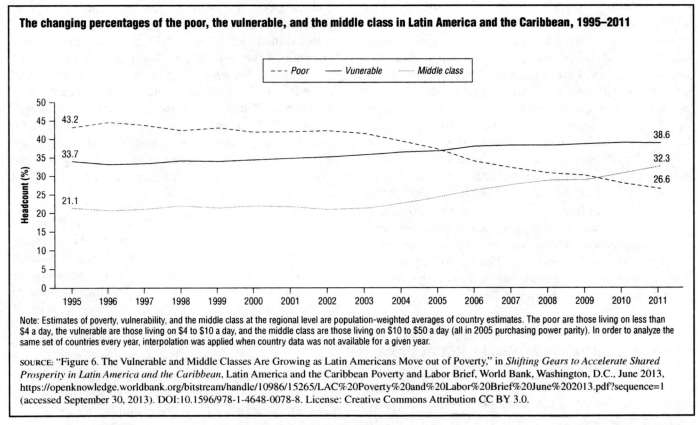

The changing percentages of the poor, the vulnerable, and the middle class in Latin America and the Caribbean, 1995–2011

--- Poor    —— Vunerable    ······· Middle class

Note: Estimates of poverty, vulnerability, and the middle class at the regional level are population-weighted averages of country estimates. The poor are those living on less than $4 a day, the vulnerable are those living on $4 to $10 a day, and the middle class are those living on $10 to $50 a day (all in 2005 purchasing power parity). In order to analyze the same set of countries every year, interpolation was applied when country data was not available for a given year.

SOURCE: "Figure 6. The Vulnerable and Middle Classes Are Growing as Latin Americans Move out of Poverty," in *Shifting Gears to Accelerate Shared Prosperity in Latin America and the Caribbean*, Latin America and the Caribbean Poverty and Labor Brief, World Bank, Washington, D.C., June 2013, https://openknowledge.worldbank.org/bitstream/handle/10986/15265/LAC%20Poverty%20and%20Labor%20Brief%20June%202013.pdf?sequence=1 (accessed September 30, 2013). DOI:10.1596/978-1-4648-0078-8. License: Creative Commons Attribution CC BY 3.0.

years, and Costa Rica also had a lower rate of extreme poverty than most LAC countries. A number of countries were clustered at a similar range of extreme poverty rates. Brazil, the Dominican Republic, Ecuador, Panama, Paraguay, and Peru all had rates of extreme poverty between 11.6% and 17% in 2011; and Mexico was also within this range in 2010, the most recent year for which data were available. The countries with particularly high rates of extreme poverty included El Salvador (22.7% in 2010), Guatemala (41.1% in 2011), Honduras (37.4% in 2011), and Nicaragua (29.3% in 2009). Though some countries saw isolated year-to-year rises in their rates of

TABLE 5.1

**Percentage of people living in extreme poverty ($2.50 per day or less), Latin America and the Caribbean, by country, 2006–11**

| Country | 2006 | 2007 | 2008 | 2009 | 2010 | 2011 |
|---|---|---|---|---|---|---|
| Argentina | 10.3 | 8.8 | 8.2 | 8.0 | 6.1 | 4.6 |
| Bolivia | 16.9 | 21.9 | 19.0 | | | |
| Brazil | 19.6 | 18.1 | 15.6 | 14.9 | | 12.6 |
| Chile | 5.1 | | | 4.1 | | |
| Colombia | | | 25.0 | 22.3 | 19.7 | 17.0 |
| Costa Rica | 11.6 | 8.2 | 7.6 | 8.1 | | |
| Dominican Republic | 18.7 | 17.9 | 18.4 | 16.4 | 16.1 | 14.0 |
| Ecuador | 20.0 | 19.8 | 19.3 | 18.9 | 15.9 | 13.6 |
| El Salvador | 20.6 | 19.5 | 21.3 | 23.1 | 22.7 | |
| Guatemala | 33.6 | | | | | 41.1 |
| Honduras | 42.0 | 37.0 | 34.0 | 31.3 | 34.0 | 37.4 |
| Mexico | 11.7 | | 13.2 | | 12.5 | |
| Nicaragua | | | | 29.3 | | |
| Panama | | 18.3 | 16.7 | 12.3 | 13.2 | 11.6 |
| Paraguay | 24.7 | 19.7 | 17.3 | 18.1 | 16.3 | 14.4 |
| Peru | 23.0 | 21.8 | 18.0 | 15.4 | 13.4 | 12.7 |
| Uruguay | 7.1 | 6.2 | 4.1 | 3.5 | 2.8 | 2.6 |

SOURCE: "Table A.4. Extreme Poverty ($2.50 a Day) by Country, 2006–2011," in *Shifting Gears to Accelerate Shared Prosperity in Latin America and the Caribbean*, Latin America and the Caribbean Poverty and Labor Brief, World Bank, Washington, D.C., June 2013, https://openknowledge.worldbank.org/bitstream/handle/10986/15265/LAC%20Poverty%20and%20Labor%20Brief%20June%202013.pdf?sequence=1 (accessed September 30, 2013). DOI:10.1596/978-1-4648-0078-8. License: Creative Commons Attribution CC BY 3.0.

TABLE 5.2

**Percentage of people living in poverty ($4 per day or less), Latin America and the Caribbean, by country, 2006–11**

| Country | 2006 | 2007 | 2008 | 2009 | 2010 | 2011 |
|---|---|---|---|---|---|---|
| Argentina | 20.6 | 19.5 | 17.3 | 16.3 | 14.1 | 11.6 |
| Bolivia | 36.7 | 39.2 | 36.4 | | | |
| Brazil | 34.8 | 31.8 | 29.1 | 27.4 | | 24.5 |
| Chile | 15.6 | | | 11.6 | | |
| Colombia | | | 42.3 | 40.1 | 36.8 | 33.1 |
| Costa Rica | 25.2 | 20.1 | 18.9 | 19.6 | | |
| Dominican Republic | 37.5 | 36.4 | 37.9 | 34.7 | 35.1 | 33.3 |
| Ecuador | 38.3 | 38.1 | 36.8 | 37.1 | 33.4 | 29.5 |
| El Salvador | 40.9 | 39.1 | 42.1 | 42.7 | 42.3 | |
| Guatemala | 53.2 | | | | | 63.1 |
| Honduras | 58.8 | 56.0 | 52.1 | 50.0 | 53.3 | 56.4 |
| Mexico | 26.7 | | 27.9 | | 28.0 | |
| Nicaragua | | | 52.2 | | | |
| Panama | | 32.2 | 28.8 | 25.3 | 24.0 | 21.2 |
| Paraguay | 43.7 | 38.7 | 35.7 | 33.0 | 30.7 | 27.7 |
| Peru | 41.4 | 38.1 | 34.2 | 30.8 | 27.7 | 25.8 |
| Uruguay | 20.0 | 18.4 | 13.8 | 11.9 | 10.7 | 8.6 |

SOURCE: "Table A.5. Moderate Poverty ($4 a Day) by Country, 2006–2011," in *Shifting Gears to Accelerate Shared Prosperity in Latin America and the Caribbean*, Latin America and the Caribbean Poverty and Labor Brief, World Bank, Washington, D.C., June 2013, https://openknowledge.worldbank.org/bitstream/handle/10986/15265/LAC%20Poverty%20and%20Labor%20Brief%20June%202013.pdf?sequence=1 (accessed September 30, 2013). DOI:10.1596/978-1-4648-0078-8. License: Creative Commons Attribution CC BY 3.0.

extreme poverty, particularly in the years when the fallout from the global financial crisis was at its peak (2009 and 2010), the overwhelming trend among all countries shown was a steady reduction in the percentage of those living on $2.50 per day or less.

At a poverty line of $4 per day, poverty rates above 25% were the norm in most LAC countries between 2006 and 2011. (See Table 5.2.) Only Argentina, Chile, and Uruguay had poverty rates sufficiently low that they approached the norms of the developed world. Brazil, with one of the region's leading economies, saw a significant reduction in its poverty rate over the period, but 24.5% of Brazil's people remained poor in 2011. The region's second-largest state, Mexico, had a poverty rate of 28% in 2010, slightly higher than in 2006. Over a third of the population in Colombia (33.1%), Dominican Republic (33.3%), and El Salvador (42.3%) fell below the $4 per day threshold in the most recent year for which data were available, as did more than half of people in Nicaragua (52.2%), Honduras (56.4%), and Guatemala (63.1%).

In 2010, for the first time in history, there were more middle-class people in the LAC region than there were people living in poverty. Figure 5.2 shows the changing proportions of the region's population who were poor (those who lived on $4 or less per day), vulnerable (those who lived on $4 to $10 per day), and middle class (those who lived on $10 to $50 per day). While the proportion of the population that was living in poverty fell to 26.6%

in 2011, the middle class grew from 21.1% of the population in 1995 to 32.3% in 2011. As more people moved out of poverty, the vulnerable population also grew, from 33.7% to 38.6%. The large size of the poor and vulnerable populations combined, however, suggested that many nations in the region remained at risk of descending into high levels of poverty in the event of a major economic crisis, violent conflict, or natural disaster.

Additionally, as the World Bank reports in *Shifting Gears to Accelerate Shared Prosperity in Latin America and the Caribbean* (June 2013, https://openknowledge.worldbank.org/bitstream/handle/10986/15265/LAC%20Poverty%20and%20Labor%20Brief%20June%202013.pdf?sequence=1), there was a dramatic disparity between levels of extreme poverty in urban and rural areas of LAC countries. In rural areas, the percentage of people living on $2.50 per day or less fell from 49.7% in 1996 to 30.5% in 2011. This was a significant improvement, but the 2011 levels continued to represent a pressing humanitarian challenge. Over the same period, extreme poverty in urban areas saw a more pronounced decline, dropping by more than half, from 18.9% to 8.9%.

The World Bank authors indicate that labor income from increased levels of employment and higher paying jobs were the main drivers of poverty reduction in the region, accounting for 61% of the decline. The second-most important factor was income from transfer payments (cash assistance from both government and private sources) and pensions (retirement income derived from either government or private sources). Together, transfers and pensions accounted for 36% of the decline in poverty between the mid-1990s and 2011.

According to the International Labour Organization (ILO), in *Global Employment Trends 2013: Recovering from a Second Jobs Dip* (2013, http://www.ilo.org/wcmsp5/groups/public/---dgreports/---dcomm/---publ/documents/publication/wcms_202326.pdf), the employment-to-population ratio (the percentage of the working-age population that is employed) in LAC countries grew steadily between 2002 and 2012, from 58.7% to 61.9%, and the labor force participation rate (the percentage of the population that is either working or looking for work) increased from 64.6% to 66.3% during those same years. The percentage of the region's workers who were both employed and yet still living on less than $2 per day (the working poor, as the ILO defines them) declined steadily during this period, from 16% to under 8%.

The percentage of all workers who were part of the informal economy (economic activity that is largely unregulated and not monitored by national governments) likewise decreased during this time. However, even in countries that performed best in moving workers from informal to formal employment the informal economy constituted 40% or more of total employment. Figure 5.3 shows both the percentage reductions and the prevalence of informal employment in selected LAC countries. In the region's largest economy, Brazil, nearly 60% of all workers were informally employed in 2010, although gains had

been made since 2000. In several other countries informal-employment levels approached 80% of all workers.

## Haiti

Haiti, the LAC region's only least developed country (LDC), is the poorest country in the Western Hemisphere. In terms of poverty data, it is an outlier in the region, its challenges more closely resembling those in the LDCs of Africa and Asia than those of other poor LAC states. Politically unstable for most of its history, Haiti in 2004 saw an armed revolt that led to the ousting of President Jean-Bertrand Aristide (1953–), and elections to replace Aristide were not held until 2006.

Although the country saw relative political stability in the years that followed, it confronted a series of major crises that caused enormous amounts of human suffering and prevented economic development. In 2008 Haiti's population experienced a sharp rise in food and fuel prices, challenging weather conditions, and steep declines in its export income due to the global financial crisis. The country then saw its already struggling economy decimated by a January 2010 earthquake whose epicenter was near the capital and largest city, Port-au-Prince. The earthquake, with a magnitude of 7.0, was the worst in the region in two centuries. In "Haiti" (2014, http://www.usaid.gov/haiti), the U.S. Agency for International Development estimates that the earthquake killed over 230,000 people and left more than 1.5 million homeless. Presidential and parliamentary elections scheduled for early 2010 had to be delayed, and when they were held later that year, as over a million people were still living in refugee camps and

**FIGURE 5.3**

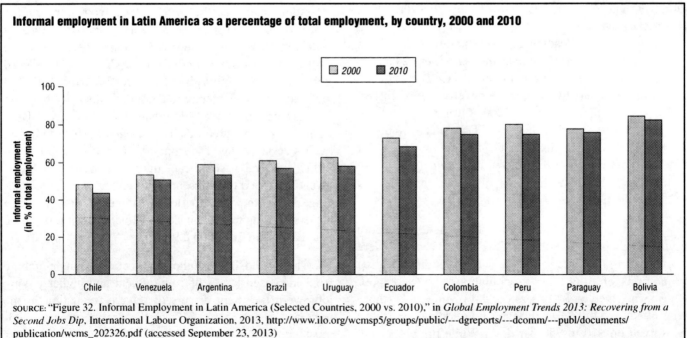

Informal employment in Latin America as a percentage of total employment, by country, 2000 and 2010

SOURCE: "Figure 32. Informal Employment in Latin America (Selected Countries, 2000 vs. 2010)," in *Global Employment Trends 2013: Recovering from a Second Jobs Dip*, International Labour Organization, 2013, http://www.ilo.org/wcmsp5/groups/public/---dgreports/---dcomm/---publ/documents/publication/wcms_202326.pdf (accessed September 23, 2013)

other makeshift dwellings, the results were contested. The country's president as of February 2014, Michel Martelly, was elected in a 2011 runoff election.

Added to these challenges, a cholera epidemic began in October 2010. As explained by Tim Witcher and Mariano Andrade in "UN Warns of Surge in Haiti Cholera Deaths" (uk.news.yahoo.com, 2014), many believe the strain of cholera involved was accidentally introduced by UN aid workers in the aftermath of the earthquake. There have been numerous riots in response to the epidemic and the continued presence of UN peacekeepers. As of February 2014, an estimated 8,330 Haitians were believed to have died from the disease and over 680,000 to have been infected.

According to the United Nations Children's Fund, in "At a Glance: Haiti" (2013, http://www.unicef.org/info bycountry/haiti_statistics.html), as of 2012 gross national income (GNI) per capita in Haiti was $760, and 61.7% of the country's population lived on $1.25 per day or less. GDP per capita had fallen an average of 0.9% between the years 1990 and 2011. The richest 20% of Haitians accounted for 63% of all household income while the poorest 40% accounted for only 9% of household income. Life expectancy at birth was 62.7. The prevalence of low birth weight and stunting both exceeded 20%, indicating the health of many children was at risk. Only 64% of Haitians had access to improved water sources and only 26.1% had access to improved sanitation facilities, both of which are important to combatting cholera. Only about three-quarters of appropriately-aged children (76.7% of boys and 77.7% of girls) attended primary school, and only 21.6% of age-eligible boys and 29.1% of age-eligible girls attended secondary school. The adult literacy rate was 48.7%.

## INCOME INEQUALITY

Although LAC countries have, on average, made rapid progress in reducing poverty since the mid-1990s, the region has long been one of the world's most unequal in terms of its distribution of wealth. Inequality is a problem in the region's poorest countries as well as in its most rapidly developing ones. A common way of quantifying inequality is through the use of a numerical index called the Gini coefficient, developed by the Italian statistician and sociologist Corrado Gini (1884–1965). Countries are assigned a Gini coefficient between 0 and 1 based on various indicators of income equality, with 0 representing perfect equality (everyone earns an equal amount) and 1 representing perfect inequality (e.g., one person earns all of the income). The more income-unequal countries of the world tend to have Gini coefficients close to 0.5, whereas the more income-equal countries tend to have Gini coefficients closer to 0.3. (Sometimes a scale of 0 to 100 is used, so that the coefficient is expressed as, for example, 50 instead of 0.5.)

Figure 5.4 compares levels of inequality from around 2011 in selected LAC countries with levels in member countries of the Organisation for Economic Co-operation and Development (OECD). The OECD is an organization of 34 developed nations whose mission is to promote worldwide economic and social well-being. Two LAC countries, Chile and Mexico, are OECD members. They had the highest Gini coefficients of any OECD nations. All of the non-OECD LAC countries also had higher Gini coefficients than any non-LAC OECD countries. Gini coefficients for LAC countries ranged from 0.43 (Argentina) to 0.57 (Honduras). In non-LAC OECD countries, Gini coefficients ranged from 0.24 (Slovenia) to 0.41 (Turkey). The largest LAC economy, that of Brazil, was among the most unequal countries in the region, its Gini coefficient nearly identical to those of Colombia and Guatemala and surpassed only by that of Honduras.

As economic growth in the LAC region accelerated after 2000, income inequality began to abate somewhat. In *Shifting Gears to Accelerate Shared Prosperity in Latin America and the Caribbean*, the World Bank notes that average incomes in the region grew by 25% between 2000 and 2010, and from 2003 to 2011 incomes for the bottom 40% of earners grew significantly faster than incomes for the population as a whole. Table 5.3 shows the progress made in selected LAC countries at reducing Gini coefficients between 2006 and 2011. Among the countries shown, only Bolivia, Chile, Costa Rica, and Honduras saw income inequality increase or remain flat during this period. Countries that made particularly significant progress included Argentina, whose Gini coefficient fell from 0.478 in 2006 to 0.436 in 2011; the Dominican Republic, whose Gini coefficient fell from 0.519 in 2006 to 0.474 in 2011; and Ecuador, whose Gini coefficient fell from 0.532 in 2006 to 0.462 in 2011. To accelerate the reduction of inequality, the World Bank recommends policies that will allow the poorest citizens of LAC countries to participate in society, including better access to health care and education. The World Bank states that "enabling people who are currently marginalized to improve their living conditions will unleash their inherent economic potential, increasing overall productivity and thus spurring growth."

### Colonization and Inequality

Latin American economic, political, and social inequality dates back to the late 15th century, when the region was first colonized by Spanish and Portuguese explorers. The indigenous peoples of what are now the Caribbean, Central America, and South America had lived there for thousands of years. When the Europeans arrived, however, they brought with them infectious diseases against which the native inhabitants had no natural immunity. Historians estimate that by the 1530s approximately 90% of the indigenous population had died—some in battle against the Europeans and others as a result of the brutal

**FIGURE 5.4**

**Income inequality in Latin America and the Caribbean (LAC) countries and Organisation for Economic Co-operation and Development (OECD) countries, ca. 2011\***

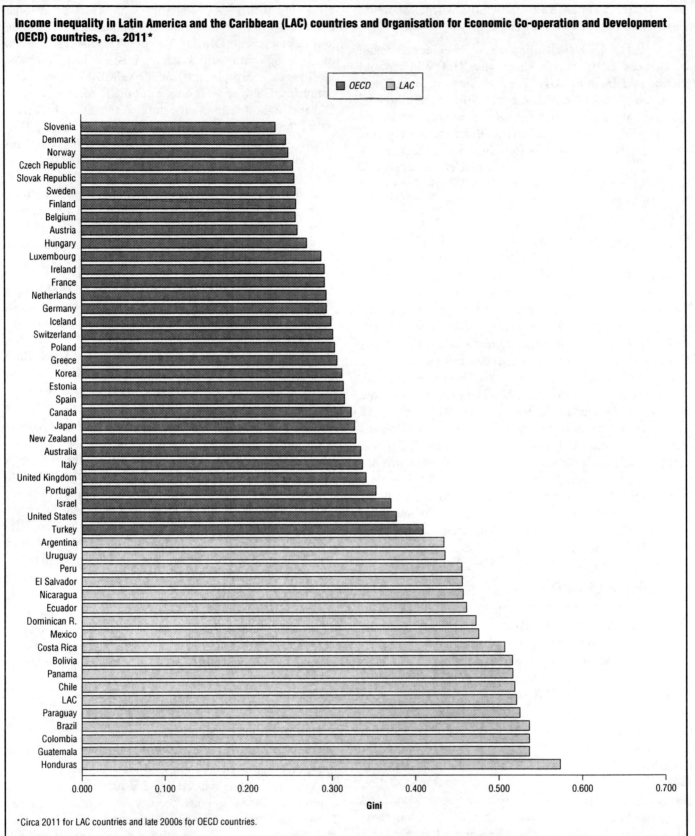

\*Circa 2011 for LAC countries and late 2000s for OECD countries.

SOURCE: "Figure 12. LAC Is One of the Most Unequal Regions in the World," in *Shifting Gears to Accelerate Shared Prosperity in Latin America and the Caribbean*, Latin America and the Caribbean Poverty and Labor Brief, World Bank, Washington, D.C., June 2013, https://openknowledge.worldbank.org/bitstream/handle/10986/15265/LAC%20Poverty%20and%20Labor%20Brief%20June%202013.pdf?sequence=1 (accessed September 30, 2013). DOI: 10.1596/978-1-4648-0078-8. License: Creative Commons Attribution CC BY 3.0.

working conditions imposed on them by the conquerors, but most because of diseases such as smallpox, typhoid fever, influenza, and measles. European colonizers began importing slaves from Africa to serve as laborers. The Europeans, Africans, and natives occasionally intermarried. However, instead of creating a society of equals, intermarriage actually resulted in a group of permanent underclasses; children of mixed unions, as well as descendants of natives, continue to be socially and economically oppressed even into the 21st century.

Besides this social and economic inequality, LAC countries have a history of unequal land distribution and of denying native peoples land rights. Native land claims were first officially addressed when LAC countries adopted the International Labour Office's C107 Indigenous and Tribal Populations Convention in 1957, which recommended methods for protecting and assimilating native peoples while recognizing their individual rights and cultures. Since the 1970s native land rights have become a central issue in Latin American legal and social reform.

## UNDERNOURISHMENT AND MALNUTRITION

LAC countries have not reduced chronic hunger levels as rapidly as China and other parts of East and Southeast Asia, but overall levels of hunger in the region are among the lowest in the developing world. As Figure 5.5 shows, LAC undernourishment levels fell from 14.6% in 1990–92 to 8.3% in 2010–12, and the region was expected to come close to meeting its UN Millennium Development Goal (MDG) of halving the prevalence of chronic hunger by 2015. As measured by another major international hunger goal, the World Food Summit target of reducing the number of hungry people by half between 1990 and 2015, LAC hunger reductions lagged significantly. The region's undernourished population numbered 65 million in 1990–92 and 49 million in 2010–12.

**TABLE 5.3**

**Gini coefficient in LAC region, by country, 2006–11**

| Country | 2006 | 2007 | 2008 | 2009 | 2010 | 2011 |
|---|---|---|---|---|---|---|
| Argentina | 0.478 | 0.474 | 0.463 | 0.452 | 0.445 | 0.436 |
| Bolivia | 0.509 | 0.519 | 0.517 | | | |
| Brazil | 0.567 | 0.559 | 0.550 | 0.545 | | 0.536 |
| Chile | 0.518 | | | 0.520 | | |
| Colombia | | | 0.558 | 0.555 | 0.551 | 0.537 |
| Costa Rica | 0.491 | 0.493 | 0.489 | 0.507 | | |
| Dominican Republic | 0.519 | 0.487 | 0.490 | 0.489 | 0.472 | 0.474 |
| Ecuador | 0.532 | 0.543 | 0.506 | 0.493 | 0.493 | 0.462 |
| El Salvador | 0.462 | 0.470 | 0.468 | 0.483 | 0.457 | |
| Guatemala | 0.559 | | | | | 0.538 |
| Honduras | 0.574 | 0.562 | 0.557 | 0.516 | 0.534 | 0.574 |
| Mexico | 0.499 | | 0.506 | | 0.478 | |
| Nicaragua | | | | 0.458 | | |
| Panama | | 0.533 | 0.527 | 0.520 | 0.519 | 0.518 |
| Paraguay | 0.536 | 0.521 | 0.510 | 0.497 | 0.518 | 0.526 |
| Peru | 0.491 | 0.497 | 0.471 | 0.463 | 0.451 | 0.457 |
| Uruguay | 0.474 | 0.479 | 0.465 | 0.465 | 0.455 | 0.437 |

SOURCE: "Table A.6. Gini Coefficient by Country, 2006–2011," in *Shifting Gears to Accelerate Shared Prosperity in Latin America and the Caribbean*, Latin America and the Caribbean Poverty and Labor Brief, World Bank, Washington, D.C., June 2013, https://openknowledge.worldbank.org/bitstream/handle/10986/15265/LAC%20Poverty%20and%20Labor%20Brief%20June%202013.pdf?sequence=1 (accessed September 30, 2013). DOI:10.1596/978-1-4648-0078-8. License: Creative Commons Attribution CC BY 3.0.

**FIGURE 5.5**

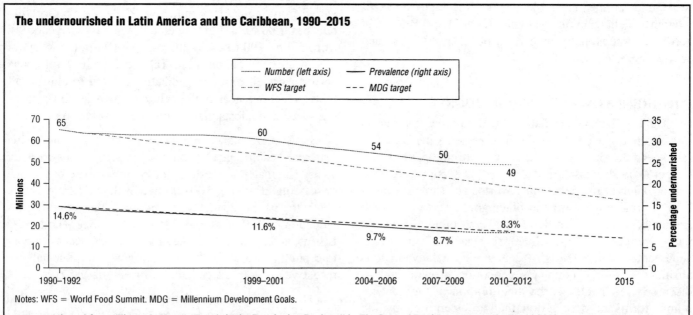

The undernourished in Latin America and the Caribbean, 1990–2015

Notes: WFS = World Food Summit. MDG = Millennium Development Goals.

SOURCE: Adapted from "Figure 2. Hunger Trends in the Developing Regions," in *The State of Food Insecurity in the World 2012: Economic Growth Is Necessary but Not Sufficient to Accelerate Reduction of Hunger and Malnutrition*, Food and Agricultural Organization of the United Nations (FAO), 2012, http://www.fao.org/docrep/016/i3027e/i3027e00.htm (accessed September 24, 2013). Reproduced with permission.

There were dramatic disparities between LAC countries when it came to undernourishment, however. The UN's Food and Agricultural Organization (FAO) notes in *The State of Food Insecurity in the World 2012: Economic Growth Is Necessary but Not Sufficient to Accelerate Reduction of Hunger and Malnutrition* (2012, http://www.fao.org/docrep/016/i3027e/i3027e.pdf) that less than 5% of people in Argentina, Chile, Cuba, Mexico, Uruguay, and Venezuela were undernourished in 2010–12. By contrast, 24.1% of Bolivians, 25.5% of Paraguayans, 30.4% of Guatemalans, and 44.5% of Haitians were chronically hungry during those years. On a positive note, most countries in the region, including several that were projected to fall well short of MDGs for hunger, had seen significant reductions in hunger levels since 1990–92. Guatemala and Paraguay, however, had seen hunger levels rise considerably over the period; and Colombia, Costa Rica, and El Salvador saw slight increases in hunger levels between the 2007–09 and 2010–12 measurement periods as a result of the global economic crisis.

Levels of stunting and other forms of malnutrition in children were lower in the LAC region during the period 2008–13 than in other parts of the developing world. As Table 5.4 shows, however, 13.4% of children in the region exhibited signs of stunting in the most recent year for which data were available, 38.5% were anemic (anaemic), 15.7% were vitamin A deficient, and 8.7% were iodine deficient. As with undernourishment, however, these overall averages disguised major variations in malnutrition levels from country to country. Compared with other LAC countries, children in Bolivia, Ecuador, Guatemala, Guyana, Haiti, and Honduras experienced relatively high rates of malnutrition across several measures. While doing relatively well on other measures, Mexico had the highest rate of vitamin A deficiency in the region (26.8%) and Brazil and Peru had exceptionally high rates of anemia (54.9% and 50.4%, respectively).

## PROGRESS TOWARD OTHER MDGS

Table 5.5 provides data related to LAC's progress toward the eight basic MDGs. The region's performance relative to the first goal ("Eradicate extreme poverty and hunger"), as discussed in the preceding sections, exceeds that of much of the developing world. The same is true of LAC's progress toward the other goals, some of which should be within reach as of 2015 and others of which, while remaining unfulfilled, represent a significant achievement nonetheless. Much of this achievement is attributable to the country's economic growth, and as discussed in Chapter 1, the amelioration of the noneconomic forms of deprivation that are identified by the MDGs reinforces economic development.

In education, the LAC region as a whole was approaching fulfillment of the MDG of providing universal primary education regardless of gender. Total enrollment in primary school reached 94% in 2000 and hovered in the mid-90% range through 2011, and among those children who started primary school, the completion rate surpassed 100% in 2010 and 2011. (See Table 5.5.) Crucially, there was no gender disparity in the region's literacy rate; 97% of both male and female 15- to 24-year-olds were literate as of 2011.

On measures of gender equity, as well, LAC outperformed most of the developing world. Although the ratio of female-to-male primary school enrollment was slightly less than equitable, at 97 females to 100 males between 1995 and 2011, more girls than boys attended secondary school and more young women than men attended college. (See Table 5.5.) Women held 41% of nonagricultural jobs in the region as of 2005, and according to the World Bank's "World DataBank: World Development Indicators" database (2013, http://databank.worldbank.org/data/views/reports/tableview.aspx#), by 2009 women accounted for 43.7% of such jobs in the region. This was halfway between the 2011 averages of 40% for the developing world and 48% of the developed world described in the UN's *The Millennium Development Goals Report 2013* (June 2013, http://www.un.org/millenniumgoals/pdf/report-2013/mdg-report-2013-english.pdf). LAC's proportion of female parliamentary members, at 23%, also exceeded the developing world average as well as the percentage in many developed countries, including the United States. By 2013, according to the UN, female representation in LAC parliaments had climbed to 24.5%, the highest such percentage for any region, developed or developing.

On health indicators, LAC countries generally outperformed most of the developing world, though progress varied from indicator to indicator. The region's mortality rate per 1,000 children under the age of five years fell from 53 in 1990 to 19 in 2011, approaching the MDG of a two-thirds reduction. (See Table 5.5.) The region also performed well on other indicators related to child mortality, reaching near-universality in measles immunization rates and substantial reductions in infant mortality.

LAC performance relative to MDGs for improving maternal health lagged behind its improvements in other areas. The maternal mortality ratio, an estimate of the rate of maternal death per 100,000 live births, fell from 140 in 1990 to 80 in 2010, well short of the three-fourths reduction specified as the 2015 MDG. (See Table 5.5.) Likewise, the MDG of achieving universal access to contraception appeared out of reach, although reliable data for recent years were unavailable as of February 2014.

HIV, malaria, and tuberculosis are diseases singled out for special concern as part of the MDG program. HIV and malaria were uncommon in LAC countries in 2011. Among those in the LAC region who did suffer from HIV, 68% had access to antiretroviral drug treatment for

# TABLE 5.4

## Malnutrition in Latin America and the Caribbean, 2008–13*

| | Prevalence of stunting among children (%) | Prevalence of micronutrient deficiencies and anaemia among children (%) | | | Prevalence of obesity among adults (%) |
|---|---|---|---|---|---|
| | | Anaemia | Vitamin A deficiency | Iodine deficiency | |
| | Most recent observation | Most recent observation | | | 2008 |
| World | 25.7 | 47.9 | 30.7 | 30.3 | 11.7 |
| Countries in developing regions | 28.0 | 52.4 | 34.0 | 29.6 | 8.7 |
| Latin America and the Caribbean | 13.4 | 38.5 | 15.7 | 8.7 | 23.4 |
| Caribbean | 6.7 | 41.3 | 17.8 | 59.8 | 20.3 |
| Anguilla | — | — | — | — | — |
| Antigua and Barbuda | — | 49.4 | 7.4 | — | 25.8 |
| Aruba | — | — | — | — | — |
| Bahamas | — | 21.9 | 0.0* | — | 35.0 |
| Barbados | — | 17.1 | 6.5 | — | 33.4 |
| British Virgin Islands | — | — | — | — | — |
| Cayman Islands | — | — | — | — | — |
| Cuba | 7.0 | 26.7 | 3.6 | 51.0 | 20.5 |
| Dominica | — | 34.4 | 4.2 | — | 25.0 |
| Dominican Republic | 10.1 | 34.6 | 13.7 | 86.0 | 21.9 |
| Grenada | — | 32.0 | 14.1 | — | 24.0 |
| Guadeloupe | — | — | — | — | — |
| Haiti | 29.7 | 65.3 | 32.0 | 58.9 | 8.4 |
| Jamaica | 5.7 | 48.2 | 29.4 | — | 24.6 |
| Martinique | — | — | — | — | — |
| Montserrat | — | — | — | — | — |
| Netherlands Antilles | — | — | — | — | — |
| Puerto Rico | — | — | — | — | — |
| Saint Kitts and Nevis | — | 22.9 | 7.1 | — | 40.9 |
| Saint Lucia | — | 32.2 | 11.3 | — | 22.3 |
| Saint Vincent and the Grenadines | — | 32.3 | 2.1 | — | 25.1 |
| Trinidad and Tobago | 5.3 | 30.4 | 7.2 | — | 30.0 |
| Turks and Caicos Islands | — | — | — | — | — |
| United States Virgin Islands | — | — | — | — | — |
| Central America | 18.6 | 29.6 | 22.3 | 10.1 | 30.4 |
| Belize | 22.2 | 35.9 | 11.7 | 26.7 | 34.9 |
| Costa Rica | 5.6 | 20.9 | 8.8 | 8.9 | 24.6 |
| El Salvador | 20.6 | 18.4 | 14.6 | 4.6 | 26.9 |
| Guatemala | 48.0 | 38.1 | 15.8 | 14.4 | 20.7 |
| Honduras | 29.9 | 29.9 | 13.8 | 31.3 | 19.8 |
| Mexico | 15.5 | 29.4 | 26.8 | 8.5 | 32.8 |
| Nicaragua | 23.0 | 17.0 | 3.1 | 0.0 | 24.2 |
| Panama | 19.1 | 36.0 | 9.4 | 8.6 | 25.8 |
| South America | 11.5 | 42.5 | 12.4 | 2.9 | 21.6 |
| Argentina | 8.2 | 18.1 | 14.3 | — | 29.4 |
| Bolivia (Plurinational State of) | 27.2 | 51.6 | 21.8 | 19.0 | 18.9 |
| Brazil | 7.1 | 54.9 | 13.3 | 0.0 | 19.5 |
| Chile | 2.0 | 24.4 | 7.9 | 0.2 | 29.1 |
| Colombia | 12.7 | 27.7 | 5.9 | 6.4 | 18.1 |
| Ecuador | 29.0 | 37.9 | 14.7 | 0.0 | 22.0 |
| French Guiana | — | — | — | — | — |
| Guyana | 19.5 | 47.9 | 4.1 | 26.9 | 16.9 |
| Paraguay | 17.5 | 30.2 | 14.1 | 13.4 | 19.2 |
| Peru | 19.5 | 50.4 | 14.9 | 10.4 | 16.5 |
| Suriname | 10.7 | 25.7 | 18.0 | — | 25.8 |
| Uruguay | 13.9 | 19.1 | 11.9 | — | 23.6 |
| Venezuela (Bolivarian Republic of) | 13.4 | 33.1 | 9.4 | 0.0 | 30.8 |

*The most recent available data for each country and condition comes from numerous surveys conducted between 2008 and 2013.

SOURCE: Adapted from "Annex Table," in *The State of Food and Agriculture 2013: Food Systems for Better Nutrition*, Food and Agriculture Organization of the United Nations, 2013, http://www.fao.org/docrep/018/i3300e/i3300e.pdf (accessed September 24, 2013). Reproduced with permission.

their disease in 2011. (See Table 5.5.) This was a higher percentage than in any other developing region, but still fell short of the MDG of universal coverage. The region had been successful at reducing the incidence of tuberculosis, a treatable disease that is often associated with poverty, by more than half since 1990.

The region's progress toward MDG environmental goals was uneven. Carbon dioxide emissions were growing, as is to be expected in a region characterized by rapid economic development. (See Table 5.5.) However, energy use per every $1,000 of GDP fell significantly between 1990 and 2010. The region's forest area was diminishing

**TABLE 5.5**

**Latin America and the Caribbean's progress in reaching Millennium Development Goals (MDGs), selected years 1990–2011**

| | 1990 | 1995 | 2000 | 2005 | 2010 | 2011 |
|---|---|---|---|---|---|---|
| **Goal 1: Eradicate extreme poverty and hunger** | | | | | | |
| Employment to population ratio, 15+, total (%) | | 58 | 59 | 60 | 61 | 62 |
| GDP per person employed (constant 1990 PPP $) | | 14,830 | 15,719 | 16,160 | 17,645 | 17,924 |
| Malnutrition prevalence, weight for age (% of children under 5) | | | | | | |
| Poverty headcount ratio at $1.25 a day (PPP) (% of population) | | | | | | |
| Poverty headcount ratio at $2 a day (PPP) (% of population) | | | | | | |
| Prevalence of undernourishment (% of population) | | 14 | 12 | 11 | 9 | 9 |
| **Goal 2: Achieve universal primary education** | | | | | | |
| Literacy rate, youth female (% of females ages 15–24) | 93 | | 97 | | | 97 |
| Literacy rate, youth male (% of males ages 15–24) | 93 | | 96 | | | 97 |
| Primary completion rate, total (% of relevant age group) | 84 | 88 | 97 | 98 | 102 | 102 |
| Total enrollment, primary (% net) | 88 | 89 | 94 | 96 | 96 | 95 |
| **Goal 3: Promote gender equality and empower women** | | | | | | |
| Proportion of seats held by women in national parliaments (%) | 12 | | 15 | 20 | 23 | 23 |
| Ratio of female to male primary enrollment (%) | 99 | 97 | 97 | 97 | 97 | 97 |
| Ratio of female to male secondary enrollment (%) | 106 | 107 | 107 | 107 | 107 | 107 |
| Ratio of female to male tertiary enrollment (%) | 97 | 107 | 118 | 120 | 127 | 127 |
| Share of women employed in the nonagricultural sector (% of total nonagricultural employment) | 37 | 39 | 40 | 41 | | |
| **Goal 4: Reduce child mortality** | | | | | | |
| Immunization, measles (% of children ages 12–23 months) | 76 | 85 | 93 | 93 | 93 | 93 |
| Mortality rate, infant (per 1,000 live births) | 42 | 35 | 28 | 22 | 17 | 16 |
| Mortality rate, under-5 (per 1,000) | 53 | 43 | 34 | 26 | 22 | 19 |
| **Goal 5: Improve maternal health** | | | | | | |
| Adolescent fertility rate (births per 1,000 women ages 15–19) | | | 83 | 77 | 72 | 71 |
| Births attended by skilled health staff (% of total) | 75 | | 86 | | | |
| Contraceptive prevalence (% of women ages 15–49) | 58 | | | | | |
| Maternal mortality ratio (modeled estimate, per 100,000 live births) | 140 | 120 | 100 | 88 | 80 | |
| Pregnant women receiving prenatal care (%) | | | | | | |
| Unmet need for contraception (% of married women ages 15–49) | | | | | | |
| **Goal 6: Combat HIV/AIDS, malaria, and other diseases** | | | | | | |
| Antiretroviral therapy coverage (% of people with advanced HIV infection) | | | | | | 68 |
| Incidence of tuberculosis (per 100,000 people) | 89 | 73 | 61 | 51 | 44 | 42 |
| Malaria cases reported | | | | | | |
| Prevalence of HIV, total (% of population ages 15–49) | 0.3 | 0.4 | 0.4 | 0.4 | 0.4 | 0.4 |
| **Goal 7: Ensure environmental sustainability** | | | | | | |
| $CO_2$ emissions (kt) | 1,021,069 | 1,147,470 | 1,352,342 | 1,510,492 | | |
| Energy use (kg of oil equivalent) per $1,000 GDP (constant 2005 PPP) | 146 | 141 | 138 | 140 | 134 | |
| Forest area (% of land area) | 52 | | 49 | 48 | 47 | 47 |
| Improved sanitation facilities (% of population with access) | 68 | 71 | 75 | 78 | 81 | 81 |
| Improved water source (% of population with access) | 85 | 88 | 90 | 92 | 94 | 94 |
| Marine protected areas (% of total surface area) | 5 | 8 | 11 | 13 | 13 | |
| Terrestrial protected areas (% of total surface area) | 10 | 12 | 15 | 20 | 20 | |
| **Goal 8: Develop a global partnership for development** | | | | | | |
| Internet users (per 100 people) | 0 | 0.1 | 4 | 17 | 35 | 39 |
| Mobile cellular subscriptions (per 100 people) | 0.03 | 0.8 | 12 | 43 | 97 | 107 |
| Net official development assistance received (current US$) | 5,151,600,000 | 6,299,220,000 | 4,856,380,000 | 6,730,490,000 | 10,563,990,000 | 11,621,680,000 |
| Telephone lines (per 100 people) | 6 | 9 | 15 | 18 | 18 | 19 |

PPP = Purchasing power parity.
GDP = Gross domestic product.

SOURCE: Adapted from "World DataBank: Millennium Development Goals," World Bank, 2013, http://databank.worldbank.org/data/views/variableselection/selectvariables.aspx?source=millennium-development-goals (accessed September 26, 2013)

slowly but steadily, a trend that was somewhat offset by a slow but steady increase in environmental protections for both marine and terrestrial areas. The proportions of the LAC population with access to improved water and sanitation sources saw steady improvement between 1990 and 2011. Access to clean water approached universality, at 94%, as of 2011; and access to improved sanitation facilities, at 81%, placed the region among the most advanced developing countries by this measure.

In general, LAC countries made significant advances in establishing the infrastructure and access to technology necessary for development. Access to cellular phones per 100 people increased from near zero in 1990 to 107 in 2011. (See Table 5.5.) The number of internet users per 100 people climbed dramatically as well, from 0 to 39. Telephone line construction lagged, but the worldwide cultural switch to mobile phones made the presence of land lines much less central to economic development.

Finally, the region saw the amount of development assistance it received grow substantially.

## VIOLENT CRIME IN LATIN AMERICA AND THE CARIBBEAN

LAC's economic growth in the late 20th and early 21st centuries made it a developing-world leader as measured by many poverty and human development indicators, but during this same time the region also became a world leader in a much more troubling arena: violent crime. The homicide rate for the region was the world's highest, and the countries of Central America were particularly beset by high rates of homicide. In "Latin America: Violence Threatens a Decade of Progress" (April 3, 2013, http://blogs.worldbank.org/latinamerica/latin-america-violence-threatens-a-decade-of-progress), Hasan Tuluy of the World Bank puts Central American violence in perspective, writing, "Spain, with 47 million inhabitants, has an average of 400 homicides per year; by contrast, Central America, with a population of 41 million, reports 18,000 violent deaths annually."

Figure 5.6 shows the homicide rate per 100,000 people in the 14 countries worldwide with the highest homicide rates in 2011. According to the World Bank, in *World Development Indicators 2013* (2013, http://databank.worldbank.org/data/download/WDI-2013-ebook.pdf), these 14 countries account for a quarter of all violent deaths worldwide. Of the eight most homicide-prone countries in the world, seven were in the LAC region. Honduras had a homicide rate of over 90 per 100,000, roughly double that of most countries in this group, followed by El Salvador, with a homicide rate of approximately 70 per 100,000. Venezuela's homicide rate was approximately 45 per 100,000, and Belize, Jamaica, Guatemala, and St. Kitts and Nevis all had homicide rates approaching 40 per 100,000. Trinidad and Tobago's homicide rate also placed it among the world's most violent countries.

In contrast to the sub-Saharan African countries that round out this group of 14 countries, the LAC countries that lead the world in homicides are not among the world's poorest. They are, however, among the world's most unequal in terms of income distribution, a factor that is believed to be associated with high crime rates. Indeed, other countries in the region, including the economic powerhouses of Brazil and Mexico, have homicide rates that are many times higher than those of most developing nations. According to the UN Office on Drugs and Crime, in "Homicide Statistics 2013" (2013, http://www.unodc.org/documents/data-and-analysis/statistics/crime/Homicide_statistics2013.xls), Mexico's homicide rate was 23.7 per 100,000 people in 2011, and Brazil's was 21.8. Brazil had the second-highest number of homicides in the world in 2011, with 42,785, exceeded only by India (42,923), whose population of 1.2 billion was approximately five times larger but whose homicide rate (3.5) was more than six times lower. Mexico was the world's third most-murderous country by absolute numbers, with 27,199 homicides in 2011. Countries with high rates of inequality tend to have high rates of youth unemployment, increasing the likelihood that young men will turn to drugs, street gangs, and other forms of crime.

Inequality is not the only explanation for the high homicide rate in LAC countries. Another major factor is the region's status as a breeding ground for criminal

**FIGURE 5.6**

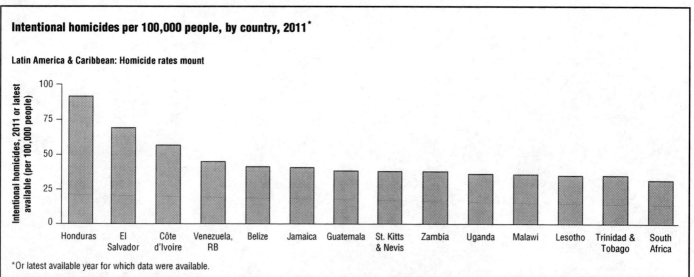

Intentional homicides per 100,000 people, by country, 2011*

Latin America & Caribbean: Homicide rates mount

*Or latest available year for which data were available.

SOURCE: "Latin America and Caribbean: Homicide Rates Mount," in *World Development Indicators 2013*, World Bank, Washington, D.C., 2013, http://databank.worldbank.org/data/download/WDI-2013-ebook.pdf (accessed October 3, 2013). DOI: 10.1596/978-0-8213-9824-1. License: Creative Commons Attribution CC BY 3.0.

organizations, including the extremely powerful Mexican and Central American drug cartels that control much of the flow of illegal substances into the United States. Additionally, the region has an abundance of firearms and comparatively ineffective systems of law enforcement and criminal justice. Finally, the LAC region is characterized by extremely high levels of violence against women. Sarah Bott et al., writing in *Violence against Women in Latin America and the Caribbean: A Comparative Analysis of Population-Based Data from 12 Countries* (2012, http://www2.paho.org/hq/dmdocuments/violence-against-women-lac.pdf), observe that intimate partner violence was widespread in all 12 countries surveyed and that "large proportions of women supported norms that reinforce gender inequality or discourage families and communities from helping women who experience violence."

Although poverty is not the sole driver of violence in the region, the poor are disproportionately affected by violent crime. Not only are they more likely to live in the most crime-ridden areas of towns and cities, they are also the least able to shield themselves from violence. In many of the LAC region's major cities, wealthier residents have responded to pervasive violence by settling in gated residences or neighborhoods and avoiding public spaces, options that are not available to the poor. This withdrawal from public life, as Tuluy notes, "ultimately weakens the interpersonal ties [that] form the foundations of society."

# CHAPTER 6
# POVERTY IN DEVELOPED COUNTRIES

## ASSESSING POVERTY IN WEALTHY COUNTRIES

Poverty in developing countries, as the preceding chapters make clear, often involves forms of deprivation so intense that they threaten survival and undermine health and opportunity across whole societies. In developed countries, poverty of this sort tends to be less widespread. Access to basic necessities such as clean water and sanitation facilities is universal or nearly so, and malnutrition is rare, with the exception of overweight and obesity, which tend to be more common than in the developing world. Most developed countries offer universal primary and secondary school, and they do not have widely divergent enrollment rates by gender. Child and maternal mortality rates are low by global standards, as are the rates of deadly communicable diseases such as HIV/AIDS, tuberculosis, and malaria. Poverty in the developed world, since it is less likely to overlap with the forms of deprivation measured by such metrics as the UN's Millennium Development Goals, is often harder to identify and to assess. It coexists alongside prosperity and is frequently less visible than in the developing world.

In the eyes of many poverty experts, the living standards of the prosperous are a key determinant of the definition of poverty in the developed world. In the wealthy countries of North America, Europe, and parts of Asia and Oceania, people can experience deprivation while having incomes that would mark them as part of the middle class in a developing country. This happens in part because the price of accessing numerous basic services and products is determined not by the cost of producing and selling those services and products, but by the economic law of supply and demand, which holds that the price for a good or service can rise or fall according to its scarcity or wide availability as well as according to the amount and intensity of the demand for it. In a country with large numbers of middle class and wealthy people, the prices of such necessities as food, shelter, and medical care can rise beyond the reach of people who otherwise would not appear poor by the standards of the developing world. Additionally, the poor in developed countries can find it extremely difficult to participate meaningfully in society. This can have effects on society and individuals that go beyond measurable levels of access to basic goods and services.

Some researchers and aid workers suggest that the poor in wealthy countries suffer more psychological problems and social isolation than those in low-income countries. In "Psychological Costs of Growing Up Poor" (*Annals of the New York Academy of Sciences*, vol. 1136, June 2008), Eric Dearing of Boston College summarizes the extensive literature available on the psychological development of youth growing up poor. He notes that "children and adolescents living in poverty often display dysfunction and delay in their cognitive, language, and social-emotional growth. In turn, these developmental problems in early life contribute to reduced earnings, involvement in crime, and mental health problems across the life span." Dearing adds that these problems usually arise when children grow up in extremely poor conditions over a prolonged period, but that living in poverty for even a brief period may result in a child developing mental health problems.

In his research synopsis, Dearing shows that poverty can affect both the social-emotional functioning and the cognitive (mental) functioning and achievement of youth by two different pathways. According to Dearing, results of studies show that poverty is associated with stress in parents who are poor. The stress of poverty is associated with mental health problems such as depression, which, in turn, is associated with parents being emotionally colder and harsher. These parental behaviors affect the social-emotional development and functioning of children. Likewise, the results of studies show another series of linked effects: poverty is associated with limited materials in the home that foster learning, such as books, and with limited parental involvement in the home learning environment. Thus, poor parents infrequently do things in the home that foster learning, such as reading to their children. The absence of these material, psychological, and social factors affects the cognitive functioning and achievement of children.

As discussed in Chapter 1, poverty measures that take into account average incomes and standards of living are called relative poverty thresholds. In most developed countries, and in most of the studies and statistics comparing poverty across the developed world, relative poverty thresholds are used to measure the prevalence of poverty.

## INCOME AND POVERTY TRENDS IN THE DEVELOPED WORLD

Across the developed world, the period from the 1980s through the first decade of the 21st century was marked by a dramatic increase both in the number of people earning high incomes and in the size of the highest incomes. Accordingly, the gap between the rich and the poor (usually defined as the amount of total income earned by the richest 10% of people versus the amount of total income earned by the poorest 10% of people) widened dramatically in most developed countries, although inequality was a much more pronounced problem in some developed countries than in others. Figure 6.1 shows the growth, over time, in the average Gini coefficient for the

## FIGURE 6.1

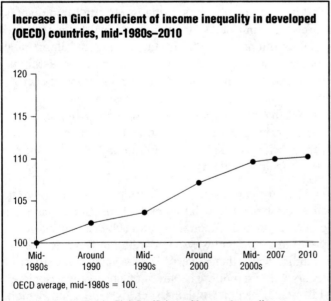

**Increase in Gini coefficient of income inequality in developed (OECD) countries, mid-1980s–2010**

OECD average, mid-1980s = 100.

SOURCE: "0. Increase in Gini Coefficient of Income Inequality at Disposable Income, Total Population," in *Statistics*, Organisation for Economic Co-operation and Development (OECD), 2013, http://www .oecd.org/els/soc/Income-Distribution-Brief-Figures&Data-Poverty.xlsx (accessed October 25, 2013). *Income Distribution and Poverty at the OECD*, http://www.oecd.org/social/inequality.htm.)

member countries of the Organisation for Economic Co-operation and Development (OECD), most of which are considered developed nations. The Gini coefficient is a measure of income inequality in a country; higher numbers indicate greater inequality.

The mid-1990s through the first decade of the 21st century were a period during which income inequality grew at a particularly rapid pace. Although the rate of Gini coefficient growth slowed between 2007 and 2010, this was not necessarily a sign that inequality in market incomes (incomes derived from work or capital) was decreasing. As the OECD notes in *Crisis Squeezes Income and Puts Pressure on Inequality and Poverty* (2013, http://www.oecd.org/els/soc/OECD2013-Inequality-and-Poverty-8p.pdf), average household market income fell by 2% per year between 2007 and 2010 due to the high unemployment and falling wages that resulted from the Great Recession of 2007 to 2009. Because of social safety-net programs such as unemployment benefits, however, and because falling incomes result in decreased tax liability (the amount of money owed in taxes), total income fell less than market income. Setting aside the effect of safety-net programs and taxes, inequality actually increased between 2007 and 2010. In the 17 countries for which the OECD had long-term data as of 2013, market income inequality increased more rapidly in those three years than it had in the preceding twelve years, suggesting that poorer workers bore the brunt of the overall declines in market income while wealthier people were less affected by the difficult economy of these years. Inequality increased most rapidly in the countries that were hardest-hit by unemployment and falling wages, such as Estonia, Ireland, Greece, Japan, and Spain. Overall, the OECD countries with the highest levels of income inequality in 2010 were, in descending order, Chile, Mexico, Turkey, the United States, and Israel. (See Figure 6.2.)

The OECD countries with the highest levels of inequality also tended to have higher-than-average percentages of people living in relative poverty (those living on less than half of the national median income). While the relative poverty rate for the OECD as a whole was 11% in 2010, the rate was between 18% and 21% in Chile, Israel, Mexico, and Turkey. (See Figure 6.3.) Spain, Japan, and the United States also had relative poverty rates that exceeded 15%. By contrast, the Czech Republic, Denmark, Finland, Hungary, Iceland, Luxembourg, the Netherlands, and Norway all had relative poverty rates of between 5% and 8%.

As with measures of inequality, however, relative poverty rates are not necessarily good indications of total poverty during a recession. Since relative poverty is pegged to median incomes, and median incomes fall during a recession, relative poverty rates can decrease even when a

**FIGURE 6.2**

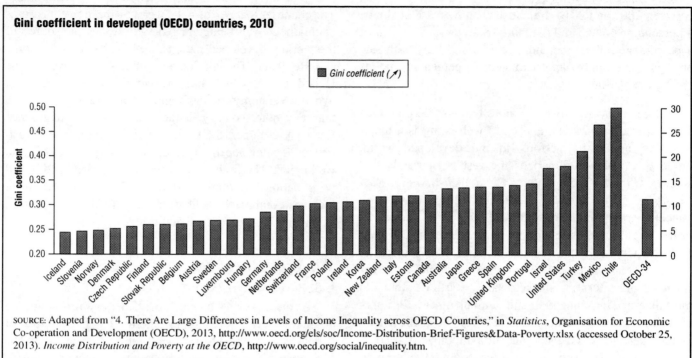

Gini coefficient in developed (OECD) countries, 2010

□ Gini coefficient (↗)

SOURCE: Adapted from "4. There Are Large Differences in Levels of Income Inequality across OECD Countries," in *Statistics*, Organisation for Economic Co-operation and Development (OECD), 2013, http://www.oecd.org/els/soc/Income-Distribution-Brief-Figures&Data-Poverty.xlsx (accessed October 25, 2013). *Income Distribution and Poverty at the OECD*, http://www.oecd.org/social/inequality.htm.

**FIGURE 6.3**

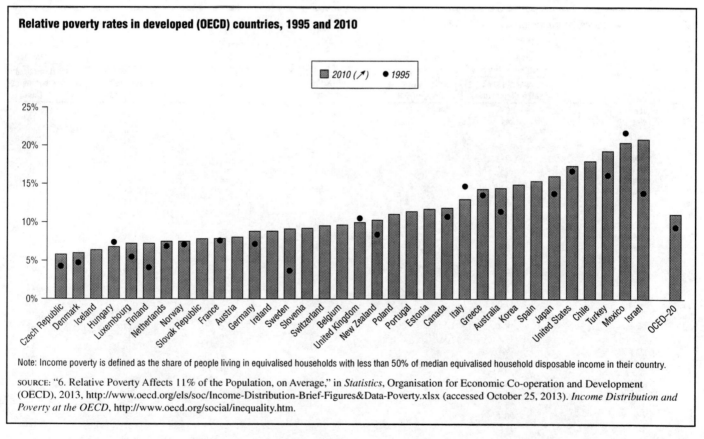

Relative poverty rates in developed (OECD) countries, 1995 and 2010

■ 2010 (↗)  ● 1995

Note: Income poverty is defined as the share of people living in equivalised households with less than 50% of median equivalised household disposable income in their country.

SOURCE: "6. Relative Poverty Affects 11% of the Population, on Average," in *Statistics*, Organisation for Economic Co-operation and Development (OECD), 2013, http://www.oecd.org/els/soc/Income-Distribution-Brief-Figures&Data-Poverty.xlsx (accessed October 25, 2013). *Income Distribution and Poverty at the OECD*, http://www.oecd.org/social/inequality.htm.

growing number of people fall into actual poverty. After controlling for this factor, the OECD finds in *Crisis Squeezes Income and Puts Pressure on Inequality and Poverty* that actual poverty rates were increasing substantially in a number of countries that had stable rates of relative poverty. Greece and Spain, for example, saw actual poverty increase by approximately 5 percentage points between 2007 and 2010; Ireland saw an increase of almost 4 percentage points; and Estonia saw an increase of almost 3 percentage points. Iceland, Mexico, and Italy each saw poverty increase by approximately 2 percentage points during this period.

Children are significantly more likely to be poor than adults in most countries, and child well-being is a major focus of antipoverty efforts in the developed world. Table 6.1, which summarizes the results of the United Nations Children's Fund study *Child Well-Being in Rich Countries: A Comparative Overview* (2013, http://www.unicef-irc.org/publications/pdf/rc11_eng.pdf), shows 29 of the world's richest countries ranked according to their performance on five measures of child well-being. The dimensions are material well-being (poverty rates and other financial indicators), health and safety (birth health, child mortality, and immunization rates, among other indicators), education (school participation as well as achievement levels), behaviors and risks (nutritional indicators, alcohol and drug use, and exposure to violence, among other indicators), and housing and environment (the quality and safety of the household and neighborhood environment). The countries that perform the worst by these five measures of childhood well-being are generally among the poorest of the world's developed nations, such as Lithuania, Latvia, and Romania. The glaring exception to this rule is the United States, which has the world's largest and most dynamic economy and has a higher concentration of wealth than any other country in the world. In spite of its vast financial resources, the United States is among the lowest-performing developed countries on these measures of child well-being. The highest-performing countries in 2009–10 were nations in northern Europe that have per capita incomes comparable to that of the United States as well as much more extensive social safety-net programs.

## THE UNITED STATES

### U.S. Poverty Statistics

As discussed in Chapter 1, the U.S. government uses an absolute poverty measure in determining the number of people who are living in poverty at any given time. The U.S. poverty measures vary by household size and composition, and they are meant to correspond to a household's

**TABLE 6.1**

Child well-being in developed countries, 2009–10

| | | Overall well-being<br>Average rank<br>(all 5 dimensions) | Dimension 1<br>Material<br>well-being<br>(rank) | Dimension 2<br>Health and<br>safety (rank) | Dimension 3<br>Education<br>(rank) | Dimension 4<br>Behaviours and<br>risks (rank) | Dimension 5<br>Housing and<br>environment<br>(rank) |
|---|---|---|---|---|---|---|---|
| 1 | Netherlands | 2.4 | 1 | 5 | 1 | 1 | 4 |
| 2 | Norway | 4.6 | 3 | 7 | 6 | 4 | 3 |
| 3 | Iceland | 5.0 | 4 | 1 | 10 | 3 | 7 |
| 4 | Finland | 5.4 | 2 | 3 | 4 | 12 | 6 |
| 5 | Sweden | 6.2 | 5 | 2 | 11 | 5 | 8 |
| 6 | Germany | 9.0 | 11 | 12 | 3 | 6 | 13 |
| 7 | Luxembourg | 9.2 | 6 | 4 | 22 | 9 | 5 |
| 8 | Switzerland | 9.6 | 9 | 11 | 16 | 11 | 1 |
| 9 | Belgium | 11.2 | 13 | 13 | 2 | 14 | 14 |
| 10 | Ireland | 11.6 | 17 | 15 | 17 | 7 | 2 |
| 11 | Denmark | 11.8 | 12 | 23 | 7 | 2 | 15 |
| 12 | Slovenia | 12.0 | 8 | 6 | 5 | 21 | 20 |
| 13 | France | 12.8 | 10 | 10 | 15 | 13 | 16 |
| 14 | Czech Republic | 15.2 | 16 | 8 | 12 | 22 | 18 |
| 15 | Portugal | 15.6 | 21 | 14 | 18 | 8 | 17 |
| 16 | United Kingdom | 15.8 | 14 | 16 | 24 | 15 | 10 |
| 17 | Canada | 16.6 | 15 | 27 | 14 | 16 | 11 |
| 18 | Austria | 17.0 | 7 | 26 | 23 | 17 | 12 |
| 19 | Spain | 17.6 | 24 | 9 | 26 | 20 | 9 |
| 20 | Hungary | 18.4 | 18 | 20 | 8 | 24 | 22 |
| 21 | Poland | 18.8 | 22 | 18 | 9 | 19 | 26 |
| 22 | Italy | 19.2 | 23 | 17 | 25 | 10 | 21 |
| 23 | Estonia | 20.8 | 19 | 22 | 13 | 26 | 24 |
| 23 | Slovakia | 20.8 | 25 | 21 | 21 | 18 | 19 |
| 25 | Greece | 23.4 | 20 | 19 | 28 | 25 | 25 |
| 26 | United States | 24.8 | 26 | 25 | 27 | 23 | 23 |
| 27 | Lithuania | 25.2 | 27 | 24 | 19 | 29 | 27 |
| 28 | Latvia | 26.4 | 28 | 28 | 20 | 28 | 28 |
| 29 | Romania | 28.6 | 29 | 29 | 29 | 27 | 29 |

Note: Lack of data on a number of indicators means that the following countries, although the Office of Economic Cooperation and Development (OECD) and/or European Union (EU) members, could not be included in the league table of child well-being: Australia, Bulgaria, Chile, Cyprus, Israel, Japan, Malta, Mexico, New Zealand, the Republic of Korea, and Turkey.

SOURCE: "Part 1. A League Table of Child Well-Being," in "Child Well-Being in Rich Countries: A Comparative Overview," *Innocenti Report Card 11*, UNICEF Office of Research, Florence, 2013, http://www.unicef-irc.org/publications/pdf/rc11_eng.pdf (accessed October 28, 2013)

ability to satisfy its nutritional and other basic needs. The official poverty guidelines issued by the U.S. Department of Health and Human Services (HHS), which are used by various federal and state agencies to determine eligibility for a wide range of government assistance programs, do not specify whether the income thresholds established each year refer to before-tax or after-tax income. This distinction, as well as others relating to the application of federal poverty guidelines, is determined by the individual agencies who administer government programs using the guidelines.

The U.S. Census Bureau, which provides the most thorough official measurements of poverty, uses its own poverty thresholds (which are closely related to the HHS poverty guidelines) to assess the extent of poverty in the United States. The Census Bureau's measurements are based on before-tax income. Carmen DeNavas-Walt, Bernadette D. Proctor, and Jessica C. Smith of the Census Bureau report in *Income, Poverty, and Health Insurance Coverage in the United States: 2012* (September 2013, http://www.census .gov/prod/2013pubs/p60-245.pdf) that 46.5 million U.S. residents were living below the national poverty line as of 2012. (See Figure 6.4.) This was roughly 15% of the population. These numbers were unchanged over the preceding two years, but they were up substantially since 2007, the year that the Great Recession began. The recession officially lasted from late 2007 through mid-2009, but its aftereffects remained pronounced through 2013.

Certain demographic groups in the United States were far more likely to live in poverty than others. In 2012, 9.7% of non-Hispanic whites lived in poverty, compared with 11.7% of Asian Americans, 25.6% of Hispanics, and 27.2% of African Americans. (See Table 6.2.) Women (16.3%) were more likely to live in poverty than men (13.6%), and children (21.8%) were far more likely to live in poverty than adults aged 18 to 64 years (13.7%) or the elderly (9.1%). Foreign-born U.S. residents as a whole (19.2%) were more likely to live in poverty than native-born residents (14.3%), but foreign-born residents who were naturalized citizens (12.4%) were less likely than the native-born to live in poverty. A quarter of foreign-born noncitizens lived in poverty.

Regionally, Table 6.2 shows that poverty was more prevalent in the South (16.5%) and West (15.1%) than the Northeast (13.6%) or Midwest (13.6%). Those living in cities (19.7%) or in rural areas (outside metropolitan

**FIGURE 6.4**

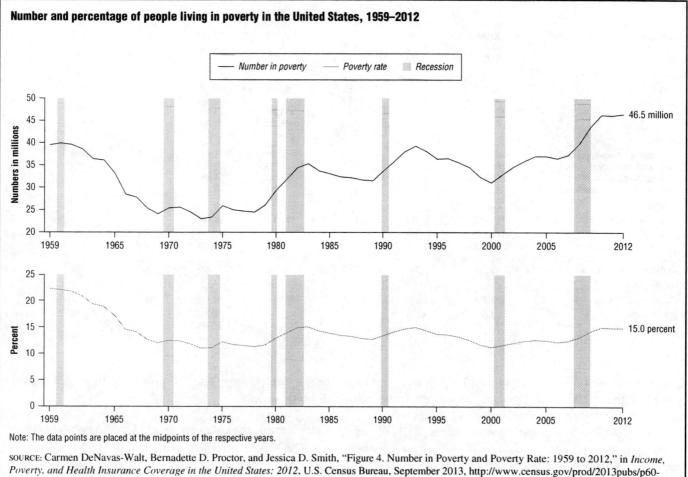

Number and percentage of people living in poverty in the United States, 1959–2012

Note: The data points are placed at the midpoints of the respective years.

SOURCE: Carmen DeNavas-Walt, Bernadette D. Proctor, and Jessica D. Smith, "Figure 4. Number in Poverty and Poverty Rate: 1959 to 2012," in *Income, Poverty, and Health Insurance Coverage in the United States: 2012*, U.S. Census Bureau, September 2013, http://www.census.gov/prod/2013pubs/p60-245.pdf (accessed November 6, 2013)

## TABLE 6.2

**People in poverty in the United States by selected characteristics, 2011 and 2012**

[Numbers in thousands. People as of March of the following year.]

| Characteristic | Total | 2011 Below poverty Number | 2011 Below poverty Percent | Total | 2012 Below poverty Number | 2012 Below poverty Percent | Change in poverty (2012 less 2011)[a] Number | Change in poverty (2012 less 2011)[a] Percent |
|---|---|---|---|---|---|---|---|---|
| **People** | | | | | | | | |
| Total | 308,456 | 46,247 | 15.0 | 310,648 | 46,496 | 15.0 | 249 | Z |
| **Family status** | | | | | | | | |
| In families | 252,316 | 33,126 | 13.1 | 252,863 | 33,198 | 13.1 | 72 | Z |
| Householder | 80,529 | 9,497 | 11.8 | 80,944 | 9,520 | 11.8 | 24 | Z |
| Related children under age 18 | 72,568 | 15,539 | 21.4 | 72,545 | 15,437 | 21.3 | −102 | −0.1 |
| Related children under age 6 | 23,860 | 5,844 | 24.5 | 23,604 | 5,769 | 24.4 | −75 | −0.1 |
| In unrelated subfamilies | 1,623 | 705 | 43.4 | 1,599 | 740 | 46.3 | 35 | 2.9 |
| Reference person | 671 | 272 | 40.6 | 641 | 278 | 43.3 | 5 | 2.7 |
| Children under age 18 | 846 | 409 | 48.4 | 855 | 440 | 51.4 | 30 | 3.0 |
| Unrelated individuals | 54,517 | 12,416 | 22.8 | 56,185 | 12,558 | 22.4 | 142 | −0.4 |
| **Race[b] and Hispanic Origin** | | | | | | | | |
| White | 241,334 | 30,849 | 12.8 | 242,147 | 30,816 | 12.7 | −33 | −0.1 |
| White, not Hispanic | 194,960 | 19,171 | 9.8 | 195,112 | 18,940 | 9.7 | −231 | −0.1 |
| Black | 39,609 | 10,929 | 27.6 | 40,125 | 10,911 | 27.2 | −18 | −0.4 |
| Asian | 16,086 | 1,973 | 12.3 | 16,417 | 1,921 | 11.7 | −52 | −0.6 |
| Hispanic (any race) | 52,279 | 13,244 | 25.3 | 53,105 | 13,616 | 25.6 | 371 | 0.3 |
| **Sex** | | | | | | | | |
| Male | 150,990 | 20,501 | 13.6 | 152,058 | 20,656 | 13.6 | 155 | Z |
| Female | 157,466 | 25,746 | 16.3 | 158,590 | 25,840 | 16.3 | 94 | −0.1 |
| **Age** | | | | | | | | |
| Under age 18 | 73,737 | 16,134 | 21.9 | 73,719 | 16,073 | 21.8 | −61 | −0.1 |
| Aged 18 to 64 | 193,213 | 26,492 | 13.7 | 193,642 | 26,497 | 13.7 | 4 | Z |
| Aged 65 and older | 41,507 | 3,620 | 8.7 | 43,287 | 3,926 | 9.1 | *305 | 0.3 |
| **Nativity** | | | | | | | | |
| Native born | 268,490 | 38,661 | 14.4 | 270,570 | 38,803 | 14.3 | 142 | −0.1 |
| Foreign born | 39,966 | 7,586 | 19.0 | 40,078 | 7,693 | 19.2 | 107 | 0.2 |
| Naturalized citizen | 17,934 | 2,233 | 12.5 | 18,193 | 2,252 | 12.4 | 19 | −0.1 |
| Not a citizen | 22,032 | 5,353 | 24.3 | 21,885 | 5,441 | 24.9 | 87 | 0.6 |
| **Region** | | | | | | | | |
| Northeast | 54,977 | 7,208 | 13.1 | 55,050 | 7,490 | 13.6 | 282 | 0.5 |
| Midwest | 66,023 | 9,221 | 14.0 | 66,337 | 8,851 | 13.3 | −370 | −0.6 |
| South | 114,936 | 18,380 | 16.0 | 115,957 | 19,106 | 16.5 | *726 | 0.5 |
| West | 72,520 | 11,437 | 15.8 | 73,303 | 11,049 | 15.1 | −388 | *−0.7 |
| **Residence** | | | | | | | | |
| Inside metropolitan statistical areas | 261,155 | 38,202 | 14.6 | 262,949 | 38,033 | 14.5 | −169 | −0.2 |
| Inside principal cities | 100,183 | 20,007 | 20.0 | 101,225 | 19,934 | 19.7 | −73 | −0.3 |
| Outside principal cities | 160,973 | 18,195 | 11.3 | 161,724 | 18,099 | 11.2 | −96 | −0.1 |
| Outside metropolitan statistical areas[c] | 47,301 | 8,045 | 17.0 | 47,698 | 8,463 | 17.7 | *418 | 0.7 |
| **Work experience** | | | | | | | | |
| Total, aged 18 to 64 | 193,213 | 26,492 | 13.7 | 193,642 | 26,497 | 13.7 | 4 | Z |
| All workers | 144,163 | 10,345 | 7.2 | 145,814 | 10,672 | 7.3 | 327 | 0.1 |
| Worked full-time, year-round | 97,443 | 2,732 | 2.8 | 98,715 | 2,867 | 2.9 | 135 | 0.1 |
| Less than full-time, year-round | 46,720 | 7,614 | 16.3 | 47,099 | 7,805 | 16.6 | 191 | 0.3 |
| Did not work at least 1 week | 49,049 | 16,147 | 32.9 | 47,828 | 15,825 | 33.1 | −322 | 0.2 |
| **Disability status[d]** | | | | | | | | |
| Total, aged 18 to 64 | 193,213 | 26,492 | 13.7 | 193,642 | 26,497 | 13.7 | 4 | Z |
| With a disability | 14,968 | 4,313 | 28.8 | 14,996 | 4,257 | 28.4 | −56 | −0.4 |
| With no disability | 177,309 | 22,105 | 12.5 | 177,727 | 22,189 | 12.5 | 84 | Z |

statistical areas; 17.7%) were more likely to live in poverty than those living in suburbs (inside metropolitan statistical areas but outside principal cities; 11.2%). Although few full-time, year-round workers (2.9%) lived below the poverty line in 2012, 16.6% of those who worked part time were poor, and 33.1% of those who worked less than one week during the year were poor. Over a quarter (28.4%) of those with disabilities lived

below the poverty line, compared with 12.5% of nondisabled people.

### Criticisms of the Calculation of U.S. Poverty Thresholds

The U.S. government uses the cost of a basic supply of food as the baseline measure for determining poverty. When the U.S. poverty threshold was established in the late 1950s, researchers estimated that a typical family spent

Z = Represents or rounds to zero.
*An asterisk preceding an estimate indicates change is statistically different from zero at the 90 percent confidence level.
<sup>a</sup>Details may not sum to totals because of rounding.
<sup>b</sup>Federal surveys give respondents the option of reporting more than one race. Therefore, two basic ways of defining a race group are possible. A group such as Asian may be defined as those who reported Asian and no other race (the race-alone or single-race concept) or as those who reported Asian regardless of whether they also reported another race (the race-alone-or-in-combination concept). This table shows data using the first approach (race alone). The use of the single-race population does not imply that it is the preferred method of presenting or analyzing data. The Census Bureau uses a variety of approaches. Information on people who reported more than one race, such as white *and* American Indian and Alaska Native or Asian *and* black or African American, is available from Census 2010 through American FactFinder. About 2.9 percent of people reported more than one race in Census 2010. Data for American Indians and Alaska Natives, Native Hawaiians and other Pacific Islanders, and those reporting two or more races are not shown separately.
<sup>c</sup>The "Outside metropolitan statistical areas" category includes both micropolitan statistical areas and territory outside of metropolitan and micropolitan statistical areas. For more information, see "About Metropolitan and Micropolitan Statistical Areas" at <www.census.gov/population/www/estimates/aboutmetro.html>.
<sup>d</sup>The sum of those with and without a disability does not equal the total because disability status is not defined for individuals in the armed forces.

SOURCE: Carmen DeNavas-Walt, Bernadette D. Proctor, and Jessica D. Smith, "Table 3. People In Poverty by Selected Characteristics, 2011 and 2012," in *Income, Poverty, and Health Insurance Coverage in the United States: 2012*, U.S. Census Bureau, September 2013, http://www.census.gov/prod/2013pubs/p60-245.pdf (accessed November 6, 2013)

one-third of its income on food. Therefore, the cost of a minimally nutritious diet, multiplied by three, was determined to be the minimum income a person or household must make to be considered capable of meeting basic survival needs. Those people and households with less than this amount of income are officially considered impoverished and are eligible for a variety of means-tested (income-based) forms of government assistance.

Many advocates for the poor consider the official U.S. poverty criteria to be outdated. They point out that housing costs were much lower in the 1950s, when the poverty guidelines were first established, than in the early 21st century. Since housing frequently accounts for much more of a 21st-century low-income household's spending than in the 1950s—in some cases far exceeding one-third of total income—a household might have triple the income required to satisfy its dietary requirements and still not be able to afford housing. Additionally, cultural changes have changed the basic financial requirements of many households. For example, in the 1950s the most common household arrangement was one in which a man worked and a woman was a homemaker who took care of her own children during the workweek. In the 21st century it is the norm—and often a financial necessity—for both partners in a couple to work, and single motherhood is far more common than at midcentury. Access to child care outside of the home has thus become a necessity for many households, and such care is frequently one of the largest single household expenses in any given month. Yet paid child care was virtually unheard of in the 1950s, when poverty researchers determined the percentages of income that must be allotted to various household expenses.

Additionally, critics of the poverty guidelines point out that they are ineffective at accounting for wide disparities in the cost of living from region to region and between urban, suburban, and rural locations. For example, Dawn Wotapka reports in "New York City

Rents Pass $3,000 Mark" (WSJ.com, October 1, 2013) that as of October 2013 the average rent in New York City was $3,049 per month. By comparison, Ilyce Glink states in "Top 10 Cheapest U.S. Cities to Rent an Apartment" (CBSNews.com, July 20, 2013) the average rent in Wichita, Kansas, was $623 per month in July 2013. Despite such a drastic disparity in living costs, households are subject to the same poverty guidelines in both places. A family of three living exactly at the 2014 U.S. poverty line of $19,790 would have a monthly income of $1,649.17, barely more than half of the average rent in New York City.

Critics also suggest that the overall picture of poverty provided by the Census Bureau is inaccurate since the agency determines poverty by computing before-tax income, not after-tax income. Although many poor people do not make enough money to be required to pay federal income tax, many are required to pay state income taxes as well as payroll taxes. After-tax income represents the money a household actually has available for satisfying its basic needs, in this view, and should therefore be the standard for determining which U.S. residents are unable to meet their needs and thereby fall below the poverty line.

These are just a few of the criticisms leveled at the U.S. federal government's standards for assessing the prevalence of poverty. In 2010, in response to an ongoing study about the need to supplement the picture of poverty provided by the official U.S. guidelines, an interagency working group consisting of representatives from various federal agencies suggested the creation of a Supplemental Poverty Measure (SPM). In 2011 the Census Bureau began releasing data on poverty using the SPM in addition to the official poverty guidelines. Although the SPM results in an altered picture of poverty, it does not address the widespread notion that the official poverty measure fails to count millions of people whose living conditions mark them as impoverished. As Mark Levinson writes in

"Mismeasuring Poverty" (Prospect.org, June 25, 2012), the official poverty measure was created as a part of President Lyndon B. Johnson's (1908–1973) War on Poverty, a combination of federal programs designed to aid "those whose basic needs exceed their means to satisfy them," but tens of millions of Americans fit this description although they do not technically qualify as poor according to the official poverty guidelines or according to the SPM. In place of the existing U.S. absolute poverty measures, Levinson and many other advocates for low-income Americans suggest that a relative poverty measure pegged to median income is necessary.

## EUROPE

The European Union (EU) is an economic and political alliance of 28 European countries (as of 2014) whose collective level of economic development is comparable to that of the United States and whose population of over 500 million is significantly larger. (See Table 6.3.) Eurostat, the EU's statistical office, collects and distributes a wide range of economic data on member countries. In assessing poverty levels, Eurostat uses an "at-risk-of-poverty threshold" set at 60% of a country's national median after-tax income. This threshold represents a much broader definition of poverty than that used by the U.S. government, so caution should be used when comparing European and U.S. statistics. Since standards of living vary widely among EU states, the Eurostat threshold is adjusted according to national purchasing power standards, an attempt to account for price differences across borders. Although Iceland, Switzerland, and Norway are not official members of the EU, they are included in the statistical portraits of poverty produced by Eurostat.

Table 6.4 shows that 16.9% of the EU population fell below the at-risk-of-poverty threshold in 2011 after social transfers (cash payments and other forms of government assistance) were taken into account. (Croatia did not join the EU until 2013, so in 2011 there were 27 member states.) At-risk-of-poverty rates varied widely among the 31 countries surveyed: rates hovered near 10% in the nations with the least poverty, such as Iceland (9.2%), the Czech Republic (9.8%), and Norway (10.5%), while

rates were at or above 20% in Lithuania (20%), Croatia (21.1%), Greece (21.4%), Spain (21.8%), Romania (22.2%), and Bulgaria (22.3%). The at-risk-of-poverty rates were either flat or growing in most EU states between 2010 and 2011, although some nations (Cyprus, Denmark, Iceland, Ireland, Latvia, Lithuania, Luxembourg, Norway, and the United Kingdom) saw decreases in their at-risk populations.

In general, European women were slightly more likely to be impoverished or at risk of impoverishment than men: 17.6% of women fell below the EU threshold in 2011, compared with 16.1% of men. (See Table 6.4.) In some countries—Bulgaria, Cyprus, Slovenia, Sweden, Switzerland, and the United Kingdom—however, the gap between the poverty rates of women and men was significantly larger. In Estonia, Hungary, Ireland, Latvia, and Poland, meanwhile, men were slightly more likely than women to be poor or at risk of being poor.

Household type was linked to the risk of poverty in EU countries in 2011. (See Table 6.5.) The households most likely to be at risk of poverty were those consisting of single parents with dependent children, 34.5% of which fell below the Eurostat poverty threshold, followed by single-person households (25.7%), and households with two or more adults and three or more dependent children (24.8%). Households with two adults and no dependent children (11.1%) as well as households with two adults and one dependent child (12.7%) were much less likely to be at risk. Two-person households without dependent children in which at least one person was 65 years of age and older were also comparatively unlikely to be in or at risk of poverty (12.7%).

Although single persons and families with three or more children were among the most likely groups to be at risk of poverty in all EU countries, the rates at which each group experienced poverty varied widely from country to country. (See Table 6.5.) For example, 78.2% of Bulgarian two-parent families with three or more children were at risk of poverty, compared with only 8% of Icelandic households of the same type. Similarly, single people in Bulgaria (50.7%), Croatia (44%), and Slovenia (40%) were much more likely

**TABLE 6.3**

### List of European Union (EU) member states (EU-28) as of July 2013

| | | | | | | | |
|---|---|---|---|---|---|---|---|
| Belgium | (BE) | Greece | (EL) | Lithuania | (LT) | Portugal | (PT) |
| Bulgaria | (BG) | Spain | (ES) | Luxembourg | (LU) | Romania | (RO) |
| Czech Republic | (CZ) | France | (FR) | Hungary | (HU) | Slovenia | (SI) |
| Denmark | (DK) | Croatia | (HR) | Malta | (MT) | Slovakia | (SK) |
| Germany | (DE) | Italy | (IT) | Netherlands | (NL) | Finland | (FI) |
| Estonia | (EE) | Cyprus | (CY) | Austria | (AT) | Sweden | (SE) |
| Ireland | (IE) | Latvia | (LV) | Poland | (PL) | United Kingdom | (UK) |

SOURCE: "Overview of Present EU Member States," in *Glossary: EU Enlargements*, Eurostat, July 11, 2013, http://epp.eurostat.ec.europa.eu/statistics_explained/index.php/Glossary:EU-27 (accessed November 7, 2013)

**TABLE 6.4**

**Percentage of EU residents at risk of poverty, by country and gender, 2009–11**

| | Total | | | Male | | | Female | | |
|---|---|---|---|---|---|---|---|---|---|
| | 2009 | 2010 | 2011 | 2009 | 2010 | 2011 | 2009 | 2010 | 2011 |
| EU-28 | — | 16.4 | 16.9 | — | 15.7 | 16.1 | — | 17.1 | 17.6 |
| EU-27 | 16.3 | 16.3 | 16.9 | 15.4 | 15.6 | 16.1 | 17.1 | 17.0 | 17.6 |
| Euro area | 15.9 | 16.1 | 16.8 | 14.9 | 15.3 | 16.1 | 16.8 | 16.9 | 17.6 |
| Belgium | 14.6 | 14.6 | 15.3 | 13.4 | 13.9 | 14.6 | 15.7 | 15.2 | 16.0 |
| Bulgaria | 21.8 | 20.7 | 22.3 | 19.8 | 19.0 | 20.8 | 23.7 | 22.3 | 23.6 |
| Czech Republic | 8.6 | 9.0 | 9.8 | 7.5 | 8.0 | 8.9 | 9.5 | 10.0 | 10.6 |
| Denmark | 13.1 | 13.3 | 13.0 | 12.8 | 13.1 | 13.0 | 13.4 | 13.4 | 13.0 |
| Germany | 15.5 | 15.6 | 15.8 | 14.7 | 14.9 | 14.9 | 16.3 | 16.4 | 16.8 |
| Estonia | 19.7 | 15.8 | 17.5 | 17.5 | 15.4 | 17.6 | 21.6 | 16.2 | 17.4 |
| Ireland | 15.0 | 16.1 | 15.2 | 14.9 | 15.9 | 15.4 | 15.1 | 16.2 | 14.9 |
| Greece | 19.7 | 20.1 | 21.4 | 19.1 | 19.3 | 20.9 | 20.2 | 20.9 | 21.9 |
| Spain | 19.5 | 20.7 | 21.8 | 18.3 | 20.1 | 21.1 | 20.6 | 21.3 | 22.4 |
| France | 12.9 | 13.3 | 14.0 | 11.9 | 12.6 | 13.5 | 13.8 | 13.9 | 14.5 |
| Croatia[b] | 17.9 | 20.5 | 21.1 | 16.0 | 19.7 | 20.0 | 19.7 | 21.3 | 22.1 |
| Italy | 18.4 | 18.2 | 19.6 | 17.0 | 16.8 | 18.3 | 19.8 | 19.5 | 20.8 |
| Cyprus | 15.8 | 15.1 | 14.5 | 13.7 | 13.5 | 12.7 | 17.8 | 16.7 | 16.2 |
| Latvia[a] | 25.7 | 21.3 | 19.1 | 24.2 | 21.7 | 20.0 | 27.0 | 21.0 | 18.4 |
| Lithuania | 20.6 | 20.2 | 20.0 | 19.1 | 20.7 | 19.8 | 21.9 | 19.8 | 20.1 |
| Luxembourg | 14.9 | 14.5 | 13.6 | 13.8 | 14.6 | 12.7 | 16.0 | 14.4 | 14.5 |
| Hungary | 12.4 | 12.3 | 13.8 | 12.8 | 12.6 | 14.1 | 12.1 | 12.0 | 13.6 |
| Malta | 15.3 | 15.0 | 15.4 | 14.7 | 14.5 | 15.0 | 15.9 | 15.5 | 15.8 |
| Netherlands | 11.1 | 10.3 | 11.0 | 10.8 | 9.7 | 10.8 | 11.3 | 10.8 | 11.1 |
| Austria | 12.0 | 12.1 | 12.6 | 10.7 | 10.7 | 11.7 | 13.2 | 13.5 | 13.5 |
| Poland | 17.1 | 17.6 | 17.7 | 16.9 | 17.4 | 17.8 | 17.4 | 17.7 | 17.6 |
| Portugal | 17.9 | 17.9 | 18.0 | 17.3 | 17.3 | 17.6 | 18.4 | 18.4 | 18.4 |
| Romania | 22.4 | 21.1 | 22.2 | 21.4 | 20.7 | 21.9 | 23.4 | 21.4 | 22.5 |
| Slovenia | 11.3 | 12.7 | 13.6 | 9.8 | 11.3 | 12.2 | 12.8 | 14.1 | 15.0 |
| Slovakia | 11.0 | 12.0 | 13.0 | 10.1 | 11.7 | 12.8 | 11.8 | 12.2 | 13.1 |
| Finland | 13.8 | 13.1 | 13.7 | 12.9 | 12.4 | 13.2 | 14.7 | 13.8 | 14.2 |
| Sweden | 13.3 | 12.9 | 14.0 | 12.0 | 11.4 | 12.2 | 14.5 | 14.3 | 15.7 |
| United Kingdom | 17.3 | 17.1 | 16.2 | 16.7 | 16.4 | 14.8 | 17.8 | 17.8 | 17.6 |
| Iceland | 10.2 | 9.8 | 9.2 | 9.3 | 9.8 | 9.0 | 11.1 | 9.8 | 9.5 |
| Norway | 11.7 | 11.2 | 10.5 | 10.1 | 10.1 | 9.9 | 13.2 | 12.2 | 11.1 |
| Switzerland | 15.1 | 15.0 | 15.0 | 13.5 | 13.8 | 13.7 | 16.7 | 16.2 | 16.3 |

[a]Break in series, 2011.
[b]Break in series, 2010.
Note: EU = European Union.

SOURCE: "Table 1. At-Risk-of-Poverty Rate after Social Transfers, 2009–2011 (%)," in *Income Distribution Statistics*, Eurostat, March 2013, http://epp.eurostat .ec.europa.eu/statistics_explained/index.php/Income_distribution_statistics (accessed November 7, 2013)

to live in or at risk of poverty than single people in most other European countries. The percentage of single-parent households who fell below the at-risk-of-poverty threshold was more consistent across EU countries; the percentage of such households surpassed 30% in 21 countries and was between 25% and 30% in another 6 countries.

European governments generally spend a greater share of their total income on social transfers—payments and subsidies to the poor, the elderly, the unemployed, and the ill and disabled—than does the U.S. government. The larger size of European countries' safety-net systems is attributable both to broader eligibility standards for assistance and to more generous benefit levels. Eurostat measures the effectiveness of social transfers at alleviating poverty by comparing poverty indicators before and after social transfer payments are made. As Figure 6.5 shows, social transfer programs do not lift everyone in Europe out of risk of poverty, but in all countries they substantially decrease the percentage of those who fall

below the at-risk-of-poverty threshold. In 2011, Denmark, Hungary, Iceland, Ireland, and Norway reduced the percentage of their populations experiencing poverty risk by half or more through social transfers, and many other European states approached this level of poverty reduction. Social transfer programs were less effective at reducing poverty risk in such countries as Bulgaria, Greece, Italy, Poland, Romania, and Slovakia.

In addition to assessing poverty levels, Eurostat also collects statistics related to social exclusion, or the inability to participate in society, which overlaps with but is not identical to poverty. According to Eurostat, people are at risk of poverty or social exclusion if they experience one of the three following conditions: their income falls below the at-risk-of-poverty threshold, they experience severe material deprivation as measured by the inability to purchase certain basic necessities, or they live in a household with very low work intensity (meaning a low ratio of months in a given year that all

TABLE 6.5

**Percentage of EU residents at risk of poverty, by country and household type, 2011**

| | Households without dependent children | | | Households with dependent children | | |
|---|---|---|---|---|---|---|
| | Single person | Two adults at least one aged 65 years or over | Two or more adults without dependent children | Single person with dependent children | Two adults with one dependent child | Two adults with three or more dependent children |
| EL-28 | 25.7 | 12.7 | 11.2 | 34.5 | 12.7 | 24.8 |
| EU-27 | 25.7 | 12.6 | 11.1 | 34.5 | 12.7 | 24.8 |
| Euro area | 25.7 | 12.4 | 11.2 | 35.1 | 12.6 | 23.2 |
| Belgium | 21.4 | 22.0 | 12.8 | 38.5 | 9.2 | 16.7 |
| Bulgaria | 50.7 | 24.4 | 14.4 | 35.4 | 13.2 | 78.2 |
| Czech Republic | 18.2 | 2.7 | 4.5 | 35.6 | 6.8 | 23.9 |
| Denmark | 27.3 | 11.2 | 8.2 | 20.6 | 5.4 | 11.7 |
| Germany | 32.3 | 10.3 | 9.7 | 37.1 | 9.8 | 16.2 |
| Estonia | 26.5 | 9.3 | 12.3 | 34.2 | 14.8 | 25.4 |
| Ireland | 24.7 | 8.4 | 11.0 | 32.9 | 10.0 | 18.0 |
| Greece | 25.2 | 22.3 | 18.5 | 43.2 | 17.7 | 20.8 |
| Spain | 24.6 | 21.3 | 17.4 | 38.9 | 16.9 | 41.6 |
| France | 19.1 | 6.8 | 7.3 | 33.9 | 10.3 | 22.1 |
| Croatia | 44.0 | 24.7 | 18.7 | 42.7 | 15.2 | 25.0 |
| Italy | 23.9 | 13.7 | 12.0 | 35.7 | 17.3 | 36.7 |
| Cyprus | 29.7 | 36.9 | 19.0 | 12.3 | 9.3 | 15.7 |
| Latvia | 20.4 | 11.0 | 15.1 | 39.1 | 17.4 | 35.2 |
| Lithuania | 26.9 | 8.3 | 12.6 | 42.4 | 16.7 | 33.1 |
| Luxembourg | 15.4 | 2.9 | 6.1 | 45.5 | 9.7 | 25.7 |
| Hungary | 15.7 | 3.0 | 6.3 | 29.9 | 11.8 | 33.0 |
| Malta | 22.7 | 21.2 | 10.4 | 47.2 | 12.4 | 32.2 |
| Netherlands | 16.4 | 6.0 | 5.2 | 33.9 | 4.5 | 19.1 |
| Austria | 23.9 | 11.7 | 8.3 | 26.2 | 6.4 | 23.0 |
| Poland | 25.5 | 11.7 | 11.7 | 29.8 | 11.3 | 34.6 |
| Portugal | 27.5 | 19.5 | 13.7 | 27.9 | 15.6 | 34.5 |
| Romania | 23.6 | 9.6 | 12.0 | 40.0 | 18.2 | 54.7 |
| Slovenia | 40.0 | 10.4 | 7.5 | 30.8 | 9.3 | 18.2 |
| Slovakia | 18.7 | 3.2 | 5.2 | 26.4 | 13.2 | 32.6 |
| Finland | 32.5 | 6.3 | 7.7 | 21.9 | 6.6 | 15.2 |
| Sweden | 30.2 | 6.6 | 6.8 | 35.9 | 8.6 | 15.4 |
| United Kingdom | 25.4 | 17.7 | 12.4 | 33.5 | 13.3 | 21.5 |
| Iceland | 19.4 | 2.7 | 4.1 | 28.4 | 6.8 | 8.0 |
| Norway | 27.1 | 1.4 | 3.5 | 19.1 | 5.9 | 9.8 |
| Switzerland | 22.5 | 23.2 | 12.3 | 32.4 | 8.9 | 26.0 |

Note: EU = European Union.

SOURCE: "Table 3. At-Risk-of-Poverty Rate by Household Type, 2011 (%)," in *Income Distribution Statistics*, Eurostat, March 2013, http://epp.eurostat.ec .europa.eu/statistics_explained/index.php/Income_distribution_statistics (accessed November 7, 2013)

working-age household members worked compared with the number of months that those members could have worked). (See Figure 6.6.) In the 27 countries that were part of the EU in 2011, 49 million people lived in households that fell below the at-risk-of-poverty threshold but did not experience severe material deprivation or very low work intensity. Another 20.2 million Europeans experienced severe material deprivation but did not experience poverty risk or very low work intensity, and 13.9 million Europeans experienced very low work intensity but not poverty risk or severe material deprivation. Approximately 29.9 million people in EU countries, meanwhile, experienced two of these three conditions, and roughly 8.1 million experienced all three.

## RUSSIA

Russia, or the Russian Federation, as it is officially known, is the largest country by land area in the world, at 6.6 million square miles (17.1 million square kilometers).

It consists of 83 territories known as federal subjects, each of which has two delegates in the Russian parliament and varying degrees of political and economic autonomy. As of 2013 the country had a population of 142.5 million, according to the U.S. Central Intelligence Agency's (CIA) *World Factbook* (2014, https://www.cia.gov/library/publi cations/ the-world-factbook/). Before the Soviet Union was dissolved, Russia was the largest of its republics. As a part of the Soviet Union, Russia accounted for more than half of the country's population and at least 60% of its gross domestic product (GDP).

The Russian Federation emerged as an independent nation late in 1991, when the Soviet Union collapsed. The Soviet Union was a communist country with a centrally planned and tightly controlled economy. In theory, this system ensured that all citizens would receive the basic necessities of life and that there would be no poverty. In reality, however, the Soviet system struggled for decades to meet the basic needs of its

**FIGURE 6.5**

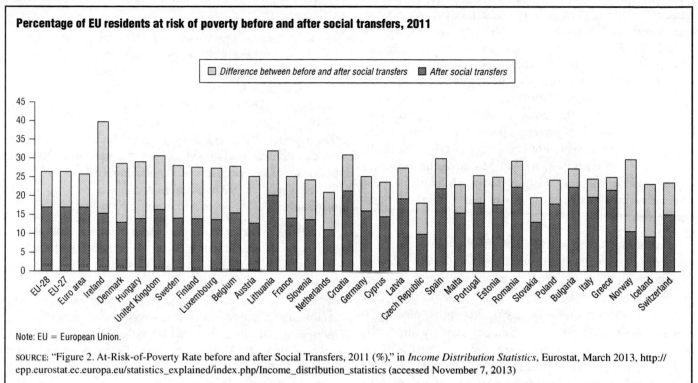

Percentage of EU residents at risk of poverty before and after social transfers, 2011

☐ Difference between before and after social transfers ▨ After social transfers

Note: EU = European Union.

SOURCE: "Figure 2. At-Risk-of-Poverty Rate before and after Social Transfers, 2011 (%)," in *Income Distribution Statistics*, Eurostat, March 2013, http://epp.eurostat.ec.europa.eu/statistics_explained/index.php/Income_distribution_statistics (accessed November 7, 2013)

**FIGURE 6.6**

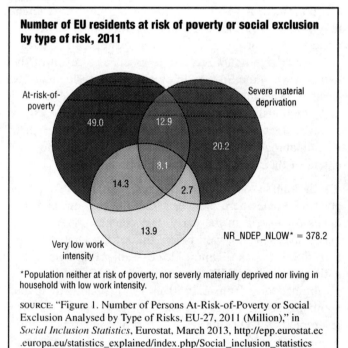

Number of EU residents at risk of poverty or social exclusion by type of risk, 2011

At-risk-of-poverty

Severe material deprivation

49.0

12.9

20.2

3.1

14.3

2.7

13.9

Very low work intensity

NR_NDEP_NLOW* = 378.2

*Population neither at risk of poverty, nor severly materially deprived nor living in household with low work intensity.

SOURCE: "Figure 1. Number of Persons At-Risk-of-Poverty or Social Exclusion Analysed by Type of Risks, EU-27, 2011 (Million)," in *Social Inclusion Statistics*, Eurostat, March 2013, http://epp.eurostat.ec.europa.eu/statistics_explained/index.php/Social_inclusion_statistics (accessed November 7, 2013)

citizens. Mikhail Gorbachev (1931–), who led the Soviet Union from 1985 to 1991, introduced the concepts of *glasnost* (openness) and *perestroika* (reconstruction) in an attempt to reform and repair the Soviet system.

The pace of reform under Gorbachev proved too slow to satisfy critics of the Soviet system, and too fast to be satisfactory to its defenders. In August 1991 communist hard-liners launched a coup d'état in an attempt to remove Gorbachev and end his reforms. They were resisted and defeated by reformers, among them Boris Yeltsin (1931–2007), the president of the Russian state within the Soviet Union. Having defeated the hard-line communists, the reformers were left as the most powerful force in the country, and they moved quickly to end the Soviet Union.

The Soviet Union was officially dissolved on December 21, 1991. Yeltsin became the president of an independent Russia. He then embarked on a program of radical economic reforms, known as shock therapy, to end the communist economic system and force the country into a Western-style free-market economy. The result of these major changes was massive economic disruption. Inflation soared, wages for Russians fell, manufacturing output declined, and many Russians became unemployed. Some Russians were able to take advantage of the new system to become quite wealthy, but many more sank into poverty. In subsequent years the economy grew rapidly, but poverty remained a serious problem.

**Poverty in Russia since the 1990s**

Russia, like the United States, uses an absolute poverty line, a minimum level of income that theoretically identifies the amount of money a person needs to meet basic survival requirements. In 2011, the Russian poverty line stood at approximately US$199 per month. In "Analysis: Economic Quandary Puts Life at $199 per Month at Risk" (MoscowTimes.com, August 6, 2012), Howard Amos states that "experts and some officials criticize [this poverty line] as insufficient and even absurd." Although the amount was almost five times lower than the U.S. poverty line at the time, living expenses in Russia were not consistently five times lower than in the United States. Indeed Moscow, the country's capital and largest city, is among the world's most expensive cities in terms of the costs of real estate and basic necessities.

According to the World Bank, in *Russian Federation: Reducing Poverty through Growth and Social Policy Reform* (February 24, 2005, http://www-wds.worldbank.org/servlet/WDSContentServer/WDSP/IB/2005/03/17/000012009_200 50317113145/Rendered/PDF/289230RU.pdf), poverty in Russia (as measured by the national poverty line) was reduced by half in a mere three years, from 41.5% in 1999 to 19.6% in 2002, with an estimated 30 million people lifted out of poverty during this period. In "Data: Russian Federation" (2013, http://data.worldbank.org/country/russian-federation?display=default), the World Bank indicates that poverty continued to fall in the years that followed, reaching 11.1% in 2006. The years of the global financial crisis brought the country's poverty reductions to a standstill, however. The proportion of the population that lived below the poverty line stood at 12.7% in 2011, according to the CIA, in *World Factbook*. As reported in "Putin: 26% of Russians Live below Poverty Line by International Standards" (KyivPost.com, January 12, 2012), in early 2012 the Russian prime minister Vladimir Putin (1952–) said that when using widely accepted international standards, the proportion of the country's population living in poverty was actually 26%.

Russia's economy grew rapidly between the 1990s and the onset of the global financial crisis, in no small part due to the country's vast reserves of oil, natural gas, coal, and other natural resources. According to the CIA, in *World Factbook*, Russia has among the world's largest reserves of oil, coal, and natural gas and is a major producer and exporter of these fuels. The Russian economy's reliance on oil and other natural-resource exports makes it extremely vulnerable to changing levels of demand in the world economy. While the country's economy averaged 7% growth between 1998 and 2008, doubling average incomes, the dramatic fall in oil prices brought on by the global financial crisis hit the Russian economy with particular force. Growth resumed in late 2009. While the Russian economy has grown faster than the economies of the developed countries of North America and Europe since that time, as of 2014 it had not begun

to approach the dynamic levels of growth of the pre-crisis years.

Like many countries with rapidly growing economies, Russia was characterized by a high degree of income inequality during these years. Tom Balmforth reports in "Dealing with the Gap between Rich and Poor" (January 4, 2013, http://rbth.ru/articles/2013/01/04/dealing _with_the_gap_between_rich_and_poor_21303.html) that between 2011 and 2013 the prevalence of poverty in the country was unchanged, even as the number of Russian billionaires (measured in U.S. dollars) climbed from 80 to 97. Collectively these 97 individuals accounted for $380 billion of wealth.

Russia's State Statistics Service uses a measure it calls a funds coefficient to assess inequality, and according to Balmforth this measure showed that the gap between the rich and the poor was growing steadily as of 2013. As measured by the Gini coefficient, however, inequality in Russia was less pronounced and was not increasing. In fact, by this standard Russia was less unequal than the United States in the most recent years for which the two countries' data were available. In a list ranking countries in order of their Gini coefficients, the CIA rates in *World Factbook* the United States as the 41st most-unequal country, and Russia as the 52nd.

Balmforth notes, however, that the Gini coefficient may not capture the true extent of inequality in Russia because of a variety of factors. For example, many Russians have significant real-estate assets as a result of the fact that when the Soviet Union collapsed, residents were granted ownership of their apartments and houses, which had previously been state-owned. Additionally, it is believed that many of the richest Russians hide their wealth abroad and outside of banks, so that the true extent of their wealth remains unknown.

In human development terms, Russia occupied a position somewhere between the developing and the developed world in the early 21st century. Average life expectancy was 69, well below that of the United States and the European Union. (See Table 6.6.) Its gross national income (GNI) per capita was $12,700 in 2012, up dramatically from $2,650 in 1995, placing it in the company of the lower-income OECD countries. It also resembled OECD countries in terms of hunger indicators, its rates of primary-school enrollment and literacy, and gender-equality indicators (although its proportion of female political representation lagged behind that of many developed countries). In terms of child and maternal mortality, along with other maternal-health indicators, Russia again ranked with lower-income OECD countries. Russia's tuberculosis prevalence and death rate was higher than that of most developed countries. Russians had nearly universal access to improved water sources, but the percentage of the population with access

**TABLE 6.6**

**Russia's progress in reaching Millennium Development Goals (MDGs), selected years 1990–2011**

| | 1990 | 1995 | 2000 | 2005 | 2010 | 2011 | 2012 |
|---|---|---|---|---|---|---|---|
| **Goal 1: Eradicate extreme poverty and hunger** | | | | | | | |
| Employment to population ratio, 15+, total (%) | — | 55 | 55 | 56 | 58 | 59 | — |
| Employment to population ratio, ages 15–24, total (%) | — | 41 | 35 | 33 | 36 | 38 | — |
| GDP per person employed (constant 1990 PPP $) | 15,281 | 10,761 | 11,991 | 15,597 | 18,268 | 19,078 | — |
| Income share held by lowest 20% | — | — | — | 7 | — | — | — |
| Poverty headcount ratio at $1.25 a day (PPP) (% of population) | — | — | — | 0.2 | — | — | — |
| Poverty headcount ratio at national poverty line (% of population) | — | — | — | 12 | — | — | — |
| Prevalence of undernourishment (% of population) | — | — | 5 | 5 | — | 5 | — |
| Vulnerable employment, total (% of total employment) | — | 2 | 8 | 6 | — | — | — |
| **Goal 2: Achieve universal primary education** | | | | | | | |
| Literacy rate, youth female (% of females ages 15–24) | — | — | — | — | 100 | — | — |
| Literacy rate, youth male (% of males ages 15–24) | — | — | — | — | 100 | — | — |
| Primary completion rate, total (% of relevant age group) | — | 92 | 91 | — | — | — | — |
| School enrollment, primary (% net) | — | 93 | — | — | — | — | — |
| **Goal 3: Promote gender equality and empower women** | | | | | | | |
| Proportion of seats held by women in national parliaments (%) | 16 | — | 8 | 10 | 14 | 14 | 14 |
| Ratio of female to male primary enrollment (%) | 100 | 100 | 99 | 99 | — | — | — |
| Ratio of female to male secondary enrollment (%) | — | — | — | 99 | — | — | — |
| Ratio of female to male tertiary enrollment (%) | — | — | — | 137 | — | — | — |
| Share of women employed in the nonagricultural sector (% of total nonagricultural employment) | — | 50 | 50 | 51 | 51 | 51 | — |
| **Goal 4: Reduce child mortality** | | | | | | | |
| Immunization, measles (% of children ages 12–23 months) | — | 85 | 97 | 99 | 98 | 98 | — |
| Mortality rate, infant (per 1,000 live births) | 22 | 22 | 20 | 14 | 10 | 9 | 9 |
| Mortality rate, under-5 (per 1,000) | 26 | 26 | 23 | 17 | 12 | 11 | 10 |
| **Goal 5: Improve maternal health** | | | | | | | |
| Adolescent fertility rate (births per 1,000 women ages 15–19) | 51 | 42 | 31 | 29 | 27 | 26 | — |
| Births attended by skilled health staff (% of total) | 99 | 99 | 99 | 99 | — | — | — |
| Contraceptive prevalence (% of women ages 15–49) | — | 63 | — | — | — | — | — |
| Maternal mortality ratio (modeled estimate, per 100,000 live births) | 74 | 72 | 57 | 37 | 34 | — | — |
| Pregnant women receiving prenatal care (%) | — | — | — | — | — | — | — |
| Unmet need for contraception (% of married women ages 15–49) | — | — | — | — | — | — | — |
| **Goal 6: Combat HIV/AIDS, malaria, and other diseases** | | | | | | | |
| AIDS estimated deaths (UNAIDS estimates) | — | — | — | — | — | — | — |
| Antiretroviral therapy coverage (% of people with advanced HIV infection) | — | — | — | — | — | — | — |
| Incidence of tuberculosis (per 100,000 people) | 47 | 96 | 127 | 135 | 106 | 97 | — |
| Malaria cases reported | — | — | — | — | 1 | — | — |
| Prevalence of HIV, total (% of population ages 15–49) | — | — | — | — | — | — | — |
| Tuberculosis case detection rate (%, all forms) | 73 | 60 | 75 | 66 | 79 | 81 | — |
| Tuberculosis death rate (per 100,000 people) | 8 | 15 | 21 | 22 | 17 | 16 | — |
| **Goal 7: Ensure environmental sustainability** | | | | | | | |
| CO2 emissions (kg per PPP $ of GDP) | — | 2 | 1.6 | 1 | 0.6 | — | — |
| CO2 emissions (kt) | — | 1,662,526 | 1,558,112 | 1,615,688 | 1,740,776 | — | — |
| Energy use (kg of oil equivalent) per $1,000 GDP (constant 2005 PPP) | 470 | 547 | 491 | 384 | 348 | 347 | — |
| Forest area (sq. km) | 8,089,500 | 8,091,092 | 8,092,685 | 8,087,900 | 8,090,900 | 8,091,500 | — |
| Improved sanitation facilities (% of population with access) | 74 | 73 | 72 | 71 | 70 | 70 | — |
| Improved water source (% of population with access) | 93 | 94 | 95 | 96 | 97 | 97 | — |
| Marine protected areas (% of total surface area) | 2 | 9 | 11 | 11 | 11 | — | — |
| Terrestrial protected areas (% of total surface area) | 5 | 8 | 9 | 9 | 9 | — | — |
| **Goal 8: Develop a global partnership for development** | | | | | | | |
| Internet users (per 100 people) | 0 | 0.1 | 2 | 15 | 43 | 49 | 53 |
| Mobile cellular subscriptions (per 100 people) | 0 | 0.06 | 2 | 83 | 166 | 179 | 184 |
| Telephone lines (per 100 people) | 14 | 17 | 22 | 28 | 31 | 31 | 30 |
| **Other** | | | | | | | |
| Fertility rate, total (births per woman) | 1.9 | 1.3 | 1.2 | 1.3 | 1.5 | 1.5 | — |
| GNI per capita, Atlas method (current US$) | — | 2,650 | 1,710 | 4,460 | 10,000 | 10,810 | 12,700 |
| Life expectancy at birth, total (years) | 69 | 65 | 65 | 65 | 69 | 69 | — |
| Literacy rate, adult total (% of people ages 15 and above) | — | — | — | — | 100 | — | — |

GDP = Gross Domestic Product.
GNI per capita = Gross National Income divided by total population.
PPP = Purchasing Power Parity.

SOURCE: Adapted from "World DataBank: Millennium Development Goals," World Bank, 2013, http://databank.worldbank.org/data/home.aspx (accessed October 28, 2013)

to improved sanitation facilities lagged significantly behind most of the developed world.

## JAPAN

Japan, with a population of approximately 127.3 million in 2013 according to the CIA, in *World Factbook*, had the fourth-largest economy of any nation that year. For much of the late 20th century, however, Japan's economy was second only to that of the United States. The country experienced rapid economic growth in the 1960s, 1970s, and 1980s, but the aftereffects of a late 1980s economic crisis led to slow growth in the 1990s, and a rapidly expanding China surpassed Japan in terms of gross GDP in 2001. Although moderate economic growth resumed in that decade, Japan's economy was surpassed by India's in 2012.

Japan was among the countries hit hardest by the global economic crisis, and it struggled to emerge from conditions of economic recession through 2010. Then it suffered another major blow in the form of a catastrophic March 2011 earthquake and tsunami, which resulted in nearly 16,000 deaths, devastated large amounts of property and infrastructure on the country's eastern coastline, and disrupted manufacturing. The country as a whole has since recovered economically, but progress has been uneven in the Tohoku region, which suffered the worst damage.

Among developed countries, Japan has above-average life expectancy (83) and GNI per capita ($47,870), according to the World Bank, in "Data: Japan" (2013, http://data.worldbank.org/country/japan), and it performs well on most quality of life indicators. Poverty has generally remained hidden in the country, however. The article "Shadowy Figures" (Economist.com, March 3, 2012) reports that "poverty rarely stares you in the face in Japan. There is almost no begging, and the homeless hide in the shadows." Tomohiro Osaki observes in "Poor Slam Anti-poverty Law as Hollow" (JapanTimes.co.jp, July 24, 2013) that "for years, the central government did not officially acknowledge that the nation was grappling with increasing poverty. Until recently, official figures on poverty rates simply did not exist. But an October 2009 push by the then-ruling Democratic Party of Japan government prompted the labor ministry to estimate for the first time poverty levels facing the nation."

The issue of poverty was forced into public consciousness by the Great Recession that began in 2007 and resulted, in Japan, in a job market that was increasingly divided into two tiers, one in which permanent workers enjoyed relative prosperity and job security and another in which a burgeoning class of workers could find only low-paying part-time or temporary work. According to *OECD Economic Surveys: Japan 2013* (April 2013, http://www.oecd-ilibrary.org/economics/oecd-economic-surveys-japan-2013_eco_surveys-jpn-2013-en), the share of nonregular workers—those who worked part time, for a contracted period, or who found work through private employment agencies—had roughly doubled since 1990, standing at 34% of total employment in 2012.

As a result of the calls for more study and attention, Osaki reports that the Japanese government began surveying poverty levels using the relative threshold of 60% of median income. It found that in 2007 15.7% of the population lived below that threshold, and that in 2011 the proportion of the population living in poverty had risen slightly, to 16%. Single-parent households became a particular cause for concern, when it emerged that they lived in poverty at a rate of 50.8%, well in excess of developed world averages. Calls for the government to undertake regular, systematic, ongoing efforts to collect and distribute poverty data were widespread during these years, but as of 2013 no such comprehensive data were available.

Japan's social safety net is among the least generous among high-income countries, according to *OECD Economic Surveys: Japan 2013*. Applicants for public assistance are subject to eligibility requirements including asset tests and verifications that the recipient has no relatives who might be able to assist him or her, and government spending on such programs lags well behind most other developed countries as a percentage of total spending. Additionally, Japan's tax code is such that the overall level of poverty for all working households and all households with children rises rather than falls after taxes and public assistance are taken into account. This was not the case in any other OECD country as of 2012.

## SOUTH KOREA

Between the 1960s and the first decade of the 21st century, South Korea (officially known as the Republic of Korea) achieved levels of sustained economic growth that were among the world's highest. In the 1960s, according to the CIA, in *World Factbook*, the country resembled the least-developed countries of Africa and Asia in terms of its economic productivity. By 2004, the country had an average annual GDP exceeding $1 trillion, and by 2013 it boasted the world's 12th-largest economy. Focused on high-technology products for export, especially to China and the United States, South Korea's economy suffered keenly in the initial stages of the Great Recession but rebounded more fully than most other developed economies beginning in 2010.

As South Korea's economy grew explosively between the 1960s and the mid-1990s, it enjoyed high levels of income equality relative to other developing countries, according to the *OECD Economic Surveys: Korea 2012* (April 2012, http://www.keepeek.com/Digital-Asset-Management/oecd/economics/oecd-economic-surveys-korea-2012_eco_surveys-kor-2012-en). However, starting with the Asian financial crisis of 1997—an economic downturn that lasted through 1999 and that was particularly severe in South Korea, Indonesia, and Thailand— inequality and poverty levels began to rise, although South Korea's economy resumed its robust growth in the years that followed.

Like Japan, South Korea's job market was characterized by two distinct forms of employment in the early 21st century: permanent employment offering strong job security and prosperity and part-time or temporary employment that often failed to lift workers out of poverty. According to *OECD Economic Surveys: Korea 2012*, more than one-third of South Korean workers were classified as nonregular workers in 2010, and on average these workers earned only 57% of what regular workers earned per hour. More than a quarter of South Korean full-time workers earned less than two-thirds of the median full-time wage, a higher proportion than in any other OECD country (slightly higher than the proportion of such workers in the United States). These workers were further imperiled by the fact that South Korea's safety-net programs for the unemployed frequently do not cover nonregular workers.

At a poverty line of 50% of national median income, approximately 15% of South Koreans were impoverished in 2010, according to the OECD, in *Crisis Squeezes Income and Puts Pressure on Inequality and Poverty*. The OECD also reported that South Korea's Gini coefficient stood at roughly 0.3 in 2010, close to the average of all OECD members. In *World Factbook*, however, the CIA rated the country's Gini coefficient as 41.9 out of 100 (or 0.42), placing it among countries with high levels of inequality, such as Russia and the United States.

## AUSTRALIA

In the early 21st century Australia was among the most highly developed and prosperous countries in the Asia-Pacific region. As of 2014, according to the CIA, in *World Factbook*, the country's population was approximately 22.3 million, and its economy had been growing steadily for more than two decades, at an average annual growth rate of 3.5%. A major producer of food and natural resources such as coal, iron, copper, gold, natural gas, and uranium, Australia benefited from years of rapidly growing demand in China, with which it had close economic ties, as well as Japan, South Korea, and India. In 2014 it boasted the world's 10th-highest life expectancy (82), universal access to clean water and sanitation facilities, and universal education and literacy rates.

Australia has no official poverty line, and the country's government does not regularly release official figures regarding the prevalence of poverty. The Melbourne Institute of Applied Economic and Social Research at the University of Melbourne provides poverty guidelines that have been updated on a quarterly basis since 1973, however, and its guidelines are used by many of the country's social scientists and other experts. The Melbourne Institute's poverty lines are relative poverty measures based on a benchmark of AU$62.70 per week in disposable (after-tax) income, which is what the organization identified as the cost, in 1973, of providing for the basic needs of a two-adult, two-child family. The poverty lines are adjusted according to household composition, and they are updated to account not only for inflation but also for per capita household income.

In "Poverty Lines: Australia, June Quarter 2013" (October 22, 2013, http://melbourneinstitute.com/downloads/publications/Poverty%20Lines/Poverty-lines-Australia-June2013.pdf), the Melbourne Institute identified the poverty line for a single person who was in the workforce as AU$490.37. The poverty line for a childless couple with one member in the workforce was AU$655.98 per week, for a single working parent with one child it was AU$629.54 per week, and the poverty line for a couple with one adult in the workforce and three dependent children was AU$1,053.60 per week. By comparison, the U.S. poverty line in 2013 for single person was roughly US$220.96 a week; for a five-person family it was US$530.19 per week. Thus, the Melbourne Institute's unofficial Australian poverty lines were set at approximately double the level of official U.S. poverty lines.

In *Poverty in Australia* (2012, http://www.acoss.org.au/uploads/ACOSS%20Poverty%20Report%202012_Final.pdf) the Australian Council of Social Service (ACOSS), a nonprofit advocacy group, produced an overview of poverty in the country using the OECD poverty line of 50% of median income. According to this measure, the poverty line in 2010 was AU$358 per week for a single adult and AU$752 per week for a couple with two children. An estimated 2.3 million people were living below this poverty line in 2010. This was 12.8% of the Australian population, up from 12.5% living in poverty in 2003. In 2010 there were 575,000 children in poverty by this measure, 17.3% of all children in Australia.

ACOSS also measured how many people were at or below 60% of the national median income, the same line used by Eurostat to measure the population at risk of poverty in the European Union. By this standard, which translated into AU$430 per week for a single adult and AU$903 per week for a couple with two children, ACOSS found that in 2010, 3.7 million Australians, or 20.9% of the population, lived in, or at risk of, poverty. Among them were 869,000 children, 26.1% of all children in Australia.

## CHAPTER 7
# WOMEN AND CHILDREN IN POVERTY

*Empowering women and girls is not only the right and fair thing to do, it also makes economic sense. Countries that invest in promoting the social and economic status of women tend to have lower poverty rates. For example, an extra year of secondary schooling for girls can increase their future wages by 10 to 20%. And evidence shows that resources in women's hands results in household expenditures that benefit children.*

—World Bank, "Millennium Development Goals—Goal 3: Promote Gender Equality and Empower Women by 2015" (2011, http://www.world bank.org/mdgs/gender.html)

International development organizations, nonprofit advocacy groups, and poverty experts across disciplinary boundaries agree that one of the most effective ways to reduce poverty is to improve the social, economic, educational, and political situation of women and, by extension, children. Women's levels of health, education, and security affect those of their families. When a mother suffers the effects of poverty, future generations of her family likely do as well, creating a cycle of impoverishment that is difficult to escape. This consensus regarding both the human rights and the developmental necessity of promoting gender equality and the protection of children has found expression in a number of landmark international agreements dating to the late 1980s.

## GLOBAL INITIATIVES TO PROTECT THE RIGHTS OF WOMEN AND CHILDREN
### Convention on the Rights of the Child

In November 1989 the United Nations (UN) adopted the treaty Convention on the Rights of the Child (CRC; http://treaties.un.org/Pages/ViewDetails.aspx?mtdsg_no =IV-11&chapter=4&lang=en). Considered to be one of the most wide-ranging and important human rights documents on which the global community has ever agreed, the CRC was charged with establishing norms and standards for the lives of children to which all countries would hold themselves accountable, including:

- Protection from violence, abuse, and abduction
- Protection from hazardous employment and exploitation
- Adequate nutrition
- Free compulsory primary education
- Adequate health care
- Equal treatment regardless of gender, race, or cultural background

The CRC has been ratified by 193 countries. Only two UN member countries had not ratified it as of 2014: Somalia and the United States. Ratification by the United States has been hampered by a number of issues. Initially, a primary reason for U.S. resistance was the CRC's insistence that capital punishment of minors be illegal. Before the U.S. Supreme Court outlawed it in *Roper v. Simmons* (543 U.S. 551 [2005]), several U.S. states had allowed the death penalty for those who were between 16 and 18 years old at the time they committed their crime. Following the Supreme Court's ruling, U.S. proponents of the CRC continued to have trouble mustering sufficient congressional support for ratification due primarily to resistance from another quarter: parents' rights organizations. Lawrence J. Cohen and Anthony T. DeBenedet explain in "Why Is the U.S. against Children's Rights?" (Time.com, January 24, 2012) the ongoing opposition to the CRC: "The opposition is primarily based on fears of U.N. interference in U.S. laws and families. The biggest worry appears to be that the treaty will undermine parental rights even though the Convention explicitly grants responsibilities and protections to parents and guardians. One of the alarms raised by ParentalRights.org, an organization that supports a parental-rights amendment to the U.S. Constitution, is that the Convention will prevent parents from spanking their children or opting them out of sex education."

## Beijing Declaration and Platform for Action

In September 1995 at the UN Fourth World Conference on Women in Beijing, China, representatives from 189 countries unanimously adopted a program intended to promote gender equality around the world, which became known as the *Beijing Declaration* (http://www.un.org/womenwatch/daw/beijing/beijingdeclaration.html) and the *Platform for Action* (http://www.un.org/womenwatch/daw/beijing/platform/index.html). One of the main goals outlined by the *Platform for Action* was addressing the enormous increase of women living in poverty during the late 20th century—a trend that has come to be known as the "feminization of poverty." The platform sought to:

- Review, adopt, and maintain macroeconomic policies and development strategies that address the needs and efforts of women in poverty

- Revise laws and administrative practices to ensure women's equal rights and access to economic resources

- Provide women with access to savings and credit mechanisms and institutions

- Develop gender-based methodologies and conduct research to address the feminization of poverty

The *Platform for Action* also required the 189 countries that adopted the platform to each develop a National Plan of Action to implement the platform locally. In June 2000, five years after the 1995 conference, the UN General Assembly adopted a resolution (http://www.stopvaw.org/sites/3f6d15f4-c12d-4515-8544-26b7a3a5a41e/uploads/Political_Dec_Beijing.pdf) that reaffirmed the member states' commitment to the objectives in the *Beijing Declaration* and the *Platform for Action*. It also agreed to regularly assess progress on these objectives. At the 10th (2005) and 15th (2010) anniversaries of the adoption of the *Beijing Declaration* and the *Platform for Action*, the UN Department of Economic and Social Affairs Commission of the Status of Women (later the Commission on the Status of Women) reaffirmed the international community's commitment to the Beijing goals and held meetings attended by representatives of member states and nongovernmental organizations. Attendees reviewed and appraised progress toward the Beijing goals, shared information and best practices, and discussed continuing obstacles to gender equality and related Millennium Development Goals (MDGs).

## Millennium Development Goals

Among the MDGs introduced in Chapter 2 and discussed throughout this book, four have particular relevance to the international efforts at addressing the challenges of women and children affected by poverty:

- Achieve universal primary education

- Promote gender equality and empower women

- Reduce child mortality

- Improve maternal health

## Global Gender Gap Index

Since 2006 the World Economic Forum (WEF), an independent Swiss-based organization that spans the international business, political, and academic communities, has released one of the most comprehensive measures of the state of gender equality across the world. The WEF's annual *Global Gender Gap Report* features a Global Gender Gap Index, which measures disparities in access to resources and opportunities between the genders; evaluates outcome variables, such as health, education, economics, and politics; and ranks countries according to gender equality. In *The Global Gender Gap Report 2013* (2013, http://www3.weforum.org/docs/WEF_GenderGap_Report_2013.pdf), the WEF ranks Iceland first among all countries in gender equality in 2013, followed by Finland, Norway, Sweden, the Philippines, Ireland, New Zealand, Denmark, Switzerland, and Nicaragua. The United States was ranked 23rd, down from 22nd the previous year and 17th in 2011. Among the countries surveyed, those ranking lowest in gender equality were all located in sub-Saharan Africa or the Middle East. The bottom 10 countries, in descending order, were Saudi Arabia, Mali, Morocco, Iran, Côte d'Ivoire, Mauritania, Syria, Chad, Pakistan, and Yemen.

## WOMEN'S EMPLOYMENT AND WAGES

Women's ability to seek and find paid employment is one of the most important measures of the level of gender equality in a region or country. The UN states in *The Millennium Development Goals Report 2013* (June 2013, http://www.un.org/millenniumgoals/pdf/report-2013/mdg-report-2013-english.pdf), "As women benefit from more regular income, they are more likely to achieve greater autonomy, self-reliance in the household and in their personal development, and decision-making power." Figure 7.1 shows the percentage of female employees in nonagricultural employment in 1990 and 2011. Globally, 40% of all paying jobs were held by women in 2011, up significantly from 1990, when 35% of jobs were held by women.

Additionally, there were dramatic disparities from region to region in the developing world in 2011. Women in Western Asia and northern Africa each accounted for only 19% of all jobs, as did 20% of women in Southern Asia. (See Figure 7.1.) Other regions whose rates of female participation fell below the global average were sub-Saharan Africa (33%), Oceania (37%), and Southeastern Asia (39%). Only two regions of the developing world—the Caucasus and Central Asia and Latin America and the Caribbean—had above-average rates of female participation. Women accounted for 44% of jobs

FIGURE 7.1

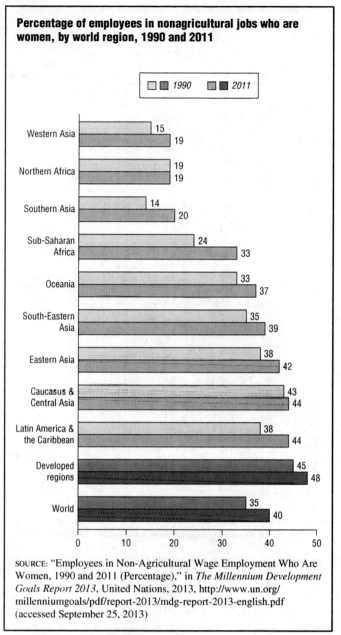

**Percentage of employees in nonagricultural jobs who are women, by world region, 1990 and 2011**

☐ ▨ *1990*     ▨ ■ *2011*

SOURCE: "Employees in Non-Agricultural Wage Employment Who Are Women, 1990 and 2011 (Percentage)," in *The Millennium Development Goals Report 2013*, United Nations, 2013, http://www.un.org/millenniumgoals/pdf/report-2013/mdg-report-2013-english.pdf (accessed September 25, 2013)

in both regions, but these rates were still below the average of 48% in the developed world.

In some parts of the world women are legally prohibited from working in the same industries as men. The UN Entity for Gender Equality and the Empowerment of Women notes in *Progress of the World's Women: In Pursuit of Justice* (2011, http://progress.unwomen.org/pdfs/EN-Report-Progress.pdf) that in 48 (25%) out of 194 countries this was the case in 2010. In the Middle East and North Africa these restrictions were most severe at 59% of the assessed countries having restrictions. In South Asia one-third (33%) of the assessed countries had restrictions on their work, in sub-Saharan Africa nearly one-third (31%) had restrictions, and in central and eastern Europe and Central Asia about 27% had restrictions.

In *Millennium Development Goals Report 2013*, the UN explains that the increased levels of labor force participation by women are not necessarily indications that working women in the developing world enjoy increasing earning capacity or job security. In every region of the developing world, among all employed people, women are far more likely to be engaged in precarious or low-paying forms of work, such as being self-employed or working on farms or in family businesses. The disparities in the types of work available to women are, according to the UN, a function of a number of factors, including discriminatory laws, women's responsibilities in the realm of unpaid family care, and a lack of child care facilities.

The International Labour Organization (ILO) notes in *Global Employment Trends 2013: Recovering from a Second Jobs Dip* (2013, http://www.ilo.org/wcmsp5/groups/public/---dgreports/---dcomm/---publ/documents/publication/wcms_202326.pdf) that women worldwide also typically find themselves unemployed at higher rates. Unemployment rates represent the share of all people who are looking for work but are unable to find it; thus, they are not always a direct indicator of gender equality. For example, a country in which women are not allowed to work in many jobs might have a low female unemployment rate because few women are looking for work. Nevertheless, the fact that women on average are more likely to be unemployed is, in combination with other evidence of discrimination, a clear sign of the overall level of inequality in most countries.

Worldwide, the average unemployment rate for women (6.2%) was slightly higher than that for men (5.7%) in 2012. (See Table 7.1.) The small size of this overall disparity disguised significant variation from region to region. Women in the Middle East and North Africa were unemployed at rates of 19.3% and 17.2%, respectively, compared with male unemployment rates of 9.3% and 7.9%. There were smaller female–male disparities in Latin America and the Caribbean (7.9% versus 5.6%), South Asia (4.6% versus 3.5%), sub-Saharan Africa (8.1% versus 7.1%), and Southeast Asia and the Pacific (4.7% to 4.1%). In non–European Union countries of Europe and the Commonwealth of Independent States (a region of Central Asia made up of the former Soviet republics), in East Asia, and in the developed world, women were slightly less likely than men to be unemployed.

## WOMEN'S REPRODUCTIVE HEALTH

Poor people suffer from more health problems and have less access to quality health care than the nonpoor, and among all poor people, women suffer disproportionately from inadequate health care. This is partly because there are more poor women than poor men in the world and partly because women face a more complicated set of

TABLE 7.1

**Unemployment rate by sex and world region, 2000 and 2005–12**

[In percent]

| Both sexes | 2000 | 2005 | 2006 | 2007 | 2008 | 2009 | 2010 | 2011 | 2012*<br>Preliminary estimate |
|---|---|---|---|---|---|---|---|---|---|
| **World** | **6.3** | **6.1** | **5.7** | **5.4** | **5.6** | **6.2** | **6.0** | **5.9** | **5.9** |
| Developed economies and European Union | 6.7 | 6.9 | 6.3 | 5.8 | 6.1 | 8.4 | 8.8 | 8.4 | 8.6 |
| Central and South-Eastern Europe (non-EU) and CIS | 10.7 | 9.1 | 9.0 | 8.3 | 8.3 | 10.1 | 9.4 | 8.7 | 8.2 |
| East Asia | 4.5 | 4.2 | 4.0 | 3.8 | 4.3 | 4.4 | 4.2 | 4.3 | 4.4 |
| South-East Asia and the Pacific | 5.0 | 6.4 | 6.1 | 5.5 | 5.3 | 5.2 | 4.7 | 4.4 | 4.4 |
| South Asia | 4.5 | 4.7 | 4.1 | 3.9 | 3.9 | 4.1 | 3.9 | 3.8 | 3.8 |
| Latin America and the Caribbean | 8.6 | 8.1 | 7.5 | 7.0 | 6.6 | 7.8 | 6.8 | 6.5 | 6.6 |
| Middle East | 11.5 | 11.2 | 10.9 | 10.3 | 10.5 | 10.7 | 11.2 | 11.1 | 11.1 |
| North Africa | 13.2 | 11.0 | 10.0 | 9.6 | 9.1 | 9.1 | 8.9 | 10.0 | 10.3 |
| Sub-Saharan Africa | 8.5 | 7.5 | 7.5 | 7.4 | 7.5 | 7.6 | 7.6 | 7.6 | 7.5 |
| **Males** | | | | | | | | | |
| **World** | **6.1** | **5.8** | **5.5** | **5.2** | **5.4** | **6.1** | **5.8** | **5.7** | **5.7** |
| Developed economies and European Union | 6.3 | 6.6 | 6.1 | 5.6 | 6.0 | 8.8 | 9.1 | 8.7 | 8.8 |
| Central and South-Eastern Europe (non-EU) and CIS | 10.5 | 9.3 | 9.2 | 8.6 | 8.6 | 10.5 | 9.7 | 8.8 | 8.4 |
| East Asia | 5.1 | 4.7 | 4.5 | 4.3 | 4.9 | 5.0 | 4.8 | 4.9 | 5.1 |
| South-East Asia and the Pacific | 5.1 | 6.0 | 5.7 | 5.3 | 5.1 | 5.2 | 4.4 | 4.1 | 4.1 |
| South Asia | 4.4 | 4.3 | 4.0 | 3.6 | 3.7 | 4.0 | 3.5 | 3.4 | 3.5 |
| Latin America and the Caribbean | 7.3 | 6.6 | 6.1 | 5.6 | 5.3 | 6.5 | 5.8 | 5.6 | 5.6 |
| Middle East | 9.8 | 9.4 | 9.0 | 8.5 | 8.7 | 9.0 | 9.3 | 9.2 | 9.3 |
| North Africa | 11.6 | 9.1 | 8.3 | 8.2 | 7.5 | 7.2 | 7.0 | 7.7 | 7.9 |
| Sub-Saharan Africa | 7.9 | 7.0 | 6.9 | 7.0 | 7.1 | 7.2 | 7.2 | 7.1 | 7.1 |
| **Females** | | | | | | | | | |
| **World** | **6.6** | **6.5** | **6.1** | **5.7** | **5.8** | **6.4** | **6.3** | **6.2** | **6.2** |
| Developed economies and European Union | 7.3 | 7.3 | 6.7 | 6.1 | 6.2 | 7.9 | 8.4 | 8.2 | 8.3 |
| Central and South-Eastern Europe (non-EU) and CIS | 10.9 | 8.9 | 8.8 | 8.0 | 8.0 | 9.6 | 9.1 | 8.5 | 8.1 |
| East Asia | 3.8 | 3.5 | 3.3 | 3.1 | 3.6 | 3.7 | 3.5 | 3.6 | 3.7 |
| South-East Asia and the Pacific | 4.9 | 6.9 | 6.6 | 5.7 | 5.4 | 5.1 | 5.1 | 4.7 | 4.7 |
| South Asia | 4.7 | 5.6 | 4.4 | 4.6 | 4.3 | 4.5 | 4.9 | 4.6 | 4.6 |
| Latin America and the Caribbean | 10.8 | 10.4 | 9.7 | 9.1 | 8.5 | 9.6 | 8.3 | 7.9 | 7.9 |
| Middle East | 19.6 | 19.0 | 18.9 | 18.2 | 18.6 | 18.4 | 19.7 | 19.5 | 19.3 |
| North Africa | 18.6 | 17.2 | 15.6 | 13.8 | 14.1 | 15.1 | 14.7 | 17.1 | 17.2 |
| Sub-Saharan Africa | 9.2 | 8.1 | 8.1 | 8.0 | 8.1 | 8.1 | 8.1 | 8.1 | 8.1 |

*2012 are preliminary estimates.
Notes: EU = European Union. CIS = Commonwealth of Independent States.

SOURCE: "Table A2. Unemployment Rate by Sex, World and Regions (%)," in *Global Employment Trends 2013: Recovering from a Second Jobs Dip*, International Labour Organization, 2013, http://www.ilo.org/wcmsp5/groups/public/---dgreports/---dcomm/---publ/documents/publication/wcms_202326.pdf (accessed September 23, 2013)

health issues during their childbearing years. The MDG targets related to maternal health underline the significance of reproduction in the overall picture of women's health and to the social and economic status of their families. Among the rights related to reproductive health that are considered vital to women and societies in the developing world are the right to freedom from sexual violence, the right to marry voluntarily, the right to time the birth of children as desired, the right to receive clear and accurate information about the reproductive process, and the right to benefit from scientific progress.

Women in low-income countries do not enjoy these rights as a matter of course. Many women are prohibited from using contraception—or from even receiving information about it—and must marry whomever their family chooses for them and at whatever age their family chooses. In some cultures resistance to these and other discriminatory conventions can place women at risk of retaliatory physical and emotional violence. However,

conceding to these conventions often increases other problems related to poverty. For example, the inability to decide how many children to have or how many years apart to have them can easily overwhelm a family's finances, making the climb out of impoverishment particularly difficult.

**Maternal Death**

In the fact sheet "Maternal Mortality" (May 2012, http://www.who.int/mediacentre/factsheets/fs348/en/index.html), the World Health Organization (WHO) provides an overview of the prevalence and characteristics of preventable deaths from pregnancy and childbirth worldwide. Maternal death is almost entirely a phenomenon in the developing world; only 1% of all such deaths occur in the developed world. Over half of preventable maternal deaths occur in sub-Saharan Africa, and another third occur in South Asia. Maternal mortality rates are higher in rural areas, where poverty is typically more widespread and quality medical care is less available. There are also disparities among lower-income and higher-income households within urban and rural locations. Teenage mothers, especially those under the age of 15 years, are at particular risk of death from pregnancy and childbirth. Complications from pregnancy or childbirth is the leading cause of death among adolescent girls in most developing countries.

The WHO notes that global maternal mortality fell by almost 50% between 1990 and 2010, a substantial reduction but well short of the 75% decrease called for by MDG Goal 5. Every day an estimated 800 women die during pregnancy or childbirth, and almost all of these deaths can be prevented if women are given access to skilled medical care before, during, and after childbirth. Eighty percent of maternal deaths are caused by severe bleeding, infections, high blood pressure, and unsafe abortions. The other 20% of maternal deaths are the product of diseases such as malaria and the acquired immunodeficiency syndrome.

Because most maternal deaths occur in already impoverished countries that are clustered together geographically, their regional impact is particularly acute. At the most personal level, children who lose their mother tend to experience emotional problems that may make them less productive as adults, and households lose valuable income without an adult female wage earner. In fact, many families, in the time leading up to a mother's death, are pushed over the brink of poverty as a result of the high cost of health care when a mother becomes sick. Communities feel the loss because women in developing countries perform so many essential unpaid tasks, such as caring for children and elders, growing and harvesting food, and gathering fuel and water. High rates of maternal deaths affect the overall economic situation in a region in terms of lost productivity and lost potential for economic, cultural, and technological expansion.

### Access to Reproductive Health Care and Contraception

The presence of a trained doctor, nurse, or midwife during pregnancy and birth increases the likelihood that a mother with life-threatening complications will get the aid she needs to prevent or manage such problems. According to the UN, in *Millennium Development Goals Report 2013*, the share of all births in the developing world attended by skilled practitioners rose from 55% in 1990 to 66% in 2011, but this left 46 million live births (of 135 million total) in which the mother delivered without adequate assistance. Within the developing world, there were dramatic disparities: in East and Central Asia skilled health care assistance at birth was nearly universal in 2011, whereas the rates of assistance in Southern Asia and sub-Saharan Africa were approximately 50%. Access to care also varied dramatically between urban and rural locations. In the developing

world as a whole, women in urban areas had access to skilled health care 84% of the time in 2011, whereas women in rural areas had adequate care in only 53% of cases. (See Figure 7.2.) In Southern Asia and sub-Saharan Africa there were similar disparities between urban and rural locations, and rates of access to care were lower overall: in 40% of rural births in both regions women delivered their children without the help of skilled health care practitioners.

The WHO recommends that pregnant women have a minimum of four prenatal visits with a skilled health care practitioner. Over the course of these visits, women should receive vaccinations, screening, and treatment for various infections and diseases. These visits should also help women identify and avoid possible complications that may threaten their own or their baby's health. Only 51% of pregnant women in the developing world met the WHO minimum of seeing a provider for four or more prenatal checkups in 2011, up from 44% in 2000 and 37% in 1990. (See Figure 7.3.) The prevalence of prenatal care in Southern Asia lagged far behind the average for the developing world, reaching only 36% by 2011; and in sub-Saharan Africa the prevalence of prenatal care had fallen from 52% in 1990 to 49% in 2011. Northern Africa made the largest gains in increasing access to prenatal care, from 23% in 1990 to 66% in 2011, but the availability of care lagged behind the Caribbean (72% in 2011), Southeastern Asia (77%), and Latin America (89%).

**FIGURE 7.2**

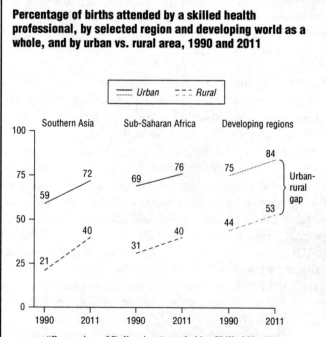

Percentage of births attended by a skilled health professional, by selected region and developing world as a whole, and by urban vs. rural area, 1990 and 2011

SOURCE: "Proportion of Deliveries Attended by Skilled Health Personnel, Urban and Rural Areas, 1990 and 2011," in *The Millennium Development Goals Report 2013*, United Nations, 2013, http://www.un.org/millenniumgoals/pdf/report-2013/mdg-report-2013-english.pdf (accessed September 25, 2013)

**FIGURE 7.3**

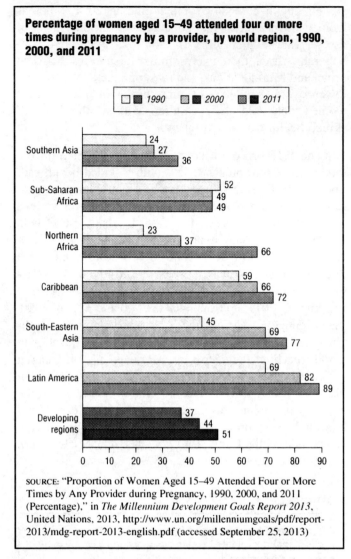

**Percentage of women aged 15–49 attended four or more times during pregnancy by a provider, by world region, 1990, 2000, and 2011**

☐■ *1990*   ☐■ *2000*   ☐■ *2011*

Southern Asia: 24, 27, 36

Sub-Saharan Africa: 52, 49, 49

Northern Africa: 23, 37, 66

Caribbean: 59, 66, 72

South-Eastern Asia: 45, 69, 77

Latin America: 69, 82, 89

Developing regions: 37, 44, 51

SOURCE: "Proportion of Women Aged 15–49 Attended Four or More Times by Any Provider during Pregnancy, 1990, 2000, and 2011 (Percentage)," in *The Millennium Development Goals Report 2013*, United Nations, 2013, http://www.un.org/millenniumgoals/pdf/report-2013/mdg-report-2013-english.pdf (accessed September 25, 2013)

**FIGURE 7.4**

**Percentage of women aged 15–49, married or in relationship, who have an unmet need for family planning, 1990, 2000, and 2011**

☐■ *1990*   ☐■ *2000*   ☐■ *2011*

Oceania: 28, 27, 25

Sub-Saharan Africa: 27.4, 26.6, 25

Caribbean: 19.3, 18.5, 17

Western Asia: 22, 20, 16

Southern Asia: 22, 18, 15

Caucasus & Central Asia: 19, 14.4, 14.1

South-Eastern Asia: 19, 16, 13

Northern Africa: 23, 14, 12

Latin America: 17, 12, 10

Eastern Asia: 6, 3, 4

Developed regions: 11, 10, 10

Developing regions: 17, 14, 13

SOURCE: "Proportion of Women Aged 15–49, Married or in Union, Who Have an Unmet Need for Family Planning, 1990, 2000, and 2011 (Percentage)," in *The Millennium Development Goals Report 2013*, United Nations, 2013, http://www.un.org/millenniumgoals/pdf/report-2013/mdg-report-2013-english.pdf (accessed September 25, 2013)

Maternal mortality tends to be lower not only in countries where access to health care during pregnancy and birth are available but also in countries with high levels of access to contraception. Contraception allows women to time the births of their children and avoid closely recurring or unintended pregnancies. Women who become pregnant unintentionally are less likely to seek out prenatal care even when it is available, and they are more likely to undergo unsafe abortions. Contraceptive prevalence has increased substantially since 1990, as the UN notes, and with this increase has come a decline in the unmet need for family planning (the percentage of women aged 15 to 49 years who are either married or in a relationship but who do not use contraception) in the developing world. As Figure 7.4 shows, in 2011 unmet family planning needs were lowest in Eastern Asia (4%) and highest in Oceania (25%) and sub-Saharan Africa (25%). In the rest of the developing world the prevalence of unmet need ranged from 10% in Latin America to 17% in the Caribbean.

Beyond the unmet need for contraception, advocates for reproductive rights point to the need for more effective forms of contraception in the developing world. In *The Impact of Contraceptive Failure on Unintended Births and Induced Abortions: Estimates and Strategies for Reduction* (September 2011, http://pdf.usaid.gov/pdf _docs/PNADX167.pdf), Sarah E. K. Bradley, Trevor N. Croft, and Shea O. Rutstein note that although it can be difficult to encourage women who have not previously used contraception to begin using it, introducing more effective forms of contraception to women who already use some form of birth control represents a more easily attainable goal. The researchers note that in 20 developing countries studied over the course of four years, 34% of all pregnancies resulted in either an unintended live birth or an abortion. They suggest that increasing the effectiveness of contraception among women who already use some form of birth control could do a great deal to bring standards of reproductive health in the developing world closer to those in the developed world.

## Childbearing in Young Women

Girls and women under the age of 19 years have a significantly higher risk of developing complications during pregnancy and birth than do older women, heightening the risks not only to their own health but to the health of their infant. According to the UN, in *Millennium Development Goals Report 2013*, of the 135 million live births worldwide in 2010, over 15 million were to adolescent mothers between the ages of 15 and 19 years. Some regions of the developing world had adolescent birth rates as low as or lower than the standards for the developed world in 2010. For example, the adolescent birth rate in Eastern Asia was only 6 per 1,000 women, compared with the average of 22 per 1,000 women in the developed world. (See Figure 7.5.) Northern Africa (29), the Caucasus and Central Asia (32), and Southeastern Asia (43) also had comparatively low rates of adolescent birth. The developing region that made the most substantial reduction in the adolescent birth rate was Southern Asia, which declined from 88 per 1,000 in 1990 to 46 per 1,000 in 2010. Western Asia (48) and Oceania (62) had also made meaningful gains, while rates remained higher and had fallen less in the Caribbean (68) and Latin America (80). Child marriage remained commonplace in sub-Saharan Africa, which helps explain why the adolescent birth rate remained at 118 per 1,000 women, down from 125 in 1990.

Besides the risk of health complications to both mother and infant, early motherhood is a major obstacle to economic development at both the family and societal levels. Furthermore, the social and economic structure of many countries reinforces the tendency of women to give birth at ages that imperil their health and their ability to provide for their children. Figure 7.6 depicts the multidirectional effects of adolescent pregnancy and numerous related social and cultural factors, showing that early pregnancy both causes and results from lower productivity and incomes, reduced levels of schooling, and poor health, among other forms of deprivation. As with other poverty indicators, adolescent pregnancy cannot be considered separately from the multiple overlapping forms of deprivation that accompany it.

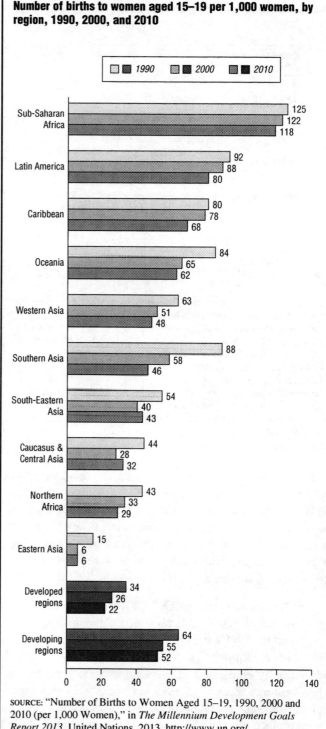

**FIGURE 7.5**

**Number of births to women aged 15–19 per 1,000 women, by region, 1990, 2000, and 2010**

SOURCE: "Number of Births to Women Aged 15–19, 1990, 2000 and 2010 (per 1,000 Women)," in *The Millennium Development Goals Report 2013*, United Nations, 2013, http://www.un.org/millenniumgoals/pdf/report-2013/mdg-report-2013-english.pdf (accessed September 25, 2013)

## Obstetric Fistula

One of the most serious health and social consequences of childbirth in poor countries—particularly in sub-Saharan Africa and South Asia—is the development of obstetric fistula. This childbirth-related injury is caused by exceptionally long labor—often as long as five to seven days—that

## FIGURE 7.6

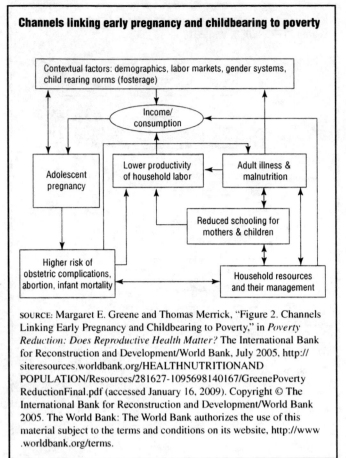

**Channels linking early pregnancy and childbearing to poverty**

Contextual factors: demographics, labor markets, gender systems, child rearing norms (fosterage)

Income/consumption

Adolescent pregnancy

Lower productivity of household labor

Adult illness & malnutrition

Reduced schooling for mothers & children

Higher risk of obstetric complications, abortion, infant mortality

Household resources and their management

SOURCE: Margaret E. Greene and Thomas Merrick, "Figure 2. Channels Linking Early Pregnancy and Childbearing to Poverty," in *Poverty Reduction: Does Reproductive Health Matter?* The International Bank for Reconstruction and Development/World Bank, July 2005, http://siteresources.worldbank.org/HEALTHNUTRITIONAND POPULATION/Resources/281627-1095698140167/GreenePoverty ReductionFinal.pdf (accessed January 16, 2009). Copyright © The International Bank for Reconstruction and Development/World Bank 2005. The World Bank: The World Bank authorizes the use of this material subject to the terms and conditions on its website, http://www .worldbank.org/terms.

cuts off blood flow to the mother's vagina, bladder, and/or rectum. Areas of tissue that are severely deprived of oxygen die due to the lack of blood flow. The resulting holes in the tissue leave women unable to control the flow of urine and feces, which leak out constantly. Nerve damage to the legs, severe infections, and kidney disease are also common among fistula sufferers.

In "Fast Facts and FAQs" (2014, http://www.fistula foundation.org/whatisfistula/faqs.html), the Fistula Foundation and the WHO state that more than 1 million women worldwide are known to suffer from obstetric fistula, which was virtually eradicated in the United States and Europe when cesarean sections (the delivery of a fetus by surgical incision through the abdominal wall and uterus) became commonplace during the late 19th century and skilled health care became available to treat birthing emergencies immediately. The actual number of women who live with this condition is unknown because it is rarely discussed, most women who suffer from it never get medical help, and it most often occurs in remote areas of the world (estimates are based on the numbers of women who seek treatment).

## GENDER EQUALITY IN EDUCATION

The *Beijing Declaration* and the *Platform for Action* identify education as an essential human right that contributes to economic development at all levels of society. This principle has won nearly unanimous support in the international community and has been endorsed by the UN, the UN Educational, Scientific, and Cultural Organization, and the World Bank, among many others. In many parts of the developing world, however, there remains a large gap between this statement of principle and the actuality of educational access among the poor.

As discussed in Chapter 2, the number of illiterate people aged 15 years and older has fallen dramatically relative to the total world population, from 880.5 million in 1990 to 773.5 million in 2011. (See Table 2.5 in Chapter 2.) Although illiteracy remains a problem across much of the developed world, it was particularly concentrated in 10 high-population countries, which together accounted for 75% of the entire world's illiterate adult population in 2005–10: India (287 million), China (62 million), Pakistan (50 million), Bangladesh (44 million), Nigeria (35 million), Ethiopia (27 million), Egypt (16 million), Brazil (14 million), Indonesia (13 million), and the Democratic Republic of the Congo (12 million). (See Figure 2.6 in Chapter 2.) Among developing regions, sub-Saharan Africa had the highest concentration of illiteracy by the percentage of total population: 10 of the 11 countries with adult literacy rates below 50% were in the region, and in four countries (Niger, Burkina Faso, Mali, and Chad) only around one out of three adults was literate.

Women were overrepresented among all illiterate adults in 2011, accounting for 493.2 million (63.8%) of the total 773.5 million illiterate people over the age of 15 years. (See Table 2.5 in Chapter 2.) In all regions of the developing world, women were more likely to be illiterate than men. Women accounted for 55.1% of the adult illiterate population in Latin America and the Caribbean, 61.2% of the illiterate population in sub-Saharan Africa, 63.8% of the illiterate population in South and West Asia, and 70.9% of the illiterate population in East Asia.

Figure 7.7 provides an overview of girls' enrollment rates relative to boys' at the primary, secondary, and tertiary levels of school in the years 1990 and 2011. Enrollment comparisons are quantified using a gender parity index (GPI) that represents the ratio of girls to boys in schools. A GPI of 1 indicates that there is one girl for every boy enrolled in a given region, numbers less than 1 indicate that there are fewer girls than boys enrolled, and numbers greater than 1 indicate that there are more girls than boys enrolled. The range of GPI values that qualifies as parity is 0.97 to 1.03. As of 2011, the developing world as a whole had achieved gender parity at the primary (0.97) and tertiary (0.98) levels and had come very close to parity at the secondary level (0.96). At all three levels of education, this represented a significant improvement over 1990 GPI values, which stood at 0.86 for primary school, 0.76 for secondary school, and 0.68 for tertiary school.

**FIGURE 7.7**

**Gender parity index in primary, secondary, and tertiary education, by region, 1990 and 2011**

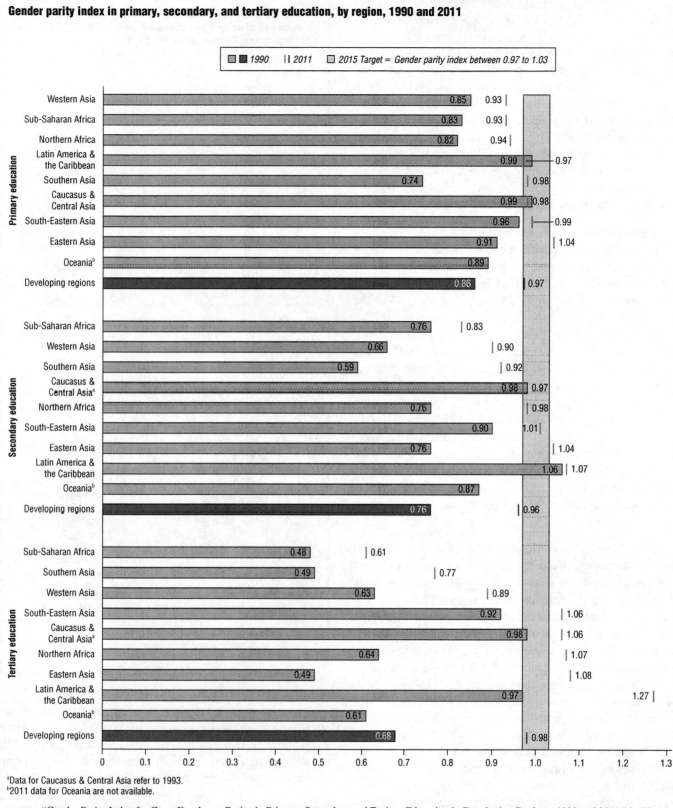

[Legend: ▨ 1990 ‖ 2011 ☐ 2015 Target = Gender parity index between 0.97 to 1.03]

**Primary education**

| Region | 1990 | 2011 |
|---|---|---|
| Western Asia | 0.85 | 0.93 |
| Sub-Saharan Africa | 0.83 | 0.93 |
| Northern Africa | 0.82 | 0.94 |
| Latin America & the Caribbean | 0.99 | 0.97 |
| Southern Asia | 0.74 | 0.98 |
| Caucasus & Central Asia | 0.99 | 0.98 |
| South-Eastern Asia | 0.96 | 0.99 |
| Eastern Asia | 0.91 | 1.04 |
| Oceania[b] | 0.89 | |
| Developing regions | 0.86 | 0.97 |

**Secondary education**

| Region | 1990 | 2011 |
|---|---|---|
| Sub-Saharan Africa | 0.76 | 0.83 |
| Western Asia | 0.66 | 0.90 |
| Southern Asia | 0.59 | 0.92 |
| Caucasus & Central Asia[a] | 0.98 | 0.97 |
| Northern Africa | 0.76 | 0.98 |
| South-Eastern Asia | 0.90 | 1.01 |
| Eastern Asia | 0.76 | 1.04 |
| Latin America & the Caribbean | 1.06 | 1.07 |
| Oceania[b] | 0.87 | |
| Developing regions | 0.76 | 0.96 |

**Tertiary education**

| Region | 1990 | 2011 |
|---|---|---|
| Sub-Saharan Africa | 0.48 | 0.61 |
| Southern Asia | 0.49 | 0.77 |
| Western Asia | 0.63 | 0.89 |
| South-Eastern Asia | 0.92 | 1.06 |
| Caucasus & Central Asia[a] | 0.98 | 1.06 |
| Northern Africa | 0.64 | 1.07 |
| Eastern Asia | 0.49 | 1.08 |
| Latin America & the Caribbean | 0.97 | 1.27 |
| Oceania[b] | 0.61 | |
| Developing regions | 0.68 | 0.98 |

[Axis: 0  0.1  0.2  0.3  0.4  0.5  0.6  0.7  0.8  0.9  1.0  1.1  1.2  1.3]

[a]Data for Caucasus & Central Asia refer to 1993.
[b]2011 data for Oceania are not available.

SOURCE: "Gender Parity Index for Gress Enrolment Ratios in Primary, Secondary and Tertiary Education in Developing Regions, 1990 and 2011," in *The Millennium Development Goals Report 2013*, United Nations, 2013, http://www.un.org/millenniumgoals/pdf/report-2013/mdg-report-2013-english.pdf (accessed September 25, 2013)

At all educational levels, all developing regions had either made progress toward gender parity or maintained gender parity since 1990, but there was substantial variation in GPI values among individual regions. At the primary level, all regions for which 2011 data were available had achieved gender parity except

Western Asia (0.93), sub-Saharan Africa (0.93), and northern Africa (0.94). (See Figure 7.7.) Eastern Asia's GPI fell outside the range of parity, but in the opposite direction, with more girls enrolled than boys. At the secondary level, sub-Saharan Africa (0.83), Western Asia (0.90), and Southern Asia (0.92) fell significantly short of gender parity, while the remaining developing regions had either achieved or exceeded parity. At the tertiary level, more significant shortcomings among the regions that had not achieved parity—sub-Saharan Africa (0.61), Southern Asia (0.77), and Western Asia (0.89)—were balanced by GPI values that exceeded parity in the rest of the developing world. In Latin America and the Caribbean (1.27), females outnumbered males by a particularly wide margin at the tertiary level.

Although Southern Asia lagged behind other developing regions in gender parity at the secondary and tertiary levels, it had made rapid progress in achieving gender parity at all levels of education since 1990. Over the course of this period, the region's GPI increased by 0.24 at the primary level, by 0.33 at the secondary level, and by 0.28 at the tertiary level. (See Figure 7.7.) Northern Africa and Eastern Asia, both of which had higher primary GPI values than Southern Asia in 1990, made extremely rapid progress at the secondary and tertiary levels: northern Africa increased its GPI by 0.22 at the secondary level and by 0.43 at the tertiary level, and Eastern Asia increased its GPI by 0.28 at the secondary level and by 0.59 at the tertiary level. The developing regions that made less progress were generally those that had already achieved parity or near-parity in 1990. The exception was sub-Saharan Africa, which made comparatively modest progress toward parity at all three levels.

In the developing world as a whole, poverty and rural/ urban location were strong predictors of a child's likelihood to be out of school in 2005–11, and gender was a slightly weaker predictor. Among the poorest 20% of the developing world's population, 31% of primary-age girls were not enrolled in school, compared with 28% of boys. (See Figure 7.8.) In contrast, among the developing world's richest 20%, only 9% of girls and 8% of boys were out of school. A similar pattern held among the children in the lower grades of secondary school: 35% of girls and 30% of boys from the poorest 20% of households were out of school, compared with 13% of girls and 9% of boys from the richest 20% of households. Furthermore, rural children in the developing world were much more likely than urban children to be out of school. At the primary level, 22% of rural children were not enrolled in school, compared with 12% of urban children; and at the lower secondary level, 24% of rural children were out of school, compared with 15% of urban children.

As the previous statistics indicate, poverty and female illiteracy broadly overlap, and female illiteracy is likewise reinforced by a number of other social factors.

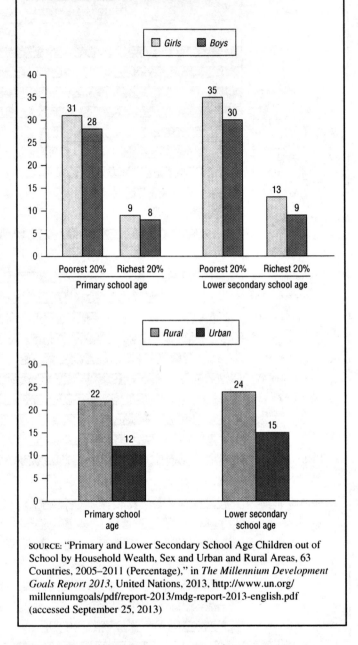

**FIGURE 7.8**

**Percentage of primary and lower secondary school-age children out of school by household wealth, sex, and urban and rural areas, 63 countries, 2005–11**

SOURCE: "Primary and Lower Secondary School Age Children out of School by Household Wealth, Sex and Urban and Rural Areas, 63 Countries, 2005–2011 (Percentage)," in *The Millennium Development Goals Report 2013*, United Nations, 2013, http://www.un.org/millenniumgoals/pdf/report-2013/mdg-report-2013-english.pdf (accessed September 25, 2013)

The costs associated with educating girls are often not seen as a worthwhile investment in regions where the opportunities for women to find paid work are rare. Additionally, generalized forms of bias against women often result in a devaluation of women's productive capacity and even, in some cases, prohibitions against girls' being educated. Especially in poor rural areas where subsistence farming is the norm, daughters and wives are frequently expected to stay home and do field work, housework, and care for elders and young siblings, without any promise of financial return. Moreover, girls in many developing areas are sometimes at risk of sexual predation and assault when they leave home, leading their families to avoid enrolling them in school. Finally, early marriage, which is particularly common in the poorest parts of the developing world, often interrupts the educational careers of girls.

Just as multiple societal norms in the world's poorest regions work to reinforce female illiteracy, female illiteracy functions to limit the economic potential not only of families but also of communities, countries, and regions. In "Educating Girls: What Works" (July 1, 2011, http://iipdigital.usembassy.gov/st/english/publication/2011/06/20110624094700aidan0.9995037.html#axzz1ik7l2 Skz), Barbara Herz notes that education for girls in developing countries is essential for economic success at all levels of society and that it may even represent the single most efficient investment a country can make. The benefits of educating girls come in the form of higher wages and faster economic growth, which in turn translate into decreased levels of malnutrition; women having smaller, healthier, and more educated families; reducing the spread of the human immunodeficiency virus; fostering participation in governmental processes; and encouraging better farming practices. Herz notes the dramatic improvements in primary school participation rates for girls, but notes that the economic and cultural benefits of female education continue to grow with each additional year of secondary school.

According to Herz, even modest increases in the number of women receiving a secondary education can lead to a slight increase in their nation's annual per capita (per person) income. As per capita growth continues, more girls achieve higher levels of education—a cycle that is ultimately beneficial for everyone. In addition, the more education women have, the lower their rates of fertility. For example, Stephan Klasen of the University of Munich explains in *Does Gender Inequality Reduce Growth and Development? Evidence from Cross-Country Regressions* (November 1999, http://siteresources.worldbank.org/INTGENDER/Resources/wp7.pdf) that a 100-country study conducted by the World Bank in 1999 showed that for every four years of extra schooling that a woman obtains, it reduces her fertility by about one birth. Likewise, in "Women and Girls: Education, Not Discrimination!" (April 2000, http://www.unesco.org/education/wef/en-docs/presskit/wome.pdf), the UN Educational, Scientific, and Cultural Organization notes that a study in Brazil found that illiterate women have approximately six children, whereas literate women have approximately 2.5 children.

Herz cites several important measures for encouraging girls to continue their education beyond primary school, including:

- Cutting or eliminating school fees
- Making school more convenient by reducing the distance between schools and residences, supplying

basic materials free of charge, and allowing for flexible hours

- Promoting girls' comfort in school through measures such as providing adequate sanitation facilities, allowing for separation from boys in societies that mandate segregation by sex, updating curricula to promote positive views of girls and women, and hiring female teachers in greater numbers
- Improving educational quality through teacher training, emphasizing interactive learning and problem solving over rote learning, and designing curricula that prepare students for jobs in the 21st century
- Mobilizing communities to prioritize female educational achievement and to provide the multifaceted support necessary for enacting reforms

Herz notes that these measures have already proved successful in a number of countries worldwide. The question, then, is not whether it is possible to improve the rates of female education and literacy and spur economic development, but whether individual countries, regions, and the international community have the political will and the readiness to use often-scarce financial resources for this purpose.

## CHILD POVERTY

Children are both more likely to live in poverty than adults and more vulnerable to the various forms of deprivation associated with poverty. Children's heightened vulnerability is a result of their lesser capacity for enduring hardships and the fact that deprivation can inhibit the all-important early years of mental and physical development. A failure to develop normally has permanent and irreversible impacts, undermining the individual's ability to live fully and participate in society as an adult. Impoverished children are frequently unable to escape poverty as adults, and they often transmit poverty to the next generation when they become parents themselves, reinforcing the cycle of poverty.

On average, fertility rates (the number of births per woman) are highest in the poorest countries in the world. This is due to a variety of factors, but the central driver of disparities in fertility is access to contraception. Adequate and affordable contraceptive methods have been commonplace in the developed world since the 1970s, but in many of the poorest countries in sub-Saharan Africa and Asia, women continue to have inadequate knowledge of and access to effective contraception. The Central Intelligence Agency indicates in *World Factbook: Country Comparison* (2013, https://www.cia.gov/library/publications/the-world-factbook/rankorder/2127rank.html) that the fertility rate in Niger was 7.03 in 2013, nearly nine times greater than that in Singapore (0.79), the country with the lowest fertility rate in the world. Most developed countries had a birth rate of around 2 births per woman or lower in 2013, whereas most countries in Africa had a birth rate of 3.5 per woman or higher. Thus, those parents who are the least able to ensure that their children will be well equipped for life are on average the ones who have the most children.

According to the Population Reference Bureau (PRB), in *2013 World Population Data Sheet* (September 2013, http://www.prb.org/pdf13/2013-population-data-sheet _eng.pdf), in 2013 there were an estimated 390,778 births per day, and 352,521 were in less developed countries. Sub-Saharan Africa's population is expected to grow from 900 million in 2013 to 2.2 billion in 2050, far outpacing growth rates elsewhere in the world. Whereas 26% of the total world population was under the age of 15 years in 2013, 43% of sub-Saharan Africa's population, compared with 31% of South Asia's population and 28% of Southeast Asia's population, was under 15 years. In developed countries, children accounted for a much smaller proportion of the total population: people under the age of 15 years accounted for only 19% of the U.S. population, 16% of the European Union population, and 13% of the Japanese population.

## Mortality Rates

In the developing world, poverty is a life-and-death matter for large numbers of children. Many children in the poorest parts of the world face deprivations such as inadequate nutrition and a lack of access to clean water, sanitation facilities, and health care—deprivations that result in developmental problems, frequent illness, and death. Because of the long-term effects of child poverty and because child mortality is frequently one of the clearest signs of the intensity and level of entrenchment of poverty, child mortality rates are among the most closely watched development indicators. How much a country invests—or does not invest—in measures to cut back preventable deaths and diseases of children is ultimately indicative of how far that country is from fully developing its economy for the benefit of its people.

Figure 7.9 shows the mortality rates for children under the age of five years (deaths per every 1,000 live births) in 1990 and 2011. Although all regions made substantial progress in reducing child mortality, the developing world as a whole lagged well behind the MDG target of reducing such deaths by two-thirds, and progress varied among regions.

Sub-Saharan Africa had reduced child mortality from a rate of 178 per 1,000 in 1990 to 109 per 1,000 in 2011, for a reduction of 39%. (See Figure 7.9.) Although this reduction was significant, the region's 2011 rate was almost 16 times higher than the rate for the developed world as a whole, at 7 per 1,000. The UN notes in *Millennium Development Goals Report 2013* that one out of every nine children in sub-Saharan Africa died before the age of five years in 2011. Southern Asia had

FIGURE 7.9

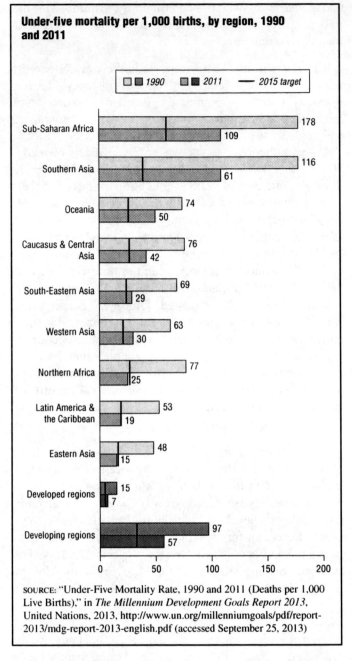

**Under-five mortality per 1,000 births, by region, 1990 and 2011**

SOURCE: "Under-Five Mortality Rate, 1990 and 2011 (Deaths per 1,000 Live Births)," in *The Millennium Development Goals Report 2013*, United Nations, 2013, http://www.un.org/millenniumgoals/pdf/report-2013/mdg-report-2013-english.pdf (accessed September 25, 2013)

made more progress and was closer to the developed world's rate, but it still had an extremely high rate of child mortality. The region's under-five death rate fell from 116 to 61 between 1990 and 2011, for a reduction of 47%, but one out of 16 children in Southern Asia continued to die before the age of five years in 2011. Combined, sub-Saharan Africa and Southern Asia accounted for 5.7 million (83%) of the 6.9 million under-five deaths worldwide in 2011.

Oceania had a lower rate of child mortality in 2011 (50) than sub-Saharan Africa or Southern Asia, but its rate of decrease since 1990 (32%) was significantly lower than that of any other developing region. (See Figure 7.9.) The Caucasus and Central Asia achieved a rate reduction of 45%, from 76 to 42, and three developing regions achieved reductions of between 50% and 65%: Western Asia, where the rate dropped from 63 to 30 (52%); Southeastern Asia, where the rate dropped from 69 to 29 (58%); and Latin America and the Caribbean, where the rate dropped from 53 to 19 (64%). Only northern Africa, where the rate dropped from 77 to 25 (68%), and Eastern Asia, where the rate dropped from 48 to 15 (69%), had met the MDG target as of 2011.

In all parts of the developing world, neonatal mortality (death during the first month of life) rates have fallen more slowly than under-five mortality rates. The UN notes that whereas the under-five mortality rate has declined by an average of 2.5% per year since 1990, the neonatal mortality rate has fallen by only 1.8% per year. Accordingly, neonatal mortality increased from 36% of total child mortality in 1990 to 43% in 2011. The UN thus recommends that, in the ongoing effort to reduce child mortality worldwide, the international community should redouble its focus on the first month of life.

## Other Health Issues

MALNUTRITION. Child malnutrition typically occurs as a result of insufficient food intake, poor feeding practices, and inadequate nutrients in the food that is available. In the poorest parts of the world, the problem frequently begins in the womb, as mothers experience chronic hunger or an insufficiently nutritious diet. Babies are born underweight and are therefore at a significant developmental disadvantage; as insufficient nutrition continues throughout their childhood, the disadvantages they face increase even further. Malnutrition correlates not only with slow physical development and increased susceptibility to disease but also to poor performance in school. Malnourished children thus frequently become adults who are less capable of contributing to society, and these problems are often passed on to the next generation.

In general, the developing world has made substantial progress in reducing malnutrition among children as measured by being underweight for one's age. The developing regions of South Asia and East Asia, led by gains in the Chinese and Indian economies, had both made rapid progress in reducing child malnutrition since 1990, but South Asia's rate of malnutrition remained the world's highest in 2011, at around 35%. (See Figure 7.10.) Meanwhile, East Asia saw the prevalence of child malnutrition fall from 20% to around 5%, slightly higher than that of Latin America and the Caribbean and Europe and Central Asia. Sub-Saharan Africa had made little progress in reducing child malnutrition; its prevalence rate in 2011 stood at approximately 25%, down from just under 30% in 1990.

CLEAN WATER AND SANITATION. According to the World Bank, in *Global Monitoring Report 2013:*

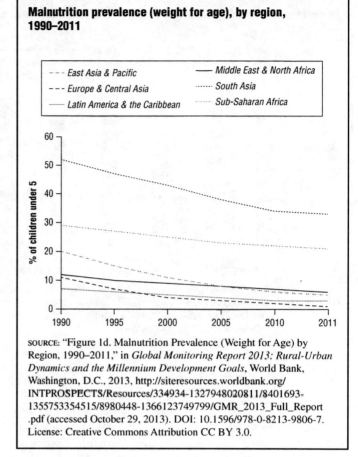

**FIGURE 7.10**

**Malnutrition prevalence (weight for age), by region, 1990–2011**

- - - East Asia & Pacific  — Middle East & North Africa
- - - Europe & Central Asia  ········ South Asia
—— Latin America & the Caribbean  ········ Sub-Saharan Africa

SOURCE: "Figure 1d. Malnutrition Prevalence (Weight for Age) by Region, 1990–2011," in *Global Monitoring Report 2013: Rural-Urban Dynamics and the Millennium Development Goals*, World Bank, Washington, D.C., 2013, http://siteresources.worldbank.org/INTPROSPECTS/Resources/334934-1327948020811/8401693-1355753354515/8980448-1366123749799/GMR_2013_Full_Report.pdf (accessed October 29, 2013). DOI: 10.1596/978-0-8213-9806-7. License: Creative Commons Attribution CC BY 3.0.

*Rural-Urban Dynamics and the Millennium Development Goals* (2013, http://siteresources.worldbank.org/INTPROSPECTS/Resources/334934-1327948020811/8401693-1355753354515/8980448-1366123749799/GMR_2013_Full_Report.pdf), approximately 1.7 million annual deaths are attributable to unsafe water or sanitation problems, and 90% of those who die for these reasons are children under the age of five years. As discussed in Chapter 3, unsafe water and sanitation facilities can result in a variety of bacterial infections, many of which lead to diarrhea, a leading cause of death among children in the developing world. In general, access to clean water and sanitation facilities has increased across the developing world, but as in many other indicators of development, South Asia and sub-Saharan Africa lag behind other regions. Additionally, in all developing regions, rural areas lag significantly behind urban areas in their levels of access to water and sanitation. According to the World Bank, almost all water- and sanitation-related deaths occur in rural areas because sanitation problems affect a higher proportion of the population and because there is less access to health care in the event of infection.

Figure 7.11 shows the levels of access to improved water sources in 1990 and 2010. Rates of access in urban areas of the developing world had increased over the course of the two decades considered and were approaching 100% except in sub-Saharan Africa, where urban access stood at

**FIGURE 7.11**

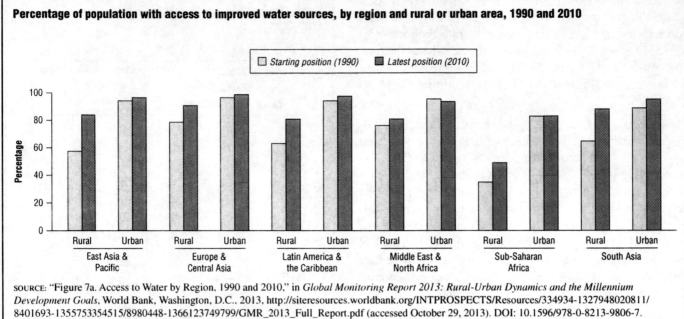

Percentage of population with access to improved water sources, by region and rural or urban area, 1990 and 2010

SOURCE: "Figure 7a. Access to Water by Region, 1990 and 2010," in *Global Monitoring Report 2013: Rural-Urban Dynamics and the Millennium Development Goals*, World Bank, Washington, D.C., 2013, http://siteresources.worldbank.org/INTPROSPECTS/Resources/334934-1327948020811/8401693-1355753354515/8980448-1366123749799/GMR_2013_Full_Report.pdf (accessed October 29, 2013). DOI: 10.1596/978-0-8213-9806-7. License: Creative Commons Attribution CC BY 3.0.

83% in both 1990 and 2010. Rates of access in rural areas had improved across the developing world, with particular gains evident in East Asia and the Pacific, where access grew from 58% to 84%. Rural areas of Latin America and the Caribbean and South Asia also saw substantial improvement, and access levels stood at over 80% in 2010, similar to the levels in rural Middle East and North Africa, where progress was slower but where access had been more widespread initially. Rural sub-Saharan Africa also made significant progress, improving access by 14 percentage points, but in 2010 less than half of the region's rural population had access to clean water.

Access to improved sanitation facilities fell much further short of universality. Only in urban areas of Europe and Central Asia, Latin America and the Caribbean, and the Middle East and North Africa were rates of access higher than 80% in 2010; and none of these regions had made substantial progress in extending urban access. (See Figure 7.12.) Only in East Asia and the Pacific was there a dramatic increase in access (of approximately 22 percentage points) among the urban population. Most regions made more progress in extending access to sanitation in rural areas, but rural access levels were much lower to begin with, and they remained dangerously low even in the higher-income parts of the developing world. Access rates were highest in the rural areas of Europe and Central Asia and the Middle East and North Africa, in both of which approximately 80% of rural residents had adequate sanitation facilities. East Asia and the Pacific made exceptionally rapid progress in extending rural access to sanitation, as levels rose from around 20% in 1990 to nearly 60% in 2010, but that still left more than

40% of the rural population exposed to preventable illnesses and death. A similar proportion of Latin America and the Caribbean's rural population was exposed to danger due to inadequate sanitation.

Meanwhile, the sanitation situation in South Asia and sub-Saharan Africa remained woefully inadequate in 2010. Rates of access in urban areas of both regions were lower than rates of access in rural areas of other developing regions: only around 50% of urban sub-Saharan Africans and around 60% of urban South Asians had access to sanitation facilities. (See Figure 7.12.) In rural areas of these regions, lack of access to sanitation facilities was the norm. Access stood at around 25% in rural sub-Saharan Africa and at around 30% in rural South Asia in 2010, underscoring the risks that children in the poorest parts of these regions faced.

**Child Labor**

Many children around the world, especially those from poor or middle-income families, work either outside the home or at home without experiencing negative impacts to their health, their development, or their educational progress. In general, such forms of child work are positive and improve both child and household welfare. Other forms of work performed by children, however, harm their mental and physical development, force them prematurely into adulthood, and undermine their dignity and their hopes for the future. These forms of work are classified as child labor, and they are primarily a phenomenon in the developing world. International groups such as the ILO are committed to eliminating them on human rights grounds.

## FIGURE 7.12

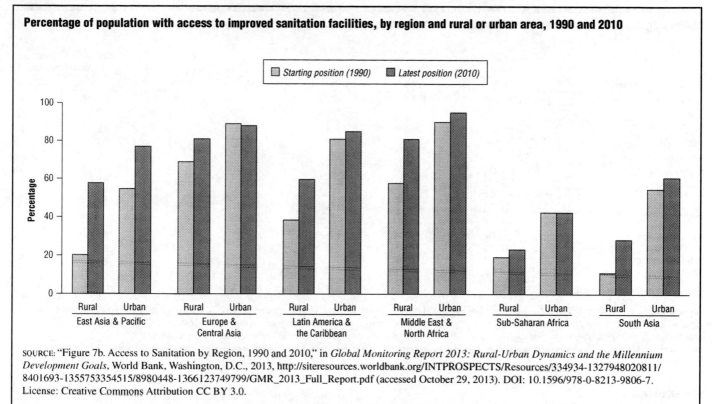

**Percentage of population with access to improved sanitation facilities, by region and rural or urban area, 1990 and 2010**

☐ Starting position (1990)　■ Latest position (2010)

SOURCE: "Figure 7b. Access to Sanitation by Region, 1990 and 2010," in *Global Monitoring Report 2013: Rural-Urban Dynamics and the Millennium Development Goals*, World Bank, Washington, D.C., 2013, http://siteresources.worldbank.org/INTPROSPECTS/Resources/334934-1327948020811/ 8401693-1355753354515/8980448-1366123749799/GMR_2013_Full_Report.pdf (accessed October 29, 2013). DOI: 10.1596/978-0-8213-9806-7. License: Creative Commons Attribution CC BY 3.0.

According to the ILO, in "What Is Child Labour" (2014, http://www.ilo.org/ipec/facts/lang--en/index.htm), child labor refers to work that:

- Is mentally, physically, socially or morally dangerous and harmful to children; and

- Interferes with their schooling by:

- Depriving them of the opportunity to attend school;

- Obliging them to leave school prematurely; or

- Requiring them to attempt to combine school attendance with excessively long and heavy work.

The worst forms of child labor are a particular focus of international organizations. They include slavery and conditions similar to slavery (such as trafficking, debt bondage, forced labor, and the use of children as soldiers); the use of children for prostitution, pornography, drug trafficking, or other illegal activities; and work that is likely to undermine a child's health, safety, or morals. The ILO and other international organizations also collect data on "hazardous work," which is a subset of child labor "that jeopardises the physical, mental or moral well-being of a child, either because of its nature or because of the conditions in which it is carried out."

Table 7.2 shows the number and percentage of children aged five to 17 years who were engaged in employment (including both child labor and forms of work that are not classified as child labor), child labor, and hazardous work

in 2012; and it breaks down these numbers and percentages by sex, age, and region. Of the nearly 1.6 billion children in this age range globally, 264.4 million (16.7%) did some form of work, 168 million (10.6%) were involved in child labor, and 85.3 million (5.4%) were engaged in hazardous work. Boys were more likely to perform all three varieties of work, and for both boys and girls, 12- to 17-year-olds were significantly more likely to be involved in all three forms of employment than were 5- to 11-year-olds.

Children in sub-Saharan Africa were far more likely to be engaged in all three varieties of work than were children elsewhere in the developed world in 2012. More than one out of five (21.4%) children in the region participated in child labor and one out of 10 (10.4%) was involved in hazardous work. (See Table 7.2.) The other three developing regions surveyed by the ILO had rates of child labor and hazardous work roughly half those of sub-Saharan Africa's. In Asia and the Pacific, 9.3% of children were engaged in child labor and 4.1% in hazardous work; in Latin America and the Caribbean, 8.8% of children were engaged in child labor and 6.8% in hazardous work; and in the Middle East and North Africa, 8.4% children were engaged in child labor and 4.7% in hazardous work.

Agricultural work was by far the most common form of child labor in 2012. Nearly six out of 10 (58.6%) child laborers worked in agriculture and another quarter (25.4%) worked in service jobs, a sector that includes informal work in hotels, restaurants, auto-repair shops, and street vending.

**TABLE 7.2**

**Children aged 5–17 in employment, child labor, and hazardous work, by sex, age group, and region, 2012**

| Sex, age group and region | Total children ('000) | Children in employment ('000) | % | Child labour ('000) | % | Hazardous work ('000) | % |
|---|---|---|---|---|---|---|---|
| **World (5–17 years)** | **1,585,566** | **264,427** | **16.7** | **167,956** | **10.6** | **85,344** | **5.4** |
| **Sex** | | | | | | | |
| Boys | 819,877 | 148,327 | 18.1 | 99,766 | 12.2 | 55,048 | 6.7 |
| Girls | 765,690 | 116,100 | 15.2 | 68,190 | 8.9 | 30,296 | 4.0 |
| **Age group** | | | | | | | |
| 5–11 years | 858,925 | 73,072 | 8.5 | 73,072 | 8.5 | 18,499 | 2.2 |
| 12–14 years | 362,146 | 70,994 | 19.6 | 47,381 | 13.1 | 19,342 | 5.3 |
| 5–14 years | 1,221,071 | 144,066 | 11.8 | 120,453 | 9.9 | 37,841 | 3.1 |
| 15–17 years | 364,495 | 120,362 | 33.0 | 47,503 | 13.0 | 47,503 | 13.0 |
| **Region** | | | | | | | |
| Asia and the Pacific | 835,334 | 129,358 | 15.5 | 77,723 | 9.3 | 33,860 | 4.1 |
| Latin America and the Caribbean | 142,693 | 17,843 | 12.5 | 12,505 | 8.8 | 9,638 | 6.8 |
| Sub-SaharanAfrica | 275,397 | 83,570 | 30.3 | 59,031 | 21.4 | 28,767 | 10.4 |
| MENA | 110,411 | 13,307 | 12.1 | 9,244 | 8.4 | 5,224 | 4.7 |

MENA = Middle East and North Africa.

SOURCE: "Table 8. Children in Employment, Child Labour and Hazardous Work by Sex, Age Group and Region, 2012," in *Marking Progress against Child Labour: Global Estimates and Trends 2000–2012*, International Labour Office, International Programme on the Elimination of Child Labour (IPEC), 2013, http://www.ilo.org/wcmsp5/groups/public/---ed_norm/---ipec/documents/publication/wcms_221513.pdf (accessed October 28, 2013)

**FIGURE 7.13**

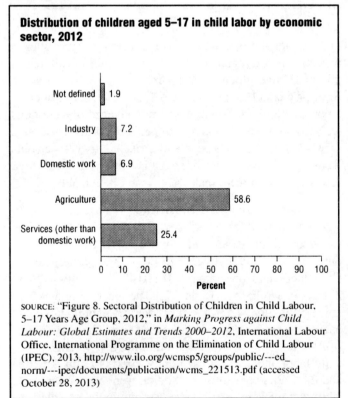

**Distribution of children aged 5–17 in child labor by economic sector, 2012**

SOURCE: "Figure 8. Sectoral Distribution of Children in Child Labour, 5–17 Years Age Group, 2012," in *Marking Progress against Child Labour: Global Estimates and Trends 2000–2012*, International Labour Office, International Programme on the Elimination of Child Labour (IPEC), 2013, http://www.ilo.org/wcmsp5/groups/public/---ed_norm/---ipec/documents/publication/wcms_221513.pdf (accessed October 28, 2013)

(See Figure 7.13.) Industry, which consists primarily of informal construction and manufacturing work, accounted for 7.2% of all child labor, and domestic work accounted for 6.9%. According to the ILO, in *Marking Progress against Child Labour: Global Estimates and Trends 2000–2012* (2013, http://www.ilo.org/wcmsp5/groups/public/---ed_norm/---ipec/documents/publication/wcms_2215 13.pdf), boys outnumbered girls in all sectors except domestic work. The ILO notes that girls in domestic work are particularly vulnerable to abuse and exploitation because their work occurs in private and cannot be monitored by workplace inspectors. Roughly seven out of 10 (68.4%) child laborers worked for family members on an unpaid basis. (See Figure 7.14.) Another 22.5% were paid for their work and 8.1% were self-employed.

The ILO indicates that since 2000 there have been substantial gains made in the reduction of child labor and hazardous work worldwide. The proportion of all 5- to 17-year-old children engaged in child labor fell from 16% in 2000 to 10.6% in 2012, for a raw numerical decline of 77.5 million, even as the total population of children was growing. Declines in the proportion of children engaged in hazardous work were even more rapid, falling from 11.1% to 5.4%, for a raw numerical decline of 85.2 million. However, progress was highly concentrated in the Asia-Pacific region, where the number of child laborers fell from 113.6 million in 2008 to 77.7 million in 2012. (See Figure 7.15.) By comparison, the population of child laborers fell modestly in Latin America and the Caribbean (from 14.1 million in 2008 to 12.5 million in 2012) and in sub-Saharan Africa (from 65.1 million to 59 million).

**FIGURE 7.14**

**Distribution of children aged 5–17 in child labor by status of employment, 2012**

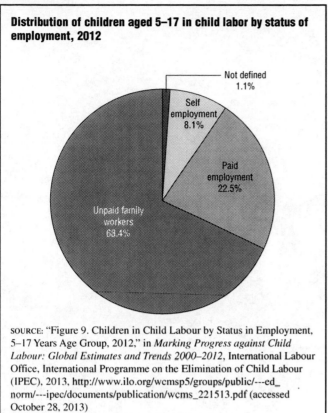

SOURCE: "Figure 9. Children in Child Labour by Status in Employment, 5–17 Years Age Group, 2012," in *Marking Progress against Child Labour: Global Estimates and Trends 2000–2012*, International Labour Office, International Programme on the Elimination of Child Labour (IPEC), 2013, http://www.ilo.org/wcmsp5/groups/public/---ed_norm/---ipec/documents/publication/wcms_221513.pdf (accessed October 28, 2013)

**FIGURE 7.15**

**Regional trends in number of children aged 5–17 involved in child labor, 2008 and 2012**

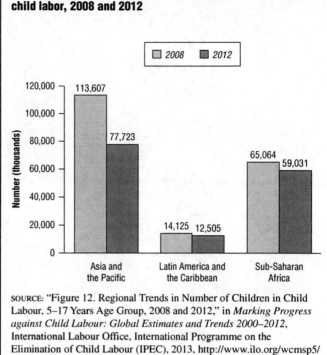

SOURCE: "Figure 12. Regional Trends in Number of Children in Child Labour, 5–17 Years Age Group, 2008 and 2012," in *Marking Progress against Child Labour: Global Estimates and Trends 2000–2012*, International Labour Office, International Programme on the Elimination of Child Labour (IPEC), 2013, http://www.ilo.org/wcmsp5/groups/public/---ed_norm/---ipec/documents/publication/wcms_221513.pdf (accessed October 28, 2013)

# CHAPTER 8
# POVERTY AND ENVIRONMENTAL HAZARDS

Residents of the developing world, and particularly of the developing world's poorest and most populous countries, suffer more often and more intensely from environmental hazards—natural disasters as well as human-caused environmental problems—than residents of wealthier countries. Additionally, the number of reported natural disasters has been rising since the 1980s, as the prevalence of climate- and weather-related disasters such as storms, floods, droughts, and wildfires have increased relative to geophysical disasters such as earthquakes and volcano eruptions. Although debate continues over the role that climate change plays in the occurrence of destructive weather events, the scientific consensus suggests that because of climate change, regularly recurring storms such as monsoons (seasonal rains) and hurricanes (also known as typhoons and cyclones) are increasingly likely to be more powerful than in previous eras. Likewise, large-scale incremental environmental problems such as drought are widely understood to have become more common and more destructive because of climate change, and rising sea levels, which threaten many of the densest coastal regions on the earth, are directly linked to climate change.

In numerical terms, the developing countries of Asia and the Pacific have suffered far more from natural disasters than the countries of any other world region since the turn of the 21st century. Krista Mahr states in "'Disaster University' Studies Ways to Minimize Death and Destruction in Asia-Pacific" (Time.com, September 24, 2013) that "in the past 10 years [2003–2013], a person in Asia was nearly 30 times more likely to be affected by a natural disaster than somebody in Europe or the U.S. During that time, some 800,000 people were killed in the tsunamis, earthquakes and storms in the region." This is due to a number of factors, including the vulnerability of many of the continent's regions to climate-related disasters, but it is also centrally related to the fact that the continent is home to numerous high-population countries that have seen rapid urbanization since the late 20th century. Many of Asia's largest cities are exponentially larger today than they were during the 1980s, so disasters are more likely to strike areas of high population density and to affect much larger numbers of people. Furthermore, cities that have experienced recent, rapid growth are more likely to have large numbers of people living in substandard housing and in areas that are physically exposed or otherwise vulnerable to flooding, storms, earthquakes, and other severe weather events.

Africa, with a much smaller population than Asia and the Pacific and relatively little exposure to earthquake risk, has not seen the same level of disaster-related suffering in numerical terms. In many ways, however, it is even more vulnerable to disasters than Asia and the Pacific, and it has seen a larger proportion of its population displaced by disasters in the 21st century, according to the Internal Displacement Monitoring Centre, in *Global Estimates 2012: People Displaced by Disasters* (May 2013, http://reliefweb.int/sites/ reliefweb.int/files/resources/global-estimates-2012-may2013 .pdf). Like Asia, Africa has many cities that have grown rapidly in a short period, many of which are particularly vulnerable to floods. It is also extremely prone to drought, the most serious form of environmental hazard on the continent in terms of the number of people affected. Due to the scarcity of resources and the impoverishment of much of the continent, regional governments have made little progress in risk preparedness, and they have little ability to fund recovery efforts in the wake of disasters. The economies of many African countries are based on agriculture, leaving them especially susceptible to the devastating impacts of climate-related events such as droughts and floods. Additionally, natural disasters in Africa are frequently compounded by the effects of the many ongoing conflicts in the region, making recovery even more difficult.

Natural disasters and environmental hazards tend to be more deadly in developing regions than in developed regions because of a lack of preparedness and early warning systems, poor construction and urban planning, and inadequate medical and social resources to care for those affected in the aftermath of catastrophe. Disasters in high-income countries tend to exact larger financial costs due to higher levels of development, but governments in these countries tend to have more ability to fund recovery efforts. Additionally, property losses in high-income countries are frequently insured, so companies and individuals in affected areas rarely face the daunting challenge of starting from scratch after a total loss. In contrast, governments in the developing world typically have far less financial flexibility to aid recovery efforts, and businesses and individuals are much less commonly insured against property loss. As a result, disasters in the developing world destroy more wealth and have longer-term effects than disasters in the developed world, and the negative economic impacts of disasters can imperil the more vulnerable national economies of poorer regions, setting back development for years or even decades.

One of the clearest measures of the levels of instability and suffering created by natural disasters and other environmental hazards is the number of people displaced by such events. Table 8.1 lists the 20 countries that experienced the most displacement as a result of disasters between 2008 and 2012. The world's most populous country, China, saw 49.8 million of its residents displaced by natural disasters during these years, and the

world's second most populous country, India, saw 23.8 million of its residents displaced. Other high-population countries in the developing world rounded out the five most afflicted countries: Pakistan, with 15 million displaced; the Philippines, with 12.3 million displaced; and Nigeria, with 6.8 million displaced. Two high-income countries, the United States and Japan, were among the top-20 countries in terms of disaster-induced displacement between 2008 and 2012. Most of the United States' displacement was associated with Hurricane Sandy, which affected the high-population coastal areas of New York, New Jersey, and other New England states in 2012; and Japan's displacement was a result of the catastrophic Tohoku earthquake and tsunami of 2011, the most costly natural disaster on record in terms of property damage. In general, natural disasters in high-income countries cause larger immediate financial losses than disasters in lower-income countries, whereas disasters in lower-income countries are more likely to have a higher human toll and to set back economic development over the long term than in higher-income countries.

Figure 8.1 shows the most severe natural disasters of 2012 and the number of people displaced by each. Flooding related to monsoons caused the most displacement globally in 2012, and India bore the brunt of these disasters, with 8.9 million people displaced over the course of two periods of monsoon activity. The monsoon season also proved devastating in neighboring Pakistan and Bangladesh, in China, and in the Philippines. Flooding displaced 6.1 million people in Nigeria and more than half a million people each in the lower-population countries of Niger and Chad. Three different typhoon events displaced nearly 3.5 million people in China, and a typhoon displaced 1.9 million people in the Philippines.

As Table 8.1 and Figure 8.1 make clear, natural disasters occur regularly and are especially devastating in the developing world. Although it is impossible to fully assess the legacy of major natural disasters on economic and human development in the developing world, this chapter will survey a number of major environmental crises whose effects continue to be felt among the world's poor.

## FAMINES AND DROUGHTS

Famine is the phenomenon of large-scale starvation in a population due to a severe shortage of food or a lack of access to food. It can be caused by natural occurrences such as drought, flooding, diseased crops, or insect infestations. It can also occur during war, when access to food is disrupted, or be the result of government policies alone or in combination with natural occurrences.

Famine is one of the most devastating events human beings can experience and one of the most dramatic and emotional from the point of view of spectators worldwide.

**TABLE 8.1**

### Countries with the most disaster-induced displacement, 2008–12

| Rank | Country | Displaced |
|------|---------|-----------|
| 1 | China | 49,782,000 |
| 2 | India | 23,775,000 |
| 3 | Pakistan | 14,991,000 |
| 4 | Philippines | 12,343,000 |
| 5 | Nigeria | 6,818,000 |
| 6 | Colombia | 3,289,000 |
| 7 | Thailand | 3,234,000 |
| 8 | Bangladesh | 2,999,000 |
| 9 | Indonesia | 2,479,000 |
| 10 | Chile | 2,133,000 |
| 11 | Haiti | 1,910,000 |
| 12 | Myanmar | 1,853,000 |
| 13 | Mexico | 1,830,000 |
| 14 | Sri Lanka | 1,578,000 |
| 15 | Brazil | 1,466,000 |
| 16 | Japan | 1,286,000 |
| 17 | Viet Nam | 1,079,000 |
| 18 | United States | 978,000 |
| 19 | Niger | 794,000 |
| 20 | Mozambique | 640,000 |

SOURCE: "Table 5.1. Top 20 Countries with the Most Displacement over 2008–2012," in *Global Estimates 2012: People Displaced by Disasters*, Norwegian Refugee Council, Internal Displacement Monitoring Centre, May 2013, http://reliefweb.int/sites/reliefweb.int/files/resources/global-estimates-2012-may2013.pdf (accessed October 28, 2013)

**FIGURE 8.1**

**Disaster-induced displacement worldwide, 2012**

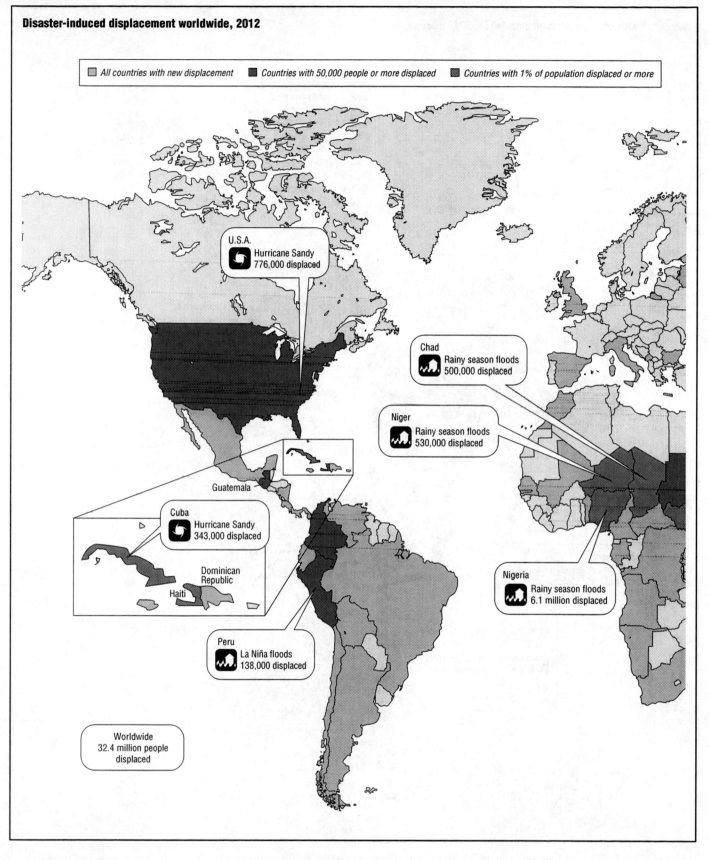

■ *All countries with new displacement*　■ *Countries with 50,000 people or more displaced*　■ *Countries with 1% of population displaced or more*

U.S.A.
Hurricane Sandy
776,000 displaced

Chad
Rainy season floods
500,000 displaced

Niger
Rainy season floods
530,000 displaced

Guatemala

Cuba
Hurricane Sandy
343,000 displaced

Dominican
Republic

Haiti

Nigeria
Rainy season floods
6.1 million displaced

Peru
La Niña floods
138,000 displaced

Worldwide
32.4 million people
displaced

For centuries, periodic famines were a more or less normal part of human existence, mostly because of crop failure. In the 21st century developed countries have sufficient wealth and infrastructure that they do not suffer from famines except under the most extraordinary of circumstances. The most recent famine in a developed country

**FIGURE 8.1**

**Disaster-induced displacement worldwide, 2012** [CONTINUED]

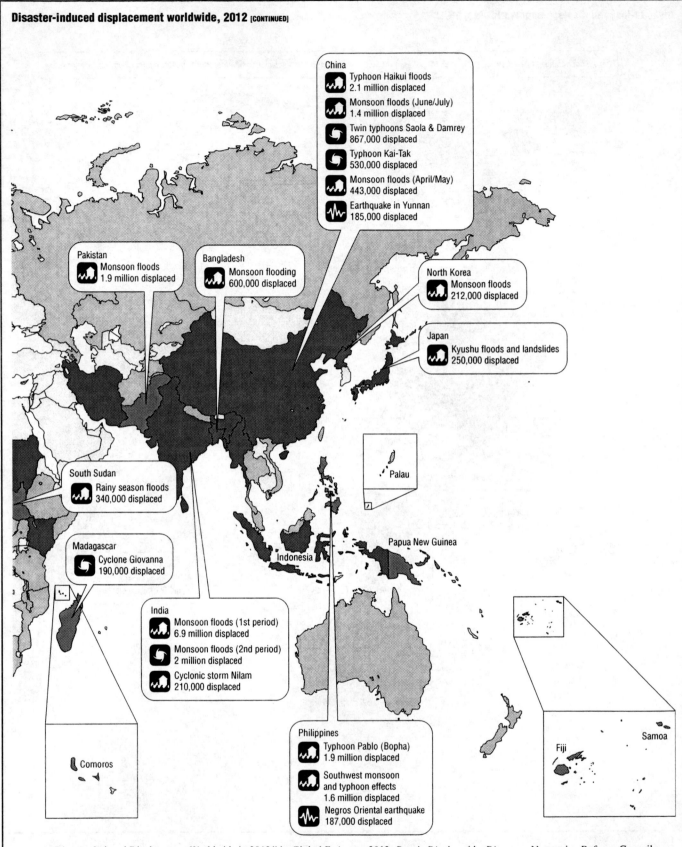

China
- Typhoon Haikui floods
  2.1 million displaced
- Monsoon floods (June/July)
  1.4 million displaced
- Twin typhoons Saola & Damrey
  867,000 displaced
- Typhoon Kai-Tak
  530,000 displaced
- Monsoon floods (April/May)
  443,000 displaced
- Earthquake in Yunnan
  185,000 displaced

Pakistan
- Monsoon floods
  1.9 million displaced

Bangladesh
- Monsoon flooding
  600,000 displaced

North Korea
- Monsoon floods
  212,000 displaced

Japan
- Kyushu floods and landslides
  250,000 displaced

South Sudan
- Rainy season floods
  340,000 displaced

Palau

Madagascar
- Cyclone Giovanna
  190,000 displaced

Papua New Guinea

Indonesia

India
- Monsoon floods (1st period)
  6.9 million displaced
- Monsoon floods (2nd period)
  2 million displaced
- Cyclonic storm Nilam
  210,000 displaced

Comoros

Samoa

Fiji

Philippines
- Typhoon Pablo (Bopha)
  1.9 million displaced
- Southwest monsoon
  and typhoon effects
  1.6 million displaced
- Negros Oriental earthquake
  187,000 displaced

SOURCE: "Disaster-Induced Displacement Worldwide in 2012," in *Global Estimates 2012: People Displaced by Disasters*, Norwegian Refugee Council, Internal Displacement Monitoring Centre, May 2013, http://reliefweb.int/sites/reliefweb.int/files/resources/global-estimates-2012-may2013.pdf (accessed October 28, 2013)

was in the Netherlands in 1944, when an exceptionally difficult winter combined with the destruction caused by World War II (1939–1945) caused at least 30,000 Dutch to starve to death. By contrast, developing regions have suffered many famines since that time. People in these areas may have difficulty meeting their basic needs during the best of times, and when disaster strikes it can become impossible for them to find enough food to eat. This is especially true for the poorest members of these societies.

In 2004 Paul Howe and Stephen Devereux of the University of Sussex provided in "Famine Intensity and Magnitude Scales: A Proposal for an Instrumental Definition of Famine" (*Disasters*, vol. 28, no. 4) a methodology for measuring both the intensity and the magnitude of famine. The ability to monitor food insecurity and make accurate judgments about its intensity is extremely important in an attempt to direct international aid to the places most in need of help, and the measurement scales developed by Howe and Devereux were influential in standardizing this process. In 2006 a consortium of international aid organizations released the Integrated Food Security Phase Classification (IPC; http://www.ipcinfo.org/ipcinfo-home/en/), a new set of procedures for measuring famine. The IPC has since become the most widely accepted way to measure food crises, and it has been subject to ongoing technical revision since its introduction.

The IPC provides scientifically based guidelines for categorizing food insecurity into five phases:

1. Minimal

2. Stressed

3. Crisis

4. Emergency

5. Famine

Each phase corresponds to specific guidelines regarding how to intervene and shape the policy response to the situation. A food-insecurity crisis is declared a famine when more than two people per 10,000 die each day, when malnutrition rates are above 30%, when all livestock is dead, and when the amount of available food drops below 2.1 million calories (2.1 megacalories) per person per day and the amount of available water drops below 1.1 gallons (4 liters) per person per day. By the time the famine phase has been declared, large-scale loss of life has already occurred, but a declaration of famine by the United Nations (UN) and other organizations allows aid to be mobilized with all possible speed and effectiveness.

## Ethiopia: The "Face of Famine"

Much of the current international understanding of famine developed as a result of the highly publicized Ethiopian famine of 1984–85, one of the most devastating of the post–World War II period. The Ethiopian famine was a result of the convergence of contributing factors: drought, war, politics, and pestilence. By 1986 over 1 million people had starved to death. Images from the famine were broadcast on television internationally and numerous high-profile benefits were staged in response to it. The international outrage and the public response to Ethiopia's famine ushered in a period of international charitable donation that continues to the present.

Ruled by a socialist faction since the overthrow of President Haile Selassie (1892–1975) in 1974, Ethiopia had experienced drought and famine during the early 1970s and began experiencing drought conditions again by the early 1980s. In 1984 drought combined with crop disease, an ongoing civil war in the country's northern provinces of Eritrea and Tigre (which in 1991 became the independent nation of Eritrea), and government mismanagement of the economy and the crisis put an estimated 6 million people at risk of starvation. By the late summer of that year, tens of thousands of Ethiopians had already died of starvation, but Western governments were reluctant to provide aid, fearing that they would fund the food needs of the Ethiopian people while the pro-Soviet national government used its resources to purchase weapons and cement its power. Aid agencies such as Oxfam made large contributions, but even as record harvests in Europe translated into a huge surplus of grain, Western governments were not directing substantial resources to Ethiopia. In fact, the aid agencies that were working to combat starvation in Ethiopia were required to buy the surplus grain on the open market.

Governments in the West slowly began providing aid during the fall of 1984, but it was private citizens in the West who changed the dynamic of the situation. As a result of media coverage, including heart-wrenching footage of starving children and their families, public donations totaling more than hundreds of millions of dollars were directed to Ethiopia that fall. However, the Ethiopian government continued to divert resources to troops fighting in the ongoing civil war, and the combination of war and famine led to widespread displacement, as refugees fled to neighboring Sudan. Prior to Christmas in 1984, a pop-music supergroup dubbing itself Band Aid recorded the benefit song "Do They Know It's Christmas?" for famine victims. This recording sold millions of copies and led to the benefit concert Live Aid, which further elevated the visibility of the cause and raised more than $200 million in relief funds. In conjunction with Live Aid, another supergroup dubbing itself USA for Africa recorded the song "We Are the World" (written by Michael Jackson [1958–2009] and Lionel Richie [1949–]), which became the fastest-selling single in U.S. music history and raised over $63 million in famine relief. As a result of these successful charitable efforts, a new era of celebrity benefit concerts, recordings, and other events began.

The famine's intensity began to wane in mid-1985, but Ethiopia's recovery, complicated by ongoing political instability and military conflict, was sporadic in the decades that followed.

### The Return of Famine to the Horn of Africa

Ethiopia and its neighbors in the Horn of Africa region—Eritrea, Djibouti, Kenya, and Somalia—were also the site of the most severe famine to have occurred thus far in the 21st century. Food security in the region had been precarious at best throughout the first decade of the 21st century, and then the total failure of the region's crops in October–December 2010, combined with crop failure and animal deaths as a result of inadequate rain during the spring of 2011, put tens of millions of people at risk of starvation. Further complicating the situation and increasing the region's vulnerability was an ongoing civil war in Somalia.

Despite wide knowledge of the region's situation among international organizations and despite specific warnings during the fall of 2010 that preemptive action was needed to prevent famine conditions, aid organizations were not able to mobilize food supplies fast enough or get them to all affected areas in a timely manner. It was only in June and July 2011, when the UN officially declared a famine in Somalia, the country most severely affected, that widespread media reports led to increased mobilization of resources. Humanitarian funding increased rapidly thereafter, and the famine subsided in early 2012. In May 2013 the UN reported in the press release "Somalia Famine Killed Nearly 260,000 People, Half of Them Children—Reports UN" (http://www.un.org/apps/news/story.asp?NewsID=44811#.UoUKpvk3urk) the final casualty figures for the crisis. In all, between October 2010 and April 2012 an estimated 260,000 Somalis died, 133,000 of whom were children under the age of five years. The UN unambiguously noted that the initial delay in responding to the famine was one of the chief reasons that casualty levels were so high.

### FLOODS
### Pakistan

Between July and September 2010 Pakistan experienced flooding on a scale it had not seen in 80 years, leaving 18 million people (almost 10% of the population of the country) to face the oncoming winter in need of food, clothing, and shelter. The flooding arrived with an unusually heavy monsoon season, beginning in Khyber Pakhtunkhwa Province in the northern part of the country. Waters overflowed the river banks in the province and flooded the best agricultural land in the region before eventually flowing south to Punjab and Sindh Provinces. The floods affected 62,000 square miles (161,000 square kilometers [km]). The Pakistanis became wary of the civilian leaders who did little to help them while the military provided substantial aid, enhancing its reputation with the

masses. The UN Development Programme was there as well, giving people food and necessary supplies. As Pakistan's government and military were stretched thin, reports emerged of aid being channeled through charities affiliated with hard-line Islamic groups and of sympathetic responses to these groups even in areas of the country that had previously resisted them.

### Nigeria

In 2012 Nigeria was disabled by the most devastating floods in its history. Unusually heavy rains between June and November of that year combined with water released from dams in Nigeria and neighboring Cameroon to bring about severe flooding across 18 countries in West and Central Africa. The Internal Displacement Monitoring Centre notes in *Global Estimates 2012: People Displaced by Disasters* that the construction of dams, irrigation channels, bridges, and other infrastructure have disrupted the normal flow of water. The diversions of water in unsustainable ways is particularly common in rapidly urbanizing parts of the region, where substandard construction, inadequate planning, blocked drainage outlets, land reclamation, and other environmentally undesirable projects greatly compounded the damage from the floods. Over 7.6 million people across 13 countries were displaced, more than 6 million of them in Nigeria.

### HURRICANES, CYCLONES, AND TYPHOONS

Hurricanes, cyclones, and typhoons are different names for the same type of storm involving extreme cyclonic (revolving) winds, heavy rains, and flooding. The usage of one name over another depends on the region of the world in which the storm is located: "hurricane" is commonly used to describe such a weather event in the Atlantic and northeast Pacific Oceans, "cyclone" in the south Pacific and Indian Oceans, and "typhoon" in the northwest Pacific Ocean. The regions of the world that are most vulnerable to these storms are the coastal regions of Asia and the Gulf and East Coasts of the United States.

The strength of a hurricane, cyclone, or typhoon is gauged using the Saffir-Simpson Scale:

- Category One storms have winds of 74 to 95 miles per hour (mph; 119 to 153 kilometers per hour [km/h])

- Category Two storms have winds of 96 to 110 mph (154 to 177 km/h)

- Category Three storms have winds of 111 to 130 mph (179 to 209 km/h)

- Category Four storms have winds of 131 to 155 mph (211 to 249 km/h)

- Category Five storms have winds in excess of 156 mph (251 km/h)

## Hurricane Katrina

On August 29, 2005, one of the costliest and deadliest hurricanes in U.S. history made landfall on the Gulf Coast states of Louisiana, Mississippi, and Alabama. Over 1,800 people were killed and nearly 93,000 square miles (241,000 sq km) of land were affected. The damage was estimated at $96 billion. Much of New Orleans, Louisiana, lies below sea level and is protected by a system of levees, which were breached by the rising water; more than 80% of the city was flooded. Residents trapped in their homes climbed to their attics and then to their roofs, but many drowned as they tried to reach safety.

The storm's damage to New Orleans resulted from factors more common in developing areas of the world than in high-income countries such as the United States. The levee breaches that caused the catastrophic flooding in the city were the result of poor design and maintenance, and ample evidence suggests that local and national officials were aware of these shortcomings well in advance of the storm. Additionally, the city had a large poor population—nearly 30% of the city's roughly 500,000 residents lived below the poverty line—many of whom had no means of transportation out of the city and were forced to weather the storm in their home or in public shelters. Finally, the response of the federal government was widely viewed as ineffective. In spite of having ample resources to aid New Orleans residents in the aftermath of the storm, federal officials in the administration of President George W. Bush (1946–) were late in mobilizing sufficient levels of aid. The suffering of thousands of poor New Orleanians, the majority of whom were African American, was meanwhile being broadcast on international media. As a result, the storm and its aftermath became a flashpoint in debates about lingering racial inequities in the United States.

The recovery in New Orleans and the Gulf Coast region was prolonged. According to Oxfam America, in "US Gulf Coast Recovery Program" (August 22, 2008, http://www.oxfamamerica.org/static/oa3/files/usgulfcoast-factsheet.pdf), as of April 2007—nearly two years after the devastation of Katrina—more than 100,000 families were still living in temporary housing. In addition, repair of approximately 82,000 rental units in Louisiana and 21,000 in Mississippi had yet to be prioritized. (Before the storm 45% of the families affected by Hurricane Katrina had been renters.) Oxfam also determined that "despite poverty rates that topped 30 percent in some storm-devastated communities, state officials sought and the federal government approved waivers reducing—and in several cases eliminating—the share of recovery grants required to benefit low- and moderate-income communities."

Much of the Mississippi Gulf Coast, where the eye of Hurricane Katrina hit, was still rebuilding as of 2014, and of the hundreds of thousands of New Orleans residents who were displaced by the storm, large numbers never returned. According to the U.S. Census Bureau (January 7, 2014, http://quickfacts.census.gov/qfd/states/22/2255000.html), as of July 2012 the population of New Orleans was 369,250, more than 100,000 people below the city's pre-Katrina population.

## Cyclone Sidr

On November 15, 2007, Cyclone Sidr made landfall on the coast of Bangladesh, which sits on the Bay of Bengal. Sidr brought with it sustained winds of 135 mph (217 km/h) and caused enormous damage to the densely populated, low-elevation coastal regions of the country. More than 3,000 people were believed to have died in the early weeks after the storm, but other estimates suggested that up to 10,000 may have died of causes related to the storm. The article "Bangladesh Gets $95 Mln W.Bank Loan for Post-Cyclone Aid" (Reuters.com, July 6, 2008) reports that damage to property, crops, and livestock was estimated at $1.7 billion, and the World Bank and national government officials estimated that the country would need $4 billion to rehabilitate the economy in the aftermath of the storm.

Although Sidr's lethality was in part a function of the inadequate preparedness and construction norms common in rapidly growing urban areas in the developing world, the Bangladeshi government worked within its resource limitations to create a rudimentary early warning system that is believed to have saved a significant number of lives. In "Hunger Threatens Three Million Bangladeshis" (Journal.ie, November 25, 2007), Andrew Buncombe notes that before Sidr made landfall, the Bangladeshi government sent volunteers on bicycles through the villages in the path of the storm and had them warn people to move to cyclone shelters. This low-tech system worked—2 million people had safely moved to the shelters by the time Sidr arrived. In addition, the storm hit at low tide, so the dikes that were built along the coast as protection provided some defense against the raging sea. Nevertheless, storm damage left 2 million people homeless.

## EARTHQUAKES AND TSUNAMIS
### Asian Tsunami of 2004

On December 26, 2004, an undersea earthquake with a magnitude of 9.1 to 9.3 on the Richter scale (a measure of an earthquake's magnitude), the third-largest earthquake ever recorded, occurred in the Indian Ocean off the west coast of Sumatra, Indonesia. Unlike most earthquakes, which last from less than 1 second to several seconds, the Sumatran earthquake lasted 8 to 10 minutes and briefly shook the entire planet, triggering smaller earthquakes around the world and a massive tsunami (a series of rolling tidal waves) that devastated 12 countries in and along the Indian Ocean and caused deaths as far away as South Africa. In "Sumatran Quake Sped Up

Earth's Rotation" (Nature.com, December 30, 2004), Michael Hopkin explains that the earthquake was so powerful that it caused the earth to shake on its axis and even slightly accelerated its rotation.

The country most directly affected by the tsunami was Indonesia, which had just under 240 million people at the time and which consists of multiple islands with densely populated coastlines. According to the World Bank, in "Indonesia: A Reconstruction Chapter Ends Eight Years after the Tsunami" (December 26, 2012, http://www.worldbank.org/en/news/feature/2012/12/26/indonesia-reconstruction-chapter-ends-eight-years-after-the-tsunami), the total death toll from the disaster was 286,000. The destruction was centered on the northeastern Indonesia province of Aceh, where 221,000 people (of a total population of approximately 4.3 million) lost their lives or went missing and an additional 500,000 or more were left homeless. A subsequent earthquake measuring 9.1 on the Richter scale struck the region three months later, resulting in further loss of life and displacement. Among the other countries that suffered most keenly from the 2004 tsunami were Sri Lanka (where more than 30,000 people died), India (where more than 10,000 people died), and Thailand (where more than 5,000 people died). Other affected countries included Bangladesh, Myanmar (Burma), Kenya, the Maldives, Tanzania, the Seychelles, and Somalia.

The 2004 tsunami was among the deadliest and costliest natural disasters on record. In February 2005 the UN Environment Programme estimated in *After the Tsunami: Rapid Environmental Assessment* (http://www.unep.org/tsunami/reports/TSUNAMI_report_complete.pdf) the damage to the region at more than $10 billion. The World Bank indicates that in Aceh alone, nearly $7 billion had been spent on the reconstruction effort as of 2012. Nearly every living creature was affected, and whole ecosystems were destroyed, including mangrove forests, coral reefs, sand dunes, and sea grasses, which served as a buffer against the strongest impact of the waves and prevented even more destruction. Fishermen lost their boats, fishing equipment, and livelihoods. Farmers lost the farm animals that are necessary to their survival, and their rice, fruit, and vegetable crops were destroyed because of saltwater contamination.

Oxfam reports in "Three Months On: New Figures Show Tsunami May Have Killed up to Four Times as Many Women as Men" (November 1, 2005, http://www.oxfam.org/node/297) that more women than men were killed because many men were out fishing on the sea, where their boats managed to survive the waves, or were working in the fields or selling crops at inland markets. By contrast, large numbers of women and children were either at home or on the beach awaiting the fishermen's return. In addition, many women lost their lives while trying to save children who were in their care at the time of the disaster.

At the time of the 2004 disaster there had been sophisticated early warning systems to detect earthquakes and tsunamis in the Pacific Ocean, but no adequate system existed in the Indian Ocean, where the earthquake and tsunami originated. In the aftermath of the catastrophe scientists and national leaders from 26 countries that bordered the Indian Ocean began collaborating on building an early warning system for the region that would be able to prevent loss of life on the scale of the 2004 disaster. The new system was unveiled in late 2008, but according to the article "Indonesia's Tsunami Warning System Failed Because It Was Broken, Say Officials as Death Toll Climbs to 340" (Dailymail.co.uk, October 28, 2010), when another tsunami struck Indonesia in 2010, it was revealed that the system had never been effectively completed and had fallen into disrepair. The UN Educational, Scientific, and Cultural Organization indicates in "Indian Ocean Tsunami Warning System Performed Well, Detailed Assessment Underway" (April 13, 2012, http://www.unesco.org/new/en/natural-sciences/ioc-oceans/single-view-oceans/news/indian_ocean_wide_tsunami_watch/) that the early warning system was functioning properly in early 2012, as judged by its response to a strong earthquake off the west coast of Sumatra, the same Indonesian island that bore the brunt of the 2004 tsunami damage.

### Northern Pakistan Earthquake

On October 8, 2005, an earthquake with a magnitude of about 7.6 on the Richter scale hit South Asia. According to Akhtar Naeem et al., in "A Summary Report on Muzaffarabad Earthquake, Pakistan" (November 7, 2005, http://reliefweb.int/sites/reliefweb.int/files/resources/A67B454BB12FFD8F852570B20070500A-eeri-pak-07nov.pdf), more than 80,000 people were killed, 200,000 were injured, and 4 million were left homeless. The earthquake set off a series of landslides that buried entire villages and blocked roadways in the mountains, impeding rescue efforts. Afghanistan and northern India suffered some damage from the earthquake, but Pakistan sustained the most, particularly the Pakistan-controlled portion of Kashmir, whose capital city, Muzaffarabad, was partially destroyed.

Already in deep poverty, Pakistan had stockpiles of food destroyed in the rubble. Due to postquake landslides, the remote Himalayan villages affected by the earthquake became even more isolated. In "World Vision Aids Pakistan Victims in Forbidden Quake Zone" (March 1, 2006, http://reliefweb.int/node/201383), Andy Goss notes that relief efforts were further complicated because certain areas of Kashmir are part of the "forbidden tribal belt." These areas are ruled by tribal leaders who forbid outsiders to visit. With more than 13,000 families in these villages in desperate need of help after the earthquake, tribal leaders contacted a trusted Pakistani aid organization that managed to send help to the area. Other aid organizations were warned not to enter the area because of the possibility of armed attack.

Months after the quake, millions of people in the mountains were still living in tents with no water, electricity, or communications systems. Snow in the high elevations and heavy rains in the valleys hampered relief efforts, as helicopters were grounded and roadways blocked. According to the World Health Organization, in "Health Situation Report #34" (February 14–28, 2006, http://www.who.int/hac/crises/international/pakistan_earth quake/Pakistan_situation_report_34_14_28Feb2006.pdf), cases of acute respiratory infection, acute diarrhea, fevers, and earthquake-related injuries were common among survivors in the winter and spring of 2006. There were also reported cases of measles, meningitis, and acute hepatitis. As of December 2006, more than a year after the disaster, 300,000 survivors were still in need of food aid, and many families who had lost everything were still living in tents in the mountains in extremely harsh conditions. Refugee camps housed some of the victims, whose homes and land had been washed away by landslides and floods.

## Java Earthquake and Tsunami

Java, the most populous island in Indonesia, experienced the most severe catastrophe in the region following the 2004 tsunami on May 27, 2006, when an earthquake measuring 6.3 on the Richter scale struck near the city of Yogyakarta. Roughly 5 million people lived within 30 miles (48 km) of the epicenter, and the quake killed nearly 6,000 people and left approximately 1.5 million homeless. Most of the people in the affected areas were poor, with annual incomes at about half the national average.

While recovering from the May earthquake, Java was hit with a tsunami two months later. According to the World Health Organization, in "Central and West Java Earthquake and Tsunami: Situation Report #5" (July 21, 2006, http://img.static.reliefweb.int/report/indo nesia/central-and-west-java-earthquake-and-tsunami-situa tion-report-5-21-jul-2006), an undersea earthquake about 100 miles (161 km) south of Java resulted in waves ranging from 6 to 23 feet (1.8 to 7 meters [m]) high. These waves traveled over 1.2 miles (2 km) inland, affecting many provinces, including Yogyakarta and Central Java.

The article "Tsunami Death Toll Increases to 668" (LATimes.com, July 23, 2006) indicates that the earthquake was much smaller than the one that triggered the 2004 tsunami, so the damage was localized. Even so, 668 people were reported dead and 287 missing. According to Shawn Donnan, in "Shelter Crisis after Indonesian Earthquake" (FT.com, September 28, 2006), the UN reported that 1.2 million people were left homeless and that international and local aid was extremely slow to help those affected.

Indonesia was hit once again before the end of 2006. In December of that year the Indonesian province of Aceh, which was still recovering from the 2004 tsunami, experienced devastating floods. Bronwyn Curran explains in "After Aceh Floods, Relief Efforts Help Families Cope with Effects of 'Tsunami from the River'" (January 12, 2007, http://www.unicef.org/infobycountry/ indonesia_38021.html) that seasonal floods are somewhat commonplace in this province, but the floods of December 2006 were much more severe than usual. Parts of Aceh Province that had not been affected by the 2004 tsunami were devastated by the floods, which killed around 70 people and affected 450,000 more.

## Haiti Earthquake

The Sumatra earthquake was soon overshadowed by a 7.0-magnitude earthquake that struck Haiti on January 12, 2010. The epicenter of the earthquake was only 10 miles (16 km) southwest of Port-au-Prince, the Haitian capital. Port-au-Prince was particularly vulnerable to earthquake damage because of its topography, construction practices, and population density. Haiti was one of the poorest nations in the world even before the earthquake, and many of the poorest residents of Port-au-Prince lived in tin-roofed shacks perched on the sides of steep ravines.

The article "Haiti Earthquake: Conflicting Death Tolls Lead to Confusion" (Associated Press, February 11, 2010) reports that at the time of the earthquake approximately 3 million people were in the capital city ready to leave schools and businesses for the day. About 250,000 houses and 30,000 commercial buildings are believed to have collapsed, crushing their occupants. Victims' bodies were piled in the streets and then buried in mass graves, and record-keeping in the aftermath of the disaster was inconsistent. As a result, the death toll remains in dispute, with estimates ranging from 170,000 to 300,000 killed.

The worldwide reaction to the Haiti earthquake was immediate. Many countries sent rescue workers to find survivors in the rubble and to bring food, water, and medical aid. Damage to the airport, the seaport, and the roads made the rescue and relief mission extremely difficult. In a tragic irony, however, some of the aid workers ended up compounding the misfortunes of the Haitian people by sparking a cholera epidemic in the country. Ivan Watson and Joe Vaccarello report in "U.N. Sued for 'Bringing Cholera to Haiti,' Causing Outbreak That Killed Thousands" (CNN.com, October 10, 2013) that cholera is not native to Haiti and that it was most likely brought to Haiti by UN peacekeepers from Nepal. The resulting cholera epidemic, which began in October 2010, killed an estimated 8,300 people and "sparked riots in several cities and towns against the force of some 8,000 U.N. peacekeepers deployed there."

The article "Still Waiting for Recovery" (Economist. com, January 5, 2013) reports that in 2013, three years after the earthquake, the grand ambitions for Haiti's reconstruction remained largely unfulfilled: "Most of the earthquake rubble is finally gone from the capital's streets. The most visible refugee camps have been emptied. Several new hotels, aimed at attracting those elusive business visitors, are due to open . . . . And yet more than 350,000 Haitians are still living in tents in scattered camps; many of those who have moved out have returned to substandard housing in hillside shanties and seaside slums." A series of tropical storms in 2012 stifled an economy that many international observers had hoped was poised for growth, and new cholera cases emerged in the aftermath of each storm. Although billions of dollars were pledged to the rebuilding effort, much of the money had failed to materialize, and much of the money that did make its way to Haiti "went to a handful of international bodies, which mainly spent it on temporary relief (tents, shelters, water-tankers and so on) and the salaries of expat staff."

## Japan Earthquake and Tsunami

On March 11, 2011, Japan was first rocked by an earthquake and then hit with a tsunami. The earthquake registered 8.9 to 9.0 on the Richter scale—the fifth-largest earthquake to be recorded since 1900 and the largest ever in Japan. The earthquake resulted in a tsunami that sent 30-foot (9-m) waves crashing into the east coast of Japan and traveled 6 miles (10 km) inland. Waves of 7 feet (2 m) or more traveled across the north Pacific Ocean at nearly 500 mph (805 km/h) toward Hawaii, which escaped with no damage, and the west coasts of Canada and the United States. The tsunami devastated the east coast of the Tohoku region of Japan, which occupies the northeastern portion of the island of Honshu, killing 15,884 people, according to Japan's National Police Agency (February 10, 2014,

http://www.npa.go.jp/archive/keibi/biki/higaijokyo_e.pdf), destroying hundreds of thousands of buildings, and heavily damaging infrastructure such as roads, railways, and a dam.

The devastation in Japan was greatly compounded by a number of explosions at the Fukushima Daiichi nuclear power plant, located near the coast in Tohoku. The plant was no longer online, but several of its reactors were seriously damaged by the earthquake and tsunami, and they began leaking radiation on March 12. People who were located within 20 miles (30 km) of the plant were evacuated. Although no short-term deaths were associated with the radiation exposure, the long-term effects on the health of those exposed as well as to the ocean were incalculable. In July 2013 the plant's owner, Tokyo Electric Power Co., admitted that radiation was still leaking from the plant into the Pacific Ocean. Martin Fackler and Hiroko Tabuchi report in "With a Plant's Tainted Water Still Flowing, No End to Environmental Fears" (NYTimes. com, October 24, 2013) that accidents and leaks at Fukushima continued through the fall of 2013, and there were concerns that even larger amounts of contaminated water were flowing into the Pacific two and a half years after the disaster than in the immediate aftermath. "And that flow may not slow until at least 2015," Fackler and Tabuchi write, "when an ice wall around the damaged reactors is supposed to be completed. Beyond that, although many Japanese believed that the plant had stopped spewing radioactive materials long ago, they have continued to seep into the air."

According to Victoria Kim, in "Japan Damage Could Reach $235 Billion, World Bank Estimates" (LATimes. com, March 21, 2011), in the weeks after the tsunami, the World Bank estimated the damage at $235 billion, making it the costliest natural disaster on record. The World Bank, however, expected the economic fallout of the disaster to be temporary because reconstruction efforts, underpinned by insurance coverage, would drive new economic growth in the highly developed country. As of 2014, full recovery remained a distant goal in parts of Tohoku, but aside from the ongoing problems with the Fukushima plant, Japan as a whole had returned to normal.

# CHAPTER 9

# POVERTY AND VIOLENCE

Poverty in the developing world is often accompanied by or caused by violence. The residents of countries that are engaged in armed conflict—whether the countries are developing or developed—almost always experience intense economic hardship. During World War II (1939–1945) much of Europe was reduced to extreme privation that in some cases approached starvation conditions. Since that time, most armed conflict has occurred in the developing world. Since the 1960s sub-Saharan Africa has seen numerous armed conflicts, many of them civil wars that have lasted for decades, and these conflicts have been central to the persistence of poverty in the region. Through the first decade of the 21st century and beyond, economic development prospects have dimmed considerably for the residents of Afghanistan and Iraq because of U.S. invasions and related internal conflicts.

Violence increases the risk of a food crisis when livestock, crops, and farmland are destroyed and when farmers are displaced and unable to work. Additionally, even in countries where combat does not affect rural farmland directly, food supply lines can be interrupted, causing shortages in other locations. Violence has played a major role in most food security crises in Africa, including the 1984–85 famine in Ethiopia and the 2011–12 famine in Somalia, both of which are discussed in Chapter 8.

War creates gender imbalances that have major consequences for human development. When large numbers of men are killed in combat, women are left to support and protect their families by themselves. This situation makes them vulnerable to physical and sexual violence during a conflict and to poverty and deprivation both during and after the conflict. Rates of violence against women tend to be highest in areas where violence in general is common, and elevated rates of gender-based violence often persist long after wars have ended. The children of women who are subjected to such forms of suffering are also negatively impacted and are likely to pass on to their own children the effects of violence, poverty, and deprivation.

Men who return from conflict present another set of challenges to their societies. Having been trained and mobilized for violent combat—sometimes as children or very young men—they may have little civilian job experience or education. They return to communities in which job prospects are scarce, and in many cases their societies lack the strong institutions necessary to achieve reconciliation between warring factions or ethnicities. Under such conditions the possibility of continued violence or a return to armed conflict is heightened.

In general, most of the human development indicators discussed over the course of this book—those related to poverty levels, nutrition, education, gender, health, and economic development—are imperiled by armed conflict. Likewise, areas with low levels of human development, as measured by these indicators, are generally at elevated risk of experiencing armed conflict.

## FRAGILE STATES

The United Nations (UN), the World Bank, the Organisation for Economic Co-operation and Development, and other international organizations use the concept of fragility to assess a country's susceptibility to violence. Fragile states are those in which armed conflict and criminal violence are most likely to take root and to exact suffering on the population at large. In a 2013 speech at the New Zealand International Institute for International Affairs, Helen Clark (1950–; http://www.undp.org/content/undp/en/home/presscenter/speeches/2013/08/12/-conflict-and-development-breaking-the-cycle-of-fragility-violence-and-poverty-/), the head of the UN Development Programme and a former three-term prime minister of New Zealand, described the characteristics of fragile states:

> As a group, the fragile states often share a number of characteristics which make it difficult for them to get ahead. These may include weak governance, poor relations between state and society, and a lack of resilience to potential internal and external shocks—including to stresses emanating from climate change and natural hazards. They may also include countries overwhelmed by rapid urbanization and the impact of burgeoning young populations without enough access to work and opportunity.

> No single factor determines fragility, and it may be masked by the existence of relatively strong, often authoritarian, institutions, as has been seen in the Arab States region. Rivalry between ethnic groups and along other lines can also drive fragility—especially where authorities lack the political will, impartiality, and/or the ability to intercede and resolve grievances.

Clark further noted that the nature of violence worldwide has evolved considerably since the 1990s. Armed conflict between states has become rarer, but levels of criminal violence and the overall numbers of violent deaths have increased. According to Clark, as of 2013, nine out of 10 (87%) reported violent deaths were the result of organized crime and gang violence, and only one out of 10 violent deaths was the result of armed conflict or terrorism. Much of the increase in violent crime since the 1990s has occurred in Latin American and Caribbean countries (among which only Haiti qualifies as a fragile state by international standards), as discussed in Chapter 5, and in parts of Africa. Battle-related deaths, although they had fallen as a proportion of total violent deaths, rose significantly in 2012, primarily as a result of the mounting death toll from the civil war in Syria. According to the article "More Than 115,000 Killed in Syrian Conflict—Monitoring Group" (Reuters .com, October 1, 2013), the death toll in Syria had surpassed 115,000 as of October 2013. Among those killed were 41,000 civilians, including 6,000 children and 4,000 women.

Table 9.1 shows violence statistics in states that the World Bank considered fragile in 2012 or the most recent year available. The countries with the highest numbers of battle-related deaths between 2000 and 2011 were Afghanistan (42,697), Iraq (25,314), Eritrea (25,057), Sudan (19,057), Somalia (9,519), Nepal (9,418), the Democratic Republic of the Congo (6,635), Burundi (5,640), and Chad (4,089). Syria's battle-related death total in the period 2000–11 did not place it among the countries with the highest numbers of battle-related deaths; the previously mentioned death toll of 115,000 applies primarily to the years 2012 and 2013, whereas the World Bank data apply to the years 2000 to 2011.

Some of these countries were also among the fragile states with the highest homicide rates (rates of murder outside battle conditions). The fragile state with the highest homicide rate per 100,000 people in 2010 (or the most recent year for which data were available) was Côte d'Ivoire, with a rate of 56.9. (See Table 9.1.) Other fragile states with high homicide rates were Malawi (36), the Central African Republic (29.3), Sudan (24.2), Burundi (21.7), the Democratic Republic of the Congo (21.7), Guinea-Bissau (20.2), Eritrea (17.8), Chad (15.8), Sierra Leone (14.9), and Zimbabwe (14.3). By comparison, the United States, which is among the developed world's most violent countries as measured by homicide rate, had a 2011 homicide rate of 4.7 per 100,000 people. The homicide rates in Côte d'Ivoire and Malawi were among the highest worldwide. Although many nonfragile states in Latin America and the Caribbean had higher murder rates than many of these fragile states, as Figure 5.6 in Chapter 5 shows, violence combined with extremely low levels of human development is particularly devastating to the general population.

Large numbers of international troops, police, and observers were present on peacekeeping missions in many of the fragile states shown in Table 9.1—an indicator of continued extreme fragility even in states where active armed conflict had ended. The countries with the most peacekeepers on the ground in 2012 (or the most recent year for which data were available) were the Democratic Republic of the Congo (19,166), Côte d'Ivoire (11,033), Sudan (10,416), Haiti (9,464), Liberia (8,862), and South Sudan (7,157).

As Table 9.2 shows, many fragile states had large numbers of internally displaced persons—people who have been forced from their homes, usually because of armed conflict or the threat of violence, and who live in refugee camps or otherwise on the margins of society, generally in extreme poverty. Sudan, which was embroiled in civil war for most of the period from 1955 to 2005 and in which smaller violent conflicts have been ongoing since that time, had by far the most internally displaced persons in 2011, at 5.2 million. As a result of the destabilization in Iraq created by the U.S.-led war of 2003–10, 2.6 million people remained internally displaced as of 2011. Other war-torn countries with exceptionally large internally displaced populations were the Democratic Republic of the Congo (1.7 million), Somalia (1.5 million), and Zimbabwe (1 million).

Fragile states generally lag behind the rest of the developing world in development indicators, and often the deprivations in these countries both cause and result from violence. Access to improved water and sanitation in these states fell far short of developing world averages and were particularly low in Chad (where 50% of people had access to clean water and 12% to sanitation facilities), the

TABLE 9.1

**Violence in fragile states, 2012 or most recent year available**

| | Peacebuilding and peacekeeping | | Intentional homicides | | | Crime | |
|---|---|---|---|---|---|---|---|
| | Troops, police, and military observers | Battle related deaths | Combined source estimates | Military expenditure | | Losses due to theft, robbery, vandalism, and arson | |
| | Number | Number (total over period) | Per 100,000 people | % of GDP | | % sales | |
| | 2012 | 2000–2011 | 2010 | 2011 | | Survey year | |
| Afghanistan | 23 | 42,697 | 2.4* | 4.7 | | 2010 | 1.5 |
| Bosnia and Herzegovina | — | — | 1.5 | 1.1 | | 2011 | 0.4 |
| Burundi | 2 | 5,640 | 21.7* | 2.4* | | 2008 | 1.1 |
| Central African Republic | 4 | 592 | 29.3* | 2.6* | | 2011 | 4.7 |
| Chad | — | 4,089 | 15.8** | 2.3 | | 2011 | 2.5 |
| Comoros | — | — | 12.2* | — | | — | — |
| Congo, Dem. Rep. | 19,166 | 6,635 | 21.7* | 1.5 | | 2011 | 1.8 |
| Congo, Rep. | — | 167 | 30.8* | 1.1 | | 2011 | 3.3 |
| Cote d'Ivoire | 11,033 | 844 | 56.9* | 1.5 | | 2011 | 3.4 |
| Eritrea | — | 25,057 | 17.8* | — | | 2011 | 0 |
| Guinea-Bissau | 18 | 0 | 20.2* | 1.8 | | 2008 | 1.1 |
| Haiti | 9,464 | 244 | 6.9 | — | | — | — |
| Iraq | 251 | 25,314 | 2.0* | 3.3 | | 2011 | 0.8 |
| Kiribati | — | — | 7.3* | — | | — | — |
| Kosovo | 16 | — | — | — | | 2011 | 0.3 |
| Liberia | 8,862 | 2,635 | 10.1* | 0.9 | | 2011 | 2.8 |
| Libya | 2 | 1,928 | 2.9* | — | | — | — |
| Madagascar | — | — | 8.1* | 0.7 | | 2011 | 1.2 |
| Malawi | — | — | 36.0* | 0.8 | | 2011 | 5.7 |
| Mali | — | 323 | 8.0** | 1.5 | | 2011 | 0.5 |
| Marshall Islands | — | — | — | — | | — | — |
| Micronesia, Fed. Sts. | — | — | 0.9* | — | | 2011 | 2.1 |
| Myanmar | — | 2,302 | 10.2* | — | | — | — |
| Nepal | 72* | 9,418 | 2.8* | 1.4 | | 2011 | 0.9 |
| Sierra Leone | 7 | 156 | 14.9* | 0.8 | | 2011 | 0.8 |
| Solomon Islands | 447 | — | 3.7* | — | | — | — |
| Somalia | 3 | 9,519 | 1.5* | — | | — | — |
| South Sudan | 7,157 | 216 | — | 5.8 | | — | — |
| Sudan | 10,416* | 19,057 | 24.2* | — | | — | — |
| Syrian Arab Republic | — | 842 | 2.3 | 3.9 | | 2011 | 0.8 |
| Timor-Leste | 1,216* | — | 6.9* | 2.6 | | 2011 | 2.7 |
| Togo | — | — | 10.9* | 1.6 | | 2011 | 2.4 |
| Tuvalu | — | — | — | — | | — | — |
| West Bank and Gaza | — | — | — | — | | 2008 | 1.2 |
| Yemen, Rep. | — | 1,399 | 4.2* | 3.5 | | 2011 | 0.6 |
| Zimbabwe | — | — | 14.3* | 2.1 | | 2011 | 0.5 |
| Fragile situations | — | 16,678 | 14.0* | 2.8 | | — | — |
| Low income | — | — | 14.5* | 2.0 | | — | — |

*Most Recent Value (MRV) if data for the specified year or full period are not available.

SOURCE: Adapted from "5.8. World Development Indicators: Fragile Situations Part 1," in *World Development Indicators: Tables*, World Bank, 2013, http://wdi .worldbank.org/table/5.8# (accessed October 29, 2013)

Democratic Republic of the Congo (46% and 31%), Madagascar (48% and 14%), Sierra Leone (58% and 13%), Somalia (30% and 24%), South Sudan (57% and 9%), Sudan (55% and 24%), and Togo (59% and 11%). (See Table 9.2.) Maternal and under-five mortality rates were also extremely high in many fragile states, including Burundi, the Central African Republic, Chad, Guinea-Bissau, Liberia, Mali, Sierra Leone, Somalia, and Sudan.

## ARMED CONFLICTS
### Civil Wars in Africa

As of February 2014, most of the violence in Africa—the developing region most consistently plagued by armed conflict in the late 20th and early 21st centuries—consisted of small civil wars or sporadic guerilla and terrorist campaigns, many of which were related

to the aftereffects of larger conflicts that had recently ended. Such was the case in Sudan and South Sudan. South Sudan declared its independence in 2011, and tensions then spilled over into the neighboring states of Chad and the Central African Republic and continued through 2013.

Similarly, the Democratic Republic of the Congo had been embroiled in civil war and related fighting since the early 1990s. Although the heaviest fighting had ended by 2013, conflicts in the eastern part of the country continued, as militias waged war against the forces of the country's central government, ensuring the region's continued instability. The various interrelated conflicts that had occurred in the region since the 1990s represented the largest interstate war in modern African history. At various points, nine African nations and more than

**TABLE 9.2**

**The effects of violence in fragile states, 2012 or most recent year available**

| | Refugees By country of origin (thousands) 2011 | Refugees By country of asylum (thousands) 2011 | Internally displaced persons (number) 2011 | Access to an improved water source (% of population) 2011 | Access to improved sanitation facilities (% of population) 2011 | Maternal mortality ratio National estimates (per 100,000 live births) 2006–11 | Maternal mortality ratio Modeled estimates (per 100,000 live births) 2010 | Under-five mortality rate Total (per 1,000 live births) 2012 | Depth of food deficit (kilocalories per person per day) 2011 | Gross enrollment ratio Primary (% of relevant age group) 2011 |
|---|---|---|---|---|---|---|---|---|---|---|
| Afghanistan | 2,664 | 3 | 456,000 | 61 | 29 | 330 | 460 | 99 | — | 98 |
| Bosnia and Herzegovina | 59 | 7 | 113,000 | 99 | 96 | 3 | 8 | 7 | 21 | 90 |
| Burundi | 101 | 36 | 78,800 | 74 | 50 | 500 | 800 | 104 | 655 | 165 |
| Central African Republic | 163 | 17 | 105,000 | 67 | 34 | 540 | 890 | 129 | 212 | 94 |
| Chad | 43 | 366 | 126,000 | 50 | 12 | — | 1,100 | 150 | 254 | 101 |
| Comoros | 0 | 0 | — | 95 | 35 | — | 280 | 78 | 677 | 98 |
| Congo, Dem. Rep. | 491 | 153 | 1,710,000 | 46 | 31 | 550 | 540 | 146 | 261 | 96 |
| Congo, Rep. | 13 | 141 | 7,800 | 72 | 18 | 426 | 560 | 96 | 130 | 116 |
| Cote d'Ivoire | 155 | 24 | 247,000 | 80 | 24 | — | 400 | 108 | — | 88 |
| Eritrea | 252 | 5 | 10,000 | — | — | — | 240 | 52 | 536 | 47 |
| Guinea-Bissau | 1 | 8 | — | 72 | 19 | 410 | 790 | 129 | 61 | 123 |
| Haiti | 34 | 0 | — | 64 | 26 | 630 | 350 | 76 | 365 | — |
| Iraq | 1,428 | 35 | 2,600,000 | 85 | 84 | 84 | 63 | 34 | 47 | 113 |
| Kiribati | 0 | — | — | 66 | 39 | 0 | — | 60 | — | — |
| Kosovo | — | — | 18,000 | — | — | — | — | — | — | — |
| Liberia | 67 | 128 | — | 74 | 18 | 990 | 770 | 75 | 219 | 103 |
| Libya | 4 | 10 | — | 97 | 97 | — | 58 | 15 | 10 | — |
| Madagascar | 0 | 0 | — | 48 | 14 | 500 | 240 | 58 | 208 | 148 |
| Malawi | 0 | 6 | — | 84 | 53 | 680 | 460 | 71 | 143 | 141 |
| Mali | 4 | 16 | — | 65 | 22 | 460 | 540 | 128 | 43 | 82 |
| Marshall Islands | — | — | — | 94 | 76 | 140 | 100 | 38 | — | 102 |
| Micronesia, Fed. Sts. | 0 | 0 | — | 89 | 55 | 0 | — | 39 | — | — |
| Myanmar | 415 | 0 | 450,000 | 84 | 77 | — | 200 | 52 | 128 | 126 |
| Nepal | 7 | 73 | 50,000 | 88 | 35 | — | 170 | 42 | 219 | 125 |
| Sierra Leone | 8 | 8 | — | 58 | 13 | 860 | 890 | 182 | 75 | 145 |
| Solomon Islands | 0 | 0 | — | 79 | 29 | 150 | 93 | 31 | — | — |
| Somalia | 1,077 | 2 | 1,460,000 | 30 | 24 | 1,000 | 1,000 | 147 | — | — |
| South Sudan | 0 | 105 | — | 57 | 9 | 2,100 | — | 104 | — | — |
| Sudan | 500 | 139 | 5,200,000 | 55 | 24 | 94 | 730 | 73 | 330 | 73 |
| Syrian Arab Republic | 20 | 1,242 | 589,000 | 90 | 95 | — | 70 | 15 | 18 | 121 |
| Timor-Leste | 0 | 0 | 400 | 69 | 39 | 560 | 300 | 57 | 231 | 124 |
| Togo | 18 | 19 | — | 59 | 11 | — | 300 | 96 | 111 | 139 |
| Tuvalu | 0 | 0 | — | 98 | 83 | — | — | 30 | — | — |
| West Bank and Gaza | 94 | 1,895 | 160,000 | 82 | 94 | — | — | 23 | 196 | 92 |
| Yemen, Rep. | 2 | 215 | 463,500 | 55 | 53 | — | 200 | 60 | 209 | 91 |
| Zimbabwe | 25 | 5 | 1,000,000 | 80 | 40 | 960 | 570 | 90 | 246 | — |
| Fragile situations | 7,646 | 4,658 | 8,644,100 | 67 | 43 | — | 450 | 91 | 211 | 104 |
| Low income | 5,612 | 2,408 | — | 67 | 37 | — | 410 | 82 | — | 108 |

Note: Most Recent Value (MRV) if data for the specified year or full period are not available.

SOURCE: Adapted from "5.8.2. World Development Indicators: Fragile Situations Part 2," in *World Development Indicators: Tables*, World Bank, 2013, http://wdi.worldbank.org/table/5.8.2.# (accessed October 29, 2013)

20 armed groups were involved in the fighting, and more than 50 million people were directly affected by the hostilities. UN peacekeepers had been trying to stabilize the region since 1999, and millions of Congolese people are believed to have died as a result of the hostilities and accompanying food shortages and disease.

Somalia has also been gripped by a civil war since the early 1990s. The most intense period of fighting was in 1991–92, following the collapse of the country's central government and the initiation of conflict over the country's farmland and resources. Intervention by the United States and other Western nations during the mid-1990s was inconclusive, and during the late 1990s regional leaders consolidated their hold on individual parts of the country in the continued absence of an effective central government. The outbreak of hostilities between factions and ethnic groups has been both consistent and unpredictable over the course of the conflict, and hostilities along with crop failures across the Horn of Africa led to the first officially declared famine of the 21st century, in 2011–12. As of 2013, an estimated 350,000 to 1 million people were believed to have died as a result of the conflict and the effects it produced.

## Afghanistan

In response to the September 11, 2001, terrorist attacks on the World Trade Center in New York City and on the Pentagon in Washington, D.C., the United States launched a war in Afghanistan. The goal was to capture or kill Osama bin Laden (1957?–2011), the terrorist leader who had planned the attacks, and to weaken his al Qaeda militant organization and its allies in the Taliban, a radical Islamist political group that ruled Afghanistan at that time. The United States quickly drove the Taliban from power, and reconstruction began in 2002 under the auspices of a new government. In the years that followed, however, the United States and its allies were not able to stabilize the country and hand over control to Afghan security forces. The Taliban regained a measure of power and succeeded in mounting a successful ongoing insurgency.

As of October 2013, a total of 86,834 North Atlantic Treaty Organization (NATO) troops, 60,000 of them American, remained in Afghanistan, according to the NATO fact sheet "International Security Assistance Force (ISAF): Key Facts and Figures" (October 8, 2013, http://www.isaf.nato.int/images/stories/File/20131014_131001-ISAF-Place mat.pdf). As Table 9.1 indicates, the death toll in Afghanistan had reached 42,697 by 2011. According to the UN High Commissioner on Refugees (UNHCR), in "2013 UNHCR Country Operations Profile—Afghanistan" (January 2013, http://www.unhcr.org/cgi-bin/texis/vtx/page?page=49e486eb6), as of January 2013 there remained approximately 4.1 million Afghan refugees and displaced people.

## The Arab Spring and Related Conflicts

On December 17, 2010, a 26-year-old Tunisian vegetable vendor, Mohamed Bouaziz, set himself on fire in his hometown of Sidi Bouzid, Tunisia, to protest his mistreatment at the hands of police. Bouaziz's act was seen as symbolic of the frustration many Tunisians felt toward their government during a time characterized by poor living standards, high unemployment, widespread corruption, and a lack of commitment to human rights. Protestors calling for change took to the streets of Sidi Bouzid, and within days protests had spread to the capital city of Tunis. As the determination of protestors and the size of demonstrations grew, President Zine el-Abidine Ben Ali (1936–) attempted to suppress the uprising with force, and security personnel killed approximately 300 protestors before Ben Ali was ousted on January 14, 2011.

The rapid success of the Tunisian uprising led Egyptians to take to the streets of central Cairo, the capital city of Egypt, to express disapproval of their own longtime leader President Hosni Mubarak (1928–). Using social media to coordinate events and to communicate with the international press, activists began the Egyptian revolt on January 25, 2011. Within a week an estimated 250,000 protestors had gathered in Cairo's Tahrir Square. As in Tunisia, the Egyptian government attempted to suppress the demonstrations by force, and violence against protestors led to mounting international pressure for Mubarak's resignation. When the Egyptian military withdrew its support for Mubarak, he stepped down, leaving office on February 11, 2011.

Protests in other Arab countries inspired by the example of the Tunisian and Egyptian revolutions fared much differently. In Algeria and Morocco, protests that began in January and February 2011 were met with firm resistance from the state, and although demonstrations led to some reforms, the ruling parties remained in power. When protests began in Libya on February 17, 2011, the country's longtime leader, Muammar Qaddhafi (1942–2011), responded by hiring mercenaries to fight demonstrators. As the violence escalated, Qaddhafi appeared on state-sponsored television to blame the uprisings on the United States, al Qaeda, and other entities, and he vowed to fight to the death rather than leave office. By the end of February, the conflict had evolved into a civil war, with rebels claiming control of several cities near the country's eastern border and setting up an opposition government. Qaddhafi ordered air attacks on the villages and towns he believed to be harboring rebels. The bombing campaign continued, and in March 2011 the UN Security Council voted to impose a no-fly zone over Libya in an attempt to prevent Qaddhafi from bombing civilians. NATO, a 28-member military alliance of countries in North America and Europe, enforced the no-fly zone with airstrikes, which enabled rebel forces to make gains against Qaddafi's troops during the spring and summer of 2011. As governments worldwide increasingly recognized the rebel organization—the National Transitional Council—as Libya's legitimate government, rebel forces continued to take more territory. In October 2011, as the National Transitional Council assumed almost complete control of the country, Qaddafi was killed by rebel forces and the Libyan civil war ended.

Protests continued across the Arab states as Libya's civil war raged. Whereas demonstrations in Bahrain and Jordan were inconclusive, protests in Syria led to a civil war on a scale that ultimately eclipsed Libya's. Large protests in March 2011 in the city of Dar'a sparked demonstrations across Syria in the months that followed, with protestors calling for the resignation of President Bashar al-Assad (1965–). The Syrian government met the protests with force from the start, sending tanks to Dar'a in the early phases of the uprising and intensifying the military response as protests spread. By December 2011 an estimated 5,000 members of the opposition had been killed, thousands more had been detained, and tens of thousands had been displaced.

In spite of mounting international pressure and economic sanctions, al-Assad's government escalated attacks on opposition forces in the months that followed, and by July 2012 the situation had developed into a full-fledged civil war. As the war progressed, the Syrian government began conducting mass bombing campaigns and massacres of civilians—actions that drew widespread condemnation from the international community. In August 2013 international pressure mounted in the wake of reports that the al-Assad government had used chemical weapons in the suburbs of the capital city of Damascus, killing 1,429 people, including 426 children. By October 2013 the death toll had surpassed 100,000. The UNHCR notes in "Stories from Syrian Refugees" (2013, http://data.unhcr.org/syrianrefugees/syria.php) that as of November 2013, more than 2.2 million former residents of Syria had fled to the neighboring countries of Lebanon, Jordan, Turkey, Iraq, and Egypt and were registered as refugees. More than three-fourths of the refugees were women and children, and almost all were entirely dependent on aid groups and charity for survival.

The ultimate consequences of the Arab Spring protests and related armed conflicts were far from certain as of February 2014. For example, in July 2013 Mohamed Morsi (1951–), Egypt's first president to be elected in the wake of Mubarak's ouster, was himself forced from power by mass demonstrations and a military overthrow. Whereas the outcomes of protests differed from country to country, all of the Arab Spring uprisings had in common a widespread refusal among citizens to accept the previous norms of authoritarian rule in the region. Although the countries in North Africa and the Middle East were not among the developing world's poorest, the citizens of the region had long been among the world's least empowered in their relations with their leaders.

## MILITARY SPENDING

Sam Perlo-Freeman et al. of the Stockholm International Peace Research Institute note in the fact sheet "Trends in World Military Expenditure, 2012" (April 2013, http://books.sipri.org/files/FS/SIPRIFS1304.pdf) that military spending worldwide dropped slightly between 2011 and 2012, but since 1988 it had increased every year prior to 2011. U.S. military spending accounted for a large share of total worldwide military spending throughout the late 20th and early 21st centuries. Although military spending worldwide fell in the immediate aftermath of the Cold War (the military standoff between the United States and the Soviet Union that lasted from 1945 to 1989 without ever erupting into actual armed conflict), it rose rapidly in the years after the September 11, 2001, terrorist attacks, powered by U.S. spending on the wars in Afghanistan and Iraq. Spending in other countries—especially China, India, and Russia—kept pace with U.S. increases during this period. The global financial crisis and resulting federal budget cuts in the United States and elsewhere led to slowed growth in military spending in 2009, and as the United States ended its wars in Iraq and, later, Afghanistan, world military spending began to decline in 2012.

As Figure 9.1 shows, the United States accounted for 39% of all global military spending in 2012. China accounted for 9.5% of total world military spending, followed by Russia, at 5.2%. The United Kingdom, Japan, France, Saudi Arabia, India, and Germany each accounted for between 2.6% and 3.5% of world military spending. Italy, Brazil, South Korea, Australia, Canada, and Turkey each accounted for between 1% and 1.9%. In all, these 15 countries accounted for more than 80% of all military spending worldwide.

Table 9.3 details the amounts that each of these 15 countries spent in 2012 both in absolute terms and as a percentage of their gross domestic product (GDP; the total value of all goods and services produced by a country in a year), and it also shows spending trends since 2003 and between 2011 and 2012. At $682 billion, U.S. spending dwarfed that of all the other countries and accounted for a comparatively large share of GDP, at 4.4%. The rapidly developing China eclipsed all the other top-spending countries in the rate of increase, however, as military spending rose 175% between 2003 and 2012. Russia (113%), Saudi Arabia (111%), India (65%), Brazil (56%), and South Korea (44%) also raised military spending dramatically during this period, suggesting an increased focus on military might in developing countries and regions.

## FIGURE 9.1

The share of world military expenditure of the 15 highest-spending countries, 2012

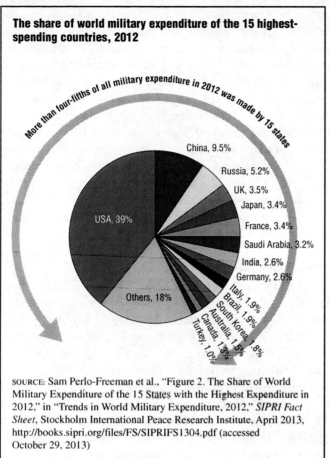

More than four-fifths of all military expenditure in 2012 was made by 15 states

- China, 9.5%
- Russia, 5.2%
- UK, 3.5%
- Japan, 3.4%
- France, 3.4%
- Saudi Arabia, 3.2%
- India, 2.6%
- Germany, 2.6%
- Italy, 1.9%
- Brazil, 1.9%
- South Korea, 1.9%
- Australia, 1.5%
- Canada, 1.3%
- Turkey, 1.0%
- USA, 39%
- Others, 18%

SOURCE: Sam Perlo-Freeman et al., "Figure 2. The Share of World Military Expenditure of the 15 States with the Highest Expenditure in 2012," in "Trends in World Military Expenditure, 2012," *SIPRI Fact Sheet*, Stockholm International Peace Research Institute, April 2013, http://books.sipri.org/files/FS/SIPRIFS1304.pdf (accessed October 29, 2013)

Perlo-Freeman et al. note that other countries in Asia and Africa not among the top-15 spenders worldwide also increased military expenditures dramatically during this period. These included Algeria (189%), Vietnam (130%), and Indonesia (73%). Although military spending in sub-Saharan Africa fell in 2012 because of decreases in Uganda and South Sudan, two-thirds of countries in the region increased military expenditures that year. In South America, Argentina saw the most rapid spending increases in the region between 2003 and 2012, at 132%.

In Central America, where countries have traditionally had low levels of military spending, such spending increased dramatically between 2003 and 2012 because of attempts to combat the epidemic of drug trafficking and the criminal violence associated with it. Military spending in the region grew 70% during this period, led by increases in Mexico, Honduras, and Guatemala. The region also dramatically increased spending on internal security as a result of the same factors. Between 2006 and 2012 Mexico's internal security spending rose 239%. Other Central American countries that increased internal security spending dramatically during this period were Costa Rica (123%), Panama (72%), Guatemala (42%), and Honduras (40%).

## VIOLENCE AGAINST WOMEN

### Intimate-Partner and Sexual Violence

In 2013 the World Health Organization (WHO), in collaboration with the London School of Hygiene and

## TABLE 9.3

Spending levels of the 15 countries with the highest military expenditures, 2012

| Rank 2012 | Rank 2011 | Country | Spending, 2012 ($b.) | Change (%) 2011–12 | Change (%) 2003–12 | Spending as a share of GDP (%)[a] 2012 | Spending as a share of GDP (%)[a] 2003 |
|---|---|---|---|---|---|---|---|
| 1 | 1 | USA | 682 | −6.0 | 32 | 4.4 | 3.7 |
| 2 | 2 | China | [166] | 7.8 | 175 | [2.0] | [2.1] |
| 3 | 3 | Russia | [90.7] | 16 | 113 | [4.4] | [4.3] |
| 4 | 4 | UK | 60.8 | −0.8 | 4.9 | 2.5 | 2.5 |
| 5 | 6 | Japan | 59.3 | −0.6 | −3.6 | 1.0 | 1.0 |
| 6 | 5 | France | 58.9 | −0.3 | −3.3 | 2.3 | 2.6 |
| 7 | 8 | Saudi Arabia | 56.7 | 12 | 111 | 8.9 | 8.7 |
| 8 | 7 | India | 46.1 | −0.8 | 65 | 2.5 | 2.8 |
| 9 | 9 | Germany | [45.8] | 0.9 | −1.5 | [1.4] | 1.4 |
| 10 | 11 | Italy | [34.0] | −5.2 | −19 | 1.7 | 2.0 |
| 11 | 10 | Brazil | 33.1 | −0.5 | 56 | [1.5] | 1.5 |
| 12 | 12 | South Korea | 31.7 | 1.9 | 44 | 2.7 | 2.5 |
| 13 | 13 | Australia | 26.2 | −4.0 | 29 | 1.7 | 1.9 |
| 14 | 14 | Canada | [22.5] | −3.9 | 36 | [1.3] | 1.1 |
| 15 | 15 | Turkey[b] | [18.2] | 1.2 | −2.1 | 2.3 | 3.4 |
| | | World total | 1,753 | −0.5 | 35 | 2.5 | 2.4 |

[ ] = Stockholm International Peace Research Institute (SIPRI) estimate.
[a]The figures for military expenditure as a share of GDP are based on data from the International Monetary Fund (IMF) World Economic Outlook database, Oct. 2012.
[b]It is possible that the United Arab Emirates (UAE) would be in 15th position in place of Turkey, but data is not available for the UAE in 2012.
Note: GDP = Gross domestic product.

SOURCE: Sam Perlo-Freeman et al., "Table 1. The 15 Countries with the Highest Military Expenditure in 2012," in "Trends in World Military Expenditure, 2012," *SIPRI Fact Sheet*, Stockholm International Peace Research Institute, April 2013, http://books.sipri.org/files/FS/SIPRIFS1304.pdf (accessed October 29, 2013)

Tropical Medicine and the South African Medical Research Council, released *Global and Regional Estimates of Violence against Women: Prevalence and Health Effects of Intimate Partner Violence and Non-partner Sexual Violence* (2013, http://apps.who.int/iris/bitstream/10665/85239/1/9789241564625_eng.pdf), the first systematic worldwide study of these two types of violence, which afflict women with alarming regularity and which have serious public health consequences. For the sake of the report, the WHO defines the term *intimate-partner violence* as physical abuse and/or unwanted sexual contact with a spouse or a domestic partner. (Other legitimate forms of intimate-partner violence, such as emotional abuse, are excluded from the report because of the difficulty of collecting relevant data.) The WHO defines the term *nonpartner sexual violence* as unwanted sexual contact with someone other than a spouse or a partner.

The WHO found that the lifetime prevalence rates of intimate-partner violence were significantly higher in low- and middle-income countries than in high-income countries. In the high-income countries of North America, Europe, and parts of Asia and Oceania, the WHO found that the lifetime prevalence of intimate-partner violence (the percentage of women aged 15 years and older who had ever been victimized by a spouse or a partner) was 23.2%. In the WHO region of the Western Pacific (based on survey data from Cambodia, China, the Philippines, Samoa, and Vietnam), women had a slightly higher lifetime prevalence rate of intimate-partner violence, at 24.6%. In the WHO region of Europe (the region centering on Russia and the other former Soviet republics), the rate was 25.4%. In the Americas (Latin America and the Caribbean), women experienced intimate-partner violence at a significantly higher rate of 29.8%. The lifetime prevalence rates of intimate-partner violence were highest in Africa (36.6%), the eastern Mediterranean (37%; the Middle East), and Southeast Asia (37.7%; Bangladesh, India, Myanmar [Burma], Sri Lanka, Thailand, and Timor-Leste).

By contrast, rates of nonpartner sexual violence were highest in the developed world, according to the WHO. In high-income countries women had a lifetime prevalence rate of 12.6%. Prevalence rates in low- and middle-income countries were highest in Africa (11.9%) and the Americas (10.7%). The WHO cautions that its data for nonpartner sexual violence were less extensive than its data for intimate-partner violence but suggests that the higher worldwide and regional rates of intimate-partner violence relative to nonpartner sexual violence are consistent across all regions of the world.

Overall, the WHO concludes that sexual violence is normative, or widely accepted as part of everyday life, in regions of the world where other forms of violence are common. Among other negative health consequences, the WHO finds that women who had experienced intimate-partner violence were more vulnerable to the human immunodeficiency virus and other sexually transmitted infections (because of forced exposure to diseases and because of the stress that comes with such violence). Women in violent relationships were also much more likely to have unintended pregnancies and to seek abortions, approximately half of which are typically conducted in unsafe conditions. Alcohol abuse, depression, and suicide were also associated with intimate-partner violence, as was the presence of a variety of injuries resulting directly from the violence. The most common locations for these injuries were the head, neck, and face.

**Female Genital Mutilation**

According to the WHO, in "Female Genital Mutilation" (February 2014, http://www.who.int/mediacentre/factsheets/fs241/en/index.html), female genital mutilation (the practice of removing or altering parts of the female genitalia, such as the clitoris, for nonmedical reasons) affects an estimated 125 million girls and women worldwide. The practice is most common in the western, eastern, and northeastern countries of Africa, and it is also common in some parts of Asia and the Middle East. Typically performed on girls younger than 15 years by traditional circumcisers who are often community leaders, the procedure harms girls by damaging healthy tissue and interfering with normal bodily functions. The procedure causes pain, shock, and bleeding and can result in tetanus, bacterial infections, open sores, and injury to other genital tissues. Possible long-term consequences include chronic bladder and urinary-tract infections, cysts, infertility, problems with pregnancy and childbirth, and the need for further surgeries.

There are no medical reasons for the various forms of the procedure; instead, the practice is typically rooted in cultural beliefs about the proper sexual identity and behavior of women. In the male-dominated communities where female genital mutilation is common, some people believe that the procedure reduces female desire and extramarital sexual behavior, and the practice is associated with notions of feminine purity and modesty. Although often performed in the name of religious tradition, female genital mutilation has no basis in any religious scripture. It is internationally regarded as an extreme form of gender discrimination and has been condemned as a human rights violation by the WHO, the UN Children's Fund, and the UN General Assembly, among other organizations.

# CHAPTER 10

# THE FIGHT AGAINST POVERTY: PROGRESS AND PROSPECTS

*We will spare no effort to free our fellow men, women and children from the abject and dehumanizing conditions of extreme poverty.*

—United Nations Millennium Declaration, September 8, 2000

Since the introduction of the Millennium Development Goals (MDGs) in 2000, the world has seen the most rapid reduction in poverty rates on record. Between 2000 and 2013 approximately 500 million people moved out of extreme poverty, under-five mortality fell by approximately 30%, and substantial progress was made toward all the other MDGs. Questions remain, however, about which factors have contributed most to these successes and which factors constitute obstacles to MDGs in regions in which rates of poverty and deprivation remain high.

The world as a whole has made substantial progress toward achieving many of the MDGs. Worldwide, the first and most basic MDG—to reduce extreme poverty (the percentage of people living on $1.25 per day or less) in half between 1990 and 2015—was reached five years ahead of schedule, in 2010. As noted throughout this book, however, this overall achievement disguises wide divergences from region to region. Furthermore, from MDG to MDG there is wide variation in the amount of progress made both across and within regions. Even in countries that have come closest to meeting all MDGs, there are typically wide disparities between urban and rural living standards. This chapter will assess MDG progress, as well as progress more generally in combating poverty, according to these and other distinctions. It will also consider various lessons learned about poverty reduction over the course of the preceding decades and address hopes for future progress in the fight against poverty and deprivation.

## MDG PROGRESS

Since 1990 the percentage of people living on $1.25 per day or less has fallen by more than the MDG of a 50% reduction. As Table 10.1 shows, all regions of the developing world met the target, with the exceptions of South Asia and sub-Saharan Africa. East Asia and the Pacific, propelled by poverty reductions in the high-population country of China, made particularly dramatic progress: the percentage of people in the region living in extreme poverty fell from 56.2% in 1990 to 12.5% in 2010. Moreover, the raw numerical decrease in this one region accounted for almost all of the total numerical decrease worldwide. Worldwide, the total number of people living in extreme poverty fell by 693.7 million during this period, from 1.9 billion to 1.2 billion, and in East Asia and the Pacific alone, the numerical reduction was 675.5 million (97% of the worldwide total), from 926.4 million to 250.9 million.

In 2010 there were still 250.9 million people living in extreme poverty in East Asia and the Pacific, however. Together, East Asia, South Asia (506.8 million people in extreme poverty), and sub-Saharan Africa (413.8 million people in extreme poverty) accounted for 1.1 billion of the 1.2 billion people living in extreme poverty worldwide. The percentage of the South Asian population living in extreme poverty fell 22.8 percentage points between 1990 and 2010, but 31% of the region's people continued to live in extreme poverty. Meanwhile, nearly half (48.5%) of sub-Saharan Africa's population continued to live in extreme poverty in 2010, down only eight percentage points since 1990.

Progress toward most of the other MDGs lags behind progress toward the extreme-poverty target, but as Figure 10.1 shows, the developing world as a whole was in a position to meet many targets as of 2010 or 2011 (the most recent year for which data were available was 2010 for some targets and 2011 for others). For each target, the bar on the left represents the percentage of progress required, as of 2010 or 2011, to be on track to meet each MDG by 2015; and the bar on the right represents the

TABLE 10.1

**Percentage and number of people living below $1.25 per day, selected years 1990–2010 and projected for 2015**

| Region | Share of population below $1.25 a day (2005 PPP) | | | | |
|---|---|---|---|---|---|
| | 1990 | 2005 | 2008 | 2010 | 2015 (forecast) |
| East Asia and Pacific | 56.2 | 16.8 | 14.3 | 12.5 | 5.5 |
| Europe and Central Asia | 1.9 | 1.3 | 0.5 | 0.07 | 0.4 |
| Latin America and the Caribbean | 12.2 | 8.7 | 6.5 | 5.5 | 4.9 |
| Middle East and North Africa | 5.8 | 3.5 | 2.7 | 2.4 | 2.6 |
| South Asia | 53.8 | 39.4 | 36.0 | 31.0 | 23.2 |
| Sub-Saharan Africa | 56.5 | 52.3 | 49.2 | 48.5 | 42.3 |
| **Total** | **43.1** | **25.0** | **22.7** | **20.6** | **15.5** |

| Region | Millions of people below $1.25 a day (2005 PPP) | | | | |
|---|---|---|---|---|---|
| | 1990 | 2005 | 2008 | 2010 | 2015 |
| East Asia and Pacific | 926.4 | 332.1 | 284.4 | 250.9 | 114.5 |
| Europe and Central Asia | 8.9 | 6.3 | 2.2 | 3.1 | 1.9 |
| Latin America and the Caribbean | 53.4 | 47.6 | 36.9 | 32.3 | 30.0 |
| Middle East and North Africa | 13.0 | 10.5 | 8.6 | 8.0 | 9.3 |
| South Asia | 617.3 | 598.3 | 570.7 | 506.8 | 406.5 |
| Sub-Saharan Africa | 289.7 | 394.9 | 399.3 | 413.8 | 408.0 |
| **Total** | **1,908.6** | **1,389.6** | **1,302.8** | **1,214.9** | **970.2** |

PPP = Purchasing Power Parity.

SOURCE: "Table BO.1.1. Poverty by Region," in *Global Monitoring Report 2013: Rural-Urban Dynamics and the Millennium Development Goals*, World Bank, Washington, D.C., 2013, http://siteresources.worldbank.org/INTPROSPECTS/Resources/334934-1327948020811/8401693-1355753354515/8980448-1366123749799/GMR_2013_Full_Report.pdf (accessed October 29, 2013). DOI: 10.1596/978-0-8213-9806-7. License: Creative Commons Attribution CC BY 3.0.

actual progress made as of 2010 or 2011. The developing world as a whole was on track to meet (or had already met) targets relating to extreme poverty, the ratio of girls to boys in primary education, access to safe drinking water, and the improvement of conditions for slum dwellers. The developing world was slightly off track to meet the target relating to gender equity in both primary and secondary education, and it was more significantly off track to meet the targets for primary completion rate, infant mortality, under-five mortality, maternal mortality, and access to sanitation.

These overall levels of progress do not reflect the fact that there were wide variations from region to region. As with the extreme-poverty target, progress in East Asia and the Pacific has a disproportionate effect on the statistics for the developing world as a whole. Because this region is so populous and has made so much more progress than any other developing region, in relation to most of the MDGs, it brings up the average levels of progress to a degree that masks serious shortfalls in other regions.

Figure 10.2 shows the amount of progress, as a percentage of the total distance to individual MDGs, that each region had made as of 2010 or 2011. To be on target for meeting MDGs, a region needed to have reached the range of 80% (for 2010) to 84% (for 2011); values above 100% indicate that a region had exceeded the necessary gains for achievement of the target. Only East Asia and the Pacific was on track to meet all the targets shown.

Sub-Saharan Africa was nowhere near achieving any of the MDGs, and South Asia was off track for meeting the targets relating to primary school completion, infant mortality, under-five mortality, and access to sanitation facilities. The Middle East and North Africa region was off track for meeting the targets relating to primary school completion, girl-to-boy ratio in education, infant mortality, and access to safe drinking water. Even regions with relatively little extreme poverty lagged significantly in certain areas. For example, Europe and Central Asia fell short in primary school completion, gender equity in primary school, maternal mortality, and access to sanitation; and Latin America and the Caribbean was projected to fall substantially short of the targets for maternal mortality and access to sanitation.

There was even more variation at the country level. As of 2013, more than 60 developing countries were "seriously off target" for four MDGs: prevalence of undernourishment, infant mortality, maternal mortality, and access to sanitation. (See Figure 10.3.) Only in relation to two targets—reduction of extreme poverty and ratio of girls to boys in education—had a majority of countries either met their target or made sufficient progress to be in a position to meet the target by 2015.

## CHINA: THE RELATIONSHIP BETWEEN ECONOMIC GROWTH AND POVERTY

The rapid progress that China has made toward reducing poverty since the 1980s has been driven largely

**FIGURE 10.1**

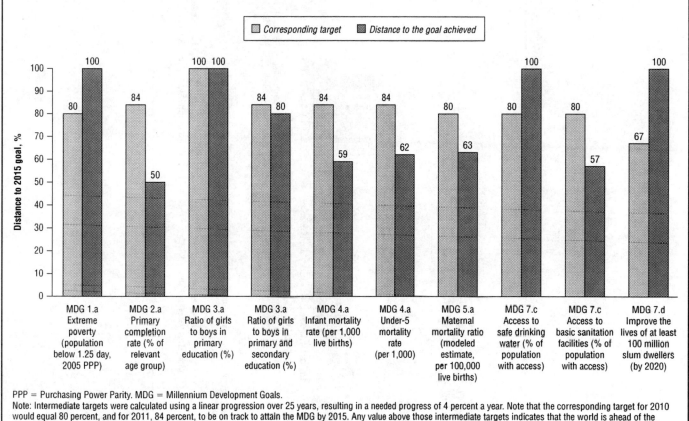

**Global progress toward achieving the MDGs, 2010 or 2011**

Developing countries, percent of total required progress between 1990 and 2015, as achieved in 2010 or 2011

PPP = Purchasing Power Parity. MDG = Millennium Development Goals.
Note: Intermediate targets were calculated using a linear progression over 25 years, resulting in a needed progress of 4 percent a year. Note that the corresponding target for 2010 would equal 80 percent, and for 2011, 84 percent, to be on track to attain the MDG by 2015. Any value above those intermediate targets indicates that the world is ahead of the required pace to meet the MDG. A value of 100 percent means that the MDG has been met.

SOURCE: "Figure 0.1. Global Progress toward Achieving the MDGs," in *Global Monitoring Report 2013: Rural-Urban Dynamics and the Millennium Development Goals*, World Bank, 2013, http://siteresources.worldbank.org/INTPROSPECTS/Resources/334934-1327948020811/8401693-1355753354515/8980448-1366123749799/GMR_2013_Full_Report.pdf (accessed October 29, 2013)

by economic growth. This fact underscores the close relationship between economic and human development. In general, as countries generate higher levels of economic productivity, they have a much greater ability to eradicate poverty. Although some observers of China's rapid progress in both economic and human development terms suggest that the country's success confirms a development model in which economic growth alone can be trusted to improve the lives of the largest numbers of people, other experts paint a more complicated picture of the relationship between economic growth and poverty.

To begin understanding China's success at combating poverty, it is important to understand the historical circumstances in which its economic growth took root. Ruled by the Communist Party of China, the country had a fully centralized command economy for approximately 30 years after its 1949 founding as a modern socialist state. A command economy is one in which land, capital (money, property, equipment, and other resources that

can be used to make more money), and most industries are either state-owned or heavily regulated by the state, and in which the state assumes a large role in deciding what goods and services should be produced and at what prices they should be sold. Although command economies typically perform well in situations requiring massive up-front investment and centralized decision making, such as large-scale infrastructure projects, they have historically performed poorly at managing the infinite number of day-to-day decisions that accompany widespread economic activity.

In a market-oriented economy, no central body makes decisions about, for example, how much land to allocate to grain production and heavy industry, how much workers in different occupations should be paid, or what the prices of everything from automobiles to pencils to apartment rents should be. These decisions are made primarily by the interlocking forces of supply and demand. In the presence of increasing consumer demand for a certain good or service, the price of that

**FIGURE 10.2**

**Global progress toward achieving the MDGs, by region, 2010 or 2011**

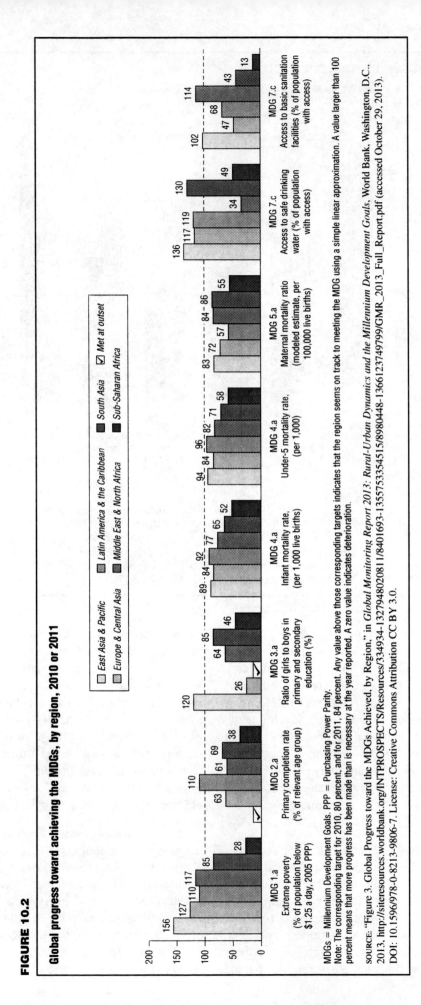

MDGs = Millennium Development Goals. PPP = Purchasing Power Parity.

Note: The corresponding target for 2010, 80 percent, and for 2011, 84 percent. Any value above those corresponding targets indicates that the region seems on track to meeting the MDG using a simple linear approximation. A value larger than 100 percent means that more progress has been made than is necessary at the year reported. A zero value indicates deterioration.

SOURCE: "Figure 3. Global Progress toward the MDGs Achieved, by Region," in *Global Monitoring Report 2013: Rural-Urban Dynamics and the Millennium Development Goals,* World Bank, Washington, D.C., 2013, http://siteresources.worldbank.org/INTPROSPECTS/Resources/334934-1327948020811/8401693-1355575335451S/8980448-1366123749799/GMR_2013_Full_Report.pdf (accessed October 29, 2013). DOI: 10.1596/978-0-8213-9806-7. License: Creative Commons Attribution CC BY 3.0.

FIGURE 10.3

**Extent of progress toward MDGs, by number of countries, 2013**

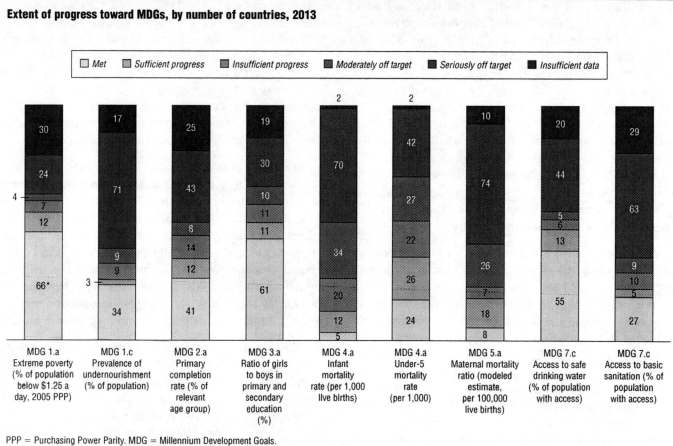

PPP = Purchasing Power Parity. MDG = Millennium Development Goals.

*In the poverty target, 11 out of the 66 countries that have met the target have less than 2% of people living below $1.25 a day.

Note: Progress is based on extrapolation of latest five-year annual growth rates for each country, except for MDG 5, which uses the last seven years. "Sufficient progress" indicates that an extrapolation of the last observed data point with the growth rate over the last observable five-year period shows that the MDG can be attained. "Insufficient progress" is defined as being able to meet the MDG between 2016 and 2020. "Moderately off target" indicates that the MDG can be met between 2020 and 2030. "Seriously off target" indicates that the MDG will not even be met by 2030. "Insufficient data" points to the fact that not enough data points are available to estimate progress or that the MDG's starting value is missing (except for MDG 2 and MDG 3).

SOURCE: "Figure 4. Number of Countries Making Progress toward the Various MDGs," in *Global Monitoring Report 2013: Rural-Urban Dynamics and the Millennium Development Goals*, World Bank, Washington, D.C., 2013, http://siteresources.worldbank.org/INTPROSPECTS/Resources/334934-1327948020811/8401693-1355753354515/8980448-1366123749799/GMR_2013_Full_Report.pdf (accessed October 29, 2013). DOI: 10.1596/978-0-8213-9806-7. License: Creative Commons Attribution CC BY 3.0.

good or service rises, encouraging producers to supply more of it. As supply increases and different producers compete for consumers' business, the price falls. The same principles apply to wages. As demand for certain types of labor rises, so do wages, and vice versa. Thus, prices are set by the collective actions of individual people acting through the market.

In a command economy, however, government officials are responsible for making all (or many) of these individual decisions, and historically this has produced inefficiency. Individuals or government agencies acting alone from a position of centralized power are typically unable to gauge what people need and want with the accuracy of market forces. The results of a high degree of central planning often include shortages of some goods and services and surpluses of others, as well as an overall constraining of the potential for economic growth. In the case of China, centralized decision making held back the

country's economic development in the decades after World War II (1939–1945). In the area of agricultural production, government policies dictating how food should be produced resulted in inefficiencies so pronounced that they played a major role in bringing about a severe famine during the late 1950s and early 1960s. With these failures in mind, Chinese leaders during the late 1970s, while still operating within the framework of the Communist Party, introduced a number of market-oriented reforms to the country's economy, such as opening up certain industries to competition among private firms, reforming landownership and other agricultural policies, and allowing for foreign investment.

As a result of the reforms, which continued in piecemeal fashion over the following decades, China's economy was transformed from a command model to a mixed economy that combined aspects of both command and market economies, and production rose dramatically.

Martin Ravallion of the World Bank notes in "A Comparative Perspective on Poverty Reduction in Brazil, China, and India" (*World Bank Research Observer*, vol. 26, no. 1, February 2011) that China's gross domestic product (GDP) per capita (the total value of goods and services produced by the Chinese economy in a given year and divided by the country's population) nearly tripled between 1981 and 1993, growing from $543.50 to more than $1,505.50, and then it nearly tripled again between 1993 and 2005, reaching $4,076.30. Overall, the Chinese economy grew by an average of 10% annually between 1978 and 2010 to become the world's second largest as measured by total output (GDP). China is expected to surpass the United States during the 2020s to become the world's largest economy.

Ravallion quantifies the success at reducing poverty that accompanied this rapid economic growth: "The data suggest that, around the time its reforms began, China had one of the highest proportions of the population living in poverty in the world. In 1981, a staggering 84 percent of the population lived below a poverty line of $1.25 per day.... The best data available suggest that only four countries (Cambodia, Burkina Faso, Mali, and Uganda) had a higher headcount index [percentage of people living in extreme poverty] than China in 1981. By 2005 the proportion of China's population living in poverty had fallen to 16 percent—well below the average for the developing world of 26 percent. The proportionate rate of poverty reduction over 1981–2005 was an impressive 6.6 percent per annum ... with the number of poor falling by 5.5 percent per annum."

Ravallion notes, however, that China's success at combating poverty hinged to a large degree on a historical circumstance not present in other developing countries: prior to the reform period, farmland in China was state-owned and cultivated for the benefit of collectives rather than for individuals. With the reform of China's agricultural industry, land was allocated to individual farmers, and the distribution of land appears to have been equitable. Chinese farmers, while not technically the owners of their land and while still subject to a substantial amount of government control, were allowed to profit from their labor. This and other agricultural reforms, according to Ravallion, "were clearly the main reason for the dramatic reduction in poverty in China in the early 1980s." Ravallion goes on to observe that over the long term, the agricultural reforms brought about what is known as "pro-poor" growth, or economic growth that benefits the poor as much as it benefits the wealthy.

China's accelerated economic growth continued to lift hundreds of millions of people out of poverty in the decades that followed, but much of the later growth came from the industrial and service sectors of the economy, and this growth benefited urban coastal areas of the country much more than the rural interior, leading to increasing income inequality between regions. In periods when China's agricultural industry performed well over the subsequent decades, both rural and urban poor people benefited. In periods when agricultural production lagged, the rural poor suffered disproportionately. While urban areas of China rapidly caught up with the living standards of the developed world, partly because they benefited from various forms of preferential treatment from the government, rural incomes languished.

Whereas China at the outset of the reform period was characterized by substantial income equality, inequality increased rapidly between the 1980s and the first decade of the 21st century. As of 2011, the country's Gini index had been increasing by an average of 7% per decade, and China was on track to become one of the world's most unequal countries by 2025. When income inequality is high, economic growth disproportionately benefits the wealthy, so increasing inequality is self-reinforcing and typically cannot be stopped by economic growth alone.

Thus, China's experience points not only to the necessity of economic growth in the attempt to reduce poverty but also to the fact that different forms of economic growth have different effects on the poor and on poverty levels. Increasingly, international advocates for human development promote pro-poor or inclusive growth. Examples include China's agricultural reforms as well as more conventional forms of economic redistribution that benefit the poor. For example, Ravallion notes that during the same period that China saw rapidly increasing inequality, Brazil, which began the 1980s as one of the world's most unequal countries, was able to reduce income inequality and poverty at the same time that it enjoyed modest economic growth. This was accomplished via transfer payments to the poor, funded by increased taxation.

Although no experts on poverty dispute the central role of economic development in poverty reduction, advocating for pro-poor or inclusive economic growth at the country level often requires overcoming substantial political opposition. Economic growth is clearly the major factor in bringing about the largest reductions in world poverty on record in the period between the 1980s and the second decade of the 21st century, and many people interpret this fact as evidence that governments and international organizations should work to promote growth without interfering in the management of economies. Most antipoverty advocates believe this to be a misunderstanding of the relationship between economic growth and poverty reduction. The United Nations Development Programme states in "Poverty Reduction" (2013, http://www.undp.org/content/undp/en/home/our work/povertyreduction/overview.html) that "economic growth will not reduce poverty, improve equality and produce jobs unless it is inclusive. Inclusive growth is also essential for the achievement of the Millennium Development Goals (MDGs). The globalization process, when properly managed, becomes an important ingredient for inclusive growth."

## THE URBAN/RURAL DIVIDE

Between 1960 and 2011 the growth of urban populations as a share of total population steadily increased worldwide in both the developed and the developing world. (See Figure 10.4.) Nearly 80% of the developed world's population lived in urban areas as of 2011, up from less than 70% in 1960. Those parts of the developing world with the highest standards of living also tended to be those with the highest rates of urbanization. The urbanized share of the population of Latin America and the Caribbean (approximately 80%) equaled that of the developed world, and both Europe and Central Asia (where approximately 65% of the population was urban) and the Middle East and North Africa (where almost 60% of the population was urban) far exceeded the average level of urbanization in the developing world (just under 50%). Meanwhile, East Asia and the Pacific has urbanized more rapidly than any other part of the world since 1960, and in 2011 its population was almost 50% urban. By comparison, the populations of both South Asia and sub-Saharan Africa were less than 40% urban.

Progress at eradicating extreme poverty has proceeded unevenly in rural and urban areas across the developing world, and rural rates of extreme poverty remained much higher than urban rates as of 2008. (See Table 10.2.) In East Asia and the Pacific, 20.4% of rural people lived on less than $1.25 per day, compared with 4.3% of urban people; and in Latin America and the Caribbean, 13.2% of rural residents lived on less than $1.25 per day, compared with 3.1% of the urban population. Even in South Asia and sub-Saharan Africa, which had extremely high rates of urban poverty, rates of rural poverty were higher still: 38% of rural South Asians and 47.1% of rural sub-Saharan Africans lived on less than $1.25 per day, compared with 29.7% of urban South Asians and 33.6% of urban sub-Saharan Africans. In all, according to the World Bank, in *Global Monitoring Report 2013: Rural-Urban Dynamics and the Millennium Development Goals* (2013, http://sitere sources.worldbank.org/INTPROSPECTS/Resources/3349 34-1327948020811/8401693-1355753354515/8980448- 1366123749799/GMR_2013_Full_Report.pdf), 76% of the extremely poor people in the developing world lived in rural areas in 2008.

The lower rates of poverty in urban areas of the developing world are closely tied to the concentration of most economic activity in cities. Worldwide, over 80% of economic activity occurs in cities, according to the World Bank. Additionally, the provision of many of the basic services that satisfy MDGs, such as clean water, sanitation, education, and health care, is much more feasible in cities than in rural areas of the developing world. The World Bank explains that "the densities that

**FIGURE 10.4**

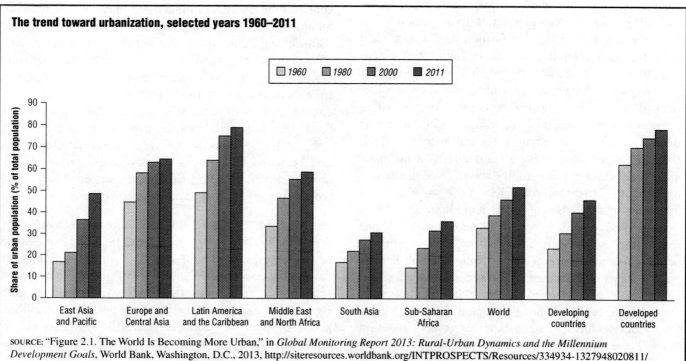

The trend toward urbanization, selected years 1960–2011

SOURCE: "Figure 2.1. The World Is Becoming More Urban," in *Global Monitoring Report 2013: Rural-Urban Dynamics and the Millennium Development Goals*, World Bank, Washington, D.C., 2013, http://siteresources.worldbank.org/INTPROSPECTS/Resources/334934-1327948020811/ 8401693-1355753354515/8980448-1366123749799/GMR_2013_Full_Report.pdf (accessed October 29, 2013). DOI: 10.1596/978-0-8213-9806-7. License: Creative Commons Attribution CC BY 3.0.

**TABLE 10.2**

**Percentage of population living below $1.25 per day, by world region and rural or urban area, selected years 1990–2008**

[Share of the population below $1.25 a day]

| | 1990 Rural | 1990 Urban | 1996 Rural | 1996 Urban | 2002 Rural | 2002 Urban | 2008 Rural | 2008 Urban |
|---|---|---|---|---|---|---|---|---|
| East Asia and Pacific | 67.5 | 24.4 | 45.9 | 13.0 | 39.2 | 6.9 | 20.4 | 4.3 |
| Europe and Central Asia | 2.2 | 0.9 | 6.3 | 2.8 | 4.4 | 1.1 | 1.2 | 0.2 |
| Latin America and the Caribbean | 21.0 | 7.4 | 20.3 | 6.3 | 20.3 | 8.3 | 13.2 | 3.1 |
| Middle East and North Africa | 9.1 | 1.9 | 5.6 | 0.9 | 7.5 | 1.2 | 4.1 | 0.8 |
| South Asia | 50.5 | 40.1 | 46.1 | 35.2 | 45.1 | 35.2 | 38.0 | 29.7 |
| Sub-Saharan Africa | 55.0 | 41.5 | 56.8 | 40.6 | 52.3 | 41.4 | 47.1 | 33.6 |
| **Total** | **52.5** | **20.5** | **43.0** | **17.0** | **39.5** | **15.1** | **29.4** | **11.6** |

SOURCE: "Table 2.1. Poverty Rates Are Falling in Both Urban and Rural Areas but Are Lower in Urban Areas," in *Global Monitoring Report 2013: Rural-Urban Dynamics and the Millennium Development Goals*, World Bank, Washington, D.C., 2013, http://siteresources.worldbank.org/INTPROSPECTS/Resources/334934-1327948020811/8401693-1355753354515/8980448-1366123749799/GMR_2013_Full_Report.pdf (accessed October 29, 2013). DOI: 10.1596/978-0-8213-9806-7. License: Creative Commons Attribution CC BY 3.0.

cities offer can create scale economies that enhance job opportunities and productivity, as well as make it cheaper to expand services.... For example, providing piped water costs $0.70–$0.80 per cubic meter in urban areas, but $2 in sparsely populated areas.... Schooling and health care can be delivered at scale in dense environments, close to where people actually live."

**The Changing Face of Urban Poverty**

In spite of the generally brighter economic and human development prospects for urban people in the developing world compared with their rural counterparts, and in spite of the rapid progress made in reducing urban poverty and living standards, a large proportion of the developing world's urban population lived in slums as of 2010. There is no technical definition of the term *slum*, but in the international community slums are typically regarded as urban areas characterized by the presence of five forms of deprivation: a lack of access to clean water, a lack of access to improved sanitation, overcrowding, impermanent construction of buildings, and transience or insecurity of residence status. According to the World Bank, in *Global Monitoring Report 2013*, an estimated 1 billion people in the developing world lived in slums as of 2013. In 2010 approximately 60% of the urban population in sub-Saharan Africa and about 35% of the urban population of Southern Asia lived in slums. (See Figure 10.5.) More than half of slum-dwellers in Southern Asia and 40% of slum-dwellers in sub-Saharan Africa were without access to improved sanitation facilities in 2010. Slums are more likely than other parts of developing cities to be built in environmentally vulnerable areas such as floodplains and steep hillsides or near industrial sites where exposure to toxic emissions or waste is common. Additionally, the temporary nature of most slum construction further exposes residents to the dangers of environmental hazards.

Although the prevalence of slum conditions in the developing world remains a major human development challenge, the giant slums in the developing world's rapidly growing "megacities" constitute only part of the overall picture of urban poverty in the 21st century. A more complex picture emerges along with a more nuanced understanding of the very definition of the term *urban*. Whereas traditional notions of the opposition between rural and urban life call to mind open countryside and agricultural lifestyles on the one hand and teeming major cities on the other, a more realistic notion of how urban populations cluster has given rise to new studies that are changing the overall picture of the urban poverty distribution in the developing world. Figure 10.6 contrasts the traditional binary notion, in which there are monolithic cities and monolithic rural areas, with a more realistic representation of the settlement types that constitute the rural–urban spectrum. Rural life remains organized in terms of villages interspersed at a distance from one another in the countryside, but urban areas consist not only of principal cities with dense populations but of complex population clusters in concentric formation, including a principal city, a metropolitan area (the principal city plus secondary cities), and a larger urban perimeter (the principal city and secondary cities plus a number of smaller cities or towns).

According to the World Bank, new research indicates that in many countries most of the urban poor live outside of the largest cities. As Table 10.3 shows, in numerous developing countries the incidence of poverty is higher in small cities and towns (and thus categorized in data sources as "urban" poverty) than in megacities of 1 million people or more. For example, in Brazil, which has one of the most urbanized populations in the world and two of South America's largest cities, São Paulo (whose population was approximately 10.9 million in 2013) and Rio de Janeiro (6.1 million), more of the urban poor

# FIGURE 10.5

**Percentage of urban population living in slums, by developing region, 1990, 2000, and 2010**

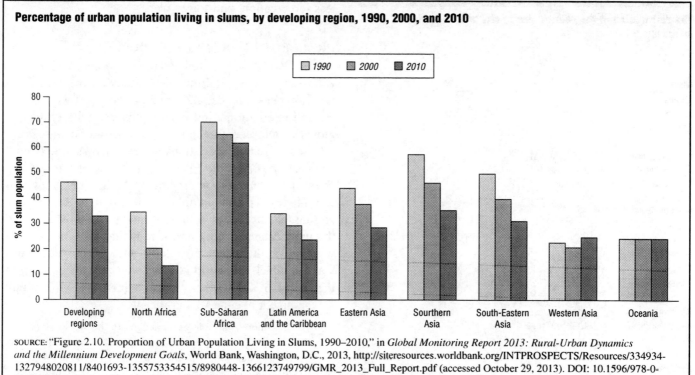

SOURCE: "Figure 2.10. Proportion of Urban Population Living in Slums, 1990–2010," in *Global Monitoring Report 2013: Rural-Urban Dynamics and the Millennium Development Goals*, World Bank, Washington, D.C., 2013, http://siteresources.worldbank.org/INTPROSPECTS/Resources/334934-1327948020811/8401693-1355753354515/8980448-1366123749799/GMR_2013_Full_Report.pdf (accessed October 29, 2013). DOI: 10.1596/978-0-8213-9806-7. License: Creative Commons Attribution CC BY 3.0. Data from United Nations-Habitat, *State of the World's Cities 2010/2011*, 2010.

# FIGURE 10.6

**The rural-urban spectrum**

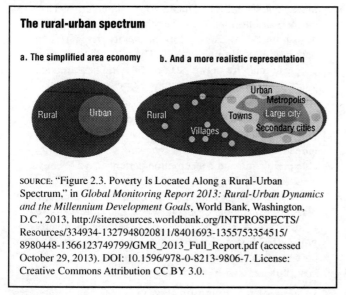

SOURCE: "Figure 2.3. Poverty Is Located Along a Rural-Urban Spectrum," in *Global Monitoring Report 2013: Rural-Urban Dynamics and the Millennium Development Goals*, World Bank, Washington, D.C., 2013, http://siteresources.worldbank.org/INTPROSPECTS/Resources/334934-1327948020811/8401693-1355753354515/8980448-1366123749799/GMR_2013_Full_Report.pdf (accessed October 29, 2013). DOI: 10.1596/978-0-8213-9806-7. License: Creative Commons Attribution CC BY 3.0.

population lived in small- and medium-sized cities than in megacities as of 2012. Brazil's population was 83% urban, divided among megacities (22%), large cities of 500,000 to 1 million people (7%), medium-sized cities of 100,000 to 500,000 people (24%), small cities/towns of 50,000 to 100,000 (1%), and extra-small cities/towns of 50,000 or fewer people (28%). Whereas 72% of Brazil's impoverished population was urban, only 9% of the impoverished population lived in megacities, compared with 17% in medium-sized cities and 39% in extra-small cities.

Similar patterns were evident in Kazakhstan and Thailand. Among the countries shown, only in Kenya, where 6% of the country's total impoverished population lived in megacities, and in Mexico, where 16% of the total impoverished population lived in megacities, did the largest cities account for the largest share of the urban poor.

## Poverty Reduction through Smart Urbanization

The changing distribution of the urban poor is consistent with theories about the economic benefits of agglomeration economies, which the World Bank defines in *Global Monitoring Report 2013* as arising "when there is a confluence of people, or population density, and firms, or economic density." The agglomeration of people and firms leads to job creation and self-reinforcing forms of economic productivity. The most productive workers are drawn to cities with high levels of agglomeration, which results in the relocation of more firms to the area, higher incomes, and more opportunities for career advancement. Because much of the poverty reduction in the late 20th and early 21st centuries is attributable to increased labor income and because the increased economic output of cities can be used to finance services at the national level, including in rural areas, the World Bank sees the promotion of agglomeration economies as a worthy tactic in the ongoing campaign to fight poverty. Moreover, in the promotion of the other MDGs, agglomeration provides for the more affordable provision of services described earlier,

**TABLE 10.3**

**The distribution of the poor by size of city or town, selected countries, 2012**

[Percent]

| Country | Urban | XL | L | M | S | XS |
|---|---|---|---|---|---|---|
| **Albania** | | | | | | |
| Population share | 42 | — | — | 15 | 13 | 14 |
| Share of the poor | 31 | — | — | 11 | 9 | 11 |
| **Brazil** | | | | | | |
| Population share | 83 | 22 | 7 | 24 | 1 | 28 |
| Share of the poor | 72 | 9 | 6 | 17 | 1 | 39 |
| **Kazakhstan** | | | | | | |
| Population share | 57 | 8 | — | 29 | 5 | 15 |
| Share of the poor | 43 | 1 | — | 21 | 5 | 15 |
| **Kenya** | | | | | | |
| Population share | 19 | 7 | 2 | 3 | 2 | 4 |
| Share of the poor | 16 | 6 | 2 | 3 | 2 | 4 |
| **Mexico** | | | | | | |
| Population share | 61 | 27 | 13 | 11 | 4 | 6 |
| Share of the poor | 39 | 16 | 6 | 7 | 3 | 7 |
| **Morocco** | | | | | | |
| Population share | 51 | 12 | 9 | 27 | 3 | 1 |
| Share of the poor | 34 | 3 | 7 | 2 | 3 | 1 |
| **Sri Lanka** | | | | | | |
| Population share | 12 | — | 3 | 3 | 2 | 4 |
| Share of the poor | 5 | — | 1 | 1 | 1 | 2 |
| **Thailand** | | | | | | |
| Population share | 31 | 12 | — | 3 | 2 | 14 |
| Share of the poor | 17 | 1 | — | 1 | 1 | 13 |

— = Not available.
Note: Population share = percent of the population living in each category; share of the poor = percent of the country's poor living in each category.
XL = > 1m; L = 500k–1m; M = 100k–500k; S = 50k–100k; XS = < 50k.

SOURCE: "Table 2.3. The Poor Are Disproportionately Concentrated in Smaller Cities and Towns," in *Global Monitoring Report 2013: Rural-Urban Dynamics and the Millennium Development Goals*, World Bank, Washington, D.C., 2013, http://siteresources.worldbank.org/INTPROSPECTS/Resources/334934-1327948020811/8401693-1355753354515/8980448-1366123749799/GMR_2013_Full_Report.pdf (accessed October 29, 2013). DOI: 10.1596/978-0-8213-9806-7. License: Creative Commons Attribution CC BY 3.0.

and it can have especially powerful impacts on the MDGs related to gender equity, provided that there are high levels of gender equity in education. Besides providing high-paying jobs for college-educated women, cities characterized by high levels of agglomeration offer numerous opportunities for poor women who have basic educations. Successfully urbanizing cities in the developing world are often home to manufacturing firms that hire large numbers of women to produce goods for export.

The World Bank indicates that successful urbanization that avoids the enlargement of slums and the increased risks associated with environmental hazards requires government involvement in urban planning, large-scale investment in infrastructure projects, and ongoing regulation of the economy and individual industries. By contrast, unregulated economic growth is likely to lead to "lower levels of investment than would be optimal and ultimately to less productivity improvement, less job creation, and lower wages."

## PROSPECTS FOR THE FUTURE

In 2013 the United Nations Secretary-General's High-Level Panel of Eminent Persons on the Post-2015 Development Agenda, a 27-member group of world leaders and international aid experts charged with crafting a global development agenda for the period beyond 2015, released its recommendations in the report *A New Global Partnership: Eradicate Poverty and Transform Economies through Sustainable Development* (2013, http://www.post2015hlp.org/wp-content/uploads/2013/05/UN-Report.pdf). Noting the success at achieving many of the MDGs and the unprecedented progress at reducing extreme poverty worldwide, the panel also took note of the numerous ways in which the world of 2013 was very different from the world of 2000 (the year in which the Millennium Development agenda was crafted):

We considered the massive changes in the world since the year 2000 and the changes that are likely to unfold by 2030. There are a billion more people today, with world population at seven billion, and another billion expected by 2030. More than half of us now live in cities. Private investment in developing countries now dwarfs aid flows. The number of mobile phone subscriptions has risen from fewer than one billion to more than six billion. Thanks to the internet, seeking business or information on the other side of the world is now routine for many. Yet inequality remains and opportunity is not open to all. The 1.2 billion poorest people account for only 1 per cent of world consumption while the billion richest consume 72 per cent.

Above all, there is one trend—climate change—which will determine whether or not we can deliver on our ambitions. Scientific evidence of the direct threat from climate change has mounted. The stresses of unsustainable production and consumption patterns have become clear, in areas like deforestation, water scarcity, food waste, and high carbon emissions. Losses from natural disasters—including drought, floods, and storms—have increased at an alarming rate. People living in poverty will suffer first and worst from climate change. The cost of taking action now will be much less than the cost of dealing with the consequences later.

In view of the changing development challenges, the panel's recommendations included going beyond reductions in extreme poverty to a goal of complete eradication of extreme poverty by 2030, a goal that had become possible for the first time in human history. Included in this poverty-eradication goal was a commitment to focusing on the challenges faced by marginalized social groups, including women, minorities, the disabled, and others whose concerns often go unheeded at the local, national, and regional political levels. In view of the challenges posed by climate change, the panel advocated putting sustainability at the core of all development efforts, and in light of the increasingly unequal distribution of income and wealth in much of the world, the panel recommended putting a greater emphasis on inclusive growth. Other post-2015 priorities included the ensuring of peace, stability, and freedom from crime and waste through the strengthening of governments with institutions that adhere to principles such as the rule of law, freedom of speech and the press, political choice, and adequate systems of justice.

Although antipoverty efforts have historically involved aid payments to poor countries by developed countries and the international community, the panel noted a growing expectation that countries, given their increased levels of economic growth, would be able to generate a majority of development funds domestically by raising revenues through better-designed tax systems. When external financing will be required, the panel suggested, much of this financing will come from private investors rather than from direct aid from developed countries. The panel notes that to ensure that such flows of investment remain stable, regulation of the global financial system must be a priority, along with the creation of new financial instruments, institutions, and laws at the national level.

Although there remained many doubts and disagreements about the best methods for fighting and measuring poverty worldwide, as of 2013 most international observers agreed that the MDGs had brought a welcome focus on the multidimensional nature of poverty. Accordingly, the international fight against poverty was likely to build on this understanding and continue the fight to reduce the complex and mutually reinforcing forms of deprivation that hold back human potential. As the post-2015 panel members observe, large-scale problems had the potential to set back antipoverty efforts considerably. The previous decades had brought much greater knowledge of the problems associated with poverty, however, and this knowledge was indisputably necessary to further progress.

# IMPORTANT NAMES
# AND ADDRESSES

**Amnesty International**
One Easton St.
London, WC1X 0DW United Kingdom
(011-44-20) 7-413-5500
FAX: (011-44-20) 7-956-1157
URL: http://www.amnesty.org/

**Asian Development Bank**
Six ADB Ave.
Mandaluyong City, 1550 Philippines
(011-63-2) 632-4444
FAX: (011-63-2) 636-2444
URL: http://www.adb.org/

**Brookings Institution**
1775 Massachusetts Ave. NW
Washington, DC 20036
(202) 797-6000
URL: http://www.brookings.edu/

**Center for Economic and Policy Research**
1611 Connecticut Ave. NW, Ste. 400
Washington, DC 20009
(202) 293-5380
FAX: (202) 588-1356
URL: http://www.cepr.net/

**Chronic Poverty Advisory Network**
**Overseas Development Institute**
203 Blackfriars Rd., Southwark
London, SE1 8NJ United Kingdom
(011-44-207) 922-0325
E-mail: chronicpoverty@odi.org.uk
URL: http://www.chronicpovertynetwork.org/

**Eurostat European Commission**
Joseph Bech Bldg.
5 Rue Alphonse Weicker
Luxembourg, 2721 Luxembourg
(011-352) 4301-35555
URL: http://www.epp.eurostat.ec.europa.eu/

**Food and Agriculture Organization of the
United Nations**
Viale delle Terme di Caracalla
Rome, 00153 Italy
(011-39) 06-57051

FAX: (011-39) 06-570-53152
E-mail: FAO-HQ@fao.org
URL: http://www.fao.org/

**Food First/Institute for Food and
Development Policy**
398 60th St.
Oakland, CA 94618
(510) 654-4400
FAX: (510) 654-4551
E-mail: info@foodfirst.org
URL: http://www.foodfirst.org/

**Global Policy Forum**
PO Box 3283
New York, NY 10163
(212) 557-3161
E-mail: gpf@globalpolicy.org
URL: http://www.globalpolicy.org/

**Human Rights Watch**
350 Fifth Ave., 34th Floor
New York, NY 10118-3299
(212) 290-4700
FAX: (212) 736-1300
URL: http://www.hrw.org/

**Institute for Economic Democracy**
13851 N. 103 Ave.
Sun City, AZ 85351
1-888-533-1020
E-mail: ied@ied.info
URL: http://www.ied.info/

**Internal Displacement Monitoring Centre**
Chemin de Balexert, 7-9
Chatelaine, Geneva, 1219 Switzerland
(011-41-22) 799-0700
FAX: (011-41-22) 799-0701
URL: http://www.internal-displacement.org/

**International Committee of the Red Cross**
19 Avenue de la Paix
Geneva, CH 1202 Switzerland
(011-41-22) 734-6001
FAX: (011-41-22) 733-2057
URL: http://www.icrc.org/

**International Crisis Group**
149 Avenue Louise, Level 14
Brussels, B-1050 Belgium
(011-32-2) 502-9038
FAX: (011-32-2) 502-5038
E-mail: brussels@crisisgroup.org
URL: http://www.crisisgroup.org/

**International Forum on Globalization**
1009 General Kennedy Ave. #2
San Francisco, CA 94129
(415) 561-7650
E-mail: ifg@ifg.org
URL: http://www.ifg.org/

**International Labour Organization**
4 Route des Morillons
Geneva 22, CH 1211 Switzerland
(011-41-22) 799-6111
FAX: (011-41-22) 798-8685
E-mail: ilo@ilo.org
URL: http://www.ilo.org/

**International Monetary Fund**
700 19th St. NW
Washington, DC 20431
(202) 623-7000
FAX: (202) 623-4661
URL: http://www.imf.org/

**MADRE**
121 W. 27th St., Ste. 301
New York, NY 10001
(212) 627-0444
FAX: (212) 675-3704
E-mail: madre@madre.org
URL: http://www.madre.org/

**New Economics Foundation**
Three Jonathan St.
London, SE11 5NH United Kingdom
(011-44-207) 820-6300
FAX: (011-44-207) 820-6301
E-mail: info@neweconomics.org
URL: http://www.neweconomics.org/

**Organisation for Economic Co-operation and Development**
2 Rue André Pascal
Paris, Cedex 16, 75775 France
(011-33-1) 45-24-8200
FAX: (011-33-1) 45-24-8500
URL: http://www.oecd.org/

**Oxfam International**
266 Banbury Road
Oxford, OX2 7DL United Kingdom
(011-44-186) 533-9100
FAX: (011-44-186) 533-9101
E-mail: information@oxfaminternational.org
URL: http://www.oxfam.org/

**Social Watch**
Avda. 18 de Julio 2095/301
Montevideo, 11200 Uruguay
(011-598-2) 403-1424
URL: http://www.socialwatch.org/

**Stockholm International Peace Research Institute**
Signalistgatan 9
Solna, SE-169 70 Sweden
(011-46-8) 655-9700
FAX: (011-46-8) 655-9733
URL: http://www.sipri.org/

**United Nations Children's Fund**
Three United Nations Plaza
New York, NY 10017
(212) 326-7000
FAX: (212) 887-7465
URL: http://www.unicef.org/

**United Nations Development Programme**
One United Nations Plaza
New York, NY 10017
(212) 906-5000
URL: http://www.undp.org/

**United Nations Economic and Social Commission for Asia and the Pacific**
Rajadamnern Nok Ave.
Bangkok, 10200 Thailand
(011-66-2) 288-1234
FAX: (011-66-2) 288-1000
URL: http://www.unescap.org/

**United Nations Economic and Social Commission for Western Asia**
PO Box 11-8575, Riad el-Solh Square
Beirut, Lebanon
(011-961) 1-981301
FAX: (011-961) 1-981510
URL: http://www.escwa.un.org/

**United Nations Economic Commission for Latin America and the Caribbean**
Av. Dag Hammarskjöld 3477
Vitacura, Santiago, Chile
(011-56-2) 2471-2000
FAX: (011-56-2) 2208-0252
URL: http://www.eclac.org/

**United Nations Educational, Scientific, and Cultural Organization**
Seven Place de Fontenoy
Paris 07 SP, 75352 France
(011-33-1) 4568-1099
FAX: (011-33-1) 4568-5639
URL: http://www.unesco.org/

**United Nations Entity for Gender Equality and the Empowerment of Women**
220 E. 42nd St.
New York, NY 10017
(646) 781-4400
FAX: (646) 781-4444
URL: http://www.unwomen.org/

**United Nations Population Fund**
605 Third Ave.
New York, NY 10158
(212) 297-5000
FAX: (212) 370-0201

E-mail: hq@unfpa.org
URL: http://www.unfpa.org/

**U.S. Bureau of Labor Statistics**
Postal Square Bldg.
2 Massachusetts Ave. NE
Washington, DC 20212-0001
(202) 691-5200
URL: http://www.bls.gov/

**U.S. Census Bureau**
4600 Silver Hill Rd.
Washington, DC 20233
(301) 763-4636
1-800-923-8282
URL: http://www.census.gov/

**Women's Environment and Development Organization**
355 Lexington Ave., Third Floor
New York, NY 10017
(212) 973-0325
FAX: (212) 973-0335
URL: http://www.wedo.org/

**World Bank**
1818 H St. NW
Washington, DC 20433
(202) 473-1000
FAX: (202) 477-6391
URL: http://www.worldbank.org/

**World Food Programme**
Via C. G. Viola 68
Parco dei Medici
Rome, 00148 Italy
(011-39-06) 65131
FAX: (011-39-06) 659-0632
URL: http://www.wfp.org/

**World Health Organization**
Avenue Appia 20
Geneva 27, 1211 Switzerland
(011-41-22) 791-2111
FAX: (011-41-22) 791-3111
URL: http://www.who.int/

# RESOURCES

Much of the data for this book comes from the World Bank and the various branches and agencies of the United Nations (UN). Together, these groups collect and distribute much of the most authoritative data on poverty in the developing world.

Besides maintaining "World Databank" (http://data bank.worldbank.org/data/home.aspx), a rich interactive data portal that provides information on poverty and development, the World Bank releases numerous reports and other publications. The publications that were particularly useful in the compiling of this book include *Global Monitoring Report 2013: Rural-Urban Dynamics and the Millennium Development Goals* (2013), *World Development Indicators 2013* (2013), *Africa Development Indicators 2012/13* (2013), and *Shifting Gears to Accelerate Shared Prosperity in Latin America and the Caribbean* (June 2013).

Of central importance to this book was the UN's *The Millennium Development Goals Report 2013* (June 2013), which provides a thorough overview of the various forms of deprivation measured by the organization's Millennium Development Goals project. Other UN agencies whose data and information about world poverty proved central to the writing of this book include the UN Development Programme's (UNDP) *Human Development Report 2013—The Rise of the South: Human Progress in a Diverse World* (2013); the UN Inter-Agency Group for Child Mortality Estimation's *Levels & Trends in Child Mortality: Report 2013* (2013); the UN Children's Fund's *Child Well-Being in Rich Countries: A Comparative Overview* (2013); the UN Educational, Scientific, and Cultural Organization's *Adult and Youth Literacy: National, Regional, and Global Trends, 1985–2015* (June 2013); the UN Food and Agriculture Organization's *The State of Food Insecurity in the World 2012: Economic Growth Is Necessary but Not Sufficient to Accelerate Reduction of Hunger and Malnutrition*

(2012) and *The State of Food and Agriculture 2013: Food Systems for Better Nutrition* (2013); and the Joint UN Programme on HIV/AIDS's *Global Report: UNAIDS Report on the Global AIDS Epidemic 2013* (2013). UN regional offices also release a range of studies and reports on the developing countries that are their focus. Particularly relevant to this book's aims were *Asia-Pacific Aspirations: Perspectives for a Post-2015 Development Agenda* (August 2013), published by the UN Economic and Social Commission for Asia and the Pacific in collaboration with the Asian Development Bank and the UNDP; *The Arab Millennium Development Goals Report: Facing Challenges and Looking beyond 2015* (2013), released by the UN Economic and Social Commission for Western Asia and the League of Arab States; and *Economic Survey of Latin America and the Caribbean, 2013: Three Decades of Uneven and Unstable Growth* (October 2013), published by the UN Economic Commission for Latin America and the Caribbean. Also of use was information from the World Health Organization, such as the *World Malaria Report 2012* (2012).

The Asian Development Bank (ADB), which resembles the World Bank in its structure and goals while focusing on Asia and the Pacific, also publishes a range of data and studies relating to poverty in its region. Besides the report *Asian Development Outlook 2013: Asia's Energy Challenge* (2013), the ADB's *Basic 2013 Statistics* (2013) provided important data for this book.

Much of the data and information on conditions for workers worldwide came from publications of the International Labour Organization, especially *Global Employment Trends 2013: Recovering from a Second Jobs Dip* (2013) and *Marking Progress against Child Labour: Global Estimates and Trends 2000–2012* (2013).

Information on poverty in the United States came primarily from the U.S. Census Bureau, in particular the report *Income, Poverty, and Health Insurance Coverage in the United States: 2012* (Carmen DeNavas-Walt, Bernadette D. Proctor, and Jessica D. Smith, September 2013). Information on poverty in Europe came primarily from Eurostat, the statistics bureau of the European Union, which presents detailed poverty data through the "Income and Living Conditions" section of its website (http://epp.eurostat.ec.europa.eu/portal/page/portal/income _social_inclusion_living_conditions/introduction). Other information on poverty in the developed world came from the Organisation for Economic Co-operation and Development, which provides a wealth of data on the "Statistics" section of its website (http://www.oecd.org/ statistics/).

Many nongovernmental organizations, think tanks, and watchdog groups provide invaluable insight and information on poverty and the poor. Among those whose reports and other work was instrumental in the compiling of this book were Oxfam International, Internal Displacement Monitoring Centre, and the Stockholm International Peace Research Institute.

*Page references in italics refer to photographs. References with the letter t following them indicate the presence of a table. The letter f indicates a figure. If more than one table or figure appears on a particular page, the exact item number for the table or figure being referenced is provided.*

# E

U.S. poverty thresholds, 2(t1.1)

violence in fragile states, 131t

violence in fragile states, effects of, 132t

water sources, percentage of population with access to improved, by region, rural/urban area, 114f

women aged 15–49, attended four or more times during pregnancy by provider, by world region, 106(f7.3)

women aged 15–49, married or in relationship, who have unmet need for family planning, 106(f7.4)

working poor indicators, US$1.25 per day, 22t

working poor indicators, US$2.00 per day, 23(t2.2)

*Statistical Update on Employment in the Informal Economy* (ILO), 23

"Still Waiting for Recovery" (Economist.com), 128

"Stories from Syrian Refugees" (UNHCR), 134

Stress, of poverty, 85–86

Structural adjustment programs (SAPs), 35

Stunted growth

Arab states children suffering from, 67

Asia-Pacific region children suffering from, 56–57

in Haiti, 77

in LAC region, 80

from malnutrition, 29

undernourishment in developing world, 31t

Sub-Saharan Africa

access to clean water/sanitation in, 113–114

adolescent birth rate in, 107

antipoverty efforts in, 19

armed conflict in, 129

births attended by skilled practitioners in, 105

child labor in, 115

child mortality in, 31, 112

contraception, access to, 111

development indicators for countries in, 39t–40t

economic growth in, 20

education/literacy, impact of, 46–50

employment restrictions for women in, 103

gender disparities in employment in, 22

gender parity index for school enrollment, 110

HIV epidemic in, 43

HIV-positive adults in, 44t

hunger, reduction of, 29

illiteracy in, 27, 108

insecticide-treated net, percentage of households with, 45f

international debt in, 35

malaria in, 43–45

malnutrition in, 42t–43t

malnutrition in children in, 113

maternal death in, 104

MDGs, failure to meet in, 138

population growth in, 112

poverty in, 37

primary education in, by country, 48t–49t

sanitation practices, percentage of population using various, 47f

sanitation/clean water, 45–46

undernourishment, people who are undernourished, by region, 41f

undernourishment/malnutrition in, 41, 43

war, impact of, 37–38, 41

water, progress toward MDG drinking-water targets in, 46f

World Bank classification of African economies by GNI, 38t

Sudan

civil war in, 131

effects of civil war on, 37, 65

"Sumatran Quake Sped Up Earth's Rotation" (Hopkin), 125–126

"A Summary Report on Muzaffarabad Earthquake, Pakistan" (Naeem et al.), 126

Supplemental Poverty Measure (SPM), 91–92

Syria

Arab Spring and, 65

civil war in, 130, 134

# T

Tabuchi, Hiroko, 128

Tajikistan, undernourishment in, 55

Taliban, 133

Taxes

Great Recession and, 86

in Japan, 98

loss of from informal economy, 24

U.S. poverty thresholds and, 91

Teenagers. *See* Adolescents

Third-world countries, 15

*See also* Developing countries

"Three Months On: New Figures Show Tsunami May Have Killed up to Four Times as Many Women as Men" (Oxfam), 126

Timor-Leste

malnutrition in, 56

primary school enrollment rates in, 57

undernourishment in, 55

Tokyo Electric Power Co., 128

"Top 10 Cheapest U.S. Cities to Rent an Apartment" (Glink), 91

Trade

agricultural subsidies/food exports and, 34

international debt and, 35

"Trends in World Military Expenditure, 2012" (Perlo-Freeman et al.), 134–135

"Tsunami Death Toll Increases to 668" (LATimes.com), 127

Tsunamis

Java earthquake/tsunami, 127

overview of, 125–126

Tuluy, Hasan, 83

Tunisia, revolution in, 65, 133

"2013 UNHCR Country Operations Profile—Afghanistan" (UNHCR), 133

*2013 World Population Data Sheet* (Population Reference Bureau), 112

Typhoons. *See* Hurricanes

# U

UN. *See* United Nations

UN Department of Economic and Social Affairs Commission of the Status of Women, 102

UN Development Programme (UNDP)

on gender equity in Asia-Pacific region, 60–63

HDI, introduction of, 4–5

on hunger in Asia-Pacific region, 55–57

"Poverty Reduction," 142–143

UN Economic and Social Commission for Western Asia (ESCWA), 51

UN Entity for Gender Equality and the Empowerment of Women, 103

UN Environment Programme, 126

UN High Commissioner for Refugees (UNHCR), 133, 134

UN Office of the High Representative for the Least Developed Countries, Landlocked Developing Countries, and Small Island Developing States, 15–18

UN Office on Drugs and Crime, 83

"U.N. Sued for 'Bringing Cholera to Haiti,' Causing Outbreak That Killed Thousands" (Watson & Vaccarello), 127–128

"UN Warns of Surge in Haiti Cholera Deaths" (Witcher & Andrade), 77

UNAIDS (Joint UN Programme on HIV/AIDS), 43

Underdeveloped countries, economic development in, 15–18

Undernourishment

in Arab states, 66–67, 67(f4.3)

in Asia-Pacific region, 55–57

definition of, 27

in Latin America and the Caribbean, 79–80, 79f

reduction of, 27, 29

in sub-Saharan Africa, 41, 41f, 43

*See also* Hunger; Malnutrition

UNDP. *See* UN Development Programme

Unemployment

among women, 103

rate by sex/world region, 104t

Watson, Ivan, 127–128
"We Are the World" (song), 123
WEF (World Economic Forum), 102
West Asia
    adolescent birth rate in, 107
    child mortality rate in, 113
    gender parity index for school
      enrollment, 110
    hunger increase in, 29
    illiteracy in, 27
"What Is Child Labour" (ILO), 115
Whites, 89
WHO. *See* World Health Organization
"Why Is the U.S. against Children's
    Rights?" (Cohen & DeBenedet), 101
Witcher, Tim, 77
"With a Plant's Tainted Water Still
    Flowing, No End to Environmental
    Fears" (Fackler & Tabuchi), 128
Women
    anti-female bias in Asia-Pacific region,
      62–63
    in Arab states, national parliament seats
      held by, 71f
    in Arab states, share of jobs held in,
      70(f4.10)
    armed conflict, effects on, 129
    births attended by skilled health
      professional, by selected region/
      developing world, by urban vs. rural
      area, 105f
    births to women aged 15–19 per 1,000
      women, number of, by region, 107f
    early pregnancy/childbearing, channels
      linking to poverty, 108f
    employees in nonagricultural jobs who
      are women, percentage of, by world
      region, 103f
    employment/wages for, 102–103
    gender disparity in Arab states, 69–70
    gender equality in education, 108–111
    gender equity in LAC region, 80
    gender parity index in primary,
      secondary, tertiary education, by
      region, 109f
    global initiatives to protect rights of
      women/children, 101–102
    in government, Asia-Pacific region, 63
    illiteracy among, 27, 108
    informal work by, 24

    literacy, adult (age 15 and over) illiterate
      population/female percentage of
      illiterate population by region, 28t
    maternal mortality rates in Asia-Pacific
      region, 63
    poverty, percentage living in, 89
    rape/murder of in India, 63
    reproductive health, 103–108
    of sub-Saharan Africa, gender equity
      and, 48–50
    unemployment rate by sex/world region,
      104t
    U.S. poverty thresholds, calculation
      of, 91
    violence against, 135–136
    violence against in LAC region, 84
    women aged 15–49, attended four or
      more times during pregnancy by
      provider, by world region, 106(f7.3)
    women aged 15–49, married or in
      relationship, who have unmet need for
      family planning, 106(f7.4)
"Women and Girls: Education, Not
    Discrimination!" (UNESCO), 111
Workers. *See* Employment; Working poor
"Workers in the Informal Economy"
    (World Bank), 24
Working poor
    indicators, US $1.25 per day, 22t
    indicators, US $2.00 per day, 23(t2.2)
    poverty status of persons/primary
      families in labor force for 27 or more
      weeks, 23(t2.3)
    wages of by region, 22
World Bank
    absolute poverty measures of, 3
    on access to clean water/sanitation, 113
    classification of African economies by
      GNI, 38t
    on costs of informal economy, 24
    on education and fertility rates, 111
    on gender equality, 101
    on gender equality in education, 108
    on gender equity in education in Africa,
      47–48
    on gender equity in LAC region, 80
    *Global Monitoring Report 2013*, 143,
      144, 145–146
    on homicide in LAC region, numbers
      of, 83

    on Indonesia, rebuilding of after
      tsunami, 126
    international debt and, 35
    on Japan's economy, 98
    on poverty in LAC region, 73
    on poverty in Russia, 96
    "Poverty Overview: Results," 3
    *Shifting Gears to Accelerate Shared
      Prosperity in Latin America and the
      Caribbean*, 75–76, 77
    Worldwide Governance Indicators
      research project, 35
    "World DataBank: Millennium
      Development Goals" (World Bank),
      47–48
    "World DataBank: World Development
      Indicators" (World Bank), 80
    *World Development Indicators 2013* (World
      Bank), 83
World Economic Forum (WEF), 102
*World Factbook* (CIA)
    *Country Comparison*, 111–112
    on population of Japan, 98
    on population of Russia, 94
    on poverty in Russia, 96
    on South Korea, 98, 99
World Health Organization (WHO)
    "Female Genital Mutilation," 136
    on Java earthquake/tsunami, 127
    on maternal death, 104–105
    on obstetric fistula, 108
    on violence against women, 135–136
    *World Malaria Report 2012*, 44
*World Malaria Report 2012* (WHO), 44
"World Vision Aids Pakistan Victims in
    Forbidden Quake Zone" (Goss),
    126–127
World War II, 129
Worldwide community. *See* Global
    community
Worldwide Governance Indicators research
    project (World Bank), 35
Wotapka, Dawn, 91

# Y

Yeltsin, Boris, 95
Youth literacy rates
    in Arab states, 70(f4.9)
    in Asia, 62t